The Road to Nusantara

The **National Research and Innovation Agency** (Badan Riset dan Inovasi Nasional, BRIN) is a cabinet-level government agency functioning directly under the President of the Republic of Indonesia that conducts integrated research, development, assessment, and application, as well as invention and innovations, and the implementation of nuclear energy and space policies. BRIN is also responsible for the regulation of science, technology, and national innovation, and is Indonesia's implementing agency for research and innovation.

BRIN Publishing is an established scientific publisher in Indonesia under The National Research and Innovation Agency (BRIN). BRIN Publishing holds a high responsibility to enlighten society's intelligence and awareness through the provision of qualified publications available to the public at large. Our main work revolves around planning, acquiring, designing, and distributing scientific knowledge to the public. BRIN Publishing has collaborated with various researchers and academicians as well as global publishers to publish high-quality publications that have passed thorough quality control mechanisms and editorial processes, including peer review.

The **ISEAS – Yusof Ishak Institute** (formerly Institute of Southeast Asian Studies) is an autonomous organization established in 1968. It is a regional centre dedicated to the study of socio-political, security, and economic trends and developments in Southeast Asia and its wider geostrategic and economic environment. The Institute's research programmes are grouped under Regional Economic Studies (RES), Regional Strategic and Political Studies (RSPS), and Regional Social and Cultural Studies (RSCS). The Institute is also home to the ASEAN Studies Centre (ASC), the Singapore APEC Study Centre and the Temasek History Research Centre (THRC).

ISEAS Publishing, an established academic press, has issued more than 2,000 books and journals. It is the largest scholarly publisher of research about Southeast Asia from within the region. ISEAS Publishing works with many other academic and trade publishers and distributors to disseminate important research and analyses from and about Southeast Asia to the rest of the world.

The Road to Nusantara
Process, Challenges and Opportunities

Edited By
Julia M. Lau, Athiqah Nur Alami,
Siwage Dharma Negara and Yanuar Nugroho

First published in Singapore in 2023 by
ISEAS Publishing
30 Heng Mui Keng Terrace
Singapore 119614
E-mail: publish@iseas.edu.sg
Website: http://bookshop.iseas.edu.sg

and

National Research and Innovation Agency
(Badan Riset dan Inovasi Nasional, BRIN)
Gedung B.J. Habibie
Jl. M.H. Thamrin No. 8
Jakarta Pusat 10340
Indonesia
E-mail: penerbit@brin.go.id
Website: penerbit.brin.go.id

All rights reserved. No part of this publication may be reproduced, stored in a retrieval system, or transmitted in any form or by any means, electronic, mechanical, photocopying, recording or otherwise, without the prior permission of the ISEAS – Yusof Ishak Institute.

© 2023 ISEAS – Yusof Ishak Institute, Singapore

The responsibility for facts and opinions in this publication rests exclusively with the authors and their interpretations do not necessarily reflect the views or the policy of the publisher or its supporters.

ISEAS Library Cataloguing-in-Publication Data

Name(s): Lau, Julia M., editor. | Alami, Athiqah Nur, editor. | Negara, Siwage Dharma, editor. | Nugroho, Yanuar, editor.
Title: The road to Nusantara : process, challenges, and opportunities / edited by Julia M. Lau, Athiqah Nur Alami, Siwage Dharma Negara and Yanuar Nugroho.
Description: Singapore : ISEAS-Yusof Ishak Institute ; Jakarta : National Research and Innovation Agency (BRIN), 2023. | All chapters started as papers presented at the conference "The Road to Nusantara: Process, Challenges and Opportunities" on 27–28 October 2022 at ISEAS in Singapore. | Includes bibliographical references and index.
Identifiers: ISBN 9789815104226 (soft cover) | ISBN 9789815104233 (ebook PDF)
Subjects: LCSH: City Planning—Indonesia. | Capitals (Cities)—Indonesia. | Economic development—Indonesia. | Indonesia—Politics and government.
Classification: LCC HT165.53 I5R62

Front cover: Photograph of Titik Nol, Nusantara, East Kalimantan. Reproduced with kind permission of Dr Agung Wicaksono, Deputy (Investment), IKN Authority.

Cover design by Refine Define Pte Ltd
Index compiled by Raffaie Nahar
Typeset by Superskill Graphics Pte Ltd
Printed in Singapore by Mainland Press Pte Ltd

Contents

List of Figures	vii
List of Tables	viii
Foreword by Dr Bambang Susantono	ix
Foreword by Dr Laksana Tri Handoko	xi
The Contributors	xiii
Glossary	xxii

Introduction: The Road to Nusantara—Process, Challenges and Opportunities   1
Athiqah Nur Alami, Siwage Dharma Negara, Yanuar Nugroho and Julia M. Lau

PART I: PROCESSES AND PATHWAYS TOWARDS NUSANTARA

1. Nusantara: A Historical Perspective   11
   Yanuar Nugroho, Wasisto Raharjo Jati, Pradita Devis Dukarno and Iryan Ali Herdiansyah

2. The New State Capital Regulations: Contending for Autonomy, Democracy and Legitimacy?   32
   Mardyanto Wahyu Tryatmoko and Koichi Kawamura

3. Nusantara and the Spatial Implications for the Practice of Indonesian Democracy   52
   Ian Douglas Wilson

4. Crowdfunding for IKN: Potential, Risk and People's Perception   75
   Riri Kusumarani and Anne Parlina

PART II: CHALLENGES IN DEVELOPING NUSANTARA

5. Addressing the Challenges in Developing Nusantara: The Roles of Spatial Planning   107
   Dimas Wisnu Adrianto and Kathleen Meira Berta

6. The Transfer of the National Capital (IKN): The Domination of the Capitalist Political Economy and the Dynamics of Local Representation   125
Septi Satriani, Pandu Yuhsina Adaba and Imam Syafi'i

7. Identifying Potential Social Challenges in IKN: Perspectives of Civil Society and Villagers in East Kalimantan   150
Deasy Simandjuntak, David Meschede and Michaela Haug

8. Population and Human Capital Redistribution: Understanding Opportunities and Challenges in Mass Migration to Nusantara   173
Meirina Ayumi Malamassam

PART III: OPPORTUNITIES FOR NUSANTARA

9. Nusantara the Green Capital: Leveraging Moment for Improved Forest Governance   197
Dini Suryani, Dian Aulia and Marcellinus Mandira Budi Utomo

10. Sustainability of the Local Community's Livelihoods and the Idea of the Modern City of Nusantara   225
Rusli Cahyadi, Deny Hidayati, Ali Yansyah Abdurrahim, Temi Indriati Miranda and Ardanareswari Ayu Pitaloka

11. Projecting A Global Identity as a Maritime Nation in the New Capital City   246
Lidya Christin Sinaga and Khanisa

Conclusion: Shaping Nusantara   267
Yanuar Nugroho and Julia M. Lau

Index   271

List of Figures

1.1	Jonggol as a Self-Contained City	19
4.1	Simplified Crowdfunding Categories	79
4.2	Conceptual Framework: Understanding Crowdfunding for the IKN	84
4.3	Projects That Are Appropriate for Crowdfunding	86
4.4	Appropriate Projects, According to Interviewed Experts	93
6.1	Map of the State Capital of Nusantara of Indonesia	130
7.1	Awareness and Impact of Proposed Capital Relocation, Respondent Summary	161
7.2	Respondents' Hopes for the Future, N=60	163
7.3	Fears of Respondents about Future Problems with IKN Relocation, N=60	164
8.1	Migrants in Indonesia, by Percentage of Total Population	180
8.2	Predicted Probabilities of Migration by Educational Attainment	184
9.1	Forest Cover in East Kalimantan (in thousand ha)	201
9.2	HWC Reports by Wildlife Species	204
9.3	Roadmap Timeline for Environmental Recovery in IKN Area	206
10.1	Map of the Existing Administrative Boundary of the IKN	228
10.2	Policies Related to IKN	236
10.3	Two Notice Boards in KIPP IKN Installed by KLHK (left) and ATR/BPN (right)	237

List of Tables

4.1	Examples of Civic Crowdfunding Projects Globally	81
4.2	Aspects of Crowdfunding Regulation in Comparison with POJK No. 16 and POJK.04/2021	83
4.3	Respondents' Demographic Information, N=285	85
4.4	Coded Examples	87
5.1	National Population Distribution in 2010, 2020, and 2035 (Projected)	109
5.2	Development Stages of Nusantara	112
9.1	Total Forest Area of East Kalimantan in 2020	200
9.2	Natural Resources Extraction Business Permits in East Kalimantan	202
9.3	Pillar 1: Policy, Legal Institutional, and Regulatory Frameworks	209
9.4	Pillar 2: Planning and Decision-Making Processes	209
9.5	Pillar 3: Implementation, Enforcement and Compliance	210
10.1	Basic Population and Area in Kelurahan Pemaluan and Bumi Harapan Village	229
10.2	Occupations in Kelurahan Pemaluan and Bumi Harapan Village, by Gender	230
10.3	Population Category by House and Land Location	239

Foreword

I welcome the publication of *The Road to Nusantara: Process, Challenges and Opportunities*, co-published by Singapore's ISEAS – Yusof Ishak Institute and Indonesia's National Research and Innovation Agency (BRIN). This book aims to capture the multi-faceted development aspects of Indonesia's future national capital, Nusantara, and critically evaluates some challenges and opportunities that the development of the city may bring.

The book provides readers with a wide range of vantage points that inform the development of this historical project. Such enriching perspectives are particularly valuable for us at the Nusantara National Capital Authority (NNCA), which is tasked to plan and coordinate the development of the city. The NNCA will subsequently oversee the government's transition to Nusantara before eventually becoming the city's administrator.

As I shared at the ISEAS-BRIN conference in October 2022, which is the foundation for this publication, Nusantara is not a typical city-building infrastructural project. A key element of the "Indonesia 2045" vision, Nusantara demonstrates Indonesia's effort to embrace new working cultures and innovative ways of thinking that will allow the nation to tackle future global challenges.

As such, the ultimate goal is to create a city that is both liveable and lovable, built atop the principles of green, smart, inclusive, resilient and sustainable. This model city can then be replicated when developing other cities in Indonesia, and ultimately help the nation to leapfrog to become a more prosperous and sustainable country.

One prime instance that illustrates the new paradigm is a grand design to make Nusantara a "sustainable forest city", which I believe will be the first in the world for a national capital. Key to this design is the plan to limit the development of the city's built-up environment to only about 25 per cent of the total land area. The remaining area will be retained as a green area, including 65 per cent that will be transformed from a production forest into a tropical forest.

To accomplish this plan, the NNCA will bring back the lush tropical forest and its thriving ecology through a "reforestation process". At the time of writing, we are collaborating closely with some organizations and community groups to distill their international expertise and local wisdom, respectively, and subsequently, to implement the concept across Nusantara.

In addition, the forest area is expected to increase water absorption, reduce the risk of flooding, and act as a carbon sink. Combined with highly controlled built-up areas, the forest will allow Nusantara to minimize emissions. With all these features, Nusantara aims to be a carbon-neutral city by 2045.

The example shows that the success of this new city will not only benefit Indonesia. The value of a "net zero" Nusantara will extend beyond the country's borders by contributing to ongoing efforts worldwide to tackle climate change. This is one of the ways in which Nusantara will play an active role at the global level. The NNCA is also working with several other international organizations to ensure Nusantara's contribution in areas such as biodiversity and the Sustainable Development Goals.

All this is made possible as Nusantara positions itself to be a "living laboratory". The NNCA is keen to make the city into a testbed for experimentation, testing, and implementation. Likewise, we continue to invite fresh ideas and perspectives to help us to shape the city and to make it more liveable, lovable and sustainable. This is exactly where the wealth of knowledge presented in this book becomes critically important and relevant.

I congratulate BRIN and ISEAS on the publication of this book. I wish to particularly acknowledge all the contributors and editors who have provided their insights for this published volume. May this book inform, inspire and spark meaningful discourse, which will eventually lead to achieving the goal of making Nusantara a green, smart, inclusive, resilient and sustainable city.

Bambang Susantono
Chairman, Nusantara National Capital Authority

Nusantara, 23 February 2023

Foreword

The upcoming capital city relocation will have an important impact on and contribution towards Indonesian development, especially to reduce the gap between Java and outside Java Island, and to emphasize the spirit of Indonesia in Indonesia's archipelago. The new capital city or *Ibu Kota Negara* (IKN) is named "Nusantara", a word representing this archipelago.

Contributing to the preparation for Nusantara in terms of policy design and a political framework, I am grateful that through this important book, our researchers at the National Research and Innovation Agency (BRIN) have contributed to the production of academic and professional knowledge on the preparation and development of Indonesia's new capital city. Their contributions will not only enrich government policies but also provide evidence-based research on the establishment of the IKN.

The contributors to the book have successfully discussed the capital city relocation from diverse perspectives and by examining wide-ranging issues. These include the historical and political perspectives on capital relocation, the ecological and socio-economic implications of the relocation, as well as the cultural and identity aspects of the new capital city. The rich, critical, and in-depth knowledge covered by the book delighted me. Through the discussion, we hope that the discussion of the capital city relocation will benefit all, in line with the main purpose of Nusantara—to be a global city for all.

Hopefully, this book will be the first and most-cited scholarly work on the current Indonesian capital city relocation project. I thank all the contributors and editors for their hard work in completing this masterpiece. I believe the readers will find this book engaging in every chapter and that the book will stimulate future discussions and deeper knowledge of Indonesia's capital city relocation.

BRIN's work on the IKN certainly does not stop with the publication of this book. In 2023, one of the signature programmes in the Institute of Social Sciences and Humanities (ISSH), for instance, is on the challenges of the IKN which need to be addressed or dealt with by the Indonesian government. These challenges include drought, floods, forest fires, landslides, improving the involvement of indigenous people, and addressing potential horizontal or vertical social conflicts. BRIN will also launch several expeditions and explorations, one of them being the Borneo Expedition, with the IKN as the focus.

Last, *The Road to Nusantara* is one of several products embodying the collaboration between BRIN and ISEAS that began in 2018 with a conference and book publication on religious authority. This collaboration continued in 2021 with a conference on "Digital Disruptions" and in 2022 on "Millennial Disruptions" and the IKN Conference that led to this publication. In August 2023, BRIN and ISEAS will organize a conference on "Social Fault-lines in Indonesia: Persistence and Change in an Evolving Landscape".

Enjoy the book! Thank you.

Laksana Tri Handoko
Chairman, National Research and Innovation Agency (BRIN)

Jakarta, February 2023

The Contributors

The Editors
Julia M. LAU is Senior Fellow and Co-Coordinator of the Indonesia Studies Programme at the ISEAS – Yusof Ishak Institute (ISEAS), Singapore. Julia is also an editor of ISEAS's commentary and analysis website, fulcrum. sg. Her research interests include Indonesia's foreign policy and domestic politics, World War II memory in Southeast Asia, the teaching and learning of political science, and gerontology. She has taught international relations and law, Asian studies, terrorism, research methods, and comparative politics courses at Georgetown University and the Catholic University of America in Washington, DC, and at McDaniel College, Westminster, MD. One of her recent publications was on designing and teaching an effective undergraduate international relations seminar, in a special issue of the *Journal of Political Science Education* (April 2022). Julia is an alumna of Georgetown University (MA Security Studies; MA Government) and the National University of Singapore (NUS) (LLB, LLM).

Athiqah Nur ALAMI is Head of the Research Center for Politics at Indonesia's National Research and Innovation Agency (BRIN) in Jakarta. Athiqah obtained her PhD in Southeast Asian Studies from the Department of Southeast Asian Studies at NUS. Her research interests focus on Indonesia's labour migration, foreign policy, diplomacy, and gender in international relations, particularly in applying a gender lens when analysing migration and foreign policy issues. Her most recent publication was on migrant care and domestic workers during the pandemic, published as a policy brief in *G20 Insights*.

Siwage Dharma NEGARA is Senior Fellow and Co-Coordinator of the Indonesia Studies Programme at ISEAS. Siwage has co-edited *The Riau Islands Province: Setting Sail* (ISEAS, 2021) and *The Indonesian Economy in Transition: Policy Challenges in the Jokowi Era and Beyond* (ISEAS, 2019). He is the author of numerous articles in academic and media publications, on the digital economy, investment, infrastructure, and development policies in Indonesia. His research has been published in the ISEAS *Perspective* and ISEAS *Trends in Southeast Asia* series, and in the *Bulletin of Indonesia*

Economic Studies, Journal of Southeast Asian Economies, Singapore Economic Review, and other international refereed journals.

Yanuar NUGROHO is Visiting Fellow of the Indonesia Studies Programme at ISEAS. Yanuar is also a senior lecturer at Driyarkara School of Philosophy, Jakarta and Honorary Research Fellow with the University of Manchester's Institute of Innovation Research, UK. His publications and research interests revolve around innovation, sustainability, knowledge dynamics and public policy. His most recent publications evaluate twenty years of decentralization in Indonesia (published in *Southeast Asia Economies*, 2021) and knowledge exchange through social capital in supply chains (published in *Supply Chain Forum: An International Journal*, 2022). He is preparing chapters on Indonesia's COVID-19 response and the historical context of Indonesia's capital relocation.

Chapter Authors (in alphabetical order)
Ali Yansyah ABDURRAHIM is a senior researcher on human ecology at the Research Center for Population, BRIN. His research topics are social-ecological systems, rural sustainable livelihoods, natural resources management, landscape governance, rural-urban dynamics, and political ecology. Some of his recent publications are "Community Champions of Ecosystem Services: The Role of Local Agencies in Protecting Indonesian Coral Reefs" (*Frontiers in Ecology and Evolution*, 2022); "Sustainable Agroforestry Landscape Management: Changing the Game" (*Land*, 2020); "Transforming Knowledge Systems for Life on Earth: Visions of Future Systems and How to Get There" (*Energy Research and Social Science*, 2020); "Opportunities in Community-Government Cooperation to Maintain Marine Ecosystem Services in the Asia-Pacific and Oceania" (*Ecosystem Services*, 2019), and "Quantitative Decision Support Tools Facilitating Social-Ecological Alignment in Community-Based Marine Protected Area Design" (*Ecology and Society*, 2019).

Pandu Yuhsina ADABA is a researcher at the Research Center for Politics, BRIN. He obtained a bachelor's in political science from UGM in 2010. He has also been a researcher at the Dignity Indonesia Berdikari Foundation since 2020. His latest publication with his team was published in the *Jurnal Penelitian Politik (Journal of Political Research)*, entitled "Kemunduran Demokrasi Tata Kelola SDA: Penguatan Oligarki dan Pelemahan Partisipasi Civil Society" [The Digression of Democratic Governance of Natural Resources: Strengthening Oligarchy and Weakening Civil Society

Participation]. Mr Yuhsina is pursuing a master's degree in rural sociology at the Faculty of Human Ecology, Bogor Agricultural Institute.

Dimas Wisnu ADRIANTO is a lecturer at the Department of Urban and Regional Planning, Universitas Brawijaya, Indonesia and was previously a Research Associate at the University of Manchester, UK. He has a bachelor's in urban and regional planning (Brawijaya), a master's in city and regional planning (Institut Teknologi Bandung, ITB), a master's in environmental management (University of Queensland, Australia), and he obtained his PhD in urban planning at the University of Manchester. His research interests focus on peri-urbanization, urban foresight and the politics of spatial planning.

Dian AULIA is a junior researcher at the Political Research Center at BRIN. She received her Bachelor of Laws degree at the University of Diponegoro. Her research interests include constitutional law, green constitution, law and politics, democracy, local autonomy, and government. Her recent published article includes "Menata Ulang Relasi Majelis Permusyawaratan Rakyat dan Presiden melalui Politik Hukum Haluan Negara" (*Jurnal Konstitusi*, 2020).

Kathleen Meira BERTA is an undergraduate student pursuing a degree in regional and urban planning at Universitas Brawijaya. Her research interests focus on marginalized community issues and informality in planning. She founded an NGO, Urbanist Indonesia, which aims to implement projects that promote city and community well-being. Her recent project attempted to address informality in the waste management process in Malang City, with scavengers as the main subject of investigation.

Rusli CAHYADI is a researcher at Human Ecology Department, at the Research Center for Population, BRIN. He is also a lecturer in the Department of Anthropology and the Tourism Vocational Program at UI. He obtained his PhD from the School of Earth and Environmental Sciences, University of Queensland, Australia. Dr Cahyadi currently pursues research related to the impact of climate change, in addition to urban issues primarily related to the urban poor, housing and environmental conditions. His recent publications include "Self-Supplied Water in Indonesia: Recent Spatial and Socio-Demographic Conditions and Its Future Development" (2022), "Lesson Learned: Riset Sosial Budaya dalam Pengendalian COVID-19" (2021) and "Community-Based Sanitation as a Complementary Strategy for the Jakarta Sewerage Development Project: What Can We Do Better?" (2021).

Pradita Devis DUKARNO earned his bachelor's in history from UGM in 2013. After graduating, he obtained a Maarif Fellowship from the MAARIF Institute for Culture and Humanity to conduct research entitled "Postcolonial Lesser Sunda Islands: Territorial Decentralization and Formation Identity". Prior to joining the Research Center for Area Studies at BRIN in 2022, he was a researcher for the Secretary-General of the Indonesian People's Consultative Assembly focusing on constitutional history. He was also a journalist at *Kontan* magazine in 2014–15.

Michaela HAUG is a Professor of Social and Cultural Anthropology at the University of Freiburg, Germany. Her research interests cover environmental anthropology, political ecology, and processes of agrarian transformations. Her current research explores how different and partly contradicting visions of the future influence forest use changes and related social, economic, and environmental transformations in the forested hinterlands of Indonesian Borneo. Some of her recent publications include "Framing the Future through the Lens of Hope: Environmental Change, Diverse Hopes and the Challenge of Engagement" (*Journal of Social and Cultural Anthropology*, 2020), "Claiming Rights to the Forest in East Kalimantan: Challenging Power and Presenting Culture" (*SOJOURN*, 2018), and the volume *Rethinking Power Relations in Indonesia: Transforming the Margins* (2017), which she edited with Martin Rössler and Anna-Teresa Grumblies.

Iryan Ali HERDIANSYAH is a graduate student at the Department of History, University of Indonesia (UI). He obtained a bachelor's in history at UGM. He has co-written several books such as *Marketing to the Middle-Class Muslim* (Gramedia, 2014), *8 Wajah Kelas Menengah* (Gramedia, 2015) and *GenM: Generation Muslim* (Bentang, 2017).

Deny HIDAYATI is a senior researcher at the Research Center for Population, BRIN. Her PhD was received from the Geographical Sciences (Human Ecology) at the Faculty of Science, ANU in 1995. Her current research focuses on reducing the risk of the elderly against the COVID-19 pandemic using a family and community approach, and the sustainable livelihoods of the local community in the IKN Nusantara. She has also conducted research on the vulnerability, preparedness and resilience of the population in facing environmental and climate changes, including natural disasters and health. Another research topic is related to the socio-economic aspects of coral reefs. Her current publications include "The Importance of the Sustainable Use of Fishery Resources to Improve the Livelihoods of Fishermen on the Islands of Sumatra and Sulawesi, Indonesia" (*Current Advances in Geography, Environment and Earth Sciences*, 2022), "The Influence of Coastal and Marine Ecosystem Conditions on Fisheries and Socio-Economic Activities of Local Fishermen" and "The Dynamic of Fishermen's Income and the Influencing Factors on the West and East" (both in IOP Conference Series, *Earth and Environmental Science*, 2021).

Wasisto Raharjo JATI is a researcher at BRIN and a research fellow on Governance and Public Policy at the Indonesian NGO Forum for International Development (INFID). He earned his bachelor's in politics and government studies from Universitas Gadjah Mada (UGM) in 2012 and a master's in political science from the Australian National University (ANU) in 2020. His research primarily focuses on voting behaviour, religion and politics, the politics of the middle class, and political movements. Besides his day-to-day research activities, Mr Jati is also a pundit in Indonesian politics.

Koichi KAWAMURA is a Senior Research Fellow at the Institute of Developing Economies (IDE), Japan External Trade Organization (JETRO). His research interests lie in the fields of constitutional politics, political institutions, and elections in Indonesia. His publications include the chapters "The Origins of the 1945 Constitution", in *Constitutional Foundings in Southeast Asia*, edited by Kevin Y.L. Tan and Ngoc Son Bui (Hart Publishing, 2019), and "President Restrained: Effects of Parliamentary Rule and Coalition Government on Indonesia's Presidentialism", in *Presidents, Assemblies, and Policymaking in Asia*, edited by Yuko Kasuya (Palgrave Macmillan, 2013).

KHANISA is a Researcher at the Research Center for Politics, BRIN. She received her bachelor's degree in international relations from UGM in 2010 and completed her MA in international relations and a master's in diplomacy at the Australian National University in 2015. She focuses on ASEAN and Southeast Asian issues.

Riri KUSUMARANI is a researcher at BRIN. She completed her PhD at the Korea Advanced Institute of Science and Technology in 2019, majoring in business and technology management. She has diverse research interests, mainly in behavioural science, social media, information systems, enterprise architecture, and crowdfunding. Her first paper on political crowdfunding was published by Elsevier and she has also published a paper on IT portfolio management. Her latest publications discuss the US elections from a crowdfunding perspective.

Meirina Ayumi MALAMASSAM is a PhD candidate in the School of Demography, ANU. She is a researcher at the Research Center for Population, BRIN, with research interests in population mobility and regional development. She holds a Master of Social Research from ANU and an MSc in Population Studies from UGM. Her PhD thesis focuses on the interrelationships between youth migration dynamics and education trajectories in Indonesia. Her recent publications include "Understanding the Migration of the Highly Educated to Sorong City, West Papua, Indonesia" (*Asian and Pacific Migration Journal*) and "Spatial Structure of Youth Migration in Indonesia: Does Education Matter?" (*Applied Spatial Analysis and Policy*).

David MESCHEDE is a PhD student in social and cultural anthropology at Cologne University, Germany. He researches socio-economic transformations and future-making practices among the rural Dayak people of East Kalimantan, Indonesia. He takes special interest in the impact of environmental changes and climate change on the lives of indigenous peoples living in the tropical rainforest in Southeast Asia as well as the history of the island of Borneo in general.

Temi Indriati MIRANDA obtained her PhD in Planning from Queensland University. She earned her master's in management of natural resources and sustainable agriculture at the Norwegian University of Life Sciences (NMBU). She prefers to call herself a sociologist due to her bachelor of sociology degree from the University of General Soedirman. A researcher at Research Center for Population, BRIN, her focus of study is the rural-urban dynamics in the form of housing, transportation and social stratification. Her PhD thesis is "Decision-Making Process Used by Middle-Middle Class Families to Access Homeownership in Greater Jakarta, Indonesia" and part of it was published at the first international seminar on family and consumer issues in Asia in 2018.

Anne PARLINA is a researcher at BRIN. She completed her doctoral programme in the Department of Electrical Engineering at UI. Her main research interests focus on text mining, information systems, and social media analysis. Her most recent works are on text mining techniques and the content analysis of academic journals.

Ardanareswari Ayu PITALOKA is a junior researcher at the Research Center for Population, BRIN. She has an MA in Sociology from UGM. Her research experience began in 2018 as a research assistant at LIPI (later BRIN). Her current research focuses on urban-rural dynamics, social and digital transformation, gender dynamics, social inclusion and social innovation. Her master's thesis "Education of Children Through Village Pre-school Education" mainly looked at the social innovation by a community of mothers in voluntarily organizing early childhood education for children living in rural areas.

Septi SATRIANI is a PhD candidate at UI and has worked as a researcher at the Research Center for Politics, BRIN since 2005. She obtained her master's degree from Gadjah Mada University in 2016. She has worked on several research topics such as local politics, conflict, and natural resource management. Her research papers have been published in various platforms such as the political research journal in LIPI (*P2P-LIPI*), the *Indonesian Journal of Political Research*, and by the national publisher in Indonesia. Her latest publication with her team is *Post-politicizing the Environment: Local Government Performance Assessments in Indonesia* (Springer, 2023).

Deasy SIMANDJUNTAK is a political scientist and a political anthropologist. She is Associate Professor at National Chengchi University, Taipei, and Associate Fellow at ISEAS. Her PhD (2010) was conferred by the University of Amsterdam. Her research interests focus mainly on Southeast Asia's politics and democratization, Indonesia's national and local politics, patronage democracy, and identity politics. Her latest publication is "Disciplining the Accepted and Amputating the Deviants: Religious Nationalism and Segregated Citizenship in Indonesia" (*Asian Journal of Law and Society*, 2021).

Lidya Christin SINAGA is a researcher at the Research Center for Politics, BRIN. She received her bachelor's degree in international relations from UGM in 2006 and completed her MA in international relations at Flinders University in 2016. Besides research on ASEAN and Southeast Asia, she also examines Chinese ethnic minority issues in Indonesia.

Dini SURYANI is a researcher at the Research Center for Politics, BRIN. She acquired her bachelor's degree from UGM in 2010 and her master's from the College of Asia and the Pacific, ANU, in 2015. Her research mainly focuses on civil society, local politics, and natural resources governance in Indonesia. Her recent publications include *Post-politicizing the Environment: Local Government Performance Assessments in Indonesia* (Springer, 2023).

Imam SYAFI'I is a researcher at the Research Center for Politics, BRIN. His bachelor's degree in history is from the State University of Malang (2011) and his master's in history from Diponegoro University (2013). His research interests focus mainly on local politics and maritime history. Some of his recent publications are "Sejarah Garam Madura: Rivalitas Pengangkutan Garam Madura 1912–1981" [The History of Madura Salt: The Rivalry of Madura Salt Transport 1912–1981], "Coastal Forest Re-Grabbing: A Case from Langkat, North Sumatera, Indonesia" (2023), and *Post-politicizing the Environment: Local Government Performance Assessments in Indonesia* (2023).

Mardyanto Wahyu TRYATMOKO is a researcher at the Research Center for Domestic Government, BRIN. His bachelor's degree from UGM is in governance studies while he was awarded his master's degree from the University of Brawijaya, Indonesia and the National Graduate Institute for Policy Studies (GRIPS) in Tokyo, Japan. In 2021, he finished his doctoral studies at the University of Queensland, Australia. His research focuses on decentralization and regional autonomy, and peace and conflict studies in Indonesia. He is also interested in scrutinizing the practice of special autonomy, which was the focus of his doctoral thesis, "The Institutionalisation of Special Autonomy as Ethnic Conflict Resolution? The Case of Papua, Indonesia".

Marcellinus Mandira Budi UTOMO is a researcher from the Research Center for Society and Culture, BRIN. Prior to his current position, he worked for the Ministry of Environment and Forestry. He holds a Bachelor of Forestry from UGM and a Master of Forestry from ANU. His current research interests are related to the politics of water resources, civil society organization of environmental safeguards, forest governance, and climate change. He actively writes scientific publications in international and national journals, and book chapters and is an invited reviewer for some international journals.

Ian Douglas WILSON is a Senior Lecturer in International Politics and Security Studies, Academic Chair of the Global Security Program, and a Co-Director of the Indo-Pacific Research Centre at Murdoch University, Western Australia. His research interests cover Indonesian politics and society, in particular the dynamics of street politics and urban social movements. He is the author of *The Politics of Protection Rackets* (2015) and *Politik Tenaga Dalam* (2020).

Glossary

adat	traditional or customary (as in law or custom, or referring to a community)
AJI	Aliansi Jurnalis Independen (Alliance of Independent Journalists)
aksi	street actions
ALKI II	Alur Laut Kepulauan Indonesia II (Indonesian Archipelagic Sea Channels)
AMAN	Aliansi Masyarakat Adat Nusantara (Alliance of Indigenous Peoples of the Archipelago)
APBN	direct government budget
APL	Area Peruntukan Lain (allocation area)
APPSI	All-Indonesian Provincial Government Association
ART	household assistant
ASN	state civil servants
BAPPEDA	Badan Perencanaan dan Pembangunan Daerah (Agency for Regional Planning and Development)
BAPPENAS	Badan Perencanaan Pembangunan Nasional (National Development Planning Agency)
binnenstad	centre, inner city
BPN	Badan Pertanahan Nasional (National Land Agency)
BPS PPU	Badan Pusat Statistik (Central Bureau of Statistics) Penajam Paser Utara (North Penajan Paser)
buitenstad	outskirts
BumDes	Badan Usaha Milik Desa (village-owned enterprise)
BWP	Botswana Pula
CBD	Central Business District
CSO	Civil Society Organizations
DAS	Daerah Aliran Sungai
DPD	Dewan Perwakilan Daerah (Regional Representatives Council)

GLOSSARY

DPR	Dewan Perwakilan Rakyat (House of Representatives)
DPRD	Dewan Perwakilan Rakyat Daerah (Regional House of Representatives)
DPR-RI	Dewan Perwakilan Rakyat Republik Indonesia
DWT	deadweight tonnage
FDI	Foreign Direct Investment
FPI	Islamic Defenders Front
FWI	Forest Watch Indonesia
GMF	Global Maritime Fulcrum
GONGO	Government-Organized Non-Governmental Organizations
GRDP	Gross Regional Domestic Product
HEI	Higher Education Institutions
HGB	Hak Guna Bangunan (right to build)
HGU	Hak Guna Usaha (right to cultivate)
HLSW	Sungai Wain Protection Forest
HPH	Hak Pengusahaan Hutan (forest concession rights)
HPK	Hutan produksi konvers (convertible production forest)
HTI	Hutan Tanaman Industri (industrial forest plantation)
HWC	Human-Wildlife Conflict
IAP	Indonesian Association of Planners
IDM	Indonesia Development Monitoring
IHM	PT ITCI Hutani Manunggal
IKN	Ibu Kota Negara (Capital City)
ITCI	International Timber Corporation Indonesia
IUP	Izin Usaha Pertambangan (Mining Licence)
IWGIA	International Working Group on Indigenous Affairs
JAL	Jaringan Advokat Lingkungan (Environmental Advocates Network)
JATAM	Jaringan Advokasi Tambang (Mining Advocacy Network)
KADIN	Kamar Dagang dan Industri (Chambers of Commerce and Industry)
KEE	Kawasan Ekosistem Esensial
Kementerian ATR/BPN	Ministry of Agrarian Affairs and Spatial Planning

KI	Kawasan Industri (industrial area)
KIA	foreign fishing vessels
KIPP	Kawasan Inti Pusat Pemerintahan (Central Government Core Area)
KKI	Kebijakan Kelautan (Marine Policy) Indonesia
KLHK	Kementerian Lingkungan Hidup dan Kehutanan (Ministry of the Environment and Forestry)
KLHS	Kajian Lingkungan Hidup Strategis (Strategic Environment Assessment)
Kodamar	Komando Daerah Maritim (Maritime Regional Command)
Konsil Perwakilan Masyarakat	Council of Community Representatives
KPBU	Kerjasama Pemerintah Dengan Badan Usaha (Government Cooperation with Business Entities)
KPIKN	Kawasan Pengembangan IKN
KSN	Kawasan Strategis Nasional
LBH	Lembaga Bantuan Hukum
LIPI	Lembaga Ilmu Pengetahuan Indonesia
LSLA	Large-Scale Land Acquisitions
Maphilindo	short-lived proposal in 1963 by Jose Rizal for Malaysia, the Philippines and Indonesia to form a loose confederation
Monas	Monumen Nasional
MSME	Micro, Small and Medium Enterprises
MP3EI 2011–2025	Masterplan Percepatan dan Perluasan Pembangunan Ekonomi Indonesia
MPR	Majelis Permusyawaratan Rakyat (People's Consultative Assembly)
Muswayarah Nasional	National Conference
NCICD	National Capital Integrated Coastal Development
NOVACAP	Companhia Urbanizadora da Nova Capital do Brasil (Development Commission for the New Capital of Brazil)
OIKN	Otorita Ibu Kota Nusantara (IKN Authority)
OJK	Financial Service Authority
OR-IPSH	Institute of Social Sciences and Humanities

Pelindo	PT. Pelabuhan Indonesia
PEN	Program Ekonomi Nasional (National Economic Programme)
PJKA	Pulang Jumat Kembali Ahad
PNBP	Penerimaan Negara Bukan Pajak
PNS	civil servants
PP	Peraturan Pemerintah (government regulation)
PPAT	land certificate makers
PPU	Penajam Paser Utara (North Penajam Paser)
PROFOR	Program on Forests
Prolegnas	Priorities in National Legislation Programme
PSN	Proyek Strategis Nasional (National Strategic Project)
PTSL	Complete Systematic Land Registration
RDPU	Rapat Dengar Pendapat Umum
RDTR	Rencana Detail Tata Ruang (Detailed Spatial Plan)
RPJMN	National Mid-Term Development Plan
RT	Rukun Tetangga (neighbourhood association)
RTH	public green open spaces
RTRW	Rencana Tata Ruang Wilayah (Regional)
RTRWN	Rencana Tata Ruang Wilayah Nasional (National)
RTRWP	Rencana Tata Ruang dan Wilayah Provinsi (Provincial)
SBSN	Surat Berharga Syariah Negara (Government Islamic Bonds)
SDGs	Sustainable Development Goals
SFM	Sustainable Forest Management
SHM	Sertifikat Hak Milik (Certificate of Right of Ownership)
SUN	Surat Utang Negara (state bonds)
TMII	Taman Mini Indonesia Indah (Beautiful Indonesia Miniature Park)
TNI	Tentara Nasional Indonesia (Indonesian Armed Forces)
TOD	Transfer-Oriented Development
UNDP	United Nations Development Programme
UU IKN	Law on the State's Capital (No. 3/2022)
Visi Indonesia 2033	Indonesia 2033 Vision

Visi Indonesia Emas 2045	Golden Indonesian Vision 2045
WALHI	Indonesian Forum for the Living Environment
WP	Wilayah Perencanaan (Planning Area)
WPP-NRI	Republic of Indonesia Fisheries Management Area

INTRODUCTION
The Road to Nusantara—Process, Challenges and Opportunities

Athiqah Nur Alami, Siwage Dharma Negara, Yanuar Nugroho and Julia M. Lau

After many years of discourse, in 2019 the Indonesian government decided to build a new capital city (*Ibu Kota Negara*, IKN) in the Penajam Paser Utara and Kutai Kartanegara municipalities, East Kalimantan province. The new capital city is named Nusantara, which means "archipelago", and it is planned that Nusantara will replace Jakarta as the main site of Indonesia's central government starting in 2024.

The capital relocation will mark significant transformations for Indonesians, not only in administrative, cultural and socio-economic aspects but significantly, in national politics. Jakarta has been the centre of gravity for Indonesia's government, business, culture and society since pre-independence days. Therefore, relocating the capital city to Nusantara, East Kalimantan, is perceived as a political commitment by the current administration to shift the national centre of gravity to a region outside Java.

Narrowing the developmental imbalance between Java and the outer islands has been at the heart of the capital city relocation narrative. Java, known for its overpopulation, is home to 152 million people (around 56 per cent of Indonesia's population), according to the most recent census in 2020.[1] This contrasts sharply with the 6 per cent of Indonesians who live in Kalimantan, which is six times larger than Java island. With its massive demographic advantage, Java produces about 59 per cent of the country's GDP. East Kalimantan is nevertheless among the provinces with the highest gross regional domestic product (GRDP) per capita, second only to Jakarta. Yet, East Kalimantan is underpopulated, with just 3.7 million inhabitants or about a third of Jakarta's.[2] The opportunity for growth is thus significant.

The other main reason cited for the capital city relocation is that Jakarta is deemed increasingly unsuitable to be the nation's capital, given its numerous cross-cutting socio-economic and environmental challenges. Despite public policy efforts to control the effects of growth, worsening traffic congestion, pollution, and the increased risk and cost of frequent flooding have all adversely affected the quality of life in the city. IKN Nusantara, in contrast, is considered by some to be less exposed to natural disasters and is strategically located in the country's geographic centre. The abundant forest lands surrounding the proposed site of Nusantara are also the inspiration for a liveable green capital city of Indonesia's future.

Despite the apparent benefits of relocating the capital city, there is significant scepticism among Indonesian and foreign observers as to whether the government can indeed realize its "dream" capital city, envisaged as a smart, innovative, inclusive and green city. Arguably, this ambitious project is unlike any other capital city project or relocation. Although Malaysia moved its administrative capital from Kuala Lumpur (KL) to Putrajaya in 2001, it took over five years to construct and Putrajaya was only 34 kilometres (km) or so away from KL. Moving the capital city from Jakarta to Nusantara, about 2,000 km away, will require massive resources and effort. It is expected to cost Rp466 trillion (approximately US$30 billion)[3] to build Nusantara's supporting infrastructure and brand-new government offices and residences for over 100,000[4] civil servants and their family members who are expected to move to Nusantara (from 2024 to 2029).

This gigantic project will not be completed within one or two presidential terms and needs to be supported by policy decisions and policymakers at the national and subnational levels for the next few decades. With the current Widodo administration having less than two years to prepare the legal and policy foundations and the basic infrastructure for this historic relocation, many questions remain about the project's feasibility and continuity.

There is a real risk that the incoming president and his or her new Cabinet and the new government in 2024 may not fully support the new capital project. This is despite the current administration's attempt to revise the IKN Law of 2022 to ensure the megaproject's continuity. There is also no guarantee that the new capital will be better than Jakarta in terms of accommodating the various and vast expectations, needs and challenges on the environmental, economic, socio-cultural and political fronts. A project of this scale will undoubtedly and significantly impact Nusantara's natural environment and local communities. These impacts may persist for a long time and change the overall development trajectory of the people and the regions. Whether this will be for better or for worse is to some extent beyond any administration's control, even with policies designed to anticipate and pre-empt some of the problems that Jakarta as a capital city has faced.

More importantly, the development of Nusantara should not be seen as a personal legacy of President Joko Widodo, who wishes to commemorate Indonesia's 79th Independence Day on 17 August 2024 in the new capital city. The IKN should be seen as the whole nation-state's endeavour to redefine Indonesia's future developmental path. Nusantara is not significant just in terms of its unprecedented cost and scale, but it is designed to accommodate various political, economic, environmental and security considerations. In many ways, the Widodo and successive administrations' success or failure in relocating the capital will define a great part of Indonesia's future trajectory and potentially impact Southeast Asia and the Asia-Pacific region.

Despite the growing interest in the capital relocation from Indonesian and external observers, only limited knowledge and information have been publicly available regarding the formation of Nusantara, its existing communities and the natural and economic environments of the proposed new capital region. Given this gap, the Indonesia Studies Programme at Singapore's ISEAS – Yusof Ishak Institute collaborated with Indonesia's Institute of Social Sciences and Humanities (OR-IPSH), National Research and Innovation Agency (BRIN), in Jakarta, to co-publish the present book. This edited volume contains what is probably the first comprehensive collection of academic writing and research findings on the complex challenges surrounding the IKN relocation.

All chapters started as papers presented at the conference "The Road to Nusantara: Process, Challenges and Opportunities" on 27–28 October 2022 at ISEAS in Singapore, co-sponsored by BRIN. This publication is made possible with the support of Konrad-Adenauer-Stiftung for the conference, which allowed the participants and audience, including all the editors and contributors to this volume, to reflect on the challenges and opportunities faced by Indonesia's central and subnational governments in implementing a more balanced, inclusive and sustainable development for Nusantara. Many of the key takeaways and policy recommendations from the multi-dimensional studies presented at the conference were refined and are presented in this edited volume.

Structure of the Book

The book is divided into three key segments: historical perspectives and political trajectories highlighting various discourses behind the relocation of the new capital city; challenges arising during the development of the IKN and transition process, including environmental and human rights issues; and opportunities that the development of Nusantara may bring, primarily economic ones but also including social innovations and green technology.

The first group of chapters gives an overview of historical processes and pathways towards Nusantara. In the first chapter, Yanuar Nugroho, Wasisto Raharjo Jati, Pradita Devis Dukarno and Iryan Ali Herdiansyah give a historical perspective of the capital city relocation idea and review the evolution of policies concerning the capital relocation plan from Sukarno to Widodo. The authors argue that since there has been a continuation of the idea of relocating Indonesia's capital throughout its post-independence, this long-term project should be able to secure the political commitment of present and future decision-makers.

Mardyanto Wahyu Tryatmoko and Koichi Kawamura discuss the regulations of the capital city relocation in Chapter 2. They argue that the relocation planning lacks a clear institutional framework in connection to the regional government system and the involvement of local people. Consequently, they argue that this is a setback for Indonesia's existing decentralization system, with potential ramifications for public resentment and conflict within society.

In Chapter 3, Ian Douglas Wilson writes that the new capital city will be crucial in influencing the spatial setting for Indonesian democracy. Drawing on insights from the theories of cities as spaces of democratic processes and reflecting on the experiences of Brazil, Malaysia and Myanmar in developing their capital cities, Wilson foresees that Nusantara will challenge the spatial practice of democracy in Indonesia.

In Chapter 4, Riri Kusumarani and Anne Parlina discuss the financing issue of the new capital city, with a special focus on crowdfunding. They identify the potential risks and the people's perception of crowdfunding for the IKN. Using an online survey and expert interviews, the authors show that there have been negative public perceptions towards crowdfunding for IKN, because most people believe that IKN financing should be the government's responsibility. The authors cite the lack of legal provisions for civic crowdfunding, which could complicate the protection of citizens and financial backers from risks that may arise from their support of the IKN project.

The book's second part focuses on the multitude of challenges in developing IKN. Dimas Wisnu Adrianto and Kathleen Meira Berta's chapter leads with a discussion of the roles of spatial planning in addressing regional development challenges, including as an instrument to manage and safeguard the environment in Nusantara. From their data and participants' responses to a workshop for policy and other officials, Adrianto and Berta show how urban problems may exacerbate the complexities of development issues in the proposed capital city and point out the need to formulate adaptive policies to be responsive to the interests of related actors.

In Chapter 6, Septi Satriani, Pandu Yuhsina Adaba and Imam Syafi'i link the relocation of the new capital city with the interests of capitalist actors such as the private sector and industry. The authors, through local field interviews, give voice to some critical attitudes of the local people, mainly representatives from civil society organizations (CSOs), who believe that the IKN relocation plan would accelerate environmental damage in East Kalimantan. However, others support the relocation, as they believe that the relocation will improve their livelihoods.

Staying on the perspective of civil society and villagers in East Kalimantan, in Chapter 7, Deasy Simandjuntak and her co-authors David Meschede and Michaela Haug argue that the relocation of the capital city will influence the livelihoods of the local *adat* (traditional or customary) communities. The authors, mostly through surveys of local CSO representatives and anonymised statements from local residents, find that there has been a lack of public consultation and local participation in policy formulation for the IKN development.

More research on the redistribution pattern of inhabitants in the new capital city is highlighted in Chapter 8, where Meirina Ayumi Malamassam analyses how in-migration flows will affect the IKN, by first examining existing studies on in-migration and then exploring trends and patterns of spatial mobility across regions in Indonesia. She argues that the capital city relocation will affect local population planning in terms of the distribution of population groups who will stay and work in the city. She points out the importance of public engagement and continuous investment in urban amenities and public infrastructure to encourage workplace relocation and spatial mobility in the IKN.

Moving from challenges to opportunity is the main theme in Part III of the book. Dini Suryani, Dian Aulia and Marcellinus Mandira Budi Utomo, in Chapter 9, argue that the relocation to IKN could be an impetus for improved forest governance. This chapter identifies critical issues concerning deforestation and forest degradation, land concessions, and human-wildlife conflict in Nusantara. The authors believe that if the criteria for good forest governance can be effectively applied and followed, the IKN relocation could strengthen the remaining forested lands in East Kalimantan.

In Chapter 10, Rusli Cahyadi, Deny Hidayati, Ali Yansyah Abdurrahim, Temi Indriati Miranda and Ardanareswari Ayu Pitaloka discuss the idea of an inclusive "smart city" in Nusantara. They argue that notwithstanding such a vision, the establishment of a new capital city is likely to disrupt the livelihoods of local people and change the value of land and population dynamics in the region. To deal with these issues, they suggest increasing the capacity of the local people to participate in the developmental processes of the new capital city.

The last chapter discusses the new capital city's potential to augment Indonesia's national and security identity. Lidya Christin Sinaga and Khanisa Krisman question whether Nusantara could help project Indonesia's maritime identity, arguing that the IKN should represent Indonesia's maritime identity, given President Widodo's vision for Indonesia as a "Global Maritime Fulcrum".

We hope that this book will provide a range of interesting perspectives and broaden the scope for the present and future Indonesian governments and other stakeholders on the myriad critical challenges facing the capital city relocation process. The collaborative research efforts of Indonesian researchers from BRIN and others, and the insights and views of some of the local inhabitants of the proposed IKN zone provide this book with noteworthy and new data, and invaluable sentiments drawn directly from the ground. This effectively provides a real-time look into the current tensions and anticipation surrounding the capital city relocation. With this volume, we aim to provide policymakers and stakeholders in and outside of Indonesia, academia, and the general public in Indonesia with a better understanding of the potential problems and solutions for this historic relocation.

In closing, we thank all the invited contributors for their writing in this volume and hope our readers will find the book thought-provoking and informative. We would also like to give special mention to Ms Rebecca Neo, research officer in the Indonesia Studies Programme at ISEAS, for her invaluable help in preparing the manuscript for publication and to our colleagues at ISEAS Publishing.

Notes
1. Badan Pusat Statistik (BPS), "Jumlah Penduduk Hasil Proyeksi menurut Provinsi dan Jenis Kelamin" [Population Projection by Province], Proyeksi Penduduk Indonesia 2015–2045 Hasil SUPAS 2015, at https://www.bps.go.id/indicator/12/1886/1/jumlah-penduduk-hasil-proyeksi-menurut-provinsi-dan-jenis-kelamin.html (accessed 4 January 2023).
2. Ibid.
3. See *Bisnis.com*, "Anggaran Pembangunan IKN Meningkat Rp15 Triliun, Buat

Apa?" [The Budget for IKN Development Has Increased to 15 trillion, What for?], 31 October 2022, https://ekonomi.bisnis.com/read/20221031/45/1593211/anggaran-pembangunan-ikn-meningkat-rp15-triliun-buat-apa (accessed 4 January 2023).

4. Prahesti Pandanwangi, "Kebijakan dan Rencana Kerja Pemindahakan Aparatur Sipil Negara ke Ibukota Nusantara" [Regulations and Workplan for the Move of the State's Civil Apparatus to IKN], webinar by BRIN, Jakarta, 14 April 2022, https://www.youtube.com/watch?v=a1Bn0VLJUBs&t=293s (accessed 4 January 2023).

Part I
PROCESSES AND PATHWAYS TOWARDS NUSANTARA

1

NUSANTARA
A Historical Perspective

Yanuar Nugroho, Wasisto Raharjo Jati,
Pradita Devis Dukarno and
Iryan Ali Herdiansyah

INTRODUCTION

The relocation of the Indonesian state capital city is not a new issue. Historically, this policy has been echoed in the eras of Indonesia's past presidents Sukarno, Suharto and Susilo Bambang Yudhoyono (SBY). The lessons that can be learnt from the relocation policies in these three presidential eras are related to top-down and reactionary policies to domestic and international problems. For example, the policymakers took into account security and geopolitical tensions (external concerns) and environmental risks (domestic concerns).

Across the different administrations, the presidents directly initiated a top-down policymaking process when responding to the changing conditions during their administrations. For President Sukarno, it was more about the need for a new identity as the glue of solidarity between Java and outside Java, and for symbols for Indonesia as a leading "third world" country post-decolonization. In the era of President Suharto, this focused on the need for a new economic centre for economic equity and for an independent city that was regionally and globally competitive. The next few transitional governments under B.J. Habibie, Abdurrahman Wahid and Megawati Sukarnoputri arguably did not prioritize capital relocation. Instead, these presidents' signature policy legacies included the first direct presidential elections (after Megawati), domestic reconciliation and anti-corruption drives. The idea of capital relocation returned under President SBY, whose policy was more of a reaction to the potential for bigger ecological disasters such as floods, the subsidence of the soil layer and uncontrolled population density in Jakarta.

Unlike the top-down relocation plans of Sukarno, Suharto and SBY, in the era of President Joko Widodo ("Jokowi") the moving of the capital city and building a new one called "Nusantara" (or *Ibu Kota Negara*, IKN) is a mixed policymaking agenda that includes both an elite-driven agenda and a bottom-up one. Advocacy for the relocation of the capital was provided by the "Vision Indonesia 2033" team (since 2008) with Andrinof Chaniago as the pioneer and initiator. When Andrinof was subsequently appointed Minister of National Development Planning/Head of National Development Planning Agency (Bappenas), this idea was further developed into a policy draft paper starting in 2015. From there, a comprehensive agenda was formed, which eventually resulted in IKN Law No. 3 of 2022 (hereafter, UU IKN).

This chapter uses archival research and various sources (including academic and non-government policy papers) to provide some historical accounts and perspectives on the relocation of the Indonesian capital city from Jakarta to Nusantara. With this, it serves as a basis for a more comprehensive discussion on specific themes, which is taken up by the subsequent chapters.

Capital City Relocation: Genealogies and Current Connections

The policy of relocating the capital city of a country has historically emphasized the ruling government or leadership's desire to build a new civilization.[1] There is a boundary between past achievements and new hopes for the construction of a new capital. This demarcation shows the efforts of a country to leave behind a political legacy. Such a legacy, in the form of the (new) capital's development, symbolically glorifies the country's greatness and development. This goal, as the philosophical foundation of the new capital city, shows that the country can adapt to world developments but still maintain its national identity. In other words, a relocation of the capital can be seen as a country's attempt to compete globally and to strengthen national solidarity.

Historically, according to Vadim Rossman, the trend of capital city relocation has become a common phenomenon.[2] Since 1900, there has been a relocation of a capital city every two to three years. In general, there are two main reasons for capital city relocation: historical and functional.[3] An example of a historical reason is post-unification Germany in the late 1990s when the German capital moved from Bonn to Berlin. An example of a functional relocation is the moving of Malaysia's capital city from Kuala Lumpur to Putrajaya, allocating the functions of state administration to a new, previously undeveloped, area. The appointment of Jakarta as Indonesia's capital city in 1961 appeared to be similarly driven by pragmatic reasons: improving Jakarta's infrastructure as part of the preparation for its hosting of the 1962 Asian Games was deemed less costly than relocating the capital.

For the relocation of Indonesia's capital city, many might think that this idea was initiated in the Sukarno era but there is no mention in any official document issued by his government in this regard.[4] A piece of information listing Palangkaraya as the projected capital city has not been convincingly verified. A study by Vitchek and Lubis noted that there was some historical evidence showing the construction of Palangkaraya with the help of the former Soviet Union, as the forerunner of the nation's capital.[5] The construction of Palangkaraya was for a pilot project of a native-planned Indonesian city. (In an article in *Kompas*, Guntur Soekarno Putra—Sukarno's son—recounted that he witnessed Dayak community leaders such as Tjilik Riwut often visiting the State Palace to meet President Sukarno in the late 1950s.[6])

However, in his memoir, Tjilik Riwut made almost no mention of the idea of a capital city relocation to Palangkaraya during his meetings with Sukarno. They instead discussed the government's efforts to embrace the Dayak community and to integrate them by awarding the establishment of a new province, Central Kalimantan, with Palangkaraya as its capital city in accordance with Law No. 27 of 1959.[7] This was confirmed by Gerry van Klinken's findings that Palangkaraya was projected to be the location for the short-lived "Maphilindo" (Malaysia, Philippines, Indonesia) grouping which was supported by Sukarno.[8]

Another relocation plan mentioned Jonggol, in West Java province, which is considered another historical point. The Jonggol plan was initiated by President Suharto's son Bambang Triatmodjo and conglomerates which wanted to develop an independent city with an area of 30,000 hectares (ha). Projected as being able to reduce "Jakarta's burden", this relocation plan was considered as potentially distributing growth. As a result, Jonggol's status as a water conservation area was revoked and it even obtained financing facilities from banks (see Presidential Decree No. 1 of 1997). With significant support from the government, this project was reported as being part of a capital city relocation plan.[9] However, this project was not actually meant to relocate the country's capital but to build an independent city, as many development companies did in the Suharto era.[10]

As explained above, previous Indonesian governments did not relocate the capital. The establishment of Palangkaraya was a form of government appreciation for the integration of the Dayak community into the Republic of Indonesia. Likewise, the development of the Jonggol area was more business-oriented and driven by economic purposes rather than government administration. However, in urban symbolism, Leclerc notes there is a "lighthouse" or symbolic framework laid out by previous governments.[11] For example, the geopolitical context developed by President Sukarno made Palangkaraya a regional hub, especially for developing countries at the time. Jonggol's development was intended to be a new economic development area that could attract foreign investors. Likewise, focusing on national development to harness potential foreign investment is the foundation of the new capital Nusantara's development policy under President Jokowi.

The current policy of capital relocation continues the "lighthouse" agenda of Indonesia's previous governments. The agenda emphasizes the Indonesian narrative where new glorification efforts are carried out by revitalizing Nusantara as the capital. As for regional and global interests, the narrative is strengthened by making the IKN the centre of a new ASEAN and for international economic growth through the promotion of Indonesia's geographical and maritime advantages.

Capital Relocation Ideas from Previous Administrations

The idea of relocating Indonesia's capital city has crossed the minds of three different presidents and administrations since the country's independence. The perception that Jakarta would become more congested due to urbanization and lack of the environment's carrying capacity were determining factors for relocating the capital city. Yet, Jakarta remains the capital city of Indonesia, given the dynamics and turbulence behind the unfinished relocation plans from previous governments.

First, there has been an absence of a clear and long-term legal basis for relocation policy specifically regulating the transfer of the capital city. During the Sukarno and Suharto administrations, the related regulations had different aims (such as planned cities or new municipalities) and were not targeted at capital relocation. The legal basis used was the Emergency Law (No. 10 of 1957) and Presidential Decree (No. 1 of 1995) which did not have permanent legal standing. According to the Indonesian legal principle of *lex superior derogate legi inferiori* (i.e., that lower or more specific regulations cannot contradict higher regulations), these two temporary regulations, having statuses short of law (*undang-undang*) are inadequate as a policy foundation. The implication is that before Jokowi, there was no strong political commitment towards moving the Indonesian capital city, only political discourse.

Second, there has been inconsistency in determining the area for the new capital city. Choices centred on the Jakarta-Jonggol-Palangkaraya region, as shown in the history of the policy of capital relocation. Every policy background study on capital relocation (prior to Jokowi's administration) merely replicated the abovementioned regions, which suggests the lack of seriousness in moving the capital. There is also uncertainty regarding the moving and the arrangement of the capital in the policy-setting agenda. There was no inclusive participation from below, which resulted in widespread public apathy regarding the capital relocation issue.[12]

Third, state capital relocation was never implemented as a long-term policy and was not a priority even for Jokowi initially.[13] From Sukarno to Jokowi, discussion of a capital city relocation appeared towards the end of each presidency. This resulted in a rushed policy-making process as the previous presidents wanted the proposed new capital to be their legacy,[14] making these merely symbolic policies. One implication of all this is the discontinuation of capital relocation policies across different administrations: these were reactive responses to the problems that arose in Jakarta or worse, only political discourse among the elites.[15]

Relocation of the Capital City from Jakarta to Palangkaraya under Sukarno

The big narrative about the capital relocation during the era of President Sukarno was decolonization, which was related to the Asian-African solidarity echoed by himself to escape colonialism. In line with that spirit, Palangkaraya initially was not projected to be the new capital city. However, its later development showed that the main policy had shifted. There were several masterminds behind the shift such as the aforementioned local elite Tjilik Riwut who advocated for Palangkaraya as a new capital and Semaun, a former exile who lived in Eastern Europe for thirty years. They called on Sukarno to relocate Indonesia's capital city to be outside Jakarta. This encouraged the development of an area to be used as a symbol of decolonization. Sukarno realized that the development of cities and settlements was unequal: those in the coastal areas are less at risk than those in the inland regions for tropical diseases such as malaria and cholera.[16]

The idea to build a modern and healthy capital city continued to grow. In 1947, Sukarno formed a *Panitia Agung* (Supreme Committee) whose task was to find a suitable city to become the nation's capital. The Committee determined the physical criteria for the city: a strategic position, being easily accessible by sea, air and land, and healthy sanitation and air.[17] In addition, the city must not be a colonial legacy. There was a change in the orientation of the future capital city as imagined by Indonesian political leaders: it was not sufficient that it would be comfortable to live in, healthy, and advanced, but must also be a symbol of independence from imperialism. There was hope for a new capital city built by the Indonesian people as a newly independent nation. Several big cities were considered, including Jakarta, Bandung, Malang, Surabaya, Yogyakarta and Surakarta, but these were already shaped by the colonial era. Other areas that met the criteria were Magelang and Temanggung, in the middle of Java Island, with cooler temperatures and a relatively lighter colonial imprint. However, the committee never completed its recommendations on these cities' level of readiness to be Indonesia's capital.[18]

The idea of building a new capital city that was not a legacy of colonialism continued to grow, driven by new hopes that were often echoed by leaders and discourses in several national newspapers. These revolved around progressive ideas against feudalism, anti-colonialism, and modernity—emphasizing social mobility. These reports were full of optimism, so the people also felt convinced of the reality of these dreams and hopes.[19] On many occasions, President Sukarno often encouraged the imagination and hopes for a new capital after Indonesia gained full sovereignty. In his 1950 speech aired nationwide after he returned from Yogyakarta and started the government in Jakarta, he envisaged the capital as a centre of power and strong leadership. He wished Indonesia could be a great nation with power equal to the Western countries—apparently alluding to the Majapahit empire.[20]

The discourse about relocating the country's capital to a relatively new area that was deeper inland attracted Sukarno. This inspiration emerged when in the mid-1950s to early 1960s, Brazil moved its capital Rio de Janeiro to an inland area, Brasilia. Pakistan also moved its capital from Karachi, a port city, to Islamabad, in the centre of the country. These examples convinced Sukarno that Indonesia needed a new capital city to forge a stronger national bond. This then became a capital city that served as a unitary geographical symbol and that was not Java-centric.[21] In his vision, Jakarta was not strong enough to become a unifying symbol of centre-region relations or, in the context of the 1950s, Java and outside Java. In 1950, regional upheaval began to emerge against Jakarta, which was seen as a representation of the central government. Issues of equitable development, military conflicts, and interethnic conflicts often arose, and new spaces (new provinces) were needed as the actualization of local elites' existence. In addition, there was a perception of Javanese dominance because most of the governorships of provinces were given to the Javanese elite.[22]

The discourse on moving the capital was raised at the National Conference (*Muswayarah Nasional*) initiated by then Prime Minister Djuanda on 10 September 1957. According to the historical record, this conference was a strategic forum and nearly all of the political party leaders, governors, military leaders, and representatives of societal groups totalling about 400 people, were present. Many important decisions were reached, including a call for balanced development between the centre and the regions, the establishment of a National Council which was expected to formulate appropriate economic policies, and the liberation of West Irian. There was discussion of the plan to move the capital from Jakarta,[23] including prerequisites that must be met, such as the strength of the state's finances, the area's history, strategic position, a city psychology that could provide peace of mind, urban planning, and the formation of a special committee to prepare for the relocation.[24]

Tjilik Riwut, who at that time was the Regent of Kotawaringin, argued that the Indonesian government should be present in remote areas by forming a new province.[25] This idea was accepted by the central government because it did not conflict with national discourse. Sukarno needed loyalists who were able to ensure that the state apparatus was in Central Kalimantan to maintain order. Tjilik's aspirations were accepted by other central elites including the military, maybe because he had a military paramedic background and was active in Indonesia's Revolutionary war. Political parties such as the Indonesian National Party (PNI) and the Indonesian Communist Party (PKI) also supported the formation of a new province, perhaps because Masyumi was already dominant in South Kalimantan. Tjilik was later appointed the first governor of Central Kalimantan.[26]

Tjilik Riwut frequently visited Jakarta to meet Sukarno; several designs for the city of Palangkaraya (as capital city) were submitted to Sukarno. The development of Palangkaraya was planned to be in synergy with the Kahayan River, which provided the main access to the city. The city is located about 50 metres from this river, while the proposed government area and the governor's palace were planned as the central point, with settlements in the areas that would become an urban forest.[27]

The initial narrative of Palangkaraya as the provincial capital which was then developed into a candidate for the country's capital outside Java Island could be traced through interviews with Roeslan Abdul Gani and A.A. Baramuli remembering Tjilik Riwut.[28] According to Roeslan and Baramuli, it was Tjilik who, at the National Council meeting, proposed to move the capital city to Palangkaraya because he saw its geographical position was in the middle of Indonesia with a large area of land. According to Presidential Decrees No. 158 of 1957 and No. 95 of 1958 (on the National Council), Roeslan was the deputy chairman and Baramuli was the representative from Sulawesi, while Tjilik represented Kalimantan. Sukarno personally inaugurated Palangkaraya as the capital of Central Kalimantan on 17 July 1957. He was also interested in the city of Palangkaraya as a symbol of national independence.

However, the idea of Palangkaraya as the new Indonesian capital was never fulfilled. One main consideration was the huge cost required to build infrastructure on peatland, which was enormous in the 1950s.[29] The other factor was political support and commitment. President Sukarno was not so serious about realizing the plan. In his speech on the 437th anniversary of Jakarta on 22 June 1964, he praised Jakarta as a historical city where the country's independence proclamation text had been read, a revolutionary city, and an international city that had hosted the Asian Games.[30] Finally, Law No. 10 of 1964 declared the Special Capital Region of Jakarta Raya as the capital of the Republic of Indonesia, which stopped further discourse on capital relocation under Sukarno.

Proposed Relocation of Capital from Jakarta to Jonggol under Suharto

Under Suharto, the discourse on the capital city relocation emerged almost coincidentally. According to Bappenas, the capital city relocation in the New Order era was linked to the construction of Jonggol, based on Presidential Decree No. 1 of 1997.[31] The decree did not mention relocating the capital and designating Jonggol as the new one, but only the development of Jonggol as an independent city in three subdistricts (Jonggol, Cileungsi, and Cariu Bogor, West Java). The assumption that Jonggol would be the capital city had existed since 1996. The government often issued statements about the importance of moving the national capital at that time but did not mention a specific location. With an area of 30,000 ha developed by the consortium of Bukit Jonggol Asri (initiated by Bambang Trihatmodjo) and with the government's support, it is understandable that some thought the government would move the capital to Jonggol.

Jonggol was projected to be an independent area that could become a centre for community activities to reduce Jakarta's burden. The concept of an independent city was more functional: the focus was the effort to build a suburb with the economy and business as its main orientation. However, the government did not explicitly stipulate that this was a relocation of the capital city and instead, it emphasized a shared function (i.e., as a "split" capital with Jakarta as the *de jure* national capital) with some functions to be transferred *de facto* to Jonggol and other supporting cities.

The developers did not deny that there was a desire to relocate government institutions to Jonggol.[32] As depicted below, Jonggol is the largest independent township development project in the Jabotabek area (see Figure 1.1). Based on Presidential Decree No. 43 of 1983, at the time Jonggol was included in the strategic water catchment area for the DKI

FIGURE 1.1
Jonggol as a Self-Contained City

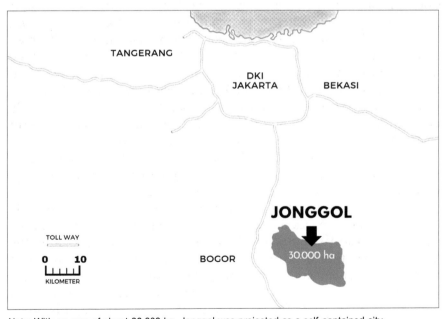

Note: With an area of about 30,000 ha, Jonggol was projected as a self-contained city.
Source: Authors' adaptation of Robert Cowherd, "Does Planning Culture Matter? Dutch and American Models in Indonesian Urban Transformations", in *Comparative Planning Cultures*, edited by Bishwapriya Sanyal (New York: Routledge, 2005).

Jakarta area and its surroundings. However, with the issuance of the Decree of the Minister of Forestry Djamaluddin Surjohadikusumo No. 1327 (Menhut-VII/1995) dated 12 September 1995, this status as a water catchment area was revoked and the construction of Jonggol was allowed. This was later strengthened by Presidential Decree No. 1 1997 and the Decree of the Governor of the First Level Region of West Java No. 536/SK.969-Huk/97 concerning the Appointment of PT Bukit Jonggol Asri as the developer of the Jonggol Area, Bogor Regency.

The huge potential of the real estate market in this suburban area connected the government of the country and entrepreneurs at that time. Cowherd and Winarso reveal that almost 80 per cent of real-estate projects in the Jabotabek area were controlled by President Suharto's family and business cronies.[33] Among these, the Jonggol development plan directly controlled by Bambang Trihatmodjo was clearly included.

From the historical perspective of regional development planning, the development of independent cities is not something new, but it is an effort to reproduce the spatial and social segregation that has occurred from the colonial era to the post-independence era. According to Freek Colombijn and Abidin Kusno, during the colonial era there was already a policy separating the centre (*binnenstad*) from the outskirts (*buitenstad*), and the development of elite settlements such as *heuvelterrein* (hill areas, synonymous with a healthier life).[34] In the 1950s, the government built the satellite town of Kebayoran Baru as a buffer for the centre of the capital city.[35] The term "satellite city" was used to indicate an area that had markets, schools, places of worship, and other public facilities, which generally distinguished itself from the village area. Then, in the 1990s, the term emerged to describe, "[a] residential area/unit of residence from various levels of society, which can already stand alone, and does not depend on other regions/cities in meeting their needs, in terms of spatial planning", which includes physical, economic, and governmental, aspects.[36]

The vision of Jonggol as an independent city emphasized economic motives rather than political ones. The development of this independent city was an anticipatory step towards the surge of urbanization in Jakarta. The narrative shows that the peripheral development policy was an important key to diverting population migration so that it would not be concentrated in Jakarta. The growing population, traffic irregularities, and other social problems became parts of a big narrative of the importance of building Jonggol. Located about 50 km from Jakarta, the independent city Jonggol, with infrastructure such as schools, business districts, recreational facilities and hospitals, among others, was believed to be able to reduce the burden of the capital. In the 1990s, the trend of similar independent cities emerged, initiated by the development of Bumi Serpong Damai by the Ciputra Group. This concept focused on the capacity of the city, to make it easier for its residents to access various public facilities, thus reducing the burden on Jakarta. Jonggol was idealized as such a city.

Relocation of Capital under SBY?

After the fall of the authoritarian New Order and at the beginning of *reformasi*, the plan on relocating the capital city had not yet become public discourse. The early transitional governments from Presidents Habibie to Megawati instead prioritized and consolidated democratic foundations such as decentralization, reconciliation and direct elections. The plan for capital relocation was rolled out only during the administration of President Yudhoyono (two terms, 2004–9 and 2009–14). However, unlike Sukarno and Suharto, he did not issue a legal framework for the relocation of the capital city.

There were nevertheless two events that pushed President Yudhoyono to carry the discourse on moving the capital city during his leadership. First, he attended the Working Meeting of the All-Indonesian Provincial Government Association (APPSI) on 2 December 2009 in Palangkaraya. This was the first time SBY discussed any plan to move the capital city. "Taking into account Jakarta and its unsolved problems, the President believes there is a comprehensive need to study capital relocation", said Velix Wanggai, then Presidential Special Advisor on regional development and decentralization.[37]

The strong reasons given were the shifting of the population burden from Jakarta, as the population growth rate (Jakarta's 28 million inhabitants was equivalent to 12 per cent of the total population in 2010) rose and the importance of economic equality (across the country). Second, President Yudhoyono became increasingly interested in relocating the capital city after returning from Astana, the new capital city of Kazakhstan. He was reportedly impressed with Astana, a city that was intentionally built to be the capital of Kazakhstan, according to then-presidential spokesperson Julian Aldrin Pasha.[38]

It is important to note that the relocation policy under SBY was partly a reaction to problems like severe traffic jams and the massive flooding in 2013 in Jakarta.[39] This means that the plan for capital relocation during his administration was not undertaken with medium- or long-term planning in mind, as was the case in the eras of Sukarno and Suharto.

However, President Yudhoyono formed a special study team to come up with policy recommendations regarding the relocation of the capital. The special study team was not under a specific ministry but was supposed to be coordinated by a presidential expert staff team. Eventually, there were three key recommendations:

1. That Jakarta remains the capital city, but be given a complete overhaul;
2. That the function of the capital city would be transferred to the Jonggol area; and
3. That the construction of a new capital city be undertaken.[40]

There was nothing new in these recommendations compared to the plans from the Sukarno and Suharto governments. These recommendations failed to be developed into government regulations or laws to legitimize the relocation, even if SBY demonstrated some intent to shift the capital by forming the special study team.

The Basic Idea of Capital Relocation and Revitalization of Past Ideas

There are various ideas behind the relocation of the Indonesian capital under the administration of President Jokowi, ranging from a green and sustainable city to a new growth centre, and from an inclusive city for all to a technology-based city. These ideas are basically answers to the classic problems of Jakarta. However, they also stem from the main ideas in the classic discourse of the capital's relocation from previous governments. Jokowi's administration intended to compile these previous ideas—"Nusantara" is an umbrella term for all the hopes for the new capital city.

This chapter has shown that the main policy narratives in previous governments and the current administration on relocating the Indonesian capital are dynamic and varied significantly. Philosophically, a relocation of a capital city is about building the character of the nation; pragmatically, it is about economic equality. The need to symbolically capture the nation's greatness and new regional economic hub narratives led to so-called "lighthouse" projects by the previous regimes. The construction of any new capital city has its own prestige, that is, it is a political legacy that will be remembered in history.

In addition, the construction of a new capital city can also be oriented towards a political legacy, such as the highest achievement of a government's policies that cannot be rivalled by subsequent governments. These two ambitious motivations are arguably behind the "lighthouse" policies in the construction of the nation's capital, both in previous governments and the current government under Jokowi.

The most important historical lesson from the unfinished capital city relocation or "lighthouse" projects in the previous administrations is the lack of legal and funding sources. These two factors are also concerns for President Jokowi's administration, which prompted them to prepare the policy foundations first before launching the capital city relocation discourse for the IKN. The current policy of capital relocation to Nusantara can thus be said to correct the shortcomings of the policies of the previous governments.

The revitalization of the capital relocation project under the Jokowi administration is certainly a challenge. Jokowi is trying to move and build a new capital city that has failed to materialize for decades. The biggest challenge is the potential discontinuity of this policy. Even though there is already a law on the establishment of the new capital city, UU IKN, the next administration may not have the political will to see the relocation through. This is a big question related to the continuity of Nusantara's future development.

How Policymakers Learn from Previous Relocation Plans

When Jokowi was elected as president, he appointed Andrinof not only as part of the transition team (also known as the "Team of 11") but also his Minister of National Development Planning/Head of Bappenas, albeit only briefly (2014–15).[41] In his brief leadership at Bappenas, Andrinof succeeded in weaving his capital city relocation discourse into policymaking processes, which was continued by his successors Sofyan Djalil and Bambang P.S. Brodjonegoro. This is what led Bappenas to routinely conduct studies on the relocation of the capital city in 2015. The president then decided in 2019 that the capital city would move to Kalimantan.[42]

The main lesson learnt for the formulators of the current capital city relocation policy is that there is a need for a comprehensive study of the current conditions of Jakarta and a projection of future problems. This is an effort to improve the formulation of the agenda and discourse on the relocation of the capital city. Geopolitical developments, economic equity, and ecological carrying capacity had not been packaged in a complete policy text prior to this time, so they remained as reoccurring discourses without resolution. Learning from history, an in-depth study was done to firmly ground the idea of a capital city relocation, for it to become a definitive policy.

As previously mentioned, a comprehensive policy study on capital relocation was prepared by the *Tim Visi Indonesia* 2033 (Indonesia 2033 Vision Team) led by Andrinof. He advocated the idea that Indonesia should have a world-class capital city.[43] The team supported the idea of relocating the capital city to Kalimantan. In fact, there had been a soft launch for such a policy on 9 December 2008, but it did not get much attention from the SBY government, which at that time already had its own discourse as explained earlier in this chapter.

The inclusion of the Vision Team into the current policymaking process for the capital city relocation shows that there is a political logic and a technocratic logic at work.[44] Since some team members have been appointed in the legislative and executive branches, it enables the policymaking process on the capital city relocation to run more smoothly than before. The political logic supports the effort to inform and include the legislative branches of government (i.e., the DPR, DPD and MPR) so that the policy of relocating the capital is not merely an initiative from the executive, but also a proposal from the people's representatives. Meanwhile, technocratic logic refers to the evidence-based policies for why the capital city should be moved from Jakarta and why Kalimantan is the right choice for the new capital.

Conclusion

An important lesson learnt from the history of Indonesia's capital city relocation policies and their relationship with the present formulation under Jokowi's administration lies in the replication of the concept. The "lighthouse" project that synergizes national and global interests has become the focus of the narrative for relocation. Jokowi's agenda for the capital city relocation is an effort to strengthen solidity and solidarity domestically and to gain international recognition for domestic achievements. The construction of a new capital city from scratch is a form of a political showcase.

The new capital city has become a symbol of transformation for the nation-state of Indonesia. Under President Sukarno, it was a symbol of the importance of a new country having a capital city which was not a legacy of colonialism. During President Suharto's era, there was an idea about the potential but partial relocation of functions of the capital city to Jonggol. The Yudhoyono administration did not firmly state that the capital should be relocated to Jonggol or other regions. During Jokowi's presidency, the plan to relocate the new capital city is a symbol of Indonesia's transformation from a Java-centric country (given the centralization of the economy and government in Java) to outside Java, to become more Indonesia-centric.

Second, historical studies show that uneven economic development triggered the desire to relocate the capital city. Since Sukarno's time, economic activity had been centralized in Jakarta, which led to massive urbanization after Indonesia's independence. This urbanization trend has increased sharply since the 1940s. Economic development was the focus of President Suharto, and he presided over the discourse about the capital city as part of economic democratization. The over-centralization of the national economy is also what prompted President Widodo to move the capital city to Nusantara, to create more equitable development.

Another reason put forward is to save Java (from ecological disasters), where agricultural land is decreasing and river quality is declining due to the large population growth. The location of Java, on a volcanic tectonic plate, also makes the capital city vulnerable to the threat of future earthquakes and tsunamis, which are expected to compound as climate change worsens. Therefore, it is projected that the capital city should be relocated to a relatively large region that is not as vulnerable as Java to the threat of ecological disaster. During the Sukarno era, the threat of environmental change was not yet visible, so environmental issues did not emerge strongly in this period. However, environmental problems began to emerge by the time of Suharto, when Jakarta was deemed increasingly unfit to be the capital due to its notorious traffic jams, periodic flooding and urban air conditions. This view grew stronger during the leadership of President Yudhoyono who discussed with the then Governor of Jakarta Widodo the idea of a capital city relocation. Jokowi's hope is that Nusantara can be a model for other environmentally friendly cities.

The three discourses on relocating the capital city have different background ideas. In the Sukarno era, the motivation to relocate the capital city was the idea of decolonization, an Indonesia that wanted to be seen globally (as outward-looking) and national integration efforts. In the Suharto era, capital city relocation focused on the development of independent areas built by the private sector or his business cronies. In the era of President Jokowi, the new capital city is predicted to be a new "showcase" for the city of the future, which is environmentally friendly and with a Nusantara (archipelagic) character.

Following Vadim Rossman's list of geographical, military, and cultural factors,[45] it can be seen that the geographical aspect is a strong factor for the various plans to relocate the capital in past eras. Political interests of the authorities in the short term determine *where* the relocation might occur, as we see in the examples of Palangkaraya (Sukarno) and Jonggol (Suharto). President SBY's three selected scenarios showed that in terms of location, he considered the aspect of financial capability of each more realistically. In the Jokowi era, the choice of location for a new capital city aims to revive the old discourse in the Sukarno era, that of an environmentally friendly city in the middle of the Kalimantan's forest but one that at the same time would benefit the politicians and others close to Jokowi who own businesses or concessions in the area.[46]

The relocation and construction of a new capital city is a long-term project where political will is the key to its continuity. The potential for policy discontinuity is certainly an important lesson for the current relocation. Although there is now a law that forms the basis for the construction of the new capital, disruption in the form of a revision of this law is certainly an unavoidable risk. Therefore, there is a need for commitment, especially from the new government that results from the 2024 elections, to prioritize this policy. This will avoid a repeat of Indonesia's history of capital relocation, where post-reform megaprojects have typically been stalled due to political reasons.

Notes

1. Vadim Rossman, *Capital Cities: Varieties and Patterns of Development and Relocation* (New York: Routledge, 2017).
2. Ibid.
3. Ibid.
4. Bagoes Wiryomartono, *Traditions and Transformations of Habitation in Indonesia: Power, Architecture, and Urbanism* (Singapore: Springer, 2020).
5. Andre Vitchek and Mira Lubis, *New Capital of Indonesia: Abandoning Destitute Jakarta, Moving to Plundered Borneo* (Jakarta: PT. Badak Merah Semesta, 2020).
6. Guntur Soekarno, "Ibu Kota Negara, Tjilik Riwut, dan Megathrust", *Kompas.id*, 10 March 2022, https://www.kompas.id/baca/artikel-opini/2022/02/15/ibukota-negara-tjilik-riwut-dan-megathrust
7. Nila Riwut, *Maneser Panatau Tatu Hiang: Menyelami Kekayaan Leluhur* (Palangkaraya: Pusakalima, 2003).
8. Gerry van Klinken, "Mengkolonisasi Borneo: Pembentukan Provinsi Dayak di Kalimantan", in *Antara Daerah dan Negara: Indonesia Tahun 1950-an. Pembongkaran Narasi Besar Integrasi Bangsa. Jakarta*, edited by S. Van Bemmelen and R. Raben (Jakarta: Yayasan Pustaka Obor Indonesia dan KITLV Jakarta, 2011).
9. Haryo Winarso, *Residential Land Developers' Behaviour in Jabotabek, Indonesia* (London, University College London, 2000); Christopher Silver, *Planning the Megacity: Jakarta in the Twentieth Century* (New York: Routledge, 2008).

10. Nyimas Aziz, "Relokasi Ibu Kota Negara: Lesson Learned dari Negara Lain", *Jurnal Kajian Wilayah* 10, no. 2 (2019): 37–64.
11. Jacques Leclerc, "Mirrors and Lighthouse: A Search for Meaning in the Monuments and Great Works of Soekarno's Jakarta, 1960–1965", in *Urban Symbolism*, edited by Peter J.M. Nas, pp. 39–57 (Leiden: Brill, 1993).
12. Wasisto Raharjo Jati, "A New Capital City for Who? Central-Local Tensions in Indonesia", *New Mandala* (blog), 23 August 2022, https://www.newmandala.org/a-new-capital-city-for-who-central-local-tensions-in-indonesia/
13. Wasisto Raharjo Jati, "A New Indonesian Capital City: Conflict Pending", *New Mandala* (blog), 21 February 2022, https://www.newmandala.org/a-new-indonesian-capital-city-conflict-pending/
14. Silver, *Planning the Megacity*; Haryo Winarso, *Residential Land Developers' Behaviour in Jabotabek, Indonesia*; Wasisto Raharjo Jati, "A New Indonesian Capital City: Conflict Pending".
15. Wasisto Raharjo Jati, "A New Capital City for Who? Central-Local Tensions in Indonesia".
16. Wiwin Ramelan, *Penyakit Menular di Batavia* (Depok: Fakultas Ilmu Pengetahuan dan Budaya, 1995).
17. *Pantjawarna*, "Malang Pantas Djadi Ibukota RI", April 1954 edition; *Merdeka*, "PM Djuanda Membuka: Indonesia Adalah Satu dan Sama", 14 September 1957.
18. Ibid.
19. Adrian Vickers, "Mengapa Tahun 1950-an Penting Bagi Kajian Indonesia", in *Perspektif Baru Penulisan Sejarah Indonesia*, edited by Henk Schulte Nordholt and Bambang Purwanto (Jakarta: Yayasan Pustaka Obor Indonesia dan KITLV Jakarta, 2013).
20. Leclerc, "Mirrors and Lighthouse".
21. Silver, *Planning the Megacity*.
22. van Klinken, "Mengkolonisasi Borneo".
23. *Merdeka*, "PM Djuanda Membuka".
24. *Merdeka*, "Pengawasan atas Sumber-Sumber Penghidupan Partai Persatuan Nasional dan Tekad Untuk Merebut Irian Barat", 21 September 1957.
25. Silver, *Planning the Megacity*.
26. Van Klinken, "Mengkolonisasi Borneo".
27. Wijanarka Wijanarka, "Tata Ruang Kota Di Kalimantan Tengah Dan Palangkaraya", in *Beberapa Ungkapan Sejarah Penataan Ruang Indonesia 1948–2000*, edited by Hardjatno Hardjatno (Jakarta: Direktorat Jenderal Penataan Ruang, 2003).
28. Diar Anwar Corner, "Prof. Dr. Roeslan Abdulgani Tentang Pemindahan Ibukota dari Jakarta ke Kalimantan", https://www.youtube.com/watch?v=XWRE74JwxcA (accessed 14 September 2022).
29. Wasisto Raharjo Jati, "Kosmologi Ibukota RI", *Harian Surya*, 12 August 2010, https://gagasanhukum.wordpress.com/2010/08/12/kosmologi-ibu-kota-ri/

30. Budi Setiyono, "Sukarno Ingin Ibukota Tetap di Jakarta", *Historia*, 8 September 2017, https://historia.id/urban/articles/sukarno-ingin-ibukota-tetap-di-jakarta-vQXAj/page/1
31. Bappenas, "Naskah Akademik RUU IKN", June 2021, https://www.dpr.go.id/dokakd/dokumen/PANSUS-RJ-20211214-125732-5084.pdf
32. *Kompas*, "Jonggol Akan Dikembangkan Sebagai Kota Mandiri Biasa", 18 November 1996.
33. Haryo Winarso, "Residential Land Developers' Behaviour in Jabotabek, Indonesia" (PhD dissertation, University of London, 2000), pp. 1–309; Robert Cowherd, "Does Planning Culture Matter? Dutch and American Models in Indonesian Urban Transformations", in *Comparative Planning Cultures*, edited by Bishwapriya Sanyal (New York: Routledge, 2005).
34. Freek Colombijn and Abidin Kusno, "Kampungs, Buitenwijken, and Kota Mandiri: Naming the Urban Fringe of Java, Indonesia", in *What's in a Name? Talking about Urban Peripheries*, edited by Richard Harris and Charlotte Vorms (Toronto: University of Toronto Press, 2017).
35. Silver, *Planning the Megacity*.
36. Bayu Saptika, *Konsep Kota Baru Mandiri* (Jakarta: Jurusan Arsitektur Fakultas Teknik Universitas Indonesia, 1997).
37. Arif Setiadi, "SBY Minta Pindah Ibukota Bukan Karena Macet", *Solopos.com*, 3 August 2010, https://www.solopos.com/sby-minta-pindah-ibukota-bukan-karena-macet-37123?utm_source=bacajuga_desktop
38. Nur Haryanto, "SBY Terinspirasi Astana Untuk Pindahkan Ibu Kota", *Tempo.co*, 13 September 2013, https://nasional.tempo.co/read/512216/sby-terinspirasi-astana-untuk-pindahkan-ibu-kota
39. Doris Ishenda and Shi Guoqing, "Determinants in Relocation of Capital Cities", *Journal of Public Administration and Governance* 9, no. 4 (2019); Greg Fealy, "Indonesian Politics in 2012: Graft, Intolerance, and Hope of Change in the Late Yudhoyono Period", *Southeast Asian Affairs 2013*, edited by Daljit Singh (Singapore: Institute of Southeast Asian Studies, 2013), pp. 103–20.
40. *Detik News*, "SBY Tawarkan 3 Skenario Pemindahan Ibu Kota", *Detik*, 21 January 2013, https://news.detik.com/berita/d-2148515/sby-tawarkan-3-skenario-pemindahan-ibu-kota
41. Wasisto Raharjo Jati, "Prosiding Webinar IKN Seri 1: Menimbang Aspirasi Pusat Dan Daerah Dalam Pembangunan IKN Kalimantan Timur" (Jakarta: Pusat Riset Politik BRIN, 2021).
42. Ibid.
43. Andrinof A. Chaniago, "Mengusung Visi Indonesia 2033", *Tokoh Indonesia*, 9 March 2011, https://tokoh.id/biografi/2-direktori/mengusung-visi-indonesia-2033/
44. Pusat Riset Politik, "Webinar Ibu Kota Negara (IKN) Baru Series I: Menimbang Aspirasi Pusat Dan Daerah", https://www.youtube.com/watch?v=7Y7UEa3I19U&t=5621s (accessed 11 December 2022).
45. Rossman, *Capital Cities*, pp. 52–55.

46. WALHI, "Ibu Kota Negara Baru Untuk Siapa, Publik Atau Elit?", 17 December 2019, https://www.walhi.or.id/ibu-kota-negara-baru-untuk-siapa-publik-atau-elit

References

Aziz, Nyimas. 2019. "Relokasi Ibu Kota Negara: Lesson Learned dari Negara Lain". *Jurnal Kajian Wilayah* 10, no 2: 37–64.

Bappenas. 2021. "Naskah Akademik RUU IKN". June 2021. https://www.dpr.go.id/dokakd/dokumen/PANSUS-RJ-20211214-125732-5084.pdf

Chaniago, Andrinof A. 2011. "Mengusung Visi Indonesia 2033". *Tokoh Indonesia*, 9 March 2011. https://tokoh.id/biografi/2-direktori/mengusung-visi-indonesia-2033/

Colombijn, Freek, and Abidin Kusno. 2017. "Kampungs, Buitenwijken, and Kota Mandiri: Naming the Urban Fringe of Java, Indonesia". In *What's in a Name? Talking about Urban Peripheries*, edited by Richard Harris and Charlotte Vorms. Toronto: University of Toronto Press.

Corner, Diar Anwar. "Prof. Dr. Roeslan Abdulgani Tentang Pemindahan Ibukota dari Jakarta ke Kalimantan". https://www.youtube.com/watch?v=XWRE74JwxcA (accessed 14 September 2022).

Cowherd, Robert. 2002. "Cultural Construction of Jakarta: Design, Planning, and Development in Jabotabek, 1980–1997". PhD dissertation, Massachusetts Institute of Technology.

———. 2005. "Does Planning Culture Matter? Dutch and American Models in Indonesian Urban Transformations". In *Comparative Planning Cultures*, edited by Bishwapriya Sanyal. New York: Routledge.

Detik News. 2013. "SBY Tawarkan 3 Skenario Pemindahan Ibu Kota". *Detik.com*, 21 January 2013. https://news.detik.com/berita/d-2148515/sby-tawarkan-3-skenario-pemindahan-ibu-kota

Fealy, Greg. 2013. "Indonesian Politics in 2012: Graft, Intolerance, and Hope of Change in the Late Yudhoyono Period". *Southeast Asian Affairs 2013*, edited by Daljit Singh, pp. 103–20. Singapore: Institute of Southeast Asian Studies.

Haryanto, Nur. 2013. "SBY Terinspirasi Astana Untuk Pindahkan Ibu Kota". *Tempo. co*, 13 September 2013. https://nasional.tempo.co/read/512216/sby-terinspirasi-astana-untuk-pindahkan-ibu-kota

Ishenda, Doris, and Shi Guoqing. 2019. "Determinants in Relocation of Capital Cities". *Journal of Public Administration and Governance* 9, no. 4: 1–200.

Jati, Wasisto Raharjo. 2010. "Kosmologi Ibukota RI". *Harian Surya*, 12 August 2010, https://gagasanhukum.wordpress.com/2010/08/12/kosmologi-ibu-kota-ri/

———. 2021. "Prosiding Webinar IKN Seri 1: Menimbang Aspirasi Pusat Dan Daerah Dalam Pembangunan IKN Kalimantan Timur". Jakarta: Pusat Riset Politik BRIN.

———. 2022a. "A New Indonesian Capital City: Conflict Pending". *New Mandala* (blog), 21 February 2022. https://www.newmandala.org/a-new-indonesian-capital-city-conflict-pending/

———. 2022b. "A New Capital City for Who? Central-Local Tensions in Indonesia". *New Mandala* (blog), 23 August 2022. https://www.newmandala.org/a-new-capital-city-for-who-central-local-tensions-in-indonesia/

Kompas. 1996. "Jonggol Akan Dikembangkan Sebagai Kota Mandiri Biasa". 18 November 1996.

Leclerc, Jacques. 1993. "Mirrors and Lighthouse: A Search for Meaning in the Monuments and Great Works of Soekarno's Jakarta', 1960–1965". In *Urban Symbolism*, edited by Peter J.M. Nas, pp. 39–57. Leiden: Brill.

Merdeka. 1957a. "PM Djuanda Membuka: Indonesia Adalah Satu dan Sama". 14 September 1957.

———. 1957b. "Pengawasan atas Sumber-Sumber Penghidupan Partai Persatuan Nasional dan Tekad Untuk Merebut Irian Barat". 21 September 1957.

Pantjawarna. 1954. "Malang Pantas Djadi Ibukota RI". April edition.

Pusat Riset Politik. 2021. "Webinar Ibu Kota Negara (IKN) Baru Series I: 'Menimbang Aspirasi Pusat Dan Daerah'". https://www.youtube.com/watch?v=7Y7UEa3I19U&t=5621s (accessed 11 December 2022).

Ramelan, Wiwin. 1995. *Penyakit Menular Di Batavia*. Depok: Fakultas Ilmu Pengetahuan dan Budaya.

Riwut, Nila. 2003. *Maneser Panatau Tatu Hiang: Menyelami Kekayaan Leluhur*. Palangkaraya: Pusakalima.

Rossman, Vadim. 2017. *Capital Cities: Varieties and Patterns of Development and Relocation*. New York: Routledge.

Saptika, Bayu. 1997. *Konsep Kota Baru Mandiri*. Jakarta: Jurusan Arsitektur Fakultas Teknik Universitas Indonesia.

Setiadi, Arif. 2010. "SBY Minta Pindah Ibukota Bukan Karena Macet". *Solopos.com*, 3 August 2010. https://www.solopos.com/sby-minta-pindah-ibukota-bukan-karena-macet-37123?utm_source=bacajuga_desktop

Setiyono, Budi. 2017. "Sukarno Ingin Ibukota Tetap di Jakarta". *Historia*, 3 August 2017. https://historia.id/urban/articles/sukarno-ingin-ibukota-tetap-di-jakarta-vQXAj/page/1

Silver, Christopher. 2008. *Planning the Megacity: Jakarta in the Twentieth Century*. New York: Routledge.

Soekarno, Guntur. 2022. "Ibu Kota Negara, Tjilik Riwut, dan Megathrust". *Kompas.id*, 10 March 2022. https://www.kompas.id/baca/artikel-opini/2022/02/15/ibukota-negara-tjilik-riwut-dan-megathrust

Van Klinken, Gerry. 2011. "Mengkolonisasi Borneo: Pembentukan Provinsi Dayak di Kalimantan". In *Antara Daerah dan Negara: Indonesia Tahun 1950-an. Pembongkaran Narasi Besar Integrasi Bangsa. Jakarta*, edited by S. Van Bemmelen and R. Raben. Jakarta: Yayasan Pustaka Obor Indonesia dan KITLV Jakarta.

Vickers, Adrian. 2013. "Mengapa Tahun 1950-an Penting Bagi Kajian Indonesia". In *Perspektif Baru Penulisan Sejarah Indonesia*, edited by Henk Schulte Nordholt and Bambang Purwanto. Jakarta: Yayasan Pustaka Obor Indonesia dan KITLV Jakarta.

Vitchek, Andre, and Mira Lubis. 2020. *New Capital of Indonesia: Abandoning Destitute Jakarta, Moving to Plundered Borneo*. Jakarta: PT. Badak Merah Semesta.

WALHI. 2019. "Ibu Kota Negara Baru Untuk Siapa, Publik atau Elit?". 17 December 2019. https://www.walhi.or.id/ibu-kota-negara-baru-untuk-siapa-publik-atau-elit

Wijanarka, Wijanarka. 2003. "Tata Ruang Kota di Kalimantan Tengah dan Palangkaraya". In *Beberapa Ungkapan Sejarah Penataan Ruang Indonesia 1948–2000*, edited by Hardjatno Hardjatno. Jakarta: Direktorat Jenderal Penataan Ruang.

Winarso, Haryo. 2000. *Residential Land Developers' Behaviour in Jabotabek, Indonesia*. University College London.

Wiryomartono, Bagoes. 2020. *Traditions and Transformations of Habitation in Indonesia: Power, Architecture, and Urbanism*. Singapore: Springer.

2

THE NEW STATE CAPITAL REGULATIONS
Contending for Autonomy, Democracy and Legitimacy?

Mardyanto Wahyu Tryatmoko and Koichi Kawamura

INTRODUCTION

The end of Indonesia's authoritarian regime in 1998 was the turning point for the state to apply substantive democracy and decentralization by devolving authority to local governments. The commitment to abandon centralization was shown in the amendment of Indonesia's 1945 Constitution by emphasizing the devolution of authority. The Constitution allows regions to have special autonomy, national recognition for those that have a history related to nation-building, and the uniqueness of local cultures and identities.[1] Thus, the autonomy granted to all local governments is not limited to administrative and fiscal aspects. Decentralization policy also allows political autonomy, where local governments can administer their regional policies after deliberations in democratically elected regional parliaments. Direct popular elections for the heads of local governments were introduced in 2005.

The commitment to adopt extensive decentralization was also shown in giving the Indonesian capital of Jakarta the status of a special region with greater autonomy under Law No. 34 of 1999 on the Provincial Government of the Special Capital Region of Indonesia. In this arrangement, Jakarta as the state's capital can exercise local government authority in all areas of government affairs excluding five national competencies: national defence and security, fiscal, monetary, judicial and religious matters. The difference (from other local governments) is that only a single structure of autonomy is applied to Jakarta at the provincial level: districts of Jakarta have only administrative power, which allows Jakarta to respond agilely, efficiently, and effectively.

In 2007, in amending Law No. 34 of 1999, the national government granted the special capital region of Jakarta more political autonomy by enacting Law No. 29 of 2007. In this regulation, the Regional House of Representatives (DPRD) no longer decides who the governor of Jakarta is. The new arrangements give more political autonomy by allowing the direct (popular) election of the governor and vice-governor of Jakarta. As a special region, however, a gubernatorial candidate must obtain a majority (50 per cent + 1) vote to win the election.[2] This differs from the electoral system in other local governments, where a candidate can win the election by earning the most votes (even if this is less than 50 per cent majority).

The democratic reform of local elections showed the nation's commitment towards substantive local democracy. However, since the Susilo Bambang Yudhoyono administration (2004–14), the commitment to have extensive local autonomy has gradually faded. For example, the amendment of the law on regional government in 2004 (Law No. 32 of 2004) strengthened the authority of the central and provincial governments over district and city governments. The enactment of Law No. 33 of 2004 on the fiscal balance between the central and local governments and Law No. 28 of 2009 on local taxes and levies also strengthened the financial authority of the central government vis-à-vis local governments. Under the Joko "Jokowi" Widodo administration, the move towards recentralization has continued. Law No. 11 of 2020 on Job Creation is an example of how the central government has clawed back some local government authority: local governments can no longer manage spatial administrations in their territories, as this authority is now assigned to the central government. The same recentralization has seemingly occurred in the arrangement of Law No. 3 of 2022 on the State Capital City (IKN), including the establishment of the IKN government. The new mode of local government for the new capital of Indonesia is likely to move away from the state's earlier commitment towards fostering local democracy and autonomy.

In this chapter, we examine two aspects of the institutional arrangements of IKN regulations. First, we look at how the arrangements of government structures under the IKN regulations have been directed towards autonomy or centralization. Second, we examine how public participation in local governance has been arranged in the new IKN. This chapter also explains how the trajectory of these two aspects will have institutional implications for local democracy and state legitimacy.

The analysis departs from the policymaking processes of IKN regulations. The data was mostly collected from primary and secondary sources, including interviews with key informants, including high-ranking officers from the Ministry of Home Affairs and the IKN Authority participating in the policymaking process. The second source comprises official documents and recordings of the deliberations in the House of Representatives (DPR) and the judicial review process in the Constitutional Court.

Our analysis shows that the regulations placed the centralized regional government structure within the decentralized frame of regional autonomy in some unreasonable and unstructured ways. Policymakers have determined the structure of the IKN government without having a strong argument based on a comprehensive study, for example, by assessing existing government models of capital cities in other countries that may fit Indonesian history and characteristics. Instead, the model of the IKN government has been developed from common sense in short debates during the formulation of the IKN Law in Indonesia's parliament. As a result, policymakers simply use the term "local government" to describe the IKN government, despite their realizing that the structure of the IKN government is characterized as that of a central government unit, without an autonomous local authority.[3] This not only makes the direction of (future) local autonomy in the IKN unclear but also causes ambiguity in determining the structures of public engagement. Thus, there is no distinct institutional framework for determining the local government structure while the central government completely disregard the roles of local society in local governance.

After the introduction, the chapter discusses the debate between centralization and decentralization in terms of democracy and the effectiveness of local governance. This part provides conceptual and theoretical perspectives on how decentralization or centralization looks promising for some states. The arguments behind state preference are the foundation of analysis in this chapter. The third section explains the arrangements of IKN government structures and public participation in relation to the direction of centralism/autonomy and democracy under IKN regulations. The fourth section analyses the possible implications of the operation of government structures framed in the IKN regulations and covers arguments on the effectiveness of the IKN's government and public participation at the local level. The last section concludes with the main findings.

Between Centralization and Decentralization: Debating Democracy and the Effectiveness of Local Governance

Decentralization or local autonomy has become a popular feature of central-local relations because it provides promising benefits, devolving far-reaching competencies to local units of government. This is extensively adopted by many countries.[4] Scholars such as Hernes and Kjellberg have raised some promising agendas favouring local autonomy to promote democracy, local (communal) liberty, and the efficiency of public provisions.[5]

In relation to democracy, many scholars have extensively examined autonomy or decentralization.[6] Some of them, including practitioners from international agencies, or what Hadiz calls neo-institutionalists,[7] conclude that local autonomy supports the consolidation of democracy at the local level.[8] This understanding supports a belief that decentralization or autonomy is the most democratic and effective way to manage local grievances such as economic, religious, and ethnic issues, which may lead to separatist insurgencies.

The notion that autonomy supports democracy at the local level seems irrelevant in some cases. In the Philippines, for instance, some scholars argue that traditional Muslim elites dominate the autonomous region of Mindanao to maintain the status quo.[9] Here, democracy is at risk because local people have limited space in articulating their preferences. Local elites, in maintaining their positions, do not rely on popular votes at the local level, since the Manila elite of the central government give them incentives (as these elites need support from the local elites in mobilizing votes) for the continuity of the regime. This shows there are cases in which autonomy can undermine the voices of local society.

A similar situation occurs in Indonesia. Local autonomy and democracy were important agendas of political transition (post-1998) in which good governance and vibrant civil society were expected to emerge.[10] But Robinson and Hadiz show that the democratization process in autonomous regions in Indonesia was hijacked by predatory interests.[11] Local actors tend to pursue or defend political powers at the local level to accumulate their wealth through corruption or rent-seeking practices.[12] Thus, the outcome of decentralization, whether democratic or not, is determined by the competition of interests among actors.[13]

These cases of negative experiences in decentralization or local autonomy may lead to bad faith in the local governance system. Thus, these experiences may lead to the trend of recentralization in local governance.

Literature explaining the benefit of centralization is extensively available, although the explanation for the ideological switch from autonomy to centralization is understudied. Hernes, for instance, argues that the increased centralization in integrated governance is influenced by demands for equal service provision, efficiency, macroeconomic control, legal protection for individuals, and the distribution of responsibilities among local authorities.[14]

Given the benefits of centralization, there has been an increasing trend of recentralization. It has become an option for some states to achieve better governance in terms of efficiency and regional integration. This may be a result of bad experiences in the practices of decentralization or local autonomy. However, other studies have found that recentralization has been driven by economic motives. In the case of Turkey, Akilli and Akilli explain that recentralization occurred as economies of scale became the main target of the expansion of metropolitan areas.[15] The attention to this economic logic, however, disregards the local democracy that was a national principle in constructing local government in Turkey. This case suggests that recentralization leads to institutional issues. As shown by Ay, due to the neglect of local entities, the recentralization of planning authority in state-led urban renewal has resulted in the lack of community participation, which causes problems for legitimacy.[16]

The formulation of IKN regulations in Indonesia may be a case where the state has switched the direction of the local governance system from decentralization to recentralization after an experiment with regional autonomy. Thus, the analysis of this chapter tries to answer the question of why a move to recentralization is justified, by looking at the formulation of the IKN Law. In addition, this chapter seeks an explanation of how the idea of recentralization is built into institutional arrangements and what implications these institutional arrangements and practices might have. These questions will be answered by the analysis of the interplay between centralization and autonomy logic or values, as the two cannot be separated.[17]

Institutional Arrangements of the New State Capital: Accommodating Autonomy and Democracy?

The decision of the central government to move the capital city from Jakarta to East Kalimantan was followed by the adoption of a new government structure operationalized at a local level. This structure is different from Indonesia's existing regional governance system in which local governments can exercise substantive autonomy. The following subsections analyse the arrangements of local government structures under the IKN Law and regulations by paying attention to the logic of centralization, autonomy and democracy.

The Problem of Autonomy in the New State Capital
The IKN Law stipulates that the IKN Authority (*Badan Otorita Ibu Kota Nusantara*) is established as the governing body for the IKN Special Region.[18] The Authority is given the same status as a ministry of the central government[19] and its Chief and Vice-Chief (*Kepala/Wakil Kepala Otorita IKN*) are directly appointed and dismissed by the president in consultation with the DPR.[20] The term of office for the Chief is five years, but the Law does not stipulate any term limits.[21]

The IKN Authority has the authority to give investment permissions, to give special facilities (especially to institutions which financially support the state capital relocation and development projects) and to develop the capital city and the surrounding areas.[22] These organizational structures and functions show that the IKN Authority is provided with no autonomous power to govern the capital city region. It is merely expected to serve bureaucratic roles to efficiently implement the relocation and administration of the state capital in accordance with the central government's order.

A comparison of the IKN Authority with other provincial governments in Indonesia reveals a stark contrast in the essence of regional governance. According to the Law on Regional Government (Law No. 23 of 2014), provincial governors are given the status of administrator for their respective regions and also serve as representatives of the central government.[23] The direct elections of governors and vice-governors by residents have been implemented since 2005. A governor's term of office is five years, and he/she is elected for only two terms.[24] The State Capital of Jakarta has been also recognized as an autonomous province since the democratization period and the governor and vice-governor of Jakarta have been elected by popular vote since 2007. Although the IKN Law stipulates that Nusantara has provincial status,[25] the IKN Authority is fundamentally different from other provincial governments which have been given autonomous status.

The centralistic nature of the IKN government structure is also seen in the IKN Law's stipulations that many detailed regulations shall be provided with several derivative or subsidiary regulations, including six government regulations (*peraturan pemerintah*),[26] two presidential decisions (*keputusan presiden*),[27] and seven presidential regulations (*peraturan presiden*).[28]

In addition to the fact that the central government has the authority to establish many derivative regulations on the IKN, the IKN Law allows the president to decide his or her regulation-making powers. The Law stipulates that changes in the Master Plan of the IKN need the approval of the president.[29] The Chief of the IKN Authority is given the authority to establish that office's own regulations (*peraturan kepala otorita IKN*), but these are limited to the administrative sphere, such as detailed spatial planning,[30] land expropriation,[31] transfers of property rights (*Hak Atas Tanah*),[32] and the implementation of special taxes or levies.[33]

As these provisions show, the IKN Law does not recognize any regional autonomy for the proposed IKN region. The region's residents, both local inhabitants and future immigrants, do not appear to have voting rights to elect any head of regional government. Although Article 38 of the Law stipulates that the DPR can monitor the law's implementation, the head of regional government is only responsible to the president. Although the IKN Authority can decide its own regulations for the administration of the IKN Special Region and the capital relocation,[34] those regulations are not the object of legislative scrutiny except for regulations which require approval of DPR as stipulated in the Law.[35]

Furthermore, since there is no provision on the local judicial system in the IKN Law, it is not clear in which courts (for criminal and civil cases) IKN citizens can be tried. Despite the stipulation that the IKN Authority will carry out the functions and roles of a special regional government,[36] it is not expected to govern a territory where several hundreds of thousands of citizens reside, but only to carry out the administrative functions for the preparation, development, and relocation of the state's capital. The IKN Authority is neither responsible for regional citizens nor controlled by any regional institution. Consequently, the aspirations of IKN citizens might be completely neglected and the fulfilment of these citizens' rights will be at risk.

The structural design of the IKN government is different from that of existing regional governments.[37] The central government justifies that its special character, that is the administration of Nusantara as the State Capital as well as the implementation of preparatory, development, and relocation activities, is in accordance with Article 18B(1) of the 1945 Constitution.[38] The Law's Elucidation points out that this special status is necessary to avoid problems such as unclear divisions of administrative matters and overlaps of administrative authority between the central and regional governments. This shows the desire and intention of the central government to implement the relocation and development of the IKN with an efficient and top-down approach without political accountability, both vertically (checks and balances) and horizontally (elections), and without administrative interference. The emphasis of the central government on efficiency and effectiveness in administering the state capital relocation and development is seen in the lack of any mention in the IKN Law of democracy or autonomy, only "efficiency" and "effectiveness".[39]

The government structure under the IKN Law has a clear direction towards centralization. But, looking thoroughly at the stipulations of the Law, the central government has framed the centralistic structure of the IKN government along the narrative of autonomy. This can be identified in phrases in the IKN Law, such as "special local governance", "distribution of authority", and managing and taking care of its own affairs. Such phrases are incompatible with the centralistic structure of the IKN government because it is merely an extension of central government authority. The mode of government relations between the central and the IKN governments is beyond the scheme of delegation[40] or the deconcentration[41] of authority. If we simply read the stipulations on the IKN government's structure in the Law, the IKN Authority is only a central government unit at the local level. The arrangements of real government structures largely contradict the narratives of autonomy in the Law.

This contradiction was noticed by the legal drafters of the central government. In the draft of the IKN Law, the IKN structures were divided into two main units: a provincial unit which exercises autonomous power and the centre of IKN which is a centralistic unit. The drafters failed to merge these two ideas into one consistent organizational structure; they simply discarded the arrangement of the autonomous unit from the institutional frame. There is no evidence that results from research or a comprehensive evaluation of government performance were referred to, to justify the use of such a centralistic bureaucratic structure for the IKN government. The structures of the IKN Authority are merely built upon assumptions that a model of government structure like Jakarta will not be effective in managing the new state capital.

The central government, nonetheless, seemed to use Brasilia of Brazil and Putrajaya of Malaysia as models of state capital relocation and the IKN Authority, after studying cases of capital relocations around the world.[42] In both cases, the relocation was conducted under the developmentalist governments, of then President Juscelino Kubitschek de Oliveira of Brazil and then Prime Minister Mahathir bin Mohamad of Malaysia. For the construction of the new state capital in Brazil, the Brazilian government established the Development Commission for the New Capital (*Companhia*

Urbanizadora da Nova Capital do Brasil, NOVACAP) in 1956 and completed the capital relocation to Brasilia in 1960. The Governor of Brasilia was directly appointed by the president with the agreement of the Senate but the regional parliament was not established. It was not until 1990 that Brasilia was granted autonomy, with the election of the governor and the establishment of a regional parliament. The Malaysian government set up the Putrajaya Authority (*Perbadanan Putrajaya*) in 1996 and successfully relocated the state capital in 2001. The Putrajaya Authority, under the Prime Minister's Office, was assigned functions for the construction and relocation of the state capital as well as for a regional administrative office. In the relocation, the Putrajaya region was separated from Selangor Province and given the status of a Federal Territory. The state relocation agencies of both countries were established by the strong leadership of the central government for the purpose of quick and efficient implementation while democratic accountability was largely ignored. The IKN Authority, arguably imitating these two agencies, has been given similar functions and has been established for the same purpose.

The organizational structure of the IKN Authority was among the most controversial issues in the deliberations of the IKN Law in the DPR. After the Jokowi government submitted the draft IKN Bill to the DPR, a Special Committee was set up for deliberations on 7 December 2021 and the bill was passed at the plenary session on 21 January 2022, just forty-three days after deliberations began. Although this is unusually quick for Indonesia's Parliament, the government and political parties could not reach an agreement on the articles on the IKN Authority until the final stage. Some parliamentary members argued that the new state capital should not follow the government structure of Jakarta, reflecting on the bad experiences of Jakarta's local government in managing the city.[43] There was no explanation as to why the new state capital needed to adopt a centralistic government structure. The argument raised was about the complexity of Jakarta in handling business and government matters; the recommendation was for the new capital city to be assigned only administrative functions. The structures of the IKN government are merely built upon an assumption that the model of government structures like Jakarta will not be effective in managing the new state capital.

On the other hand, the opposition parties, like the Prosperous Justice Party (PKS) and Democratic Party, rejected the idea of setting up the IKN Authority due to its questionable constitutionality. They pointed out that there was no stipulation on such an Authority to govern a region in the 1945 Constitution, arguing that the Constitutional Court may judge its stipulation as unconstitutional if judicial review was requested. Against these oppositions, the central government insisted that it was in accordance with Articles 18 and 18B of the Constitution, arguing that the IKN would be given the status of a special region. In the end, most of parliament, excluding the PKS, agreed with the government's argument. Outside the DPR, academics and civil society organizations (CSOs) strongly criticized the idea of establishing the IKN Authority. They argued that the governance structure would not be democratic if there were no regional parliament or governor's election. They demanded that the government explained why the IKN Authority was necessary for the new state capital.[44] However, the Jokowi government completely ignored those critics.

The centralistic structures may be suitable in the phases of preparation, development, and relocation of the state capital, but not in the normal operations of local government and provisions of public services, which need more public engagement in day-to-day government activities. The central government, mixing different needs in the four phases, has prioritized the operational efficiency and effectiveness of the new capital's relocation. It has resulted in institutional arrangements that do not have any local government in place.

The Problem of Public Participation in the New Capital

The problem of governance in the Nusantara region can be found not only in the aspects of autonomy but also in public participation. There will be no formal political channel for residents to express, collect, and realize their aspirations and interests at any level. In the Special Region of Nusantara, a regional parliament will not be established and elections in the IKN region will be conducted only for the DPR and the president at the national level. In deliberations for the draft IKN Law, the PKS and Democratic Party had demanded the establishment of a regional parliament. Even Golkar and the National Awakening Party (PKB), both of which are in the ruling coalition, argued for this.[45] However, the Jokowi government and the ruling coalition did not take those voices seriously.

In Indonesia's provinces, elections for members of the regional parliaments (DPRD) are held once every five years, simultaneously with the general elections for the national DPR. The regional parliaments function as local legislatures, deliberating regional regulations and budgets, and overseeing governors and regional administrations. In the existing State Capital of Jakarta, its "provincial" parliament, whose members are directly elected, is set up with the same functions of legislation and administrative oversight as other provinces' parliaments. Yet, since there will be no regional parliament for the IKN, the checks and balances between the executive and the legislative at the regional level will be lacking. Therefore, the lack of public participation in the formal political institutions in the IKN region reveals a glaring difference when seen against the nationwide regional governance system.

Article 37 of the IKN Law stipulates that society can participate in the process of preparation, development, relocation, and management of the IKN in the form of public consultation, conference, partnership, delivery of aspirations, and other involvement. However, the central government has not provided any effective arrangements for such societal participation to ensure the active involvement of diverse groups, especially in the policymaking processes for the new capital city. Presidential Regulation No. 62 of 2022 on the IKN Authority provides for the establishment of an Advisory Council (*Dewan Penasihat*).[46] This Regulation also stipulates that participation in the preparation, development, relocation and administration of the IKN will be made possible through social consultative forums[47] but there are no clear provisions on how local society can give inputs to the IKN administration in concrete and effective ways. This indicates that the central government has only the intention of accommodating rather than seriously considering the diverse interests and needs of local society.

In the deliberations on the IKN Law, academics, CSOs and local communities criticized the lack of public participation. The DPR held a public hearing at Mulawarman University in Samarinda City, East Kalimantan in January 2022, but it was reported that participants were highly limited and that the general public as well as customary (*adat*) communities were not invited.[48] Jati argues that "local voices, especially those of *adat* communities (including the Sultanate of Kutai Kartanegara) have been excluded from discussions of the capital draft bill".[49] In defence, the Chairman of the Special Committee of the DPR, Ahmad Doli Kurnia Tandjung, commented that the Special Committee had heard opinions from thirty-one specialists and academic researchers in the eastern and western parts of the country, denying lack of public participation at the deliberation process.[50] President Jokowi, in response to those criticisms, held a short meeting with *adat* community leaders during his visit to East Kalimantan, but this was done ten days after the passage of the IKN Law.[51]

In drafting the Presidential Regulation on the IKN Authority, the central government had the idea to establish a Council of Community Representatives (*Konsil Perwakilan Masyarakat*), a public forum in which local representatives from *adat* communities, academics and other organizations could participate to give input to public policy. This was a response to public pressure questioning what institutions would make up for the absence of the proposed IKN's DPRD. Initially, the Council was supposed to consist of seventeen members selected by the Chief of the IKN Authority. However, during the discussion of the draft, this idea was criticized; the public argued that without giving it the proper authority, the Council would be powerless in providing input to the Chief of the IKN Authority.[52]

The institutional arrangement of public participation is difficult to synchronize with a proposed governmental structure that is centralistic and weighted towards the executive. Since the term "local governance" as stated in the IKN Law is not in line with such an executive arrangement, the idea of establishing an institution to deliver public voices to the local executive could not be realized in the final Presidential Regulation.

Possible Implications of Institutional Practices

The previous section argued that the lack of an institutional framework for autonomy has resulted in the unstructured local governance system of the proposed new capital, IKN. This unclear form of governance might have serious implications for institutional practices. This section discusses the implications of centralistic bureaucratic patterns and limited public channels in the arrangements of the IKN regulations.

The administrative predilection of a centralistic bureaucracy at the local level might be that it would be ineffective in addressing local issues, including ethnicity, psychology, sociology, and culture. A case of failure can be found in Papua, where inappropriate central government interventions have hindered fundamental settlements of issues of underdevelopment and regional identities. These issues ideally need to be addressed by a local state apparatus which understands the local culture and psychology. When the structure of government at the local level is overly beholden to a centralistic consideration, decision and order, these issues will not be resolved effectively.

The IKN regulations define the operations of local government in four phases: development, preparation, relocation and implementation. In pushing forward with various projects in each phase, the centralistic structures of the IKN government might bring positive results since these can lead to effective development and administrative operationalization at the local level, especially in the first three phases. Strong decision-making structures with support from the central government are necessary to speed up the infrastructural development of the new state capital. However, such arrangements might not work for day-to-day local government operations. This is because local people need their voices to be heard and their needs and expectations to be accommodated.

Furthermore, the area where the proposed IKN is being built is not an empty space—it includes areas that are previously part of the districts of Penajam Paser Utara and Kutai Kartanegara. Some subethnic groups such as the Paser, Dayak Kenyah, Dayak Modang, Kutai, Benuaq, Tunjung, Punan and Basab are living in this area,[53] where traditional society lives with customary norms and values (*adat*). Local people feel that the central government has ignored their voices, especially in the planning of the IKN development.[54] Some local people do not even know about the planning of the IKN. But even those who know about the capital relocation do not understand what impacts the IKN's construction might have (on them) and how they can be involved in the operationalization of the IKN government at the local level.[55]

The IKN regulations do not provide a space for indigenous people to express their political rights at the local level. Moreover, the central government prefers public consultation to public engagement for their participation in local governance. In the public consultation, local people can deliver their aspirations only to the local government, without participating in official political decision-making processes.[56] Since local communities are so diverse, such public consultation will not be effective in bringing the voices of the local people into these local regulations. The IKN government needs more than public consultation since the local people are used to having their representatives in the existing regional parliaments. In responding to the desire of local society to defend its rights, the central government should prepare an appropriate political system to reduce local grievances and increase the government's legitimacy. The absence of representative institutions at the local level will irritate local society, especially the natives who will have little chance for their voices to be accommodated if there are no institutions representing them.[57]

In the meantime, the structural conflict between customary communities and industry or government at the local level has frequently occurred. As the IKN project opens the possibility of massive inbound migration in the coming years, it is likely to alienate the local people. If the construction of the new capital is carried out without public engagement in a complex society, people's discontent will possibly increase. Considering that the IKN project will use a large area of land, which is in part communal,[58] this social discontent will likely transfer to other economic issues. Since the central government has decided not to provide an effective deliberative institution, the limited arrangements for social involvement in the content and implementation of the IKN regulations are likely to lead to grievance and conflict in the new capital region. Conflict will be likely to occur not only between the state and society but also among communities. In the long run, the institutional arrangement of the IKN will pose serious challenges to the continuity of democracy and autonomy in Indonesia.

Conclusion

This chapter has discussed the arrangement of local governance structures under the IKN regulations from the perspectives of regional autonomy and democracy after Indonesia's *Reformasi* period. In contrast with most analyses focusing on the motives or justifications of autonomy or recentralization in determining policy direction, this chapter has paid more attention to institutional arrangements, particularly local government structures and public participation in local governance. We analysed two issues of institutional arrangements. First, the form of centralistic executive-heavy structures determined by the central government has no strong institutional justification to be the arrangement of local governance in the new IKN. This form of local governance is estranged from the political commitment of Indonesia's post-democratization governments to foster local democracy and autonomy. Rather, the arrangement of local government structures for the IKN shows the tendency of the current government towards recentralization. The central government has no willingness to ensure that institutional arrangements for public participation exist in the IKN's local governance.

Second, the problematic arrangement of the local government structure and the lack of a viable public participation channel in the IKN will have serious institutional implications. The centralistic and bureaucratic pattern of local government might make bureaucracy at the local level follow the central government's direction rather than understand local characteristics, needs, and expectations. The IKN's bureaucracy is likely to fail to address local issues because it might tend to adhere to central direction, resulting in ineffective local governance. Furthermore, since local decision-making processes might be coloured with such a centralistic bureaucratic pattern, the involvement of non-state political actors at the local level will be limited. Hindering local participation can lead not only to legitimacy issues but also worsen social resentment and conflict in the implementation of the IKN regulations.

Notes

1. See articles 18A and 18B of the Indonesian Constitution of 1945 (2nd amendment).
2. Article 11 of Law No. 29 of 2007 on the Special Provincial Government of Jakarta as the State Capital City of the Republic of Indonesia.
3. Authors' interview with high-ranking officers in the Ministry of Home Affairs, Jakarta, on 20 October 2022.
4. Andreas Ladner, Nicolas Keuffer, and Harald Baldersheim, "Measuring Local Autonomy in 39 Countries (1990–2014)", *Regional & Federal Studies* 26, no. 3 (2016): 321–57; UN-Habitat. *Planning Sustainable Cities: Global Report on Human Settlements* (United Nations Human Settlements Programme, 2009); World Bank, *Decentralisation and Local Democracy in the World: First Global Report by United Cities and Local Governments* (Barcelona: United Cities and Local Governments, 2008).
5. Vilde Hernes, "The Case for Increased Centralisation in Integration Governance: The Neglected Perspective", *Comparative Migration Studies* 9, no. 32 (2021); Francesco Kjellberg. "The Changing Values of Local Government", *Annals of the American Academy of Social Sciences* 540, no. 1 (1995): 40–50.
6. Richard Robison and Vedi R. Hadiz, *Reorganising Power in Indonesia: The Politics of Oligarchy in an Age of Markets* (London: Routledge Curzon, 2004); James Manor, *The Political Economy of Democratic Decentralisation* (Washington, DC: World Bank, 1999); Steven Rood. "Interlocking Autonomy: Manila and Muslim Mindanao", in *Autonomy and Armed Separatism in South and Southeast Asia*, edited by Michelle Ann Miller (Singapore: Institute of Southeast Asian Studies, 2012), pp. 256–77; James Wunch, "Decentralisation, Local Governance and the Democratic Transition in Southern Africa: A Comparative Analysis", *African Studies Quarterly: Online Journal for African Studies* 2, no. 1 (1998): 19–45; Henk Schulte Nordholt, "Decentralisation and Democracy in Indonesia: Strengthening Citizenship or Regional Elites?", in *Handbook of Southeast Asian Politics*, edited by Richard Robison (Oxford: Routledge, 2011), pp. 229–41; Nancy Thede, "Decentralisation, Democracy and Human Rights: A Human Rights-Based Analysis of the Impact of Local Democratic Reforms on Development", *Journal of Human Development and Capabilities* 10, no. 1 (2009): 103–23.
7. Robison and Hadiz, *Reorganising Power in Indonesia*.
8. Richard Crook and James Manor, *Democracy and Decentralization in South Asia and West Africa* (Cambridge: Cambridge University Press, 1998); Manor, *The Political Economy of Democratic Decentralisation*; Thede, "Decentralisation, Democracy and Human Rights"; Joern Altmann, Ledivina Carino, Richard Flaman, Manfred Kulessa, and Ingo Schulz, *The UNDP Role in Decentralisation and Local Governance: A Joint UNDP-Government of Germany Evaluation* (New York: Evaluation Office UNDP, 2000), http://web.undp.org/evaluation/documents/decentralisation_final_report.pdf (accessed 18 August 2022).
9. Rood, "Interlocking Autonomy".
10. Nordholt, "Decentralisation and Democracy in Indonesia?".

11. Robison and Hadiz, *Reorganising Power in Indonesia*.
12. The involvement of hundreds of local government heads in corruption cases indicates and supports scholars' arguments. The authors, by calculating data from annual reports of the Corruption Eradication Commission (KPK), found a total of 170 local government heads, including provincial governors, district heads, and city mayors, have been arrested for corruption charges by KPK between 2003 and 2021.
13. Robison and Hadiz, *Reorganising Power in Indonesia*.
14. Hernes, "The Case for Increased Centralisation in Integration Governance".
15. Husniye Akilli and H. Serkan Akilli, "Decentralisation and Recentralisation of Local Governments in Turkey", *Procedia—Social and Behavioral Sciences* 140 (2014): 682–86.
16. Deniz Ay, "Diverging Community Responses to State-led Urban Renewal in the Context of Recentralisation of Planning Authority: an Analysis of Three Urban Renewal Projects in Turkey", *Habitat International* 91 (2019).
17. According to Kjellberg (1995), the contesting values between autonomy and centralization cannot be resolved by taking utterly one of the two and discarding one of them. The two have important positions in shaping democracy and legitimacy.
18. Article 1(9) of Law No. 3 of 2022 on the State Capital City Nusantara (hereafter IKN Law).
19. Article 4(1)-a of the IKN Law.
20. Article 9 of the IKN Law.
21. Article 10 of the IKN Law. Article 10(3) provides that the first IKN Authority Chief and the Vice-Chief can be nominated and appointed by the president. President Jokowi appointed a technocratic figure, Bambang Susantono, as the first Chief and the executive of Sinar Mas Land, a big property development conglomerate, Dhony Rahajoe, as the first Vice-Chief on 3 October 2022.
22. Article 12(2) of the IKN Law.
23. Law No. 23 of 2014 is a revision of the pass-breaking law for regional autonomy, Law No. 22 of 1999, established in the early democratization period. The Regional Government Law provides "wide and complete autonomy" with second-tier regional governments, district (*kabupaten*) and city (*kota*), while provincial governments are given limited autonomy since governors are expected to play a role of coordinators of lower regional governments as well as representatives of the central government.
24. Article 60 of the Law on Regional Government.
25. Article 1(2) of the IKN Law.
26. Articles 12(3), 24(7), 25(3), 26(2), 35 and 36(7) of IKN Law. As of December 2022, the national government has only enacted Government Regulation No. 17 of 2022 on Funding and Budget Management in the Context of Preparation, Development and Relocation of the State Capital City and Administration of the Special Region of State Capital City Nusantara.
27. Articles 4(2) and 39(1) of the IKN Law.

28. Articles 5(7), 7(4), 7(6), 11(1), 14(2), 15(2) and 22(5) of the IKN Law. As of December 2022, the national government has enacted only four of seven presidential regulations: Presidential Regulation No. 62 of 2022 on the State Capital Authority, Presidential Regulation No. 63 of 2022 on Details of the Nusantara State Capital City Master Plan, Presidential Regulation No. 64 of 2022 on Spatial Plans for the National Strategic Areas of the Nusantara State Capital City for 2022–42, and Presidential Regulation No. 65 of 2022 on Land Acquisition and Management of Land in the Nusantara State Capital City.
29. Article 7(5) of IKN Law.
30. Article 15(4) of IKN Law.
31. Article 16(5) of the IKN Law.
32. Article 23(1) of the IKN Law.
33. Article 24(6) of the IKN Law.
34. Article 5(6) of the IKN Law.
35. Elucidation of the IKN Law. Article 24(6) stipulates that the implementation of special taxes and levies in the IKN requires the approval of the DPR. Article 29(4) stipulates that transfers of government-owned goods have to be reported to the DPR.
36. Article 5(5) of the IKN Law.
37. Elucidation of the IKN Law.
38. Article 18B(1) of the 1945 Constitution provides that the state recognizes and respects units of regional authorities that are special and distinct.
39. See Article 3 of the IKN Law. Moreover, the Elucidation of the IKN Law states that the principle of effectiveness and efficiency of the government means that the arrangements of the Law are aimed at constructing an IKN city which is convenient and efficient in the management of governance, business, and citizens through the application of information, communication, and the technology of a smart city.
40. Delegation is commonly defined as the transfer of management and decision-making authority from the higher level of government to the lower autonomous regions that are under indirect supervision or control from higher government institutions (Rondinelli 1981).
41. Deconcentration means transferring the field of administration from a higher tier of government to lower-level arenas by which local staff are part of or responsible for central government institutions (Manor 1999; Rondinelli 1981).
42. Brasilia is often picked up in the research report made by the National Development Planning Agency (Bappenas), see Henley and Frigo (2020). Putrajaya was mentioned as a model by Imron Bulkin, the chief of the research team for the state capital relocation at Bappenas. See "Badan Otorita di Ibu Kota", *Tempo*, 31 August 2019.
43. The discussion at a hearing meeting with the Special Committee on the draft law for the IKN in the DPR.
44. See, for example, *GATRA.com*, "Tanpa DPRD dan Pemilu Kepala Otorita, IKN Disebut Tak Demokratis", 28 January 2022, https://www.gatra.com/news-534568-

Nasional-tanpa-dprd-dan-pemilu-kepala-otorita-ikn-disebut-tak-demokratis.html (accessed 24 November 2022). Critical views on the IKN Authority were already expressed for the academic draft of the IKN Law. See *Koran Tempo*, "Naskah Akademik Sarat Kritik", 22 January 2022.
45. *Kompas*, "Pemerintahan IKN Nusantara Diawasi DPR", 22 January 2022, p. 4.
46. Article 20 of Presidential Regulation No. 62 of 2022 on the State Capital Authority.
47. Article 32 of Presidential Regulation No. 62 of 2022 on the State Capital Authority.
48. *Tempo*, "Kenapa Jokowi Ingin RUU Ibu Kota Negara Buru-buru Disahkan", 22 January 2022, https://majalah.tempo.co/read/nasional/165133/kenapa-jokowi-ingin-ruu-ibu-kota-negara-buru-buru-disahkan
49. Wasisto Raharjo Jati, "A New Indonesian Capital City: Conflict Pending", *New Mandala*, 21 February 2022, https://www.newmandala.org/a-new-indonesian-capital-city-conflict-pending/ (accessed 3 September 2022).
50. Rini Kustiasih, "Ibu Kota Negara Baru untuk Siapa?", *Kompas*, 21 January 2022, https://www.kompas.id/baca/polhuk/2022/01/20/ibu-kota-baru-untuk-siapa
51. *Tempo*, "Safari Mendulang Dukungan Masyarakat Adat di Ibu Kota Baru", 2 February 2022, https://koran.tempo.co/read/nasional/471472/presiden-jokowi-temui-sejumlah-tokoh-adat-di-kalimantan-timur-perihal-proyek-ibu-kota-baru
52. *Kompas*, "Tanpa Kewenangan Kuat, Konsil Perwakilan Masyarakat IKN Berpotensi 'Mandul'", 24 March 2022, https://www.kompas.id/baca/polhuk/2022/03/24/tanpa-kewenangan-kuat-konsil-perwakilan-masyarakat-ikn-nusantara-berpotensi-mandul
53. Presentation of Erasmus Cahyadi, the deputy secretary general of AMAN (Alliance of Indigenous Peoples of the Archipelago), for hearing with the Special Committee on the IKN Law at the DPR.
54. About twenty-one groups of customary communities are living in the area of IKN, including the groups called Paser and Paser Balik. Nurhadi Sucahyo, "Hak Masyarakat Adat di Tengah Mega Proyek IKN", *VOA Indonesia*, 23 March 2022, https://www.voaindonesia.com/a/hak-masyarakat-adat-di-tengah-mega-proyek-ikn/6504396.html (accessed 28 August 2022).
55. Authors' interview with high-ranking officers of the Provincial Government of East Kalimantan (29 November 2022), the District Government of Kutai Kartanegara (29 November 2022), and the District Government of Penajam Paser Utara (30 November 2022). This was also stated by a prominent figure of Council of Paser Community in the authors' interview (30 November 2022).
56. The omission of local parliament from the structures means allowing public consultation only. See also Article 37 of the IKN Law.
57. *Kompas*, "Sebut IKN Dibangun Tanpa Legitimasi Kuat Masyarakat Adat di Kalimantan, AMAN: Yang Diajak Bicara Kan Elite", 18 February 2022, https://nasional.kompas.com/read/2022/02/18/16091911/sebut-ikn-dibangun-tanpa-legitimasi-kuat-masyarakat-adat-di-kalimantan-aman (accessed 28 August 2022).
58. Sucahyo, "Hak Masyarakat Adat di Tengah Mega Proyek IKN".

References

Akilli, Husniye, and H. Serkan Akilli. 2014. "Decentralisation and Recentralisation of Local Governments in Turkey". *Procedia—Social and Behavioral Sciences* 140: 682–86.

Altmann, Joern, Ledivina Carino, Richard Flaman, Manfred Kulessa, and Ingo Schulz. 2000. *The UNDP Role in Decentralisation and Local Governance: A Joint UNDP-Government of Germany Evaluation*. New York: Evaluation Office UNDP. http://web.undp.org/evaluation/documents/decentralisation_final_report.pdf (accessed 18 August 2022).

Ay, Deniz. 2019. "Diverging Community Responses to State-led Urban Renewal in the Context of Recentralisation of Planning Authority: An Analysis of Three Urban Renewal Projects in Turkey". *Habitat International* 91. https://doi.org/10.1016/j.habitatint.2019.102028 (accessed 17 August 2022).

Crook, Richard, and James Manor. 1998. *Democracy and Decentralization in South Asia and West Africa*. Cambridge: Cambridge University Press.

GATRA.com. "Tanpa DPRD dan Pemilu Kepala Otorita, IKN Disebut Tak Demokratis". 28 January 2022. https://www.gatra.com/news-534568-Nasional-tanpa-dprd-dan-pemilu-kepala-otorita-ikn-disebut-tak-demokratis.html (accessed 24 November 2022).

Henley, David, and Giulia Frigo. 2020. "Lessons from Brasilia: on the Empty Modernity of Indonesia's New Capital". *New Mandala*, 14 April 2020. https://www.newmandala.org/lessons-from-brasilia-on-the-empty-modernity-of-indonesias-new-capital/ (accessed 28 August 2022).

Hernes, Vilde. 2021. "The Case for Increased Centralisation in Integration Governance: The Neglected Perspective". *Comparative Migration Studies* 9, no. 32. https://doi.org/10.1186/s40878-021-00247-z (accessed 25 August 2022).

Jati, Wasisto Raharjo. 2022. "A New Indonesian Capital City: Conflict Pending". *New Mandala* (blog), 21 February 2022. https://www.newmandala.org/a-new-indonesian-capital-city-conflict-pending/ (accessed 3 September 2022).

Kjellberg, Francesco. 1995. "The Changing Values of Local Government". *Annals of the American Academy of Social Sciences* 540, no. 1: 40–50. https://doi.org/10.1177/0002716295540000004 (accessed 28 August 2022).

Kompas. 2022a. "Pemerintahan IKN Nusantara Diawasi DPR". 22 January 2022, p. 4.

———. 2022b. "Tanpa Kewenangan Kuat, Konsil Perwakilan Masyarakat IKN Berpotensi 'Mandul'". 24 March 2022. https://www.kompas.id/baca/polhuk/2022/03/24/tanpa-kewenangan-kuat-konsil-perwakilan-masyarakat-ikn-nusantara-berpotensi-mandul

Koran Tempo. 2022. "Naskah Akademik Sarat Kritik". 22 January 2022.

Kustiasih, Rini. 2022. "Ibu Kota Negara Baru untuk Siapa?". *Kompas*, 21 January 2022. https://www.kompas.id/baca/polhuk/2022/01/20/ibu-kota-baru-untuk-siapa

Ladner, Andreas, Nicolas Keuffer, and Harald Baldersheim. 2016. "Measuring Local Autonomy in 39 Countries (1990–2014)". *Regional & Federal Studies* 26, no. 3:

321–57. https://doi.org/10.1080/13597566.2016.1214911 (accessed 1 September 2022).

Manor, James. 1999. *Political Economy of Democratic Decentralization*. Washington, DC: World Bank.

May, Ronald J. 2012. "History, Demography and Factionalism: Obstacles to Conflict Resolution through Autonomy in the Southern Philippines". In *Autonomy and Armed Separatism in South and Southeast Asia*, edited by Michelle Ann Miller, pp. 278–95. Singapore: Institute of Southeast Asian Studies.

Nordholt, Henk Schulte. 2011. "Decentralisation and Democracy in Indonesia: Strengthening Citizenship or Regional Elites?". In *Handbook of Southeast Asian Politics*, edited by Richard Robison, pp. 229–41. Oxford: Routledge.

Robison, Richard, and Vedi R. Hadiz. 2004. *Reorganising Power in Indonesia: The Politics of Oligarchy in an Age of Markets*. London: Routledge Curzon.

Rondinelli, Dennis A. 1981. "Government Decentralisation in Comparative Perspective: Theory and Practice in Developing Countries". *International Review of Administrative Sciences* 47, no. 2: 133–45. https://doi.org/10.1177/002085238004700205 (accessed 2 September 2022).

Rood, Steven. 2012. "Interlocking Autonomy: Manila and Muslim Mindanao". In *Autonomy and Armed Separatism in South and Southeast Asia*, edited by Michelle Ann Miller, pp. 256–77. Singapore: Institute of Southeast Asian Studies.

Sucahyo, Nurhadi. 2022. "Hak Masyarakat Adat di Tengah Mega Proyek IKN". *VOA Indonesia*, 23 March 2022. https://www.voaindonesia.com/a/hak-masyarakat-adat-di-tengah-mega-proyek-ikn/6504396.html (accessed 28 August 2022).

Tempo. 2019. "Badan Otorita di Ibu Kota". 31 August 2019.

———. 2022a. "Kenapa Jokowi Ingin RUU Ibu Kota Negara Buru-buru Disahkan". 22 January 2022, https://majalah.tempo.co/read/nasional/165133/kenapa-jokowi-ingin-ruu-ibu-kota-negara-buru-buru-disahkan

———. 2022b. "Safari Mendulang Dukungan Masyarakat Adat di Ibu Kota Baru". 2 February 2022, https://koran.tempo.co/read/nasional/471472/presiden-jokowi-temui-sejumlah-tokoh-adat-di-kalimantan-timur-perihal-proyek-ibu-kota-baru

Thede, Nancy. 2009. "Decentralisation, Democracy and Human Rights: A Human Rights-Based Analysis of the Impact of Local Democratic Reforms on Development". *Journal of Human Development and Capabilities* 10, no. 1: 103–23.

UN-Habitat. 2009. *Planning Sustainable Cities: Global Report on Human Settlements*. United Nations Human Settlements Programme. World Bank.

World Bank. 2008. *Decentralisation and Local Democracy in the World: First Global Report by United Cities and Local Governments*. Barcelona: United Cities and Local Governments.

Wunch, James. 1998. "Decentralisation, Local Governance and the Democratic Transition in Southern Africa: A Comparative Analysis". *African Studies Quarterly: Online Journal for African Studies* 2, no. 1: 19–45. https://asq.africa.ufl.edu/wunsch_98/ (accessed 25 August 2022).

3

NUSANTARA AND THE SPATIAL IMPLICATIONS FOR THE PRACTICE OF INDONESIAN DEMOCRACY

Ian Douglas Wilson

Introduction

The plan to move Indonesia's national capital from its historic site in Jakarta to a new purpose-built city in East Kalimantan Province is undoubtedly the most ambitious state infrastructure project of modern Indonesian history in terms of scale, logistics and cost. It has understandably provoked divergent responses, from praise as a visionary attempt to reimagine and modernize the nation, to criticism of the massive expenditure required and its environmental impacts, and scepticism that it is driven by political interests. Beyond issues of the economic and logistical feasibility of the plan's implementation at a time of investor wariness and economic uncertainty, significant questions emerge regarding how a purpose-built capital will impact the ways that Indonesia's national politics is imagined and conducted.

Purpose-built capitals are by no means a new or unique phenomenon. There have been twelve capital cities built since the 1960s, with several others underway or in pre-planning stages. Pojani notes that, regardless of whether the political setting is democratic, a hybrid regime or authoritarian, new capital cities have been almost entirely planned by those in power as "totalizing projects", rather than being developed and built piecemeal over time through processes involving a range of social political and economic interests.[1] This has generally resulted in a tendency for purpose-built capitals to reinforce and embody state and elite conceptions and "utopian" visions, of nation, state and spatializations of political order. In particular, the crucial role played by non-state and civil society actors in shaping political praxis and popular resistance in capital cities has often been omitted, by oversight or intent, from this state or elite vision, such as in Myanmar's junta-built capital of Naypyidaw or Nursultan, Kazakhstan's capital named after its former autocratic president.

This chapter will reflect upon two central questions in considering the implications of Nusantara for political praxis in Indonesia. The first is historical: What has been the relationship among space, *rakyat* and political change in Jakarta, the nation's capital and biggest city? Particular attention is given to the centrality of Jakarta's streets as political space, producing social and political movements and dialectical tensions that have shaped and constrained the political direction of the nation-state. The second considers the implications of a pre-planned capital and the disentangling of national government from the complexity and messiness of a dynamic megacity for the direction and substance of Indonesian democracy heading in to the 2024 elections and beyond.

The political drive to realize Nusantara has occurred within a specific socio-political context marked by what many analysts have characterized as democratic regression alongside growing executive illiberalism.[2] Indonesia's electoral democracy is, broadly speaking, institutionally consolidated; however, it has remained subject to ongoing political attack.[3] In contrast to the early to mid-2000s, Indonesian civil society has become increasingly fragmented and polarized, and as such less able to provide coherent opposition and checks and balances. Despite this, protests, rallies, mobilizations, advocacy, and self-organization in Jakarta, often via established networks of activists and driven by young people, have continued to be crucial barometers and shapers of public opinion, if not facilitators of change.

The interaction between the historic and national symbolism of public spaces in Jakarta and the public sphere, such as rallies and protests, together with the proximity to national and international media serve to amplify the reach and impact of ideas, issues and meanings, or what Padawangi has referred to as a "megaphonic function".[4] The function of capital cities as "containers" of sovereignty makes them central rallying points for struggle and contentious claims.[5] As a political stage and megacity capital of Indonesia, Jakarta continues to highlight the realities of mismanagement, poor governance, and infrastructural inequality, which has left it as a notorious example of uneven development. As Harvey states, "Cities are constituted not by one but by multiple spatio-temporalities, producing multiple frameworks within which conflictual social processes are worked out".[6]

This chapter argues that separating Indonesia's historical centre of executive power and national government from a cosmopolitan "nation in microcosm" megacity will re-spatialize, and in doing so consolidate, trends towards more unaccountable and inaccessible forms of state power. This is due to two main factors. The first is spatial proximity: as seen in purpose-built capitals elsewhere, greater distances of the seat of executive government from large diverse populations and concentrations of organized and disorganized civil society have been associated with higher levels of unaccountability and unreceptiveness to public sentiment.[7] The second is the disentanglement of the administrative capital from the heterotopia (spaces of otherness and difference) of the megacity.[8] Rather than being a place in which national government operates, the contestations and cosmopolitanisms of Jakarta, together with the spatial dialectics of inclusion and exclusion, connection, and segregation, have generated social movements and dynamic forms of political agency shaped by the needs and wants of its residents.

Capital Cities, Democracy and Political Space

All politics occurs in space, and spaces do not just exist but are produced through complex political relations.[9] Territory and space matter for the balance of power, and for how dominance and efforts to achieve it are constituted. As the sociologist Lefebvre articulated it:

> Socio-political contradictions are realized spatially. The contradictions of space thus make the contradictions of social relations operative. In other words, spatial contradictions 'express' conflicts between socio-political interests and forces; it is only in space that such conflicts come effectively into play, and in doing so they become contradictions of space.[10]

These contradictions of space are reproduced and controlled by practices associated with the prevailing systems of control but can be challenged by repertoires of contention, such as those forged in social movements or counter-hegemonic groups like the United States' Occupy movement. These also occur at different levels of scale, such as the centre-periphery divide experienced by many post-colonial states.[11]

The work of Lefebvre, Soja, and others highlights the political nature of space, which can be taken to mean both the public sphere in which political claims are made, contested, and decided, as well as the physical space of buildings, monuments, streets, and neighbourhoods. Cities are both symbolic and actual concentrations of power and wealth. As such, cities are not static entities or simply places in which formal politics and the exercising of power occur but are productive of social and political relations, types of claim-making, alliances and negotiations, and struggles by different kinds of people to inhabit and gain access to the city and public realm, which can also challenge and transform state power, as well as a traditional conception of politics in which only certain types of activity can be recognized as political.

Cities, and especially capital cities, play crucial roles in the production and maintenance of dominance and as sites of popular resistance and claim-making. In the context of demographic changes to urban-majority populations, major cities have emerged as key sites within which struggles over the legitimacy of governments and regimes are played out and where opposition movements seek to gain support and influence.[12] The past decade has demonstrated the importance of urban mobilization in capital cities beyond conventional political boundaries, with new actors and instigators of protest and claim-making, such as seen in the Arab Spring, Occupy movements, and pro-democracy protests in Hong Kong. Despite the differences between these, a common characteristic has been the movements' occupation or repurposing of prominent public space.

Capital cities in institutionalized democracies are confronted with tensions around the representation and facilitation of the democratic sovereign. Minkenberg argues that the urban form and function of capital cities of democratic countries must, in some way, correspond to, or facilitate, the values, needs and processes of democracy, which extends beyond the symbolic to the actual.[13] For countries that have undergone transitions from authoritarian to democratic systems, this often occurs through the contestation of the meaning and function of "official space" by various groups. The Arab Spring, for example, saw the transformation of Tahrir Square in Cairo into a space of democratic self-government by ordinary civilians that was both real and imaginary in so far as it symbolically encompassed all of Egypt.[14] Similarly in Indonesia, rallies and protests in Jakarta's Merdeka Square have contested official inscriptions of historical meaning, while games of cat and mouse between public order officials and informal traders using it as a space of livelihood generation have challenged authority and rights to space.

Capital cities are places particularly associated with the state; hence it is unsurprising that they should also be primary sites of resistance to it. Being densely populated can mean that cities are "conduits where movements connect and develop" and where ideas and discourse ferment.[15] Urban populations tend to be more highly educated and capital cities are often opposition strongholds or percolators of alternative political visions and ideologies.

Decentralization of political and economic power has been a prominent part of the official rationale in many countries undertaking this type of new capital project. However, even with the best of democratic intentions, the complex dynamism and potentialities of urban life are difficult to reproduce.[16] In the case of Brazil for example, its planned capital Brasilia was intended as a model for significant social democratic reform that would facilitate more egalitarian social relations and usher in a new era of economic development in the nation's interior.[17] In practice, however, it soon reproduced extreme forms of social inequality and segregation and failed to generate social transformation.

Pojani argues that purpose-built capitals emerge out of political power rather than developing over an extended period in dialectic tension with the needs and wants of residents.[18] Proposals to reposition a capital city are often stimulated by the antinomies and tensions between the contested reality of "organic" capital cities, and their normative definitions as upheld by the political leadership.[19] As Martin and Byron Miller note, "Social relations are spatial as well as historical and altering the spatial or historical constitution of social processes will likely alter how they play out."[20]

Population density facilitates collective action. The heterogeneity of cities such as Jakarta and its densely populated districts and *kampung* has been, as Simone has observed the "precondition for politics—not just a by-product"; the proximity of different ways of doing things, the intertwining of social relations, collisions of strategies of survival with vested material interests, and processes of adaptation which may, in some instances, consolidate into forms of claim-making and either atomized or collective struggles with government institutions.[21]

Nation-Building, and the Everyday Politics of Jakarta's Streets

> Jakarta is a city that is both powerful and painful ... all the progress in the nation can be seen here. The national politics is here. Technologies begin here. New lifestyles develop here. Hedonism triumphs here. Big businesses proliferate here. And poverty also reproduces very well here.
> (Joko Widodo, Governor of Jakarta, 2012)[22]

The street is a specific social space with its distinct kind of politics, forms of organization, conviviality, and networks. Jakarta's streets have been sites of collective action and contestation and spaces where the interests of citizens and the state interact. Populations have mobilized en masse at particular stages of their histories into nation-state–building processes and have been mobilized by political authorities seeking to bolster or install their regimes.[23] The country's first president Sukarno, a trained architect, envisioned Jakarta as a showpiece for the greatness of the nation and a "portal of the country", explicitly linking the construction of spaces such as the National Monument and Sudirman-Thamrin to the process of nation-building itself.[24] Grand symbolism however camouflaged increasingly dire socio-economic realities and political tensions between ideological blocs. Populist mass mobilizations that made use of monumental public space were however encouraged by Sukarno's populist and revolutionary rhetoric, with Jakarta as the locus for popular mobilization, where even the lower classes were organized in civil society and political organizations.[25]

The upheavals of 1965 played out violently in the capital, leaving in the aftermath unspoken trauma and fear. In its wake, Jakarta's streets and spaces of populist mass mobilization were hyper-securitized. In contrast to the Sukarno era, where Jakarta's national monuments and spaces were frequent sites of populist mobilizations and rallies, the New Order harboured a deep institutional paranoia towards the *massa*, the meaning of which shifted from "the masses" to something closer to "mob".[26] The New Order's campaign for the depoliticization of society and the transformation of popular sovereignty into the "floating mass" resulted in a severe curtailment of the possibilities for oppositional forms of political organization. Fear of the streets increasingly dominated the city's spatial organization, with a greater focus on controlling Jakarta's population than on developing a viable city.[27] At the same time, the growth of an urban middle class living in apartments and gated estates saw a shift in political space away from the street.

This shaped the urban governance of the capital with a significant reduction in public infrastructure and public space. Expanding neoliberalization and the lobbying power of developers and industry also left their mark. The automobile industry, for example, successfully blocked plans for expanding public transportation infrastructure, which was further exacerbated by cheap motorcycles and subsidized fuel, while shopping malls became de facto public spaces for the middle class.[28] This worsened problems such as gridlock and flooding, routinely blamed on poor and new migrants, who largely self-built their own neighbourhoods and communities.[29]

The New Order regime considered the poor and the unplanned informal spaces such as *kampung* in which many lived, as both an unsightly impediment to the realization of its modernizing and developmentalist rhetoric, unsuitable for Jakarta as a symbolic centre of the nation, and as potential sites of crime and political unrest. Jakarta's governor from 1966 to 1977, Ali Sadikin, characterized the city's poor as lacking "urban rationality" and as such, constituting a threat to the New Order's nation-state developmentalism.[30] Elite imaginings of Jakarta as a modernist city resulted in patterns of segregation and surveillance towards the poor together with discipline campaigns and the construction of new spaces of exclusivity.[31] This "nationalist urbanism" explicitly linked the governance of the city to the power of Jakarta as the seat of national power and prestige, so that, "If a *kampung* had to be demolished and the master plan changed, the further development of the nation provides sufficient justification."[32]

For the hundreds of thousands of people absorbed into the capital's ever-expanding peri-urban fringe, Jakarta was and is a place of possibility, but also precarity. Jakarta's official population increased from just 3 million in the 1960s to well over 10 million by the early 2000s.[33] Faced with little in the way of public infrastructure and often hostile policies from the city administration, the poor engaged in complex everyday politics to acquire the necessities of such as housing, work, and access to utilities, in the process transforming the city.[34] These atomized mobilizations and localized struggles constitute a distinct form of collective action through repetition by large numbers that, by its very scale, has significantly shaped the physical but also political contours of Jakarta. This is readily evident, from the appropriation of state or privately-owned land for livelihood generation by street vendors, to informal settlements that make use of available empty land.[35]

To paraphrase Benedict Anderson, cities, like nations, are more "imagined communities" than actual ones, in so far as it is not possible to experience each one in its totality. What this does is provide space for struggles and contestations over the meaning and identity of each city. The struggles of the city's poor for rights and a place in the capital have also been struggles for defining the meaning of moral as opposed to legal constructions of citizenship.[36] Jakarta has been a "privileged place for democratic innovation" and has produced new modes of democratic engagement, such as the sophisticated use of political contracts with electoral candidates by urban poor communities to bargain and gain concessions.[37]

AKSI AND DEMOCRACY

Jakarta's position as a national political stage has served to magnify the symbolic and political impact of street-based political actions. Throughout the New Order mobilization in Jakarta's streets became a high-risk strategy of resistance by various opposition groups to authoritarian power. As a symbolic space for the contestation of meaning and identity, and through their criminalization, demonstrations in the capital generated powerful reverberations that extended around the nation.[38] *Aksi* street actions in Jakarta (and other regional centres) throughout the 1990s had immediate and cumulative impacts.[39] It was in part due to this symbolic power of people rallying in Jakarta's streets that the New Order routinely orchestrated counter-demonstrations in support of state policies or as a strategy to intimidate opposition groups.[40]

A key driver was, and remains, young people. Jakarta's university and college campuses have long been spaces of networking, discussion and political activism, as have the *kos* (hostels), *kafe*, *warnet* and *warung* (cafes, Internet cafes, and eating places) where students live and congregate. Key transformative moments were driven by a complex and extended organization and information sharing. *Aksi*, mass mobilizations and rallies did not take place only in spaces associated with the state, such as national government buildings, but in streets, boulevards, roundabouts and *kampung*, industrial zones and campuses. As Magnusson writes, "The state is always of some importance in relation to [political] issues ... it is rarely the case that the crucial battle will be fought on the terrain of the state itself."[41]

The protests, street clashes and riots of May 1998 which toppled the rule of Suharto witnessed the streets of the city as virtual battlegrounds. The economic crisis of 1997, which precipitated the political crisis, increased the numbers of the poor and precarious in the capital. Street vendors, beggars, drivers of public transport, and others seeking to make ends meet occupied public parks, private land, sidewalks, overpasses and any available space.[42] These bolstered mobilizations by student activists against the regime in 1998, turning even mundane spaces of the city into protest sites of central significance. Key sites of state power such as the national parliament building were occupied by student protestors, emerging as powerful symbols of popular sovereignty.

Post-New Order, the streets and neighbourhoods of Jakarta became a renewed space of contestation between various social classes and interests. New organizations, networks, political voices and information-sharing practices formed, and an invigorated sense of a right to the city prevailed, with Jakarta witnessing a euphoria of claim-making on the state. State control fragmented, leading to the rise of new and different groups vying for legitimacy and influence.

The immediate post-1998 era also saw some shifts away from overtly authoritarian approaches to planning in Jakarta, with some notable exceptions. Governor Sutiyoso continued policies aimed at social control, albeit in the name of beautification, such as enclosing Monas (the National Monument) with a tall fence and rebuilding Bundaran HI, both important sites for protests. This period marked an important shift in the political dynamics of the capital as "residents of Jakarta, from various classes, found themselves in more advantageous positions to criticize developmental projects in the city that "seek to represent the image of the nation".[43] Protests and rallies became daily fare and, as Padawangi documents, spanned a broadened set of issues, claims and concerns.[44] Civil society flourished with NGOs, and social, religious and community organizations establishing offices, networks, and presences throughout the capital near the executive government and a diverse national media which "strengthened Indonesia's diagonal accountability mechanisms".[45] Political parties followed suit, with early post-1998 electoral campaigns focused on the mobilization of crowds and street-based shows of force by party *satgas* (task force) units.

Since 2014, street protests and mass mobilizations in Jakarta have continued to constitute an important part of political contestation and popular political participation. The huge rallies in Jakarta of 2016–17 organized by the 212 Movement, which was sparked by allegations of blasphemy by Jakarta's governor Basuki Tjahaja Purnama, or Ahok, were driven by divergent political agendas and interests that spanned classes, interests and groups.[46] The success of these mobilizations in deposing the popular governor reignited political elite interest in the potential of street politics, but in largely undemocratic terms. The subsequent government crackdowns on Islamist groups linked to the 212 Movement reflected older government paranoias of the disruptive potential of the *massa*, whereas political co-option of 212 Movement leaders by rival contenders for the presidency was informed by New Order notions of street mobilizations as means to power.

Mass protests and riots in Jakarta throughout 2019 bore strong resonances with those of almost twenty years earlier in May 1998. Large mobilizations of students and workers, under the banner of "*reformasi dikorupsi*" ("Reform has been corrupted"), responded to government efforts to push through controversial revisions to the Corruption Eradication

Commission (KPK) Law, and the criminal code (KUHP).[47] These and similar actions have remained crucial forms of popular social opposition and participation, in a context in which grand coalition government has undermined oppositional dynamics within the legislature and autocratic legalism replaced substantive public consultation, but where the president remains sensitive to perceptions of unpopularity. In each case, protests by students and workers have served to delay contentious draft legislation packages that the government has attempted to rush through, forcing some form of public debate via social and commercial media. As Bayat has noted, "centrality, proximity, and accessibility ... are crucial features of any street of discontent".[48]

Glaeser and Steinberg have postulated a positive relationship between urbanization, the megacity and democracy, suggesting that cities facilitate coordinated public action and enhance the effectiveness of dissent, increase the demand for democracy relative to autocracy, and engender the development of "civic capital"; the social skills and networks that collectively enable citizens to improve their own institutions.[49] Jakarta has historically functioned as a central rallying point of struggles, political claims, and regime change. It has also fostered the mobilization of marginal groups, such as the urban poor, at times in disparate alliances with the middle class or Islamists.[50]

Democratic Decline and its Infrastructural Reconfiguration

Numerous scholars have characterized Indonesia as undergoing an extended process of state-driven "democratic regression" over the past decade, characterized by a gradual erosion of formal rights and protections gained post-1998.[51] Autocratic legalism has been a distinctive feature, whereby key legislative packages with wide-ranging implications for personal and political freedoms and rights, anti-corruption efforts, and environmental protection such as the Omnibus Law on Job Creation, have been passed into law with minimal to no public consultation.[52] Physical infrastructure development has been a prevailing concern of the Jokowi administration, intended to redress spatial inequities in development throughout the archipelago, but largely untethered from any agenda for bureaucratic, legal, rights or anti-corruption reform.[53]

In the context of executive illiberalism and constrictions on civil democratic space, the continuation of largely free and fair elections has been cited as a sign of Indonesia's democratic "resilience".[54] Autocratic nostalgia for a rolling back of direct elections within the Jokowi administration has however remained strong. Key government figures such as Minister of Home Affairs Tito Karnavian, head of the MPR Bambang Soesatyo, and Coordinating Minister Luhut Panjaitan among others have routinely questioned the utility, value, and future of direct elections.[55] Karnavian, for example, has advocated for so-called "asymmetrical" elections whereby local elections are limited to areas with a high democracy index rating.[56] Areas with low index ratings are, according to Karnavian, susceptible to manipulation and poor electoral outcomes with the lower classes in particular "unable to understand democracy".[57]

Nusantara will establish a new benchmark for "asymmetrical" electorally limited governance. Unlike other special status regions, such as Yogyakarta, Papua, Aceh or Jakarta, Nusantara will not have direct local elections nor a regional parliament (DPRD). Instead, local issues are to be facilitated via the national-level legislature (DPR) and regional representatives (DPD), in effect, an institutional convergence of national and local representation. The new capital is to be led by a Head of Capital Authority, likened to a "city manager", appointed directly by the President.[58] The rationale for this governance structure has been framed in depoliticized, technocratic terms, like embracing efficiency and effectiveness to deliver development outcomes. Despite government predictions that it will have a population of up to 2 million, the seat of national government Nusantara is envisioned as not having a "population" that requires direct political representation.[59] The IKN project is too important to be left to the machinations and "divisiveness" of popular electoral politics, particularly as its initial population would consist primarily of civil servants and their families.[60] In doing so, IKN establishes a space of governmentality that is less susceptible to civil society dynamics. The centre of state power is re-spatialized as a special zone of technocratic and rationalist modernity, distanced from the possibility of popular disruption.

As discussed above, the intersection between local and national has been a consistent feature of Jakarta. Popular forces in the streets have regularly disrupted state authority and challenged state narratives. Despite the pivotal role of social and political movements in Jakarta's streets in bringing down the New Order and ushering in democracy post-1998, Jakarta was a relative latecomer to post-New Order electoral reforms due to its special capital region status. Direct municipal elections for governor and parliament were not held until 2007, several years behind the rest of the country.[61] Subsequent gubernatorial elections have had significant reverberating impacts on national politics, from the rise of Joko Widodo to the turmoil of 2017 and the 212 Movement.[62] The absence of local elections or a regional parliament for Nusantara will mean a lack of direct representation for local concerns and tiers of citizenship; an effective democratic vacuum.[63]

National and regional elections in 2024 will nonetheless see the politicization of Nusantara whose success requires commitment extending over at least two presidential terms.[64] Public scepticism towards the feasibility and need for a new capital city has remained high, with numerous surveys indicating that significant majorities doubt it will be successfully completed and view it as economically detrimental.[65] Accusations of wasted resources have commonly plagued new capital city projects. In the case of Naypyidaw, for example, resentment at huge state expenditure while the country was mired in poverty flowed into greater support for democratic opposition figure Aung San Suu Kyi.[66] It remains unclear if, how, and where widespread scepticism and disillusionment towards Nusantara will find expression.

In contrast to Glaeser and Steinberg, Goodfellow and Jackman contend that cities can hold certain advantages for ruling elites attempting to consolidate their control and thwart the potential for effective resistance, and that the control of capital cities has been crucial to the production of political dominance and how ruling coalitions seek to perpetuate it.[67] Nusantara, in this respect, could be seen as a spatial consolidation of elite-driven erosions of Indonesia's democratic gains. The political process around IKN to date has arguably reflected this, with minimal public consultation, rushed legislation, and a timeline driven by political imperatives. Indigenous populations in East Kalimantan, who may be displaced from traditional lands by the project, have been excluded from planning discussions.[68] This sees a risk of reproducing patterns of informality like dispossession, as seen in Jakarta, where indigenous Betawi populations were disenfranchised by the city's development and pushed to the city's peripheries.[69]

Potter argues that moving capital cities outside of the largest urban population centres is often driven by a motivation to mitigate the potential for urban uprisings or civil conflicts, such as in the cases of Myanmar and Kazakhstan.[70] Considering the pivotal role played by *aksi* ("action") protests, mobilizations, and riots in Jakarta, this may be a consideration. More compelling is Potter's observation that when the government is located outside of the country's largest urban area, it limits its control and influence over the government. He contends this may in some cases enable the government to better manage competing geographically concentrated political and economic interests, particularly in contexts where this is a driver of civil conflict.[71] Indeed, a key argument for Nusantara has been as a corrective to Jakarta and Java-centrism, both politically and in terms of centre-periphery patterns of development.[72] In this regard, a new capital allows for the bypassing of old economic, transportation, and administrative structures and the development of new ones.[73]

There is no certainty however that this results in better governance or more equitable development. In a comparative analysis of purpose-built capitals, Campante, Do, and Guimares found that more geographically isolated capitals built away from established major population centres are both symptoms and enablers of misgovernance, and more prone to corruption and unaccountable government, particularly in the context of weakly-institutionalized, non-democratic or hybrid regimes.[74] This is owing to the national government being less politically constrained by proximity to large populations where various factors come into play. This includes sensitivity to the potential for an immediate widespread public reaction such as protests or strikes, the "megaphone" effect of civil society mobilization in capital cities, higher levels of scrutiny, and demands for accountability provided by concentrations of media, and greater general levels of interest from the public regarding government machinations.[75]

The spatial proximity of executive government to urban populations operates as a facilitator of oversight scrutiny and sensitivity to public perception. The reconstituting of effective and dynamic civil society networks within a new capital, particularly one designed by those in power, will take considerable time and effort. For civil society organizations in Jakarta, the logistics of moving or commuting will be daunting. This is likely to result in a significantly reduced civil society presence in Nusantara compared to Jakarta, with pre-existing local organizations alongside several larger and better-resourced national organizations, many of which may have close or clientelist ties to the government. It is perhaps unsurprising that the first organizations to announce they will open offices in Nusantara are two of the country's oldest, best-resourced, and most politically connected: Nahdlatul Ulama and Pemuda Pancasila.[76]

The vision of Nusantara, as articulated by the national government as a green, sustainable, tech-enabled, and poverty-free smart-city capital appears admirable but stands in grating contrast with the realities of current-day Jakarta and many other urban centres throughout the country.[77] Rossman notes that purpose-built capitals have often "laid the utopian and futuristic paradigms of national development serving as a foundation for more ambitious blueprints of social transformation".[78] Building Nusantara with state-of-the-art facilities and services when other major population centres in Indonesia are conspicuously lacking these may, however, inadvertently produce new patterns of political resentment, uneven development, segregation and clientelism, while insulating national decision-makers from these realities and voices of discontent.[79]

Conclusions

Despite significant investment by Indonesia's first president, Sukarno, in grand modernist developments in Jakarta, he remained strongly attracted to the idea of building a new capital from scratch in Kalimantan. Silver has suggested this was, in part, reflective of a more general indifference to the everyday needs of Jakarta required to make it a liveable city, such as water infrastructure and social housing, and a penchant for large-scale capital projects.[80] A capital should be, according to Sukarno, a grand statement of national unity and identity. Such a vision was challenged by the realities of rapid urbanization, failed economic strategies and political disintegration. It is difficult not to see a similar set of predilections in relation to Nusantara.

Regardless of the shape and form Nusantara may eventually take, the infrastructural and socio-economic challenges of Jakarta will remain. Building a new capital will do nothing to stem subsidence, traffic congestion, air pollution or deepening infrastructural inequality. Symbolically, it could be interpreted by political opposition as an expensive escape plan, considering that the technocratic utopian vision of Nusantara is, in many respects, all that Jakarta is not.[81]

Nusantara as currently proposed will entail a political disentangling of executive power from a heterogeneous urban context that has historically functioned as a check and balance on power, a means to power, as well as the source and driver of fundamental change, including the overthrowing of state authoritarianism. Without direct elections, a potentially ring-fenced notion of inclusion/exclusion, and geographically divorced from the contradictions and inequalities of development readily apparent in the megacity, there is a danger that Nusantara will serve to incubate the autocratic tendencies of political elites, as evidenced in the experiences of purpose-built capitals elsewhere.

Notes

1. Dorina Pojani, *Trophy Cities: A Feminist Perspective on New Capital* (Cheltenham: Edward Elgar Publishing, 2021).
2. Marcus Mietzner, "Sources of Resistance to Democratic Decline: Indonesian Civil Society and Its Trials". *Democratization* 28, no. 1 (2021): 161–78.
3. This has ranged from the 2014 law that abolished regional elections, only to be

overturned by a presidential decree, to more recent calls from senior figures in the Jokowi administration for a return to parliamentary appointment of regional leaders.
4. Rita Padawangi, "The Cosmopolitan Grassroots City as Megaphone: Reconstructing Public Spaces through Urban Activism in Jakarta", *International Journal of Urban and Regional Research* 73 (2013): 849–63.
5. Jo Beall, Tom Goodfellow, and Dennis Rodgers, "Cities and Conflict in Fragile States in the Developing World". *Urban Studies* 50, no. 5 (2013): 3065–83.
6. David Harvey, "Contested Cities: Social Process and Spatial Form", in *Transforming Cities New Spatial Divisions and Social Transformation*, edited by Nick Jewson and Susanne MacGregor (London: Routledge, 1997).
7. Filipe R. Campante, Quoc-Anh Do, and Bernardo Guimares, "Capital Cities, Conflict, and Misgovernance", *American Economic Journal: Applied Economics* 11, no. 3 (2019): 298–337.
8. Michiel Dehaene and Lieven De Cauter, "Heterotopia in a Postcivil Society", in *Heterotopia and the City: Public Space in a Postcivil Society*, edited by Michiel Dehaene and Lieven De Cauter (London: Routledge, 2008).
9. Jeroen Gunning and Ilan Z. Baron, *Why Occupy a Square? People, Protests and Movements in the Egyptian Revolution* (Oxford University Press, 2014).
10. Henri Lefebvre, *The Production of Space* (New Jersey: Wiley-Blackwell, 1991), p. 365
11. Nic Cheeseman, *Democracy in Africa: Successes, Failures, and the Struggle for Political Reform*. Cambridge (Cambridge: Cambridge University Press, 2015).
12. Danielle Resnick, *Urban Poverty and Party Populism in African Democracies* (Cambridge: Cambridge University Press, 2014).
13. Michael Minkenberg, *Power and Architecture: The Construction of Capitals and the Politics of Space* (Berghahn Books, 2014). For example, large public spaces that are fully accessible to the public and not restricted to official state ceremonies.
14. Gunning and Baron, *Why Occupy a Square?*
15. Justus Uitermark, Walter Nicholls, and Maarten Loopmans, "Cities and Social Movements: Theorizing Beyond the Right to the City", *Environment and Planning* 44, no. 11 (2012): 2549.
16. Vadim Rossman, *Capital Cities: Varieties and Patterns of Development and Relocation* (London: Routledge, 2016).
17. Isabel Maria Madaleno, "Brasilia: The Frontier Capital", *Cities* 13, no. 4 (1996): 273–80.
18. Pojani, *Trophy Cities*.
19. Rossman, *Capital Cities*.
20. Deborah Martin and Byron Miller, "Space and Contentious Politics", *Mobilization: An International Quarterly* 8, no. 2 (2003): 144–45.
21. AbdouMaliq Simone, *Jakarta, Drawing the City Near* (Minneapolis: University of Minnesota Press, 2014), p. 214.
22. As cited in Abidin Kusno, "Power and Time Turning: The Capital, the State and

the *Kampung* in Jakarta", in *Cities and Power: Worldwide Perspectives*, edited by Göran Therborn (London: Routledge, 2016).
23. Donald J. Porter, "Citizen Participation Through Mobilization and the Rise of Political Islam in Indonesia", *Pacific Review* 15, no. 2 (2002): 201–24.
24. Abidin Kusno, "Whither Nationalist Urbanism? Public Life in Governor Sutiyoso's Jakarta", *Urban Studies* 41, no. 12 (2004): 2377–94.
25. Abidin Kusno, "Power and Time Turning: The Capital, the State and the *Kampung* in Jakarta", *International Journal of Urban Sciences* 19, no. 1 (2015): 53–63.
26. T. James Siegel, "Suharto, Witches", *Indonesia* 71 (April 2001): 27–78.
27. Simone, *Jakarta, Drawing the City Near*.
28. Paul A Barter, "An International Comparative Perspective on Urban Transport and Urban Form in Pacific Asia: The Challenge of Rapid Motorisation in Dense Cities", PhD thesis, Murdoch University, 1999.
29. Ian D. Wilson, "Urban Poor Activism and Political Agency in Post-New Order Jakarta", in *Activists in Transition: Progressive Politics in Democratic Indonesia*, edited by Thushara Dibley and Michelle Ford, pp. 99–116 (New York: Cornell University Press, 2019).
30. Kusno, "Whither Nationalist Urbanism?".
31. This pattern has been a recurring one, the city's middle classes perceiving the poor and their living spaces as a danger to both their own hopes, the development of the nation-state, and the realization of Jakarta as a modernist technocratic dreamland *à la* Singapore, albeit minus the public housing.
32. Kusno, "Whither Nationalist Urbanism?", p. 2377.
33. BPS (2021).
34. Wilson, "Urban Poor Activism and Political Agency in Post-New Order Jakarta".
35. Jane Hutchison and Ian D. Wilson, "Poor People's Politics in Urban Southeast Asia", in *The Political Economy of Southeast Asia: Politics and Uneven Development under Hyperglobalisation*, edited by Toby Carroll, Shahar Hameiri, and Lee Jones, pp. 271–91 (Springer International Publishing AG, 2020).
36. Sheri Lynn Gibbings, "Street Vending as Ethical Citizenship in Urban Indonesia", *Anthropologica* 58, no. 1 (2016): 77–94.
37. Borja and Castells (1997), p. 251. In the 2012 gubernatorial election, political contracts between a coalition of urban poor groups and Joko Widodo were pivotal to his electoral support among the city's poor. See Edward Aspinall and Amalinda Savirani, "Adversarial Linkages: The Urban Poor and Electoral Politics in Jakarta", *Journal of Current Southeast Asian Affairs* 36, no. 3 (2017): 3–34.
38. Padawangi, "The Cosmopolitan Grassroots City as Megaphone".
39. Max Lane, *Unfinished Nation: Indonesia before and after Suharto* (London: Verso, 2008).
40. Ian D. Wilson, *The Politics of Protection Rackets: Coercive Capital, Authority and Street Politics* (London: Routledge, 2015).
41. Warren Magnusson, *Politics of Urbanism: Seeing Like a City* (London: Routledge 2011), p. 60.

42. Prior to this, in 1996, thousands of poor *kampung* youth destroyed police stations, banks and government offices in a display of deep-seated animosity towards the regime provoked by its violent intervention in the leadership of the nominally oppositional Indonesian Democratic Party, which has been argued as a turning point in the momentum against the New Order (see Eklof 1999).
43. Kusno, "Whither Nationalist Urbanism?", p. 2378.
44. Padawangi, "The Cosmopolitan Grassroots City as Megaphone".
45. Marcus Mietzner, "Sources of Resistance to Democratic Decline: Indonesian Civil Society and Its Trials", *Democratization* 28, no. 1 (2021): 173.
46. Ian D. Wilson, "Making Enemies Out of Friends", *New Mandala*, 3 November 2016, https://www.newmandala.org/making-enemies-friends/ (accessed 25 September 2022).
47. The RUU KPK was ratified less than two weeks after its initiation in the DPR and involved a considerable weakening of the KPK in independently investigating and prosecuting corruption cases. The revised criminal code (RUHKP) contains several controversial provisions, such as the criminalization of premarital sex, and Article 273 which threatens to criminalize protests conducted without prior approval of the authorities.
48. Asef Bayat, *Life as Politics: How Ordinary People Change the Middle East* (Cairo: American University Cairo Press, 2009), p. 168.
49. Edward L. Glaeser and Bryce Millett Steinberg, "Transforming Cities: Does Urbanization Promote Democratic Change?", *Regional Studies* 51, no. 1 (2017): 58–68.
50. Wilson, "Urban Poor Activism and Political Agency in Post-New Order Jakarta".
51. Edward Aspinall, Diego Fossati, Burhanuddin Muhtadi, and Eve Warburton, "Elites, Masses, and Democratic Decline in Indonesia", *Democratization* 27, no. 4: 505–26; Marcus Mietzner, "Fighting Illiberalism with Illiberalism: Islamist Populism and Democratic Deconsolidation in Indonesia", *Pacific Affairs* 91, no. 2 (2018): 261–82; Eve Warburton, "A New Developmentalism in Indonesia?", *Journal of Southeast Asian Economies* 35, no. 3 (2018): 356–68.
52. Iqra Anugrah, 2019. "Out of Sight, Out of Mind? Political Accountability and Indonesia's New Capital Plan", *New Mandala*, 23 July 2019, https://www.newmandala.org/out-of-sight-out-of-mind-political-accountability-and-indonesias-new-capital-plan/ (accessed 3 September 2022). It is worth noting that under the Omnibus Law package, certain regional powers have been recentralized, such as control over spatial planning, the issuing of environmental impact assessments, and regulatory authority over the operations of mining companies.
53. Warburton, "A New Developmentalism in Indonesia?".
54. Ken M.P. Setiawan, "Vulnerable but Resilient: Indonesia in an Age of Democratic Decline", *Bulletin of Indonesian Economic Studies* 58, no. 3 (2022): 273–95.
55. Other examples include current defence minister and repeat presidential candidate Prabowo Subianto, who in 2014 led a parliamentary coalition which passed a law

that abolished direct elections for local government heads, only overturned by then President Bambang Yudhoyono after intense pushback from civil society (Mietzner 2021).
56. Karniavan rearticulates infantilizing notions of political order integral to the New Order, viz., that political engagement by the masses was undesirable due to their lack of intellectual maturity.
57. Rakhmad H. Permana, "Mendagri Tito Usul Lagi Pilkada Asimetris, Ini Alasannya", *Detik.com*, 20 June 2020, https://news.detik.com/berita/d-5061454/mendagri-tito-usul-lagi-pilkada-asimetris-ini-alasannya (accessed 25 September 2022).
58. Chandra Iswinarno and Ria Rizki Nirmala Sari, "Usung Konsep City Manager, Tidak Akan Ada DPRD di Ibu Kota Negara Nusantara", *Suara.com*, 21 February 2022, https://www.suara.com/news/2022/02/21/150214/usung-konsep-city-manager-tidak-akan-ada-dprd-di-ibu-kota-negara-nusantara (accessed 25 August 2022).
59. Firmansyah, "Kata Staf KSP soal Kepala Otorita IKN Dipilih Tanpa Pilkada", *Tempo.co*, 21 February 2022, https://nasional.tempo.co/read/1563058/kata-staf-ksp-soal-kepala-otorita-ikn-dipilih-tanpa-pilkada. (accessed 30 August 2022).
60. Vendy Yhulia Susanto, "Jumlah Penduduk IKN Nusantara Direncanakan Mencapai 1,9 Juta Jiwa", *Kontan.co.id*, 20 September 2022, https://nasional.kontan.co.id/news/jumlah-penduduk-ikn-nusantara-direncanakan-mencapai-19-juta-jiwa (accessed 25 September 2022).
61. It did, however, retain a system whereby mayors are appointed by the regional parliament and chosen from existing civil servants.
62. Ian D. Wilson, "Jakarta: Inequality and the Poverty of Elite Pluralism", *New Mandala*, 19 April 2017, https://www.newmandala.org/jakarta-inequality-poverty-elite-pluralism/ (accessed 20 September 2022).
63. See K. Fahmi, "Pemilu 2024 di IKN" [Election 2024 in the IKN], *Sindonews*, 5 July 2022.
64. A possibility that has unsettled some government ministers. See, for example, *Republika*, "Tito Harap Siapa Pun Presiden Terpilih pada 2024 Dukung IKN" [Tito Hopes Whomever Is Chosen President in 2024 Supports IKN], 16 February 2022.
65. Tim Detikcom, "Survei Litbang Kompas: Pemerintah Lebih Fokus IKN Dibanding Ekonomi Rakyat", *Detik.com*, 25 April 2022, https://news.detik.com/berita/d-6049820/survei-litbang-kompas-pemerintah-lebih-fokus-ikn-dibanding-ekonomi-rakyat
66. Pojani, *Trophy Cities*.
67. Glaeser and Steinberg, "Transforming Cities"; Tom Goodfellow and David Jackman, "Control the Capital: Cities and Political Dominance", ESID Working Paper No. 135 (2020).
68. Wasisto Raharjo Jati, "A New Capital City for Who? Central-Local Tensions in Indonesia", *New Mandala*, 23 August 2022, https://www.newmandala.org/a-new-capital-city-for-who-central-local-tensions-in-indonesia/ (accessed 30 August 2022).

69. Wilson, *The Politics of Protection Rackets*.
70. Alan Potter, "Locating the Government: Capital Cities and Civil Conflict", *Research & Politics* 4, no. 4 (2017): 1–7.
71. In the case of Canberra, for example, its position midway between Australia's two largest cities, Sydney and Melbourne, was chosen as a politically "neutral" space between centres of competing political and economic interest.
72. *Jakarta Post*, 2020. East Kalimantan, the chosen site for Nusantara, has a GRDP almost on par with that of Jakarta, contradicting arguments that relocating the capital to this region will serve to address underdevelopment. The most significant underdevelopment is in the east of the country.
73. Canberra, for example, was actively designed to prevent the existence of dynamic street life, described by its Chief Planner Peter Harrison as a "third world nation". See "Peter Harrison interviewed by James Weirick", (1990), at https://catalogue.nla.gov.au/Record/1984234
74. Campante, Do, and Guimares, "Capital Cities, Conflict, and Misgovernance".
75. Ibid.
76. *Beritakaltim.com*, "Menyusul NU, Pemuda Pancasila Ingin Bangun Kantor Pusat di IKN", 4 February 2022.
77. See, for example, the renderings of Nusantara provided on the official IKN website, https://ikn.go.id/en/about-ikn
78. Rossman, *Capital Cities*, p. 272.
79. The provision of significantly better services and living conditions for civil servants has been offered by the government as an incentive to move to Nusantara, with surveys showing up to 95 per cent of civil servants do not wish to relocate. See *BBC*, "PNS dan 'Kekhawatiran' Pindah ke Ibu Kota Baru di Kalimantan Timur: Menguatkan Diri Tinggal di Tempat Yang Tidak Selengkap Jakarta" [Civil Servants and 'Concerns' at Moving to New Capital in East Kalimantan: Preparing to Live in a Place Less Complete than Jakarta], 28 August 2019, https://www.bbc.com/indonesia/indonesia-49487400
80. Christopher Silver, *Planning the Megacity: Jakarta in the Twentieth Century* (Routledge: London, 2008).
81. Something perhaps intimated by the governor of Jakarta on his visit to IKN. See *Kompas*, "Bawa Tanah Kampung Akuarium ke IKN Baru, Pengamat Sebut Anies Ingin Sentil Jokowi" [Bringing Soil from Kampung Akuarium to the New Capital City, Commentators Suggest Anies Wishes to Provoke Jokowi], 15 March 2022, https://megapolitan.kompas.com/read/2022/03/15/13234201/bawa-tanah-kampung-akuarium-ke-ikn-baru-pengamat-sebut-anies-ingin-sentil

References

Anugrah, Iqra. 2019. "Out of Sight, Out of Mind? Political Accountability and Indonesia's New Capital Plan". *New Mandala*, 23 July 2019. https://www.newmandala.org/out-of-sight-out-of-mind-political-accountability-and-indonesias-new-capital-plan/ (accessed 3 September 2022).

Aspinall, Edward, and Amalinda Savirani. 2017. "Adversarial Linkages: The Urban Poor and Electoral Politics in Jakarta". *Journal of Current Southeast Asian Affairs* 36, no. 3: 3–34.

———, Diego Fossati, Burhanuddin Muhtadi, and Eve Warburton. 2020. "Elites, Masses, and Democratic Decline in Indonesia". *Democratization* 27, no. 4: 505–26.

Barter, Paul A. 1999. "An International Comparative Perspective on Urban Transport and Urban Form in Pacific Asia: The Challenge of Rapid Motorisation in Dense Cities". PhD thesis, Murdoch University.

Bayat, Asef. 2009. *Life as Politics: How Ordinary People Change the Middle East*. Cairo: American University Cairo Press.

BBC. 2019. "PNS dan 'Kekhawatiran' Pindah ke Ibu Kota Baru di Kalimantan Timur: 'Menguatkan Diri Tinggal di Tempat Yang Tidak Selengkap Jakarta" [Civil Servants and "Concerns" at Moving to New Capital in East Kalimantan: Preparing to Live in a Place Less Complete than Jakarta]. 28 August 2019. https://www.bbc.com/indonesia/indonesia-49487400

Beall, J., T. Goodfellow, and D. Rodgers. 2013. "Cities and Conflict in Fragile States in the Developing World". *Urban Studies* 50, no. 5: 3065–83.

Beritakaltim.com. 2022. "Menyusul NU, Pemuda Pancasila Ingin Bangun Kantor Pusat di IKN". 4 February 2022.

Borja, Jordi, and Manuel Castells. 1997. *Local and Global: The Management of Cities in the Information Age*. London: Routledge.

Badan Pusat Statistik. 2021. *Provinsi DKI Jakarta Dalam Angka 2021*. Jakarta: BPS.

Campante, Filipe R., Quoc-Anh Do, and Bernardo Guimares. 2019. "Capital Cities, Conflict, and Misgovernance". *American Economic Journal: Applied Economics* 11, no.3: 298–337.

Cheeseman, Nic. 2015. *Democracy in Africa: Successes, Failures, and the Struggle for Political Reform*. Cambridge: Cambridge University Press.

Dehaene, Michiel, and Lieven De Cauter. 2008. "Heterotopia in a Postcivil Society". In *Heterotopia and the City: Public Space in a Postcivil Society*, edited by Michiel Dehaene and Lieven De Cauter. London: Routledge.

Eklof, Stefan. 1999. *Indonesian Politics in Crisis: The Long Fall of Suharto 1996–98*. Copenhagen: NIAS Press.

Fahmi, K. 2022. "Pemilu 2024 di IKN" [Election 2024 in the IKN]. *Sindonews*, 5 July 2022.

Firmansyah. 2022. "Kata Staf KSP Soal Kepala Otorita IKN Dipilih Tanpa Pilkada". *Tempo.co*, 21 February 2022. https://nasional.tempo.co/read/1563058/kata-staf-ksp-soal-kepala-otorita-ikn-dipilih-tanpa-pilkada (accessed 30 August 2022).

Gibbings, Sheri Lynn. 2016. "Street Vending as Ethical Citizenship in Urban Indonesia". *Anthropologica* 58, no. 1: 77–94.

Glaeser, Edward L., and Bryce Millett Steinberg. 2017. "Transforming Cities: Does Urbanization Promote Democratic Change?". *Regional Studies* 51, no. 1: 58–68.

Goodfellow, Tom, and David Jackman. 2020. "Control the Capital: Cities and Political Dominance". ESID Working Paper No. 135.

Gunning, Jeroen, and Ilan Z. Baron. 2014. *Why Occupy a Square? People, Protests and Movements in the Egyptian Revolution*. Oxford University Press.

Harvey, David. 1997. "Contested Cities: Social Process and Spatial Form". In *Transforming Cities New Spatial Divisions and Social Transformation*, edited by Nick Jewson and Susanne MacGregor. London: Routledge.

Hutchison, Jane, and Ian D. Wilson. 2020. "Poor People's Politics in Urban Southeast Asia". In *The Political Economy of Southeast Asia: Politics and Uneven Development under Hyperglobalisation*, edited by Toby Carroll, Shahar Hameiri, and Lee Jones, pp. 271–91. Springer International Publishing AG.

Iswinarno, Chandra, and Ria Rizki Nirmala Sari. 2022. "Usung Konsep City Manager, Tidak Akan Ada DPRD di Ibu Kota Negara Nusantara". *Suara.com*, 21 February 2021. https://www.suara.com/news/2022/02/21/150214/usung-konsep-city-manager-tidak-akan-ada-dprd-di-ibu-kota-negara-nusantara (accessed 25 August 2022).

Jakarta Post. 2020. "New Capital City to Contribute Little to Indonesia's Economic Growth: Indef". 22 January 2020.

———. 2022. "Theater State". 18 March 2022. https://www.thejakartapost.com/opinion/2022/03/17/theater-state.html (accessed 20 August 2022).

Jati, Wasisto Raharjo. 2022. "A New Capital City for Who? Central-Local Tensions in Indonesia". *New Mandala*, 23 August 2022. https://www.newmandala.org/a-new-capital-city-for-who-central-local-tensions-in-indonesia/ (accessed 30 August 2022).

King, Ross. 2007. "Re-writing the City: Putrajaya as Representation". *Journal of Urban Design* 12, no.1: 117–38.

Kompas. 2022. "Bawa Tanah Kampung Akuarium ke IKN Baru, Pengamat Sebut Anies Ingin Sentil Jokowi" [Bringing Soil from Kampung Akuarium to the New Capital City, Commentators Suggest Anies Wishes to Provoke Jokowi], 15 March 2022. https://megapolitan.kompas.com/read/2022/03/15/13234201/bawa-tanah-kampung-akuarium-ke-ikn-baru-pengamat-sebut-anies-ingin-sentil

Kusno, Abidin. 2003. "Remembering/Forgetting the May Riots: Architecture, Violence, and the Making of 'Chinese Cultures' in Post-1998 Jakarta". *Public Culture* 14, no.1: 149–77.

———. 2004. "Whither Nationalist Urbanism? Public Life in Governor Sutiyoso's Jakarta". *Urban Studies* 41, no.12: 2377–94.

———. 2015. "Power and Time Turning: The Capital, the State and the *Kampung* in Jakarta". *International Journal of Urban Sciences* 19, no. 1: 53–63.

———. 2016. "Power and Time Turning: The Capital, the State and the *Kampung* in Jakarta". In *Cities and Power: Worldwide Perspectives*, edited by Göran Therborn. London: Routledge.

Lane, Max. 2008. *Unfinished Nation: Indonesia before and after Suharto*. London: Verso.

Lefebvre, Henri. 1991. *The Production of Space*. New Jersey: Wiley-Blackwell.

Madaleno, Isabel Maria. 1996. "Brasilia: The Frontier Capital". *Cities* 13, no.4: 273–80.

Magnusson, Warren. 2011. *Politics of Urbanism: Seeing Like a City*. London: Routledge.

Martin, Deborah, and Byron Miller. 2003. "Space and Contentious Politics". *Mobilization: An International Quarterly* 8, no.2: 143–56.
Mietzner, Marcus. 2018. "Fighting Illiberalism with Illiberalism: Islamist Populism and Democratic Deconsolidation in Indonesia". *Pacific Affairs* 91, no. 2: 261–82.
———. 2021. "Sources of Resistance to Democratic Decline: Indonesian Civil Society and Its Trials". *Democratization* 28, no. 1: 161–78.
Minkenberg, Michael. 2014. *Power and Architecture: The Construction of Capitals and the Politics of Space*. Oxford: Berghahn Books.
Permana, Rakhmad H. 2020. "Mendagri Tito Usul Lagi Pilkada Asimetris, Ini Alasannya". *Detik.com*, 20 June 2020. https://news.detik.com/berita/d-5061454/mendagri-tito-usul-lagi-pilkada-asimetris-ini-alasannya (accessed 25 September 2022).
Padawangi, Rita. 2013. "The Cosmopolitan Grassroots City as Megaphone: Reconstructing Public Spaces through Urban Activism in Jakarta". *International Journal of Urban and Regional Research* 73: 849–63.
Pojani, Dorina. 2021. *Trophy Cities: A Feminist Perspective on New Capitals*. Cheltenham: Edward Elgar Publishing.
Porter, Donald J. 2002. "Citizen Participation Through Mobilization and the Rise of Political Islam in Indonesia". *Pacific Review* 15, no. 2: 201–24.
Potter, Alan. 2017. "Locating the Government: Capital Cities and Civil Conflict". *Research & Politics* 4, no. 4: 1–7.
Republika. 2022. "Tito Harap Siapa Pun Presiden Terpilih pada 2024 Dukung IKN" [Tito Hopes Whomever Is Chosen President in 2024 Supports IKN]. 16 February 2022.
Resnick, Danielle. 2014. *Urban Poverty and Party Populism in African Democracies*. Cambridge: Cambridge University Press.
Rossman, Vadim. 2016. *Capital Cities: Varieties and Patterns of Development and Relocation*. London: Routledge.
Setiawan, Ken M.P. 2022. "Vulnerable but Resilient: Indonesia in an Age of Democratic Decline". *Bulletin of Indonesian Economic Studies* 58, no.3: 273–95.
Siegel, James T. 2001. "Suharto, Witches". *Indonesia* 71 (April): 27–78.
Silver, C. 2008. *Planning the Megacity: Jakarta in the Twentieth Century*. Routledge: London.
Simanjuntak, Joanthan. 2022. "Survei: Mayoritas Publik Tak Percaya Ibu Kota Nusantara Akan Berhasil". *SindoNews*, 4 June 2022. https://nasional.sindonews.com/read/788269/15/survei-mayoritas-publik-tak-percaya-ibu-kota-nusantara-akan-berhasil-1654315607 (accessed 25 August 2022).
Simone, AbdouMaliq. 2014. *Jakarta, Drawing the City Near*. Minneapolis: University of Minnesota Press.
Susanto, Vendy Yhulia. 2022. "Jumlah Penduduk IKN Nusantara Direncanakan Mencapai 1,9 Juta Jiwa". *Kontan.co.id*, 20 September 2022. https://nasional.kontan.co.id/news/jumlah-penduduk-ikn-nusantara-direncanakan-mencapai-19-juta-jiwa (accessed 25 September 2022).
Tim Detikcom. 2022. "Survei Litbang Kompas: Pemerintah Lebih Fokus IKN Dibanding Ekonomi Rakyat". *Detik.com*, 25 April 2022. https://news.detik.com/

berita/d-6049820/survei-litbang-kompas-pemerintah-lebih-fokus-ikn-dibanding-ekonomi-rakyat

Uitermark, J., W. Nicholls, and M. Loopmans. 2012. "Cities and Social Movements: Theorizing Beyond the Right to the City." *Environment and Planning* 44, no. 11: 2546–54.

Warburton, Eve. 2018. "A New Developmentalism in Indonesia?". *Journal of Southeast Asian Economies* 35, no. 3: 356–68.

Wilson, Ian. D. 2015. *The Politics of Protection Rackets: Coercive Capital, Authority and Street Politics*. London: Routledge.

———. 2016. "Making Enemies Out of Friends". *New Mandala*, 3 November 2016. https://www.newmandala.org/making-enemies-friends/ (accessed 25 September 2022).

———. 2017. "Jakarta: Inequality and the Poverty of Elite Pluralism". *New Mandala*, 19 April 2017. https://www.newmandala.org/jakarta-inequality-poverty-elite-pluralism/ (accessed 20 September 2022).

———. 2019. "Urban Poor Activism and Political Agency in Post-New Order Jakarta". In *Activists in Transition: Progressive Politics in Democratic Indonesia*, edited by Thushara Dibley and Michelle Ford, pp. 99–116. New York: Cornell University Press.

4

CROWDFUNDING FOR IKN
Potential, Risk and the People's Perception

Riri Kusumarani and Anne Parlina

Introduction

"Citizen participation" can be defined as the active involvement of the general public in the government's decision-making process to influence and address issues of public concern.[1] It covers a range of practices, from volunteering to political participation. Civic participation is similar, although it includes involvement in non-political activities. The advancement in digital technologies has enabled collective participation and civil actions, encouraging greater participation, better decision-making and more trust.[2]

Among different forms of civic participation, crowdfunding has emerged as one type of public participation in a democratic environment. The ability to accept small amounts of money from a larger number of people positions crowdfunding as a platform for citizens to express their views on services that they require and their civic rights. It allows citizens to participate in society and the government by donating their resources as an act of support for particular programmes or projects.[3] It also allows social movements to pool financial resources from the public relatively quickly.[4] This potential should be emphasized because a system that handles and provides civic services would result in increased citizen participation.[5] Crowdfunding also allows citizens residing outside the country, or diaspora, to participate in the projects. The diaspora community is said to be more willing to participate in smaller-scale but beneficial initiatives that many larger project backers would not pursue.[6] With an expected number of 8 million Indonesians in the diaspora with an average monthly income of US$1,999,[7] this potential should not be overlooked.

In August 2019, the Indonesian government announced its plan to move the capital from Jakarta to a new city in East Kalimantan province. The new capital is named Nusantara (also called IKN) and its construction is targeted to be completed by 2045.[8] Government officials are set to move to the new capital in stages. The development is divided into three main stages: developing the urban infrastructure, developing the city along with the economic sector and moving government officials to the new capital, then finally increasing connectivity with other cities near the IKN.

For financing, there are at least six funding schemes: direct government budget (*Anggaran Pendapatan dan Belanja Negara*, APBN), public-private partnership (PPP), investment from private companies, cooperation with business entities (KPBU), international/foreign investment, and creative financing. In 2020, Luhut Binsar Pandjaitan, the Coordinating Minister for Maritime Affairs and Investment, reported that Japan's SoftBank Corporation would contribute US$100 billion (Rp1,400 trillion) to IKN.[9] However, in 2022, Softbank decided to cancel its participation.[10] This decision changed the course of the IKN's funding journey. Bambang Susantono, chief for IKN development, initiated the idea that the public could gather funds as a form of contribution to build the new capital.[11] His statement triggered public debate on the pros and cons of civic crowdfunding in IKN development.

As an example, the Mayor of London has used crowdfunding to fund the city's development programme.[12] The programme is considered an innovation in gathering public funding for civic projects. The Mayor of London acted as the project backer and pledged up to £20,000 in funds for projects designed and uploaded by local community groups (the initiator). Projects that were funded through the Mayor's programmes are said to have positive impacts on the community, such as promoting grassroots innovations, strengthening local capacity and supporting resilience.[13] The maximum number of project backers on one of the projects was 928 (Peckham Coal Line, a 900-m long park linking two parts of the city[14]), while public facilities dominated the project types.

There are some examples of crowdfunding projects related to city development programmes. Yet, not much is known regarding the use of crowdfunding to fund a new city's development, especially for a nation's capital. This chapter aims to explore crowdfunding as an alternate funding resource for the IKN. It discusses the basis of the IKN financing scheme and expected problems. Next, the literature review discusses several examples of crowdfunding projects. An online survey was done to understand people's perceptions of the idea of crowdfunding the IKN. From this, the authors asked for experts' opinions regarding crowdfunding as a potential alternative funding resource for the IKN and the potential risks. This chapter shows the experts' and public respondents' perspectives on what types of projects on the IKN are appropriate for crowdfunding.

LITERATURE REVIEW

Funding Schemes

Presidential Regulation (PP) No. 17 of 2022 provides a legal basis for the IKN financing scheme. This PP covers issues related to IKN financing, and in Chapter II Article 3, it states that IKN funding comes from the State Budget (APBN) and other sources. The APBN does not bear the entire burden of the IKN project costs. In general, financing from the APBN can be sourced from non-tax state revenues and state securities such as state sharia securities (*Surat Berharga Syariah Negara*, SBSN) and state debt securities (*Surat Utang Negara*, SUN).

President Joko Widodo has said that what will be built first in the IKN is a core zone consisting of the presidential palace, the state secretariat, and the ministries of home affairs, foreign affairs, and defence.[15] The entire budget for developing this core area will be sourced from the APBN.

Another financing source for IKN development is expected to be private investment. Widodo has stated that 20 per cent of the total funds needed to develop the new capital city would come from the APBN, while the estimated budget (for the IKN's completion) might reach as much as Rp486 trillion (approximately US$31.45 billion). Of this, the state budget will contribute around Rp97 trillion (approximately US$6.27 billion).[16]

An alternative funding source is the Government and Business Entity Cooperation, or the PPP scheme, where the government invites the participation of entrepreneurs. The PPP can fund the construction and running of projects like parks, convention centres, and public transit systems. PPP may include giving up tax or other operating funds, liability protection, or a portion of ownership rights over public items or entities.[17]

Besides the above, the participation of other parties, either private funding or international funding support, can be tapped. A private funding model is a pure investment from the private sector which can be given incentives. In this case, the government invites the private sector to jointly build the IKN. Meanwhile, international funding draws from multilateral institutions wishing to participate in developing the IKN as a "green capital city" through grants or grant bailouts. In addition, IKN funding can also be sourced from taxes or special IKN levies, which may be applied after the transfer of the position, function, and role of the capital from Jakarta to Nusantara, as well as through "creative financing". However, PP17/2022 does not specifically mention crowdfunding as a financing option.

The Limitations of APBN

The initial utilization of APBN for infrastructure development in Nusantara is critical to send positive signals to private investors. Nevertheless, the government has limited state spending on the IKN's development to just 20 per cent of the total cost.[18] Even so, some parties have criticized the use of the APBN for the construction of the IKN. Bhima Yudhistira, director of the Center for Economic and Legal Studies (CELIOS), asserts that because of limited government funds, using the state budget to build the IKN would be challenging, especially when the country is still trying to recover from the COVID-19 pandemic.[19]

In the authors' view, the first risk of allocating the state budget to the IKN's development is that the budget for social assistance, particularly for micro, small and medium enterprises (MSMEs), may be impacted. An increase in national debt is the second risk. Unproductive debt loads can force Indonesia into a debt trap or indirectly increase taxes for Indonesians.

The Reasoning for Crowdfunding for the IKN

Given the limitations of the APBN, the government has introduced the idea of crowdfunding for the IKN to the general public. Several reasons why the government is considering this option are discussed below.[20]

According to an excerpt of an interview with Sidik Pramono, a spokesperson of Bappenas and the Head of Communications for IKN, published on Bisnis.com, "Crowdfunding creates an opportunity for the community to participate in the IKN development process actively." He added, "Crowdfunding, in its purest form, can be understood as from, by, and for the community." In his view, crowdfunding is a valid funding strategy for the development of the IKN and falls under the category of creative financing. If designed properly, it can complement state budget financing.

Crowdfunding is similar to crowdsourcing, which emphasizes public participation to source common knowledge. However, crowdfunding is more specific in its usage for fundraising.[21] Therefore, it depends more on the size of public funding.[22] Crowdfunding is classified into several categories based on how the money is donated: it can be based on rewards, donations, equity or lending (see Figure 4.1). Reward-based crowdfunding allows project backers to receive a reward in exchange for their contribution. In contrast, project backers receive nothing in exchange for their donation in donation-based crowdfunding. Those who participate in equity crowdfunding receive

FIGURE 4.1
Simplified Crowdfunding Categories

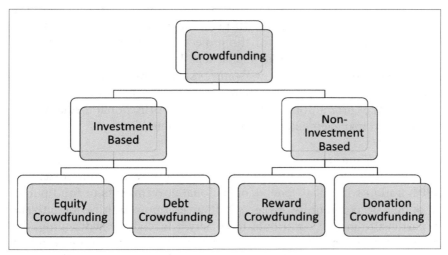

Source: Reproduced and simplified from Raphael Sedlitzky and Yvonne Franz, "'What If We All Chip In?' Civic Crowdfunding as Alternative Financing for Urban Development Projects", *Built Environment* 45, no. 1 (2019): 26–44.

a portion of the project's equity, while debt crowdfunding allows project initiators to use funds as a form of investment, with the obligation to return the funds to the project backers after a specified time and in accordance with regulations.

The foundation of crowdfunding is that the action is entirely voluntary. The possibility of raising funds from the public inspires a plethora of crowdfunding applications. It can be as simple as a donation or as complex as supporting a presidential campaign. However, the entrepreneurial sector is often the most active. This chapter focuses on civic crowdfunding for the IKN, which is gaining attention not only from entrepreneurs but also from governments due to the prospect of gathering funds to realize projects.[23] Governments have started to look into crowdfunding as a potential source to fund public projects.[24]

Risk in Crowdfunding

Like other financial activities, crowdfunding has risks and challenges. Despite the typically limited amount of money that project backers put into a single project, projects can pose risks that must be understood before anyone commits to a project. In general, crowdfunding investments are frequently influenced by various decision biases and a high level of emotion, which can pose risks. Furthermore, crowdfunding risk affects not only the project backers but also the project initiators. Crowdfunding platforms typically charge platform fees of around 10 per cent of capital raised. They also frequently charge extra fees for the project's due diligence or insurance requirements, to mitigate risks for backers. In addition, project initiators must consider the costs of potential returns such as interest, mutual benefits, discounts, or other forms of compensation. Other costs associated, such as the creation of promotional videos and other informational media, as well as campaign management, must also be considered.[25]

Civic Crowdfunding

Civic crowdfunding can be defined as funding directly from citizens in collaboration with local, federal, or national governments to fund public or public or community projects.[26] It gives opportunities for citizens to participate in and contribute to society.[27] In civic crowdfunding, the government acts as the co-founder of the project. Civic crowdfunding platforms gained attention as an alternate funding source from the public when there is a limited budget for development while allowing collaboration to shape future cities.[28] Civic crowdfunding can also provide or initiate new services that did not previously exist or were beyond the capabilities of the government.[29] Project backers can be individuals or businesses.[30]

Some examples of civic projects launched on crowdfunding platforms provide diverse opportunities for the government and the public to collaborate. Spacehive.com is one of many platforms that allow citizens to fund projects such as upgrading toilet facilities at a community centre or transforming an abandoned park into a new learning space.

This is not to say that crowdfunding projects can only be carried out on civic crowdfunding platforms. Kickstarter.com, a popular crowdfunding platform for entrepreneurship projects, recently completed a successful civic crowdfunding project in Detroit, USA. The project, which aimed to build a Robocop statue as a city landmark, received over US$67,000 in funding from over 2,700 project backers.[31] A similar model was seen in Brighton, UK, which aimed to restore the city's iconic historical arches. "Save Madeira Terrace" successfully raised £463,007 from 2,095 project backers.[32] (Table 4.1 shows some examples of civic crowdfunding projects across platforms.)

The trend of crowdfunding as a funding scheme for public projects is not common only in developed countries. Indonesia's crowdfunding platform Kitabisa (kitabisa.com) offers project backers chances to donate

TABLE 4.1
Examples of Civic Crowdfunding Projects Globally

Project	Platform	Amount Funded	Backers	Country
Wooden Luchtsingel Footbridge	N.A.	N.A.	N.A.	Netherlands
Community Center	Spacehive	£792,021	107	England
Medellin Metrocable	N.A.	N.A.	N.A.	Colombia
Madeira Terrace	Spacehive	£463,007	2095	England
Wind Turbines	Crowdfunder	£881,705	298	England
Dartmoor Zoo	Crowdfunder	£339,930	740	England
Garden	ioby.org	US$3,681	N.A.	US

Sources: Authors' compilation from Spacehive, "Crowdfunding For Local Projects", 2022, https://www.spacehive.com/; Ioby.org, "Ioby Brings Neighborhood Projects to Life, Block by Block", 2022, https://www.ioby.org/; Crowdfunder UK, "Crowdfunder UK - Where Ideas Happen", 2022, at https://www.crowdfunder.co.uk/

to infrastructure projects such as bridges, water wells, water pumps, or school buildings. A project for clean water wells in Papua, for example, secured a fund of approximately Rp2.86 billion from more than 74,000 project backers, with donations ranging from Rp1,000 to Rp25 million.[33]

Some key characteristics of civic crowdfunding projects are summarized below. First, civic crowdfunding is known to have higher success rates compared to conventional crowdfunding and a project size of less than US$10,000.[34] Davies in 2014 compared crowdfunding project types on the Kickstarter platform[35] and found that more than 80 per cent of civic crowdfunding projects on it were distributed below US$10,000. Even though the data is outdated, the authors have compared it with recent civic crowdfunding projects on Kitabisa.com and found that most projects also fall below the US$10,000 threshold.

The second characteristic of civic crowdfunding according to Werbner is related to project backers who tend to be locally distant but have a sense of relation to the project and a community to support it.[36] Related to this, Stiver et al. showed that civic crowdfunding is more suitable for geographically proximate communities.[37] Contradicting Stiver et al., however, other studies show that civic crowdfunding has the ability to attract project backers from distant locations.[38] Crowdfunding the IKN's development can fall into the category of civic crowdfunding, as it involves the development of public places.

Legal Aspects

Governments react differently to legal aspects of crowdfunding. Juredieu and Mayoux have elaborated on crowdfunding laws across countries,[39] emphasizing the diversity of approaches that each country has taken. Indonesia has a significant amount of catching up to do in terms of crowdfunding regulations compared to countries that are already mature. The Indonesian Financial Service Authority (OJK) tries to regulate equity crowdfunding initiatives, including capping the maximum amount of funds that could be raised through any initiative (approximately Rp10 billion per project). It also limits the maximum amount that citizens can invest in equity crowdfunding projects and penalizes rule-breakers with administrative sanctions.

In Indonesia, however, there is currently no regulation governing civic crowdfunding. One of the reasons for this is a lack of projects deemed suitable for such schemes. Separately, Alhammad, Al Othman and Tan have reviewed crowdfunding regulations across twenty-six countries.[40] Table 4.2 summarizes their findings and links them with Indonesia's current regulations (POJK No. 16 and POJK.04/2021).

Project Scale

Despite the potential of crowdfunding as an alternative funding scheme for the IKN's development, it should not be considered a substitute for traditional government spending.[41] One of the main reasons that its limited ability to gather funds.[42] However, when combined with suitable crowdfunding projects, the IKN's development can be divided into smaller-scale projects. For instance, allowing donation-based crowdfunding for projects such as religious sites, parks, and sports facilities could reduce the burden on APBN while allowing more individuals to participate in fundraising.

Conceptual Framework and Methodology

Figure 4.2 shows the authors' conceptual framework. It captures people's perceptions of the concept of crowdfunding to detect current public opinion in Indonesia on crowdfunding for the IKN's development. The literature review on the potential and risk of civic crowdfunding for city development foreshadows the gathering of experts' opinions on crowdfunding the IKN's development and the survey findings by the authors.

TABLE 4.2
Aspects of Crowdfunding Regulation in Comparison with POJK No. 16 and POJK.04/2021

Aspects	Definition	POJK #
Authorization	Operators of crowdfunding platforms must be licensed in order to act as an intermediary in securities investments.	Chapter 2, A.7, 8
Fund seekers limit	Additional fundraising or offering limits on the amount of money that businesses can raise through crowdfunding platforms.	Chapter 1, A.12
Project backer limits	Limitation for project backers to crowdfund projects	None
Disclosure obligations	Documents that are required to be submitted by parties who are acting as crowdfunding project owner	Required
Crowdfunding advertising law	Obligations related to advertising crowdfunding offers	None
Capital requirements policies	Minimum capital requirement for crowdfunding platforms and project owners	Chapter 2, A.12
Protection of client funds	In terms of the management of project backers' funds, regulatory authorities have established guidelines for how project backers' funds should be handled.	Not available
Platform-specific regulation	Specific regulation that is not covered by other aspects	Not available

Source: Adapted from M.M. Alhammad, R. Al Othman, and C. Tan, "Review of Crowdfunding Regulations across Countries: A Systematic Review Study", *Journal of Information Systems Engineering and Management* 6, no. 4 (2021).

Methodology, Results and Discussion

Public Opinion on Crowdfunding for IKN

The authors administered an online survey with twenty-five questions to collect public opinion on crowdfunding for IKN, between June 2022 and early September 2022. Two hundred eighty-five respondents took the survey

FIGURE 4.2
Conceptual Framework: Understanding Crowdfunding for the IKN

Understanding Crowdfunding
the IKN

but compared to Indonesia's population, this is a tiny sample with limited scope. Future research must be done to increase the accuracy of the findings.

The questionnaire is divided into four sections. After gathering demographic data, the survey captures general knowledge of the crowdfunding concept and ascertains people's perception of crowdfunding for the IKN's development. The survey then asks respondents' opinions of crowdfunding projects and what they believe to be the right percentage of IKN funding that would be appropriate for crowdfunding. Respondents were allowed to freely respond to the survey and crowdfunding for IKN in the last section. (Table 4.3 shows the demographic information of the respondents.)

Over 60 per cent of respondents were men between 35 and 44 (those aged 25–34 were the second-largest group). Over 47 per cent are civil servants. Surprisingly, less than 30 per cent of respondents claimed they were familiar with crowdfunding. However, when asked to choose at least one among six options which they thought was a crowdfunding platform, only 8 per cent of respondents chose incorrectly.

When asked what they thought could be a minimum contribution for crowdfunding, more than 40 per cent said "No Idea". Roughly 60 per cent

TABLE 4.3
Respondents' Demographic Information, N=285

Gender, % (n)		Occupation, % (n)		Education Level, % (n)	
Female	42.1 (120)	Public sector employee	47.3 (133)	Doctoral	8.1 (23)
Male	57.9 (165)	Private sector employee	24.6 (69)	Master's degree	32.6 (93)
Age Range in Years % (n)		Entrepreneur	12.5 (35)	Bachelor's degree or equivalent	46 (131)
18–24	8.1 (23)	Housewife	11.4 (32)	High school or equivalent	12.3 (35)
25–34	43.3 (123)	Other	4.3 (12)	Below high school	1.1 (3)
34–45	31.7 (90)				
> 45	16.9 (48)				
Total	X (100)				

were unaware that crowdfunding has been used for civic development in other countries. Concerning people's perceptions of crowdfunding for IKN, more respondents had a negative view.

More than half of the respondents felt that crowdfunding was inappropriate for financing the IKN project. A similar proportion claimed they would not support the IKN through crowdfunding or encourage others to do the same. About 50 per cent believed that the public would not participate in the IKN crowdfunding with enthusiasm or respond favourably. Meanwhile, more than 40 per cent disagreed that crowdfunding (for the IKN) would improve foreign impressions of Indonesia, while up to 41 per cent disagreed that such crowdfunding will be handled effectively. 47 per cent of respondents believed that their participation in crowdfunding (generally) will be risky, while 64 per cent believed that crowdfunding (for the IKN specifically) will have risks.

According to the respondents, educational facilities, community places (e.g., religious facilities), and parks or sports facilities were the top three crowdfunding-friendly projects (see Figure 4.3). These findings were perhaps foreshadowed by the fact that #orasudisumbangikn (a hashtag roughly translated as "I do not want to donate for IKN") trended in Twitter

FIGURE 4.3
Projects That Are Appropriate for Crowdfunding

discussions right after the government mentioned crowdfunding for the IKN. Eleven thousand Twitter discussions using the hashtag were observed on 24 March 2022, the same day the term was first introduced to the public. It can be seen that there is still much residual discomfort or even distrust when the Indonesian public considers crowdfunding for public purposes. The authors see that public trust in the government and their sentiments towards the IKN project are reflected in how they negatively see crowdfunding. As public trust in government capacity is low, when combined with the people's sentiment toward IKN development, their opinion towards crowdfunding tends to be negative.

Expert Opinion on Crowdfunding for the New Capital

Several experts on crowdfunding were contacted for face-to-face interviews between July 2022 and September 2022. Five experts agreed to participate and signed interview consent forms. Two experts are from private institutions related to crowdfunding while the other three are academics, with one being a non-Indonesian and working as a professor. All the experts were briefed about crowdfunding for the IKN topic.

The main method was content analysis for the transcribed responses of the interviewees:[43] a coding scheme was developed to categorize words and sentences using four main criteria. These are (1) potential, (2) risk, (3) strategy, and (4) sectors. The experts' words and sentences were coded for analysis. (Table 4.4 shows the coded examples.)

TABLE 4.4
Coded Examples

Criterion	Details	Coded Example (Author's Translation)
Potential	This refers to the potential of crowdfunding that experts perceive. Instances of this category are coded verbatim from the transcripts.	"I feel like they're really kind and they're very generous too. ... So they will be generous in contributing the money." "Sebetulnya juga ide kreatif untuk crowdfunding itu juga." ("As a matter of fact, crowdfunding is a creative idea.")
Risk	This refers to the risk of crowdfunding that experts perceived. Instances of this category are coded verbatim from the transcripts.	"Political crowdfunding on this scale may bring a huge risk to national security." "Resikonya mungkin barangkali tidak memenuhi target pendanaan saja." (The failure to reach the funding goal is probably one of the risks.")
Strategy	This criterion is strategies the experts cited that may make a successful crowdfunding campaign for the IKN. Instances of this category are coded verbatim from the transcripts.	"... perlu ada ketegasan juga dari pemerintah formatnya ... dan SOPnya .... Pembagiannya peran pemerintah dimana, platform dimana, pengusaha dimana ... diperjelas dahulu ...." ("The government has to decide the crowdfunding format starting from the SOP (standard operating procedure), the division of roles between government, the crowdfunding platform, and private entities. Otherwise, it will be difficult for the project to succeed.")
Sectors	This refers to sectors that experts suggested as appropriate for crowdfunding schemes. Instances from this category are further classified into designated sectors.	"They should allocate this fund for public parks, roads, community centres, public schools, religious sites, and other programs or infrastructure that people will get the benefit the most."

Experts' General Opinion
All of our experts stated their enthusiasm toward the idea of crowdfunding. Expert C said, "Crowdfunding is a creative idea". Further, he said that the idea (of IKN crowdfunding) should be supported since the other funding schemes were dependent on other parties: "The idea to support infrastructure development with alternative funding should be cultivated, which so far have only been APBN, foreign loans or G2G (government to government), B2B (business to business), and so on, which may be considered by the public to be burdensome because it burdens the State Budget."

Expert A, the foreigner, perceived that Indonesians are known to be generous and hoped that Indonesians would behave similarly in terms of monetary contribution. "I have been to Indonesia once and I have met Indonesian people; I feel like they are kind and very generous too.... So they will be generous in contributing the money. I understand that the income level is not so high, but still, crowdfunding does not ask for much money."

Likewise, expert B said that the idea of crowdfunding the IKN was interesting as it can benefit the project backers (read: the public). Expert C further commented that the idea needed to be accompanied by legal and other assurance from the government, while the government needs to decide which crowdfunding mechanism is appropriate for the IKN. Said expert C, "The idea of crowdfunding to build IKN is an interesting idea ... if the government can clarify the certainty of the legality and what kind of crowdfunding mechanism will be used in building IKN. It should not rule out the possibility of entrepreneurs and people who are keen to contribute to IKN projects." (Authors' translation of C's comments.)

A Successful Crowdfunded IKN Project
The discussion on what makes a successful crowdfunded IKN project is interesting, as each expert had a different focus on which aspect was important. The key themes or keywords that each expert used throughout their interview include: legal foundation, political sentiment, nationalism, literacy, citizens' participation, and pitching strategy.

Legal Aspect
All experts stated that the legal aspect was a necessary first step for a successful civic crowdfunding project for the new IKN. All believe that for a successful crowdfunding scheme, the government needs to set up regulations on civic crowdfunding schemes before executing the projects.

Expert C said, "There is a need to be assertive by the government as to what format and SOPs (standard operating procedures) should be used for civic crowdfunding. The division of the role of the government, which platform, which entrepreneurs, must be clarified first, otherwise it will be difficult to (make) progress." (Authors' translation.) Expert B, who believed that backers would only have a sense of security in investing money only when there is a legal basis, highlighted its importance: "There is a need to give assurance or security to investors (project backers) as well as in the form of a written agreement in case there is a policy change"; "... There will be guarantees that the state can give (assurance) that it will still be able to return the capital to the crowdfunders. So when the political situation changes, there is still a valid agreement that protects the people who crowdfund their money." (Authors' translation and insertions.)

Political Sentiment
Only one expert, C, mentioned the political environment: "I think political situations influence the success of crowdfunding to fund activities such as infrastructure. If the political situation is positive, then people will support it." The authors argue that political sentiments need special attention due to the negative sentiment revealed in the online survey of the public. Previous research shows that people who are disappointed, for example, in the government or a president's performance, have a higher level of citizen participation such as participating in voting or attending political campaigns.[44] For political crowdfunding, a study by Kusumarani and Zo showed that people with negative perceptions toward politics would tend to participate in political crowdfunding only if they saw themselves as similar to the candidate.[45]

A similar situation arguably happens in the case of the IKN. Citizens with negative perceptions of the existing political situation are reluctant to support crowdfunding for the IKN because they do not see a connection between themselves and the proposed IKN. This topic is related closely to the subsequent discussion on literacy on crowdfunding, citizen participation, and pitching strategy.

Citizens' Crowdfunding Literacy
Expert C mentioned that it was necessary to ensure that the public understands crowdfunding before continuing with the idea of crowdfunding the IKN. "The public must understand the four existing schemes of crowdfunding (reward, donation, equity and lending-based) if the government wants to collect funds from the public." Expert B highlighted

the need to increase the public's literacy on crowdfunding: "First, there is a need for socialization to the public to increase knowledge and literacy regarding how crowdfunding works."

It is not known how well Indonesians understand crowdfunding. Notably, as mentioned above, the authors' survey revealed that only 30 per cent of the respondents understand the concept. (The real figure is likely to be smaller due to the limited sample size.) Research on crowdfunding projects' success factors generally focuses on the founder and project characteristics; not much research has been done on the importance of the level of crowdfunding literacy to a project's eventual success.

Citizens' Participation
Expert A sees crowdfunding the new capital as an opportunity for letting citizens express their contribution, making people feel connected to the project: "You must let people decide the design, for example, the parks. Show them the designs and ask them to vote for which they like or do not like. Once they have done it, they will think they have a right to monitor the progress. So they will take pride that they are part of the process of making this new city." Most of the experts believe that crowdfunding is a tool for citizen participation that allows them to participate in society and government projects.

Pitching Strategy—Public Communication—Information Asymmetry
Project narration is a significant factor affecting a crowdfunding project's success rate.[46] For instance, Zhou et al. analysed Kickstarter's over 140,000 projects from 2009 to 2014 and found that project descriptions had a significant impact on the funding success of a project.[47] Crowdfunding for the IKN is more than a typical crowdfunding project—it is a national-level crowdfunding project run by the government. Therefore, it needs to be supported by an effective public communications strategy.

There are different findings on the likelihood of success of language narratives in crowdfunding projects. Parhankangas and Renko found conflicting results on social crowdfunding and commercial crowdfunding in which linguistic style affects the success of social crowdfunding campaigns but not commercial ones.[48] Aligned with the above finding, expert E highlighted the importance of project pitching. If the government of Indonesia decides to use a social crowdfunding scheme, an appropriate pitching strategy is a must. Quoting E, "In this case, the government must have good public communication strategy … that can attract people and make them feel that they have become part of the contributor(s) to the IKN."

The pitching strategy generally consists of two parts: how messages are communicated (substance) and how one communicates (linguistic style).[49] In the case of civic crowdfunding, the government or project initiator will need to adjust their communication strategy to attract not only citizens but also wider community groups, private sectors, and foreign investors.

Information asymmetry is a related major concern in crowdfunding.[50] While a crowdfunding project's creator may know the project's quality, project backers may not know the project initiators' credibility or ability to deliver a product or service as promised. Such information asymmetry between project initiators and project backers can be minimized by providing information that can be used by backers to evaluate the potential of the projects. Given this, the pitching strategy needs to be adjusted by considering information asymmetry in each of the IKN's potential crowdfunding projects.

Risk of Crowdfunding the IKN
Every action that is related to finance is subject to risk. Regarding crowdfunding the IKN, the experts interviewed agreed that the risk is similar to that of general crowdfunding. First, any crowdfunding project's risk of not fulfilling campaign targets is pervasive. Expert E, who focuses on crowdfunding for business purposes, mentioned the risk of the government failing to give rewards to project backers. He also suggested the importance of creating a loan insurance scheme to protect backers from this kind of risk. "There will be a risk of crowdfunding in IKN; for example, in the business crowdfunding sector, there may be a risk of the government failing to repay the capital to entrepreneurs or the public who participate in crowdfunding. (One way of) mitigating this risk is to make loan insurance, so project backers do not lose." Expert C mentioned the need for strong commitment from the funding body and backers if the project is designed to be a reward-based scheme. However, if the chosen scheme is donation-based, expert C suggested collaborating with mass media to share progress and updates on the projects: "... There is a need for a firm commitment from the recipients of funds so that the agreed promises can be executed...while for channelling funds ... it is necessary to cooperate with the mass media to monitor the success of the activities carried out on their projects." (Authors' translation). One expert suggested a similar risk of not delivering the project according to the actual project plan. Therefore, there is a need for a specific governmental or other body dedicated to managing and monitoring IKN crowdfunding projects.

Third, money laundering is another risk that needs to be mitigated. Expert C mentioned the possibility that there might be people who want to evade tax using crowdfunding, suggesting that "crowdfunding might be used for money laundering to avoid taxes ... To avoid this, there is a need for stringent regulations related to crowdfunding." Expert D suggested a need to limit the number of funds to which a single entity or person can donate. Currently, the OJK Law limits the number of funds based on the annual income of project backers. Similarly, crowdfunding the IKN should have limitations similar to the existing law.

Fourth, corruption is seen as a risk that must be mitigated carefully. As expert B notes, "There is a potential risk ... such as misappropriation of funds, the potential for corruption. Therefore ... it is necessary to have laws and regulations concerning the requirement for reporting, transparency, and disclosure of information to the public so that potential risks that may occur can be monitored carefully."

It is known that Indonesia's public infrastructure projects are prone to corruption.[51] A study by Kusumarani and Zo showed the impact of an individual's corruption perception on his or her level of trust in the government, which influences people's intention to donate to civic crowdfunding projects[52] Therefore, the authors recommend that this risk be considered carefully for crowdfunding campaigns for IKN projects.

Projects Suitable for Crowdfunding

The experts were asked about the type of projects suitable under crowdfunding schemes for the IKN. Two experts agreed that small business-related projects are more suitable, while all agreed that public infrastructure projects such as highways and schools are the government's responsibility. Three mentioned religious places, transportation facilities and public spaces as being more appropriate for crowdfunding. There is some dissonance between the experts' opinions and those of the general public: only one expert felt that crowdfunding was suitable for providing educational facilities compared to 64 per cent of the survey respondents. A possible explanation is their different perspective on what kinds of educational facilities are suitable. The survey respondents might see educational facilities as the responsibility of the government while the experts might see them as an opportunity for citizen initiatives through crowdfunding.

Expert C highlighted the need to develop a new crowdfunding scheme specially designed for IKN projects, to cover aspects that cannot be done through the usual scheme of crowdfunding. Expert E noted that almost every type of sector could be crowdfunded under business crowdfunding, noting that the sector is not a public service (that is, public facilities that are part of the government's responsibility). (Figure 4.4 presents the experts' views on what appropriate crowdfunding projects are.) The experts and online respondents concurred that projects involving community spaces (including religious sites) and open areas like parks and sporting venues could be financed by crowdsourcing.

Crowdfunding as Alternate Funding for the New Capital
Crowdfunding for the new IKN was proposed by the government after Japan's SoftBank Group Corp opted not to invest in the project. The total project cost, estimated to be around US$31.45 billion, cannot be covered by the APBN alone. All experts interviewed agreed that crowdfunding could not replace the main funding from the APBN as it is intended as a supplement. This subsection elaborates on how crowdfunding as alternate funding for the new capital can be realized based on the experts' opinions.

Type of Crowdfunding
To date, there is still no decision on what kind of crowdfunding scheme has been chosen for the IKN but it can be considered civic crowdfunding,

FIGURE 4.4
Appropriate Projects, According to Interviewed Experts

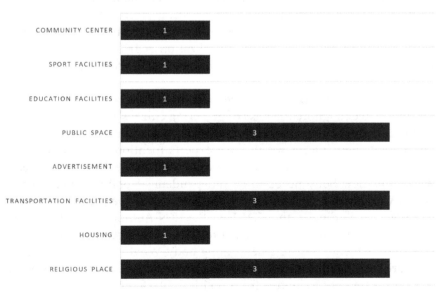

which focuses more on public facilities development. There is some urgency for the central government to decide on the appropriate crowdfunding scheme for the IKN development. Crowdfunding for the IKN can take different forms, such as equity-based, donation-based, and reward-based schemes. The experts agreed that reward-based projects are appropriate for funding projects that have business value (e.g., supermarkets, restaurants, gas stations), while for critical sectors (like health, infocomm, food and agriculture), equity-based crowdfunding will be able to attract more project backers.

Familiarity with Crowdfunding
As argued earlier, the lack of understanding of and familiarity with crowdfunding might explain the generally negative perception of survey respondents towards crowdfunding for the IKN. Familiarity refers to a project backer's degree of acquaintance with the crowdfunding model, which includes knowledge and understanding of relevant procedures, types, and outcomes.[53] Familiarity is a significant factor affecting people's intention to crowdfund and a characteristic of crowdfunding sustainable projects.[54] For instance, in one study, familiarity was linked with positive perceptions toward renewable energy crowdfunding projects.[55]

Our survey finds that many Indonesians are not familiar with crowdfunding. Crowdfunding the new IKN appears to be unpopular and is understood as passing on what should be the government's financial burden to citizens. This understanding is the opposite of crowdfunding, which ideally should be done voluntarily. Based on this, the authors recommend that the government promotes the socialization of IKN crowdfunding by consulting various stakeholders to get broader public support.

A New Authority for the IKN's Crowdfunding?

It is impossible to ignore the risks of gathering citizens' funds at a national level to finance a large-scale, multiyear megaproject for a new capital city. Throughout their interviews, the five experts mentioned the need for a single authority, perhaps, to manage crowdfunding for the IKN development. Ideally, this new body needs to be independent of political interference and to work with industry and practitioners. However, this is unlikely to happen. According to the IKN Law, the IKN Authority has the power to manage finance and assets related to IKN. Therefore, there is no legal basis upon which to create a new ruling body. What is important now is to ensure that the IKN Authority has the independence to effectively work with businesses and to be free from political interference.

Conclusion

This chapter analyses the feasibility of the alternative funding scheme known as crowdfunding for future IKN development, while seeking expert and general opinions on the concept's feasibility for Indonesia's new capital. Indonesians' poor familiarity with and understanding of crowdfunding might explain why there is much negative perception toward the idea of using it for the proposed IKN projects. There also needs to be robust government rationales for choosing crowdfunding as an alternate funding scheme for the IKN and this must be done in coordination with related stakeholders, including the private sector. The government must use an effective public communications strategy to spread the idea to citizens and a strong legal basis must underpin crowdfunding for the IKN. The legal basis, whatever form it takes, should protect Indonesia's citizens from potential risks that might arise, including project failure or untimely delivery of goods, infrastructure, or services.

The interviews and surveys cited in this chapter point to further directions for research for scholars interested in the intersection of crowdfunding and public policy. If Indonesia's government seriously uses crowdfunding as part of the funding scheme for the new IKN megaproject, future studies can focus on understanding crowdfunding models at the national level and beyond.

Acknowledgements

The authors would like to thank all of the experts who were interviewed and Ms Dinda Febriani, who helped to transcribe the interview recordings. They would also like to thank BRIN, ISEAS, and KAS for the opportunity to conduct this research.

Notes

1. American Psychological Association, "Civic Engagement", No Longer Invisible, 2009, https://doi.org/10.1093/acprof:oso/9780199844739.003.0008; Aroon Manoharan, Lamar Vernon Bennett, and Tony Carrizales, "M-Government: An Opportunity for Addressing the Digital Divide", in *Citizen 2.0: Public and Governmental Interaction through Web 2.0 Technologies*, pp. 87–98. (IGI Global, 2012.)
2. Francesca Bria, Esteve Almirall, Peter Baeck, Harry Halpin, Jon Kingsbury, Frank Kresin, and S. Reynolds, "Digital Social Innovation Interim Report" (London: Nesta, 2014); Matt Stokes, Peter Baeck, and Toby Baker, "What Next for Digital Social Innovation", *NESTA, Mayo*, 2017, https://www.nesta.org.uk/report/what-next-for-digital-social-innovation-realising-the-potential-of-people-and-technology-to-tackle-social-challenges/#:~:text=Focusing%20instead%20on%20investment%20

in,within%20existing%20civil%20society%20organisations; and *The Economist*, "Declining Trust in Government Is Denting Democracy", 25 January 2017, https://www-economist-com.proxy.library.upenn.edu/graphic-detail/2017/01/25/declining-trust-in-government-is-denting-democracy

3. Rodrigo Davies, "Civic Crowdfunding: Participatory Communities, Entrepreneurs and the Political Economy of Place", *Entrepreneurs and the Political Economy of Place (May 9, 2014)* (2014); Roberto Esposito, "Civic Crowdfunding Can Revive the Citizens-Politics Relationship", *Crowdsourcingweek.com*, 19 January 2015, http://crowdsourcingweek.com/blog/civic-crowdfunding-can-revive-the-citizens-politics-relationship/; Lee Chang Heon, J. Leon Zhao, and Ghazwan Hassna, "Government-Incentivized Crowdfunding for One-Belt, One-Road Enterprises: Design and Research Issues", *Financial Innovation* 2, no. 1 (2016): 1–14; Angelo Miglietta, Emanuele Parisi, Matteo Pessione, and Flavio Servato, "CrowdFunding and Local Governments: A Financial Opportunity for a New Liaison with Citizens", paper presented at Toulon-Verona Conference on "Excellence in Services", 2013; Alexandra Stiver, Leonor Barroca, Shailey Minocha, Mike Richards, and Dave Roberts, "Civic Crowdfunding Research: Challenges, Opportunities, and Future Agenda", *New Media & Society* 17, no. 2 (2015): 249–71.

4. Javier Ramos Diaz and Bruno González Cacheda, "Financing Social Activism: Crowdfunding and Advocatory Social Movement in Spain in Times of Crisis", in *Proceedings of the 9th International Conference on Theory and Practice of Electronic Governance*, edited by John Bertot, Elsa Estevez and Sehl Mellouli, pp. 139–48, paper presented at ICEGOV 15-16: 9th International Conference on Theory and Practice of Electronic Governance, Montevideo Uruguay, 1–3 March 2016.

5. Byungjun Kim, Minjoo Yoo, Keon Chul Park, Kyeo Re Lee, and Jang Hyun Kim, "A Value of Civic Voices for Smart City: A Big Data Analysis of Civic Queries Posed by Seoul Citizens", *Cities* 108 (2021): 102941.

6. Jennifer M. Brinkerhoff, "David and Goliath: Diaspora Organizations as Partners in the Development Industry", *Public Administration and Development* 31, no. 1 (2011): 37–49.

7. Humas Brin, "Pemetaan Karakteristik Diaspora Di 90 Negara Sebagai Strategi Penguatan Ekonomi Diaspora Indonesia", *BRIN*, 2022, https://brin.go.id/news/96246/pemetaan-karakteristik-diaspora-di-90-negara-sebagai-strategi-penguatan-ekonomi-diaspora-indonesia

8. Indonesia Government, *Lampiran II, Undang-Undang RI No. 3 Tahun 2022 about Rencana Induk IKN* (Jakarta: Sekretariat Negara, 2022).

9. Cantika Adinda Putri, "Jalan Panjang SoftBank Investasi di IKN Hingga Akhirnya Batal", *CNBC Indonesia*, 12 March 2022, https://www.cnbcindonesia.com/news/20220312135913-4-322219/jalan-panjang-softbank-investasi-di-ikn-hingga-akhirnya-batal

10. Yoga Sukmana, "Softbank Batal Investasi di IKN Nusantara, Begini Kata Ekonom", *Kompas.com*, 15 March 2022, https://money.kompas.com/

read/2022/03/15/152042126/softbank-batal-investasi-di-ikn-nusantara-begini-kata-ekonom
11. Laila Afifa, "Govt Explores Potential of Crowdfunding for New Capital Project", *Tempo.co*, 22 March 2022, https://en.tempo.co/read/1573683/govt-explores-potential-of-crowdfunding-for-new-capital-project
12. London City Hall, "Civic Crowdfunding Programme", 2022, https://www.london.gov.uk/programmes-strategies/business-and-economy/supporting-londons-sectors/smart-london/civic-crowdfunding-programme#:~:text=The%20Mayor's%20Crowdfunding%20Pilot%20offers,and%20pledges%20from%20the%20Mayor
13. London City Hall, "The Impact of Community Crowdfunding", 2022, https://www.london.gov.uk/programmes-strategies/shaping-local-places/funding-opportunities/make-london/impact-community-crowdfunding
14. London City Hall, "The Peckham Coal Line Urban Park", 2022, https://www.london.gov.uk/programmes-strategies/shaping-local-places/funding-opportunities/crowdfunding-pilot-programme/peckham-coal-line-urban
15. Dian Erika Nugraheny, "Jokowi: Anggaran Pembangunan Kawasan Inti IKN Seluruhnya dari APBN", *Kompas.com*, 22 March 2022, https://nasional.kompas.com/read/2022/02/22/13105671/jokowi-anggaran-pembangunan-kawasan-inti-ikn-seluruhnya-dari-apbn
16. Fitria Chusna Farisa, "Berapa Dana APBN Yang Akan Dipakai Untuk Membangun IKN? Ini Hitung-Hitungan Jokowi", *Kompas.com*, 23 February 2022, https://nasional.kompas.com/read/2022/02/23/14282541/berapa-dana-apbn-yang-akan-dipakai-untuk-membangun-ikn-ini-hitung-hitungan
17. Public-Private Partnership Knowledge Lab, "PPP Contract Types and Terminology", 2020, https://ppp.worldbank.org/public-private-partnership/ppp-knowledge-lab
18. Wibi Pangestu Pratama, "Jokowi Akui Biaya Bangun IKN 20 Persen Pakai APBN", *Bisnis.com*, 16 August 2022, https://ekonomi.bisnis.com/read/20220816/9/1567591/jokowi-akui-biaya-bangun-ikn-20-persen-pakai-apbn
19. Angga Ulung Tranggana, "Bhima Yudhistira: Pendanaan Pembangunan IKN Makin Memberatkan APBN", *Politik.rmol*, 4 February 2022, https://politik.rmol.id/read/2022/02/04/522021/bhima-yudhistira-pendanaan-pembangunan-ikn-makin-memberatkan-apbn
20. Wibi Pangestu Pratama, "Otorita IKN Tegaskan Crowdfunding Itu Mekanisme Sah Untuk Pendanaan Ibu Kota Baru", *Bisnis.com*, 25 March 2022, https://ekonomi.bisnis.com/read/20220325/9/1514957/otorita-ikn-tegaskan-crowdfunding-itu-mekanisme-sah-untuk-pendanaan-ibu-kota-baru
21. Ethan Mollick, "The Dynamics of Crowdfunding: An Exploratory Study", *Journal of Business Venturing* 29, no. 1 (2014): 1–16.
22. Jeff Howe, *Crowdsourcing: How the Power of the Crowd Is Driving the Future of Business* (Random House, 2008).
23. Stiver et al., "Civic Crowdfunding Research"; Ben Matthews and Paul Taylor, "Head to Head Is Crowdfunding the Way Forward for Councils Local Government

Network", *The Guardian*, 29 May 2013, https://www.theguardian.com/local-government-network/2013/may/29/crowdfunding-way-forward-for-councils%0A

24. Lee Chang Heon, Yiyang Bian, Rajaa Karaouzene, and Nasreen Suleiman, "Examining the Role of Narratives in Civic Crowdfunding: Linguistic Style and Message Substance", *Industrial Management & Data Systems* 119, no. 7 (2019): 1492–514.
25. Michael M. Gierczak, Ulrich Bretschneider, Philipp Haas, Ivo Blohm, and Jan Marco Leimeister, "Crowdfunding: Outlining the New Era of Fundraising", in *Crowdfunding in Europe*, edited by Dennis Bruntje and Oliver Gajda (Cham: Springer, 2016), pp. 7–23.
26. Rodrigo Davies, "Three Provocations for Civic Crowdfunding", *Information, Communication & Society* 18, no. 3: 342–55.
27. Esposito, "Civic Crowdfunding Can Revive the Citizens-Politics Relationship"; Miglietta et al., "CrowdFunding and Local Governments"; Stiver et al., "Civic Crowdfunding Research".
28. Davies, "Three Provocations for Civic Crowdfunding".
29. Davies, "Civic Crowdfunding"; Angelo Miglietta and Emanuele Parisi, "Civic CrowdFunding: Sharing Economy Financial Opportunity to Smart Cities," in *Smart Cities Atlas: Western and Eastern Intelligent Communities*, edited by Eleonora Riva Sanseverino, Raffaella Riva Sanseverino, Valentina Vaccaro (Cham: Springer International Publishing, 2016), pp. 159–72; Stiver et al., "Civic Crowdfunding Research".
30. Veronica De Crescenzo, Dolores Botella-Carrubi, and María Rodríguez García, "Civic Crowdfunding: A New Opportunity for Local Governments", *Journal of Business Research* 123 (2021): 580–87.
31. Imagination Detroit Station, "Detroit Needs A Statue of Robocop!", *Kickstarter.com*, January 2020, https://www.kickstarter.com/projects/imaginationstation/detroit-needs-a-statue-of-robocop
32. VisitBrighton, "Save Madeira Terrace", Spacehive.com, November 2017, https://www.spacehive.com/madeira-terrace
33. Baitul Wakaf, "Krisis Air Bersih: Wakaf Sumur Tuk Santri Papua", *Kitabisa.com*, January 2023, https://kitabisa.com/campaign/wakafsumuruntukpesantren
34. Daniel A. Brent and Katie Lorah, "The Economic Geography of Civic Crowdfunding", *Cities* 90 (2019): 122–30.
35. Davies, "Civic Crowdfunding".
36. Pnina Werbner, "The Place Which Is Diaspora: Citizenship, Religion and Gender in the Making of Chaordic Transnationalism", *Journal of Ethnic and Migration Studies* 28, no. 1 (2002): 119–33.
37. Stiver et al., "Civic Crowdfunding Research".
38. Brent and Lorah, " The Economic Geography of Civic Crowdfunding"; Mai Anh Doan and Margalit Toledano, "Beyond Organization-Centred Public Relations: Collective Action Through a Civic Crowdfunding Campaign", *Public Relations Review* 44, no. 1 (2018): 37–46.

39. Franck Juredieu and Sébastien Mayoux, "Crowdfunding Legal Framework: An International Analysis", *International Perspectives on Crowdfunding* (2016): 81–97.
40. M.M. Alhammad, R. Al Othman, and C. Tan, "Review of Crowdfunding Regulations across Countries: A Systematic Review Study", *Journal of Information Systems Engineering and Management* 6, no. 4 (2021).
41. Brent and Lorah, " The Economic Geography of Civic Crowdfunding".
42. Davies, "Civic Crowdfunding".
43. Klaus Krippendorff, *Content Analysis: An Introduction to Its Methodology* (Sage Publications, 2018).
44. Michael M. Gant and Sigelman Lee, "Anti-candidate Voting in Presidential Elections", *Polity* 18, no. 2 (1985): 329–39; Sigelman Lee and Michael M. Gant, "Anticandidate Voting in the 1984 Presidential Election", *Political Behavior* 11, no. 1 (1989): 81–92.
45. Riri Kusumarani and Hangjung Zo, "Why People Participate in Online Political Crowdfunding: A Civic Voluntarism Perspective", *Telematics and Informatics* 41 (2019): 168–81.
46. Annaleena Parhankangas and Maija Renko, "Linguistic Style and Crowdfunding Success Among Social and Commercial Entrepreneurs", *Journal of Business Venturing* 32, no. 2 (2017): 215–36.; Mi Zhou, Baozhou Lu, Weiguo Fan, and G. Alan Wang, "Project Description and Crowdfunding Success: An Exploratory Study", *Information Systems Frontiers* 20 (2018): 259–74.
47. Zhou et al., "Project Description and Crowdfunding Success".
48. Parhankangas and Renko, "Linguistic Style and Crowdfunding Success Among Social and Commercial Entrepreneurs".
49. Lee Chang Heon et al., "Examining the Role of Narratives in Civic Crowdfunding: Linguistic Style and Message Substance".
50. Wang Nianxin, Huigang Liang, Yajiong Xue, and Shilun Ge, "Mitigating Information Asymmetry to Achieve Crowdfunding Success: Signaling and Online Communication", *Journal of the Association for Information Systems* 22, no. 3 (2021): 4.
51. Susanne Kühn, and Laura B. Sherman, *Curbing Corruption in Public Procurement: A Practical Guide* (Transparency International, 2014).
52. Kusumarani and Zo, "Why People Participate in Online Political Crowdfunding".
53. Krystallia Moysidou and J. Piet Hausberg, "In Crowdfunding We Trust: A Trust-Building Model in Lending Crowdfunding", *Journal of Small Business Management* 58, no. 3 (2020): 511–43.
54. Mohammed Alharbey and Stefan Van Hemmen, "Investor Intention in Equity Crowdfunding: Does Trust Matter?", *Journal of Risk and Financial Management* 14, no. 2 (2021): 53; Isabell Tenner and Jacob Hörisch, "Crowdfunding Sustainable Entrepreneurship: What Are the Characteristics of Crowdfunding Investors?", *Journal of Cleaner Production* 290 (2021): 125667.
55. Ariel Bergmann, Bruce Burton, and Matthias Klaes, "European Perceptions on Crowdfunding for Renewables: Positivity and Pragmatism", *Ecological Economics* 179 (2021): 106852.

References

Afifa, Laila. 2022. "Govt Explores Potential of Crowdfunding for New Capital Project". *Tempo.co*, 22 March 2022. https://en.tempo.co/read/1573683/govt-explores-potential-of-crowdfunding-for-new-capital-project

Alhammad, M.M., R. Al Othman, and C. Tan. 2021. "Review of Crowdfunding Regulations across Countries: A Systematic Review Study". *Journal of Information Systems Engineering and Management* 6, no. 4: 1–13.

Alharbey, Mohammed, and Stefan Van Hemmen. 2021. "Investor Intention in Equity Crowdfunding. Does Trust Matter?". *Journal of Risk and Financial Management* 14, no. 2: 1–20.

American Psychological Association. 2009. "Civic Engagement". *No Longer Invisible.* https://doi.org/10.1093/acprof:oso/9780199844739.003.0008

Baitul Wakaf. 2023. "Krisis Air Bersih: Wakaf Sumur Tuk Santri Papua". *Kitabisa.com*, January 2023. https://kitabisa.com/campaign/wakafsumuruntukpesantren

Bergmann, Ariel, Bruce Burton, and Matthias Klaes. 2021. "European Perceptions on Crowdfunding for Renewables: Positivity and Pragmatism". *Ecological Economics* 179: 1–9.

Brent, Daniel A., and Katie Lorah. 2019. "The Economic Geography of Civic Crowdfunding". *Cities*, 90: 122–30.

Bria, Francesca, Esteve Almirall, Peter Baeck, Harry Halpin, Jon Kingsbury, Frank Kresin, and S. Reynolds. 2014. "Digital Social Innovation Interim Report". London: Nesta.

Brinkerhoff, Jennifer M. 2011. "David and Goliath: Diaspora Organisations as Partners in the Development Industry". *Public Administration and Development* 31, no. 1: 37–49.

Crowdfunder UK. 2022. "Crowdfunder UK – Where Ideas Happen". https://www.crowdfunder.co.uk/

Davies, Rodrigo. 2014. "Civic Crowdfunding: Participatory Communities, Entrepreneurs and the Political Economy of Place". Master thesis, Massachusetts Institute of Technology.

———. 2015. "Three Provocations for Civic Crowdfunding". *Information, Communication & Society* 18, no. 3: 342–55.

De Crescenzo, Veronica, Dolores Botella-Carrubi, and María Rodríguez García. 2021. "Civic Crowdfunding: A New Opportunity for Local Governments". *Journal of Business Research* 123: 580–87.

Diaz, Javier Ramos, and Bruno González Cacheda. 2016. "Financing Social Activism: Crowdfunding and Advocatory Social Movement in Spain in Times of Crisis". In *Proceedings of the 9th International Conference on Theory and Practice of Electronic Governance*, edited by John Bertot, Elsa Estevez and Sehl Mellouli, pp. 139–48. Paper presented at ICEGOV '15-16: 9th International Conference on Theory and Practice of Electronic Governance, Montevideo Uruguay, 1–3 March 2016.

Doan, Mai Anh, and Margalit Toledano. 2018. "Beyond Organisation-Centred Public

Relations: Collective Action Through a Civic Crowdfunding Campaign". *Public Relations Review* 44, no. 1: 37–46.

Economist, The. 2017. "Declining Trust in Government Is Denting Democracy". 25 January 2017. https://www-economist-com.proxy.library.upenn.edu/graphic-detail/2017/01/25/declining-trust-in-government-is-denting-democracy

Esposito, Roberto. 2015. "Civic Crowdfunding Can Revive the Citizens-Politics Relationship". *Crowdsourcingweek.com*, 19 January 2015, http://crowdsourcingweek.com/blog/civic-crowdfunding-can-revive-the-citizens-politics-relationship/

Farisa, Fitria Chusna. 2022. "Berapa Dana APBN Yang Akan Dipakai Untuk Membangun IKN? Ini Hitung-Hitungan Jokowi". *Kompas.com*, 23 February 2022. https://nasional.kompas.com/read/2022/02/23/14282541/berapa-dana-apbn-yang-akan-dipakai-untuk-membangun-ikn-ini-hitung-hitungan

Gant, Michael M., and Lee Sigelman. 1985. "Anti-candidate Voting in Presidential Elections". *Polity* 18, no. 2: 329–39.

Gierczak, Michael M., Ulrich Bretschneider, Philipp Haas, Ivo Blohm, and Jan Marco Leimeister. 2016. "Crowdfunding: Outlining the New Era of Fundraising". In *Crowdfunding in Europe*, edited by Dennis Bruntje and Oliver Gajda, pp. 7–23. Cham: Springer.

Howe, Jeff. 2008. *Crowdsourcing: How the Power of the Crowd Is Driving the Future of Business*. Random House.

Humas Brin, 2022. "Pemetaan Karakteristik Diaspora Di 90 Negara Sebagai Strategi Penguatan Ekonomi Diaspora Indonesia". *BRIN*, 2022. https://brin.go.id/news/96246/pemetaan-karakteristik-diaspora-di-90-negara-sebagai-strategi-penguatan-ekonomi-diaspora-indonesia

Imagination Detroit Station. 2020. "Detroit Needs A Statue of Robocop!". *Kickstarter.com*, January 2020. https://www.kickstarter.com/projects/imaginationstation/detroit-needs-a-statue-of-robocop

Indonesia Government. 2022. *Lampiran II, Undang-Undang RI No. 3 Tahun 2022 about Rencana Induk IKN*. Jakarta: Sekretariat Negara.

Ioby.org. 2022. "Ioby Brings Neighborhood Projects to Life, Block by Block". 2022. https://www.ioby.org/

Juredieu, Franck, and Sébastien Mayoux. 2016. "Crowdfunding Legal Framework: An International Analysis". *International Perspectives on Crowdfunding*, pp. 81–97.

Kim, Byungjun, Minjoo Yoo, Keon Chul Park, Kyeo Re Lee, and Jang Hyun Kim. 2021. "A Value of Civic Voices for Smart City: A Big Data Analysis of Civic Queries Posed by Seoul Citizens". *Cities* 108, 102941: 1–9.

Krippendorff, Klaus. 2018. *Content Analysis: An Introduction to Its Methodology*. Sage Publications.

Kühn, Susanne, and Laura B. Sherman. 2014. *Curbing Corruption in Public Procurement: A Practical Guide*. Transparency International.

Kusumarani, Riri, and Hangjung Zo. 2019. "Why People Participate in Online Political Crowdfunding: A Civic Voluntarism Perspective". *Telematics and Informatics* 41: 168–81.

Lee, Chang Heon, J. Leon Zhao, and Ghazwan Hassna. 2016. "Government-Incentivized Crowdfunding for One-Belt, One-Road Enterprises: Design and Research Issues". *Financial Innovation* 2, no. 1: 1–14.

———, Yiyang Bian, Rajaa Karaouzene, and Nasreen Suleiman. 2019. "Examining the Role of Narratives in Civic Crowdfunding: Linguistic Style and Message Substance". *Industrial Management & Data Systems* 119, no. 7: 1492–514.

London City Hall. 2022a. "Civic Crowdfunding Programme". https://www.london.gov.uk/programmes-strategies/business-and-economy/supporting-londons-sectors/smart-london/civic-crowdfunding-programme

———. 2022b. "The Impact of Community Crowdfunding". https://www.london.gov.uk/programmes-strategies/shaping-local-places/funding-opportunities/make-london/impact-community-crowdfunding

———. 2022c. "The Peckham Coal Line Urban Park". https://www.london.gov.uk/programmes-strategies/shaping-local-places/funding-opportunities/crowdfunding-pilot-programme/peckham-coal-line-urban

Manoharan, Aroon, Lamar Vernon Bennett, and Tony Carrizales. 2012. "M-Government: An Opportunity for Addressing the Digital Divide". In *Citizen 2.0: Public and Governmental Interaction through Web 2.0 Technologies*, pp. 87–98. IGI Global.

Matthews, Ben, and Paul Taylor. 2013. "Head to Head Is Crowdfunding the Way Forward for Councils Local Government Network". *The Guardian*, 29 May 2013. https://www.theguardian.com/local-government-network/2013/may/29/crowdfunding-way-forward-for-councils%0A

Miglietta, Angelo, and Emanuele Parisi. 2016. "Civic CrowdFunding: Sharing Economy Financial Opportunityto Smart Cities". In *Smart Cities Atlas: Western and Eastern Intelligent Communities,*, edited by Eleonora Riva Sanseverino, Raffaella Riva Sanseverino, Valentina Vaccaro, pp. 159–72. Cham: Springer International Publishing.

———, Emanuele Parisi, Matteo Pessione, and Flavio Servato. 2013. "CrowdFunding and Local Governments: A Financial Opportunity for a New Liaison with Citizens". Paper presented at Toulon-Verona Conference on "Excellence in Services".

Mollick, Ethan. 2014. "The Dynamics of Crowdfunding: An Exploratory Study". *Journal of Business Venturing* 29, no. 1: 1–16.

Moysidou, Krystallia, and J. Piet Hausberg. 2020. "In Crowdfunding We Trust: A Trust-Building Model in Lending Crowdfunding". *Journal of Small Business Management* 58, no. 3: 511–43.

Nugraheny, Dian Erika. 2022. "Jokowi: Anggaran Pembangunan Kawasan Inti IKN Seluruhnya dari APBN". *Kompas.com*, 22 March 2022. https://nasional.kompas.com/read/2022/02/22/13105671/jokowi-anggaran-pembangunan-kawasan-inti-ikn-seluruhnya-dari-apbn

Parhankangas, Annaleena, and Maija Renko. 2017. "Linguistic Style and Crowdfunding Success Among Social and Commercial Entrepreneurs". *Journal of Business Venturing* 32, no. 2: 215–36.

Pratama, Wibi Pangestu. 2022a. "Otorita IKN Tegaskan Crowdfunding Itu Mekanisme Sah Untuk Pendanaan Ibu Kota Baru". *Bisnis.com*, 25 March 2022. https://ekonomi.bisnis.com/read/20220325/9/1514957/otorita-ikn-tegaskan-crowdfunding-itu-mekanisme-sah-untuk-pendanaan-ibu-kota-baru

———. 2022. "Jokowi Akui Biaya Bangun IKN 20 Persen Pakai APBN". *Bisnis.com*, 16 August 2022. https://ekonomi.bisnis.com/read/20220816/9/1567591/jokowi-akui-biaya-bangun-ikn-20-persen-pakai-apbn

Public-Private Partnership Knowledge Lab. 2020. "PPP Contract Types and Terminology". https://ppp.worldbank.org/public-private-partnership/ppp-knowledge-lab

Putri, Cantika Adinda. 2022. "Jalan Panjang SoftBank Investasi di IKN Hingga Akhirnya Batal". *CNBC Indonesia*, 12 March 2022. https://www.cnbcindonesia.com/news/20220312135913-4-322219/jalan-panjang-softbank-investasi-di-ikn-hingga-akhirnya-batal

Sedlitzky, Raphael, and Yvonne Franz. 2019. "'What If We All Chip In?' Civic Crowdfunding as Alternative Financing for Urban Development Projects". *Built Environment* 45, no. 1: 26–44.

Sigelman, Lee, and Michael M. Gant. 1989. "Anticandidate Voting in the 1984 Presidential Election". *Political Behavior* 11, no. 1: 81–92.

Spacehive. 2022. "Crowdfunding For Local Projects". https://www.spacehive.com/

Stiver, Alexandra, Leonor Barroca, Shailey Minocha, Mike Richards, and Dave Roberts. 2015. "Civic Crowdfunding Research: Challenges, Opportunities, and Future Agenda". *New Media & Society* 17, no. 2: 249–71.

Stokes, Matt, Peter Baeck, and Toby Baker. 2017. "What Next for Digital Social Innovation". *NESTA. Mayo*, https://www.nesta.org.uk/report/what-next-for-digital-social-innovation-realising-the-potential-of-people-and-technology-to-tackle-social-challenges/#:~:text=Focusing%20instead%20on%20investment%20in,within%20existing%20civil%20society%20organisations

Sukmana, Yoga. 2022. "Softbank Batal Investasi di IKN Nusantara, Begini Kata Ekonom". *Kompas.com*, 15 March 2022. https://money.kompas.com/read/2022/03/15/152042126/softbank-batal-investasi-di-ikn-nusantara-begini-kata-ekonom

Tenner, Isabell, and Jacob Hörisch. 2021. "Crowdfunding Sustainable Entrepreneurship: What Are the Characteristics of Crowdfunding Investors?". *Journal of Cleaner Production* 290 (2021): 1–9.

Tranggana, Angga Ulung. 2022. "Bhima Yudhistira: Pendanaan Pembangunan IKN Makin Memberatkan APBN". *Politik.rmol*, 4 February 2022. https://politik.rmol.id/read/2022/02/04/522021/bhima-yudhistira-pendanaan-pembangunan-ikn-makin-memberatkan-apbn

VisitBrighton. 2017. "Save Madeira Terrace". *Spacehive.com*, November. https://www.spacehive.com/madeira-terrace

Wang, Nianxin, Huigang Liang, Yajiong Xue, and Shilun Ge. 2021. "Mitigating Information Asymmetry to Achieve Crowdfunding Success: Signaling and Online

Communication". *Journal of the Association for Information Systems* 22, no. 3: 773–96.

Werbner, Pnina. 2002. "The Place Which Is Diaspora: Citizenship, Religion and Gender in the Making of Chaordic Transnationalism". *Journal of Ethnic and Migration Studies* 28, no. 1: 119–33.

Zhou, Mi, Baozhou Lu, Weiguo Fan, and G. Alan Wang. 2018. "Project Description and Crowdfunding Success: An Exploratory Study". *Information Systems Frontiers* 20: 259–74.

Part II
CHALLENGES IN DEVELOPING NUSANTARA

5

ADDRESSING THE CHALLENGES IN DEVELOPING NUSANTARA
The Roles of Spatial Planning

Dimas Wisnu Adrianto and Kathleen Meira Berta

INTRODUCTION

The plan to relocate Indonesia's capital city (IKN) has finally come to its realization under President Joko Widodo's leadership. Jakarta claims that Nusantara, the new capital city now under construction, will be one of the most sustainable cities in the world. The term "Forest City" has been emphasized as the designated design slogan to accentuate an integrated human-nature approach, where about 75 per cent of the total landscape will be green open spaces. Walking and public transport will be the main modes of mobility in a city where main attractions and services can be accessed within 10 minutes of travel time for any commuter. Besides creating a sustainable city, the planners' agenda aims to distribute or more evenly transfer economic and population growth out of Indonesia's main island of Java. The central government aims to create approximately 5 million local jobs by 2045,[1] which will potentially attract massive in-migration from Java and other islands to the IKN area.

To successfully develop Nusantara, planners must engage in thorough planning. In the initial stage, the government made the plan to relocate the capital a priority in the National Mid-term Development Plan (RPJMN) 2020–2024. This was followed by the enactment of Decree No. 3 of 2022[2] on the IKN, which highlighted the cruciality of spatial planning as an instrument to guide the construction of a safe, convenient, productive, and sustainable capital city. The General Spatial Plan for the IKN (Presidential Decree 64/2022) will provide a macro-level reference for urban planning, which marks the inauguration of developing Nusantara. Considering the commencement of this megaproject, this chapter reviews and further discusses the related opportunities and challenges and identifies how spatial planning can play significant roles in Indonesia's urban development.

Conceptual Framework and Methodology

This chapter will emphasize the importance of spatial planning as an instrument for development planning in the megaproject of Nusantara. In doing so, the authors observe the social and environmental issues concerned, to provide initial information to identify the potential implications for spatial planning. Separately, the authors initiated a workshop using the Synergistics method[3] to observe institutional issues within the planning framework and to identify the potential forward pathways for spatial planning.

The workshop involved twenty-two participants representing national public and private actors encompassing policymakers and practitioners in spatial planning, infrastructure, housing, transportation, environmental protection, agriculture and governance. The workshop was conducted on 19 September 2019 at Indonesia's presidential staff office in Jakarta. The participants were asked to reflect on their experience in conducting the practice of spatial planning in Indonesia and to suggest plausible problems and challenges they foresaw in developing Nusantara.

Rationale for Relocation to Nusantara

Growth Distribution

The Indonesian archipelago consists of more than 17,000 islands, with economic growth poorly distributed across the country. Most of the country's development has been concentrated on the main island of Java, which covers 15 per cent of the national territory but is home to approximately 56 per cent of the total population (see Table 5.1).

Geographically spreading out the national population as well as economic growth away from Java to the outer islands will become increasingly essential, particularly given the rapidly increasing urbanization in Java and worsening inter-region inequalities. Approximately an average of 55.32 per cent of the total Indonesian population and 65.4 per cent of the population in Java live in urban areas. For Java, this is expected to escalate to 81 per cent by 2035.[4] The urban population increases alongside the expansion of urban areas have contributed to the significant loss of agricultural lands and other important ecosystem services provided by Java's rural areas.

TABLE 5.1
National Population Distribution in 2010, 2020, and 2035 (Projected)

Major Islands	Population (in thousands)					
	2010	%	2020	%	2035 Projection	%
Sumatra	50,860	21.32	58,600	21.68	68,500	22.41
Java	137,033	57.45	151,600	56.10	167,326	54.74
Bali and Nusa Tenggara	13,130	5.50	15,000	5.54	17,496	5.72
Kalimantan/Borneo	13,851	5.81	16,500	6.15	20,318	6.65
Sulawesi	17,437	7.31	19,900	7.36	22,732	7.44
Maluku	2,585	1.08	8,600	3.17	3,831	1.25
Papua	3,622	1.52			5,450	1.78
National	238,519	100.00	270,200	100.00	305,652	100.00

Source: Indonesian National Bureau of Statistics, 2014 and 2021.

Overall, urbanization has been the primary cause of the loss of 7,435 ha of prime agricultural lands each year between 2003 and 2015.[5] The growth of Jakarta's urban areas alone has contributed to the loss of farming parcels at the rate of about 2.71 per cent per annum,[6] while other secondary cities (such as Malang and East Java) were experiencing a higher rate of conversion at 4.51 per cent every year.[7] These figures are expected to remain high and are likely to accelerate, as a greater proportion of national economic investments, either through foreign direct investment (FDI) or domestic investment, continue to be concentrated in Java.

Dismantling Java's supremacy as the centre of national economic growth has been one of the top priorities of every government since Dutch colonialism, reaching its peak in the New Order (*Orde Baru*) of President Suharto. Through the *transmigrasi* (transmigration) programme, the New Order government initiated the establishment of new settlements across several remote areas out of Java, aimed at distributing the population and creating opportunities to boost national economic development.[8] The programme was quite successful (in some ways) and was able to nationally distribute an estimated 10 per cent of Java's population.[9] However, the transmigration programme was controversial and was eventually terminated after the impeachment of Suharto in 1998, as Indonesia entered the reformation (*reformasi*) era, with the ensuing struggles towards political stabilization and the establishment of a decentralized government.

The Search for a Liveable City: Not Jakarta
The prolonged and worsening flood disasters in Jakarta indicate the severity of Jakarta's urban problems. Recent floods have affected most of the vital locations, including the high-valued Central Business District (CBD) and government office buildings.

According to the NCICD Master Plan (2014), there are three different typologies of Jakarta's flooding, which were cited as why the government cannot overcome this natural hazard. These are:

(1) The overflow of rivers, where the massive discharge from the high rainfall in the upstream areas flows towards the urban centre, exceeding the storage capacity of the river;
(2) flooding due to high local rainfall, where the urban drainage system cannot sufficiently support rainwater discharge towards rivers; and
(3) coastal flooding, caused by seawater intrusion inward to the northern coastal areas, where the area lies under the sea level.

Meanwhile, intractable problems in the transportation sector—with Jakarta's urban population still heavily relying on automobiles despite endless government efforts to improve the public transport system—have contributed to the wicked problem of commuting and congestion. Although Jakarta had recently improved its overall public transport system (such as through the provision of rapid transit facilities on railways and buses),[10] managing 3.2 million daily commuters who spend an average of an hour travelling distances of just 10–20 kilometres[11] remains a significant challenge. Given these problems, Jakarta's liveability index had fallen below the national average levels, according to research conducted by the Indonesian Association of Planners (IAP) in 2014. Two of the significant determining factors were the environmental conditions (the series of flood disasters and air pollution) and transport (commuting). The transportation problems and the prolonged history of flood disasters and continuous failures to mitigate and overcome the impacts highlight the wicked problems in managing Jakarta's urbanization. Difficulties in implementing spatial policies (for instance, preventing land use conversion into high-class apartments and real estate in protected areas) and executing the construction of flood mitigation infrastructures (such as the construction of the east river canal that took more than forty years) are among the complexities in managing Jakarta.[12] Considering this, the relocation of the capital has become increasingly urgent in the sense that the central government offices need to be established in a more liveable urban environment. It is also believed that separating government functions from business interests will have a positive outcome for urban development, although many might disagree with this statement.

An Overview of Nusantara

General Characteristics

Nusantara borders the Regency of North Penajam and the City of Balikpapan in the south, the Regency of Kutai Kartanegara in the west and north, and the Strait of Makassar in the east. The city spans approximately 256,142 ha from the inland to the eastern coastal area of East Kalimantan. According to Nusantara's general spatial plan,[13] the IKN is designated as a national strategic economic zone and consists of two main regional zones. The first (56,180 ha) is the main capital city zone which includes the Core zone for the seat of the government (KIPP) with an area of 6,671 ha and inner-city zones. Meanwhile, a further 199,962 ha are the extended capital city zones which will be developed in the later stages of urban development.[14] Additionally, Nusantara is surrounded by several satellite cities such as Bontang, Samarinda, Balikpapan and Tenggarong. This regional structure serves as an advantage for the strategic economic agenda, where there will be opportunities for spatial integration and to strengthen connectivity among regions with different economic specializations.

The Proposed Urban Design

The Indonesian government under President Joko Widodo has already committed to delivering a green and sustainable city as the foreground of the conceptual urban design of the new capital since the preliminary study for the capital relocation was conducted (Table 5.2). There are at least four principal designs as the foundation of the development of the new capital city:[15] a city that (1) symbolizes Indonesia's diverse culture; (2) is modern and sustainable; (3) is globally competitive; and (4) is capable of supporting an efficient system of governance.

The urban gradient of the new capital city encompasses four urban zones that will be constructed in four different stages. The first stage (2022–24) will focus on developing the urban core, which will accommodate the main functions of the government, including the Presidential Palace and the ministry offices. The second stage is the construction of the inner-city zone, which includes public housing provided for government officials and other essential public services (like education, health and commercial

TABLE 5.2
Development Stages of Nusantara

Stage	Year	Planning Area(s)
Stage 1	2022–24	• KIPP Stage 1A sub-BWP 1
Stage 2	2025–29	• KIPP Stage 1A and part of 1B sub-BWP 1 • West IKN area • East IKN area
Stage 3	2030–34	• KIPP Stage 1B Sub-BWP 1, part of Stage 2A sub-BWP II • West IKN area • East IKN area
Stage 4	2035–39	• KIPP Stage 2A, and part of Stage 2B sub-BWP II • West IKN area • East IKN area • North IKN area
Stage 5	2040–45	• KIPP Stage 2B sub-BWP II, Stage 3A, and 3B sub-BWP III • West IKN area • East IKN area • North IKN area

Source: Indonesia's Presidential Regulation no. 3 of 2022.

activities). The expansion of the new capital city will be conducted in the third stage, where commercial housing will be built while carrying out the establishment of a national park dedicated to the conservation of the orangutan and other essential ecosystem services. The last stage will bring about a second planned expansion of the city, which functions as the regional frontier of strategic economic development (industrial and commercial) to be integrated with the urban agglomeration in the surrounding cities and provinces.

To obtain feedback from the public, a competition for the urban design was held in 2020, which attracted 755 architects and urban planners. The winning award design was "Negara Rimba Nusa"[16] (by Urban+, an urban design consulting firm)—a utopian urban design expressing the diverse culture of the Indonesian archipelago integrated within the theme of a sustainable forest city. This concept is now being adopted formally in the planning stages and implemented in the undergoing construction of urban fabrics.

In terms of transport and mobility, the city will have a walkable environment, while travel or commutes between urban zones will be served by mass public transportation. Green infrastructures, the use of renewable energy, and the provision of large green open spaces are also central to the "Forest City" theme, where 75 per cent of the city will be maintained as forests and green open spaces. These proposed themes altogether represent an ideal format for future Indonesian cities and are claimed to be the benchmark for Indonesian urban planning and development.

Problems and Implications for Spatial Planning

Indeed, building a city from scratch means having the liberty to implement innovative urban designs that meet the desire of having socially, economically, and environmentally viable neighbourhoods.[17] This option can sometimes be more feasible (such as in the context of budgeting or dealing with the complexity of actors' vested or competing interests) than redeveloping a city that is already suffering from severe urban problems.[18] However, this is not a simple practice, particularly considering the challenges and the imminent problems likely to be encountered in the absence of a robust planning and execution framework. This section highlights some of the crucial issues for the development of Nusantara.

Population and Urbanization

Population projections estimate that by 2045, Nusantara will be inhabited by approximately 1.9 million people,[19] which means the new capital city will reach the size of a metropolis. Additionally, the new capital city is designed to be attractive not only in social terms but also economically, it will be part of the Balikpapan-Samarinda urban agglomeration, which will provide a strong incentive for rapid urbanization. Therefore, there is a strong possibility that the actual population of IKN might be significantly higher due to the government's commitment to creating around 5 million jobs by 2045.[20] The prevalence of jobs alone will attract massive in-migration of the working class from across the country. Consequently, this means that there will be an imminent surge in the demand for spaces for housing, infrastructure, and the provision of various public services, which will potentially trigger urban expansion and sprawl.

For spatial planning purposes, there are at least two implications. First, there will be a need to allocate sufficient spaces for the growth of residential areas whilst ensuring that housing is provided at an affordable price for the working class. Second, planners need to adopt a design of an urban structure that can slow the pace of urban expansion and, most importantly, prevent sprawl.

Potential Conflicts Regarding Customary Lands and Concessions

According to the Alliance of Indigenous Peoples of the Archipelago (AMAN), there are twenty-one indigenous community groups (nineteen from Penajam Paser and two from Kutai Kartanegara) inhabiting the area of IKN, in which eleven of them are located within the core government area (*Kawasan Inti Pusat Pemerintahan*, KIPP).[21] The existence and protection of these tribes and their customary ownership of lands are undoubtedly of paramount importance. Most of these community group members rely on the surrounding nature as part of their source of income (e.g., farming and plantations), which is now under an imminent threat of displacement due to the expected urban development. Conflicts involving customary lands are a common phenomenon in Indonesia but at times resolutions are quite unsatisfactory given various factors. These include the overlapping of and differences between the formal legal framework and customary laws, the lack of political will in fully recognizing customary laws as part of the formal legal framework,[22] and problems relating to the lack or the inadequacy of empirical research supporting policies that failed to capture the details and accuracy of customary land geographical distributions.[23]

Some of this resonates in the IKN process. For instance, the Balik ethnic community of the Sepaku subdistrict, which has occupied the lands in the designated KIPP zone for generations, has not yet been given full recognition and protection of its rights, including in matters of land acquisition and dispossession.[24] (See Chapter 6 for a more detailed treatment of this issue.) In relation to this matter, however, the national government should be appreciated for enacting Presidential Decree no. 65 of 2022 regarding acquisition and land management, but it is unclear how this will be executed thoroughly and whether it will be done through inclusive communication with the ethnic groups. Consequently, spatial planners for IKN need to be fully aware of this issue, to ensure that the areas designated for urban development shall not violate these customary jurisdictions.

Another crucial related issue is the fact that a significant portion of lands within the IKN is still under mining and palm oil plantation concessions. These two business sectors are the main causes of deforestation and land conversions.[25] Until recently, there had been around 180,000 ha of land holding such concession statuses, of which 5,644 ha are situated in the KIPP zone and 42,000 ha in the inner-city zone.[26] Given how crucial customary lands are, spatial planning needs to address its full attention to such land concessions to prevent imminent conflicts from hindering the construction phases of urban development.

Local Economy
The mining sector is currently the biggest contributor to the regional GDP of Penajam Paser Utara Regency (25 per cent), followed by agriculture (21 per cent) and manufacturing (16 per cent).[27] Being designated as a national economic strategic area, the IKN's prospect for manufacturing activity is quite promising, particularly considering the intended expansion area of the IKN, which is designated to accommodate industrial growth, some of which is likely to be labour-intensive.

The greater concern, however, over the development of Nusantara is the potential disruption to the agricultural sectors (crops, livestock and fisheries). In Java, urban expansion has caused displacements of significant numbers of farming communities following the influx of secondary (manufacturing) and tertiary (retail) economic sectors.[28] The experience of Java has also shown the difficulties in controlling urban growth, particularly under the enormous pressure of economic development motives, due to the complexity of actors' interests and uneven power relations between government, private institutions, and farming (and/or other grassroots) communities.[29]

Spatial planning for the IKN needs to take on a strategic role to deploy control mechanisms to prevent potential social segregation, displacement and marginalization. Importantly, the commitment to build a socially inclusive city in IKN means the need to safeguard the local people and ensure to maintain their access to equitable or fair income, livelihoods, and resources. Hence, local economic development is as important to any of the proposed futuristic and sustainable urban designs as other aspects of planning.

THE ROLE OF SPATIAL PLANNING

Through the enactment of the 2007 Spatial Planning Act (Law No. 26/2007[30]), Indonesia marked its transformation from an authoritarian to a more decentralized system of spatial planning. Consequently, the local government has more power under this Act to plan and authorize development than before. As an adaptation to institutional changes, this planning act gave stronger recognition to sustainable development goals, institution-actor collaboration, and the integration of multisector and multiscalar jurisdictions, which were not sufficiently addressed in the previous 1992 planning Act.[31]

The Indonesian spatial planning framework applies a hierarchical system of policies where policies trickle down to the local level. For instance, the national general spatial plan (*Rencana Tata Ruang Wilayah Nasional*,

RTRWN) serves as the point of reference for planning at the provincial level (*Rencana Tata Ruang Wilayah Provinsi*, RTRWP). Meanwhile, local spatial planning (the RTRWK for the *Kabupaten/Kota*) is substantially driven by policies of the RTRWP, and so on. The policies of a smaller spatial unit plan provide more operational and detailed policies to guide development.

In this regard, Ministerial Regulation no. 11/2021 highlighted the importance of spatial planning (in particular the detailed planning/zoning regulation provided by the *Rencana Detail Tata Ruang*, RDTR) as a key instrument to regulate development in three functions: (1) Planning (*perencanaan tata ruang*), which involves conducting empirical studies to construct policies; (2) Utilization (*pemanfaatan tata ruang*), focusing on the enforcement of spatial policies in development programmes; and (3) Control (*pengendalian pemanfaatan ruang*), which supervises the implementation of spatial policies. The aim of operationalizing these functions is to ensure consistency between planning and implementation to accentuate convenient, safe, productive and sustainable spaces with a strong emphasis on the integration of the natural and built environments. Considering these functions, spatial planning can contribute to the development of Nusantara in several crucial areas, including but not limited to: (1) multiscalar and multisectoral integration; (2) a "clean and clear" development; and (3) devotion to sustainable development goals.

Multiscalar and Multisectoral Integration
As mentioned earlier, the framework of spatial planning centres on the practice of multidimensional integration. This involves multiscalar synergy channelling the integration of national and provincial spatial policies in local land use allocation. For Nusantara, this function is vital considering that the IKN represents the national interest to ensure the establishment of a green and sustainable city. In its practice, the Ministry of Agrarian Affairs and Spatial Planning (Kementerian ATR/BPN) is responsible for enforcing planning documents to meet a significant standard of quality. Meanwhile, the multisectoral conduit ensures spatial planning will produce policies that integrate the needs of various sectors. For this, the national authorities in ATR/BPN review the proposed local planning to ensure policies have considered multisectoral dynamics. Additionally, spatial planning itself is a multidisciplinary approach and thus, with planners' commitment towards thorough practice, spatial planning provides an avenue to synergize actors with different interests.

Ensuring a "Clean and Clear" Development

One of the important stages in constructing zoning regulation policies is the mapping of land status. Here, planners ensure the provision of accurate data through cross-referencing different sources. Public participation plays a key role here, which opens the opportunity to discover layers of customary land ownership. This exercise focuses on identifying ecosystem services, investigating disaster risks, and defining further mitigation options. Additionally, physical aspects of the receiving environment are scrutinized to map the baseline information to analyse the potential carrying capacity of the city region. All these components are then synthesized to conclude what is "go" and "no-go" development. Areas defined as "developable" imply that they are "clean and clear" (of endangering the environment and raising potential social conflicts).

Devotion to Sustainable Development Goals

The recognition of sustainable development goals in the current spatial planning act denotes the encouragement to adopt sustainable designs in urban development. Hence, spatial planning emphasizes controlling imminent urban growth and expansion. In the context of Nusantara, besides applying the concept of a "Forest City", the government is also committed to applying transfer-oriented development (TOD) design. The advantage of this TOD concept is the potential of reducing emissions due to the application of a more efficient mode of mobility like mass public transport.[32] In morphological terms, this neotraditional development encourages compaction and mixed land use in the neighbourhoods around transit locations.[33] This serves as a disincentive for urban expansion, which can result in the prevention or reduction of sprawl in the long run.

CHALLENGES TO THE CONDUCT OF SPATIAL PLANNING

In pursuit of creating a liveable capital city for IKN, the authors felt the need to contemplate whether planners had the capacity to thoroughly plan and execute this agenda. Can Indonesia plan a city, control its growth, and meet the expected outcomes of developing Nusantara under the current state of the spatial planning framework?

To find the answers, a workshop was conducted using the Synergistics approach, involving twenty-two participants encompassing private stakeholders (that is, housing developers) and various public sector actors at the national level who are likely to be involved in developing the new capital city. The workshop deployed three stages of "synergistic mapping": (1) mapping of the system and its problems/symptoms; (2) the identification of changes or intervention to the system; and (3) mapping of potential forward pathways.

To obtain insightful information, participants were asked to reflect on case studies of planning in other Indonesian cities and to consider how past problems are likely to resonate for the new capital city's planning and implementation.

System and Problem Mapping
The discussion at this workshop stage revealed at least three main issues. The first relates to the urbanization phenomenon, particularly in secondary cities of Java, which involves the uncontrollable expansion of urban areas. In most cases, the spread of low-density development in the urban outskirts has taken the most valuable lands for food production and the provision of other ecosystem services (e.g., catchment areas). The transformation of landscapes from predominantly rural to urban was not in line with the recommendations of spatial planning, which means that there is a substantial mismatch between planning and the actual development in the field.

The second issue was the gap between the CBD and the urban outskirts in terms of policy coverage—excessive policies in the CBD, as opposed to insufficient planning and urban growth control in peri-urban areas.

The third issue concerns the impact of uncontrollable urban growth, where the influx of urban development caused the displacement of local communities (e.g., farmers), social exclusion (due to cultural alienation), and environmental degradation caused by the rapid land conversion in protected areas.

Changes to and Interventions in the System
This stage of the workshop aimed to obtain insights into the possible drivers of the outlined problems. While urban problems may exhibit the complexities of the many aspects related to development, in this opportunity, the discussion covered whether the problems are likely rooted in the current state of planning. Participants expressed their concern about the prevalence of potential disruptions towards planning by "informal processes" that involve the conflicting interests of actors. This was addressed based on their reflection on existing cities' struggles to manage urban expansion.

The process of urbanization connects strongly with the dynamics of the political dimension and business sectors. The coalition of elite actors in Indonesia has been close to the process of plan-making (even if not directly involved) and through their power and connections, they could influence the direction of policies. For instance, in a vastly growing Surabaya around the late 1990s, developers were able to convince the city council to revise the land use map. As soon as developers acquired around 2,000 ha of land, the local governor instructed the city council to adjust the land use map according to the interest of the developer, changing the plan from previously green open space to a designated residential area. This case was raised in the workshop as a potential problem that is likely to occur in Nusantara.

Conclusions and Forward Pathways for Spatial Planning

The relocation of the capital city is undisputedly the biggest urban development project in Indonesia's history of spatial planning. The design of Nusantara adopts the concept of a modern and sustainable city with strong exposure to the cultural diversity of the Indonesian archipelago. From the viewpoint of the potential level of in-migration, the new capital city is likely to rapidly grow. In this regard, establishing a framework to ensure sustainable urban growth is of paramount importance. This is increasingly essential, considering the important nature reserves surrounding the designated location of IKN. The biodiversity within the 8.3 million ha of the East Kalimantan forest, the prevalence of customary lands, and the imminent population growth are the key components demanding the appropriate management of urban growth.

On the other hand, Indonesia needs to be vigilant of similar processes happening in the cities of Java, where capitalistic urbanization has prevented the production of socially inclusive and environmentally sound urban spaces. Many of these capitalistic modes of development have worsened or created social segregation and unequal access to basic infrastructures. Therefore, to make policies adaptive to change and responsive to the interests of various actors, the planning process for IKN needs to be integrative and inclusive in terms of sectors and actors, followed by continuous control and evaluation.

Notes

1. See Ibu Kota Nusantara, at https://ikn.go.id/
2. Undang-Undang Nomor 3 Tahun 2022 Tentang Ibu Kota Negara (UU No. 3/2022), full text of law available at https://peraturan.bpk.go.id/Home/Details/198400/uu-no-3-tahun-2022 (accessed 18 November 2022).

3. Joe Ravetz, *Deeper City: Collective Intelligence and the Pathways from Smart to Wise* (New York: Routledge: 2020).
4. World Bank, "East Asia's Changing Urban Landscape: Measuring a Decade of Spatial Growth", *Urban Development Series* (Washington, DC: World Bank, 2015), https://doi.org.10.1596/978-1-4648-0363-5
5. Ibid.
6. Dimas Wisnu Adrianto, "The Local Food System as a Strategy for the Rural-Urban Fringe Planning: A Pathway Towards Sustainable City Regions", in *Urban Environment Proceedings of the 10th Urban Environment Symposium* edited by S. Rauch and G.M. Morrison (Springer, 2012), pp. 83–95. https://doi.org.10.1007/978-94-007-2540-9
7. Dimas Wisnu Adrianto, Baqi Rindang Aprildahani, and Aris Subagiyo, "Tackling the Sprawl, Protecting the Parcels: An Insight into the Community's Preference on Peri-urban Agricultural Preservation", *Spaces and Flows: An International Journal of Urban and Extra Urban Studies* 3, no. 3 (2013): 115–25, http://ijf.cgpublisher.com/product/pub.203/prod.14
8. Brian A. Hoey. "Nationalism in Indonesia: Building Imagined and Intentional Communities Through Transmigration", *Ethnology* 42, no. 2 (2003): 109. doi: 10.2307/3773777.
9. Graham K. Brown. 'Trade, Employment and Horizontal Inequalities in New Order Indonesia', *European Journal of Development Research* 24, no 5 (2012): 735–752. https://doi.org.10.1057/ejdr.2012.29
10. Aiya Nurbaiti, "Jakarta Wins Global 2021 Sustainable Transport Award for Integrated Public Transportation", *Jakarta Post*, 31 October 2020, https://www.thejakartapost.com/news/2020/10/31/jakarta-wins-global-2021-sustainable-transport-award-for-integrated-public-transportation.html
11. Badan Pusat Statistik (National Bureau of Statistics), 2019.
12. Bosman Batubara, Michelle Kooy, and Margreet Zwarteveen, "Uneven Urbanisation: Connecting Flows of Water to Flows of Labour and Capital Through Jakarta's Flood Infrastructure", *Antipode* 50, no. 5 (2018): 1186–1205. https://doi.org.10.1111/anti.12401
13. "PERPRES No. 64 Tahun 2022 tentang Rencana Tata Ruang Kawasan Strategis Nasional Ibu Kota Nusantara Tahun 2022-2024", *Presidential Decree No. 64/2022*, https://peraturan.bpk.go.id/Home/Details/207620/perpres-no-64-tahun-2022 (accessed on 18 December 2022).
14. "Rencana Detail Tata Ruang IKN Timur dan IKN Barat" (Detailed Spatial Plan of East IKN and West IKN), 2022, https://ikn.go.id/tag/rdtr-ikn
15. Berita Pembangunan, "Bappenas Tekankan Tujuan Besar IKN untuk Mewujudkan Visi Indonesia 2045", Kementarian PPN/Bappenas, 11 March 2022, https://www.bappenas.go.id/berita/bappenas-tekankan-tujuan-besar-ikn-untuk-mewujudkan-visi-indonesia-2045-q6ojv (accessed on 12 November 2022).
16. Kementerian Pekerjaan Umum dan Perumahan Rakyat, "Konsep Negara Rimba Nusa Jadi Pemenang Lomba Desain Ibu Kota Negara Baru", Biro Komunikasi

Publik Kementerian PUPR, 23 December 2019, https://pu.go.id/berita/konsep-nagara-rimba-nusa-jadi-pemenang-lomba-desain-ibu-kota-negara-baru (accessed 21 December 2022).

17. *The Economist*, "Building a Megacity from Scratch", Economist Intelligence Unit 423, no. 9035 (2017): 38.
18. Ibid.
19. "Estimated Population Projection", *Bappenas*, 2022, https://www.bappenas.go.id/files/6e021d1d-85d0-4588-b8a9-c89bf08ea7cd/download#:~:text=Berdasarkan%20hasil%20proyeksi%2C%20jumlah%20penduduk,%E2%80%93%20318%2C9%20juta%20jiwa (accessed 21 December 2022).
20. "Delapan Prinsip Ibukota Negara" [Eight Principles of the National Capital], https://ikn.go.id/ (accessed 20 December 2022).
21. Richaldo Harianja, "Masyarakat Adat di Tengah Proyek IKN Nusantara", *Mongabay*, 17 August 2022, https://www.mongabay.co.id/2022/08/17/masyarakat-adat-di-tengah-proyek-ikn-nusantara/ (accessed 12 November 2022).
22. Andrew McWilliam, "Historical Reflections on Customary Land Rights in Indonesia", *Asia Pacific Journal of Anthropology* 7, no. 1 (2006): 45–64, https://doi.org.10.1080/14442210600551859
23. Ibrahim Ahmad, "Prinsip Keadilan Dalam Penyelesaian Sengketa Tanah Untuk Kepentingan Pembangunan", *Jurnal Legalitas* 3, no. 2: 15–25.
24. Wasisto Raharjo Jati, "A New Indonesian Capital City: A Conflict Pending", *Organisasi Riset Ilmu Sosial dan Humaniora BRIN*, 21 February 2022, https://ipsh.brin.go.id/2022/02/24/a-new-indonesian-capital-city-conflict-pending/ (accessed 13 November 2022).
25. Muhammad Refiansyach Dwiyanto, Astrid Damayanti, Tito Latif Indra and Muhammad Dimyati, "Land Use Changes Due to Mining Activities in Penajam Paser Utara Regency, East Kalimantan Province", *IOP Conference Series: Earth and Environmental Science. Bristol: IOP Publishing*, 1811, no. 1 (2021): 12088, https://doi.org.10.1088/1742-6596/1811/1/012088
26. WALHI, "Ibu Kota Negara Baru untuk Siapa, Publik atau Elit?", 17 December 2019, https://www.walhi.or.id/ibu-kota-negara-baru-untuk-siapa-publik-atau-elit
27. See https://ppukab.bps.go.id/
28. Adrianto, "The Local Food System as a Strategy for the Rural-Urban Fringe Planning"; Adrianto, Aprildahani and Subagiyo, "Tackling the Sprawl, Protecting the Parcels".
29. Dimas Wisnu Adrianto, "Peri-urbanisation and the Emergence of Integrated Spatial Planning and Governance – Managing the Growth of Peri-urban Areas in the Secondary City-regions of Indonesia" (PhD dissertation, University of Manchester, UK, 2022).
30. "Undang-undang (UU) tentang Penataan Ruang", *Database Peraturan*, 26 April 2007, https://peraturan.bpk.go.id/Home/Details/39908/uu-no-26-tahun-2007
31. Delik Hudalah and Johan Woltjer, "Spatial Planning System in Transitional Indonesia", *International Planning Studies* 12, no. 3 (2007): 291–303, https://

doi.org.10.1080/13563470701640176; Deden Rukmana, "The Change and Transformation of Indonesian Spatial Planning after Suharto's New Order Regime: The Case of the Jakarta Metropolitan Area," *International Planning Studies* 20, no. 4 (2015): 350–70, https://doi.org.10.1080/13563475.2015.1008723

32. Michael Lewyn, "Sprawl As How We Grow, Or How Government Makes Suburbia Sprawling" In *Government Intervention and Suburban Sprawl: The Case for Market Urbanism*, edited by Micheal Lewyn (New York: Palgrave Macmillan, 2017), pp. 95–128, https://doi.org.10.1057/978-1-349-95149-9_4

33. Yosef Rafeq Jabareen, "Sustainable Urban Forms: Their Typologies, Models, and Concepts", *Journal of Planning Education and Research* 26, no. 1 (2006): 38–52, https://doi.org.10.1177/0739456X05285119

References

Adrianto, Dimas Wisnu. 2012. "The Local Food System as a Strategy for the Rural-Urban Fringe Planning: A Pathway Towards Sustainable City Regions". In *Urban Environment Proceedings of the 10th Urban Environment Symposium*, edited by S. Rauch and G.M. Morrison, pp. 83–95. Springer. https://doi.org.10.1007/978-94-007-2540-9

———. 2022. "Peri-urbanisation and the Emergence of Integrated Spatial Planning and Governance: Managing the Growth of Peri-urban Areas in the Secondary City-Regions of Indonesia". PhD dissertation, University of Manchester, UK.

———, Baqi Rindang Aprildahani, and Aris Subagiyo. 2013. "Tackling the Sprawl, Protecting the Parcels: An Insight into the Community's Preference on Peri-urban Agricultural Preservation". *Spaces and Flows: An International Journal of Urban and Extra Urban Studies* 3, no. 3: 115–25.

Ahmad, Ibrahim. 2010. "Prinsip Keadilan Dalam Penyelesaian Sengketa Tanah Untuk Kepentingan Pembangunan". *Jurnal Legalitas* 3, no. 2: 15–25.

Badan Pusat Statistik (National Bureau of Statistics), 2019.

Bappenas. 2018. "Estimated Population Projection", 24 August 2018. https://www.bappenas.go.id/files/6e021d1d-85d0-4588-b8a9-c89bf08ea7cd/download#:~:text=Berdasarkan%20hasil%20proyeksi%2C%20jumlah%20penduduk,%E2%80%93%20318%2C9%20juta%20jiwa (accessed 21 December 2022).

Batubara, Bosman, Michelle Kooy, and Margreet Zwarteveen. 2018. "Uneven Urbanisation: Connecting Flows of Water to Flows of Labour and Capital Through Jakarta's Flood Infrastructure". *Antipode* 50, no 5: 1186–205. https://doi.org.10.1111/anti.12401

Berita Pembangunan. 2022. "Bappenas Tekankan Tujuan Besar IKN untuk Mewujudkan Visi Indonesia 2045". Kementerian PPN/Bappenas, 11 March 2022, https://www.bappenas.go.id/berita/bappenas-tekankan-tujuan-besar-ikn-untuk-mewujudkan-visi-indonesia-2045-q6ojv (accessed 12 November 2022).

Brown, Graham K. 2012. "Trade, Employment and Horizontal Inequalities in New Order Indonesia". *European Journal of Development Research* 24, no 5: 735–52. https://doi.org/10.1057/ejdr.2012.29

Dwiyanto, Muhammad Refiansyach, Astrid Damayanti, Tito Latif Indra, and Muhammad Dimyati. 2021. "Land Use Changes Due to Mining Activities in Penajam Paser Utara Regency, East Kalimantan Province". *IOP Conference Series: Earth and Environmental Science.* Bristol: IOP Publishing, 1811, no. 1 (2021): 12088. https://doi.org.10.1088/1742-6596/1811/1/012088

Economist, The. 2017. "Building a Megacity from Scratch". *Economist Intelligence Unit* 423, no. 9035.

Harianja, Richaldo. 2022. "Masyarakat Adat di Tengah Proyek IKN Nusantara". *Mongabay*, 17 August 2022. https://www.mongabay.co.id/2022/08/17/masyarakat-adat-di-tengah-proyek-ikn-nusantara/ (accessed 12 November 2022).

Hoey, Brian A. 2003. "Nationalism in Indonesia: Building Imagined and Intentional Communities Through Transmigration". *Ethnology* 42, no. 2: 109. https://doi.org.10.2307/3773777

Hudalah, Delik, and Johan Woltjer. 2007. "Spatial Planning System in Transitional Indonesia". *International Planning Studies* 12, no. 3: 291–303. https://doi.org.10.1080/13563470701640176

Ibu Kota Negara. 2022. "Delapan Prinsip Ibukota Negara" [Eight Principles of the National Capital]. 2022. https://ikn.go.id/ (accessed 20 December 2022).

———. 2022. "Ibu Kota Nusantara". 2022. https://ikn.go.id/ (accessed 20 December 2022).

———. 2022. "Rencana Detail Tata Ruang IKN Timur dan IKN Barat" [Detailed Spatial Plan of East IKN and West IKN], 2022. https://ikn.go.id/tag/rdtr-ikn

Jabareen, Yosef Rafeq. 2006. "Sustainable Urban Forms: Their Typologies, Models, and Concepts". *Journal of Planning Education and Research* 26, no. 1: 38–52. https://doi.org.10.1177/0739456X05285119

Jati, Wasisto Raharjo. 2022. "A New Indonesian Capital City: A Conflict Pending". *Organisasi Riset Ilmu Sosial dan Humaniora BRIN*, 21 February 2022, https://ipsh.brin.go.id/2022/02/24/a-new-indonesian-capital-city-conflict-pending/ (accessed 13 November 2022).

Kementerian Pekerjaan Umum dan Perumahan Rakyat. 2019. "Konsep Negara Rimba Nusa Jadi Pemenang Lomba Desain Ibu Kota Negara Baru". Biro Komunikasi Publik Kementerian PUPR, 23 December 2019. https://pu.go.id/berita/konsep-nagara-rimba-nusa-jadi-pemenang-lomba-desain-ibu-kota-negara-baru (accessed 21 December 2022).

Lewyn, Michael. 2017. "Sprawl as How We Grow, or How Government Makes Suburbia Sprawling". In *Government Intervention and Suburban Sprawl: The Case for Market Urbanism,* edited by Micheal Lewyn, pp. 95–128. New York: Palgrave Macmillan. https://doi.org.10.1057/978-1-349-95149-9_4

McWilliam, Andrew. 2006. "Historical Reflections on Customary Land Rights in Indonesia". *Asia Pacific Journal of Anthropology* 7, no. 1: 45–64, https://doi.org.10.1080/14442210600551859

Nurbaiti, Aiya. 2020. "Jakarta Wins Global 2021 Sustainable Transport Award for Integrated Public Transportation". *Jakarta Post*, 31 October 2020. https://www.

thejakartapost.com/news/2020/10/31/jakarta-wins-global-2021-sustainable-transport-award-for-integrated-public-transportation.html

Pemerintah Pusat. "Rencana Tata Ruang Kawasan Strategis Nasional Ibu Kota Nusantara Tahun 2022-2024" [National Strategic Plan for the IKN Region, 2022-2024]. BPK RI, 18 April 2022. https://peraturan.bpk.go.id/Home/Details/207620/perpres-no-64-tahun-2022 (accessed 16 December 2022).

———. "Undang-Undang Nomor 3 Tahun 2022 Tentang Ibu Kota Negara (UU No. 3/2022)". BPK RI, 15 February 2022. https://peraturan.bpk.go.id/Home/Details/198400/uu-no-3-tahun-2022 (accessed 18 November 2022).

"PERPRES No. 64 Tahun 2022 tentang Rencana Tata Ruang Kawasan Strategis Nasional Ibu Kota Nusantara Tahun 2022–2024". Presidential Decree No. 64/2022, https://peraturan.bpk.go.id/Home/Details/207620/perpres-no-64-tahun-2022 (accessed 18 December 2022).

Ravetz, Joe. 2020. *Deeper City: Collective Intelligence and the Pathways from Smart to Wise*. New York: Routledge.

Rukmana, Deden. 2015. "The Change and Transformation of Indonesian Spatial Planning after Suharto's New Order Regime: The Case of the Jakarta Metropolitan Area". *International Planning Studies* 20, no. 4: 350–370. https://doi.org.10.1080/13563475.2015.1008723

"Undang-undang (UU) tentang Penataan Ruang", *Database Peraturan*, 26 April 2007, https://peraturan.bpk.go.id/Home/Details/39908/uu-no-26-tahun-2007.

WALHI. "Ibu Kota Negara Baru untuk Siapa, Publik atau Elit?". 17 December 2019. https://www.walhi.or.id/ibu-kota-negara-baru-untuk-siapa-publik-atau-elit

World Bank. 2015. "East Asia's Changing Urban Landscape: Measuring a Decade of Spatial Growth". *Urban Development Series*. Washington, DC: World Bank. https://doi.org.10.1596/978-1-4648-0363-5.

6

THE TRANSFER OF THE NATIONAL CAPITAL (IKN)
The Domination of the Capitalist Political Economy and the Dynamics of Local Representation

Septi Satriani, Pandu Yuhsina Adaba and Imam Syafi'i

INTRODUCTION

Maaf ya pak, kalau suku Jawa kan bisa kembali ke Jawa. Suku Balik ini kemana kalau tanahnya tidak ada. Kita (tanah airnya) hanya di sini. Sejarah Orang Balik kemana? Hilang!

"I'm sorry, sir ... if the Javanese can return to Java, where do the Balik tribe return to if their land is not available? We (our tribal homeland) are only here. Where is the history of the Balik tribe? It is lost!"[1]

The opening is a direct quote from an interview with a person ("M") from the Balik tribe, one of the indigenous groups that have resided for generations in the new IKN location. There are concerns that the IKN development project could further marginalize the Balik tribe, who were already marginalized due to the development of Balikpapan City as an oil-producing and oil-processing town. The Balik tribe has argued that the transfer of IKN is an elitist, centralized policy, as it is lacking meaningful participation from the community in the planning process. This opinion is based on their experience of being excluded at all stages of construction, including when the government of the subdistrict marked the land for the planned location of the national capital. When the Balik tribe informed the government of the subdistrict about the capital transfer's possible effect on this tribe, the subdistrict government claimed not to understand the matter because the determination was in the hand of the central government.[2]

The IKN Law was ratified on 7 December 2021, after Indonesia's legislature considered and passed the proposed law in just forty-two days. The bill had incurred public resistance because public involvement in the deliberation process was insignificant. Procedurally speaking, indigenous peoples should have been involved in the initial consultation on IKN because they have long resided in the area to which the national capital will be moved. Apart from that, the IKN Law substantially contradicts at least eight articles in the 1945 Constitution. For instance, Article 1(2) of the Constitution stipulates that "sovereignty is in the hands of the people and implemented according to the 1945 Constitution" while Article 18B(2) stipulates that the State recognizes and respects customary law communities and their traditional rights, as long as they exist and abide by the principles of the unitary state of the Republic of Indonesia. Various individuals and groups (including the Alliance of Indigenous Peoples of the Archipelago (*Aliansi Masyarakat Adat Nusantara*, or AMAN), the Indonesian Forum for Living Environment (*Wahana Lingkungan Hidup Indonesia*, or WALHI), and *Poros Nasional Kedaulatan Negara* (PNKN) have petitioned the Constitutional Court, objecting to the IKN Law.[3]

When the IKN Law was discussed by the Indonesian House of Representatives (DPR) Special Committee (*Panitia Khusus Dewan*),[4] two supporting reasons for the capital transfer were given. First, there was a necessity for legal certainty to support the IKN transfer as the basis for the private sector and investors to immediately move into IKN development. Second, there was a need to cope with Java's, specifically Jakarta's, unsustainably high population growth. The IKN transfer is expected to overcome these issues while creating new economic growth outside Java and the transfer is expected to encourage such equitable development.

Several criticisms emerged in the process of ratifying the IKN Law. Inadequate public participation has been the key problem, as discussed above. One notable example is how a public hearing (*Rapat Dengar Pendapat Umum*, RDPU) purported to provide a public space for the people's input but was conducted only briefly.[5] Hence, the IKN regulation is viewed as accommodating the aspirations of some elite groups but overlooking public criticism against it.[6] This regulation continues to stir criticism, including the vast project's potential for environmental damage and accusations of land grabbing, "whitewashing" the obligations of mining companies, and the exclusion of indigenous peoples.[7]

Prior studies have raised related issues regarding the IKN transfer. Silalahi[8] and Hasibuan and Aisa[9] have highlighted the problem of potential construction costs for the new IKN, which could burden the national budget. Jati,[10] Nugroho,[11] Massola, Rosa, and Rompies[12] highlight how the Jakarta elites have not accommodated local aspirations, the lack of protection for indigenous peoples, and how the proposed IKN would potentially affect the residents. These authors argue that IKN's residents would be under pressure due to ambitious state projects that will result in the loss of their livelihoods and rights as indigenous peoples.

Prior studies such as Dewi et al.[13] and Taufik[14] have discussed community readiness in proposed IKN locations, which remains low. The local community has concerns due to unclear information from the national government regarding the IKN project. Similarly, WALHI and Kontras[15] have reported that the IKN project threatens the living spaces of inland (upstream) communities and communities along the coast of Balikpapan Bay. Another study conducted by Henley and Frigo[16] suggests that the proposed transfer of IKN will hurt the poor if they are moved to the outskirts of the new capital with minimal facilities.

This chapter argues that Jakarta's policy on the IKN transfer is an integral part of the operation of the new capital to solely create new investment space. In line with David Harvey's argument,[17] the role of the Indonesian state is deemed pivotal in facilitating the operation of this capital. Facilities provided by the state include regulatory design, spatial planning, regional planning, various financing incentives, and institutional designs. The present authors consider the transfer of the IKN as negatively affecting the local communities. In addition, this chapter observes the extent to which the IKN transfer policy has impacted the local communities and how the local communities have responded to it.

The Concept of a Capitalist Political Economy and Local Communities

The government has suggested that the transfer of IKN would lead to a multiplier effect. On various occasions, senior state officials have pointed out that the new IKN would serve as the epicentre of economic growth and equity, particularly outside Java. President Widodo has claimed that the construction of the new IKN will create new job opportunities as well as market potential.[18] As economics is inseparable from politics,[19] the IKN transfer may conflate more of the government and the elite group that holds economic power in Indonesia.

Harvey has argued that nonetheless, obstacles arise during the process of a capital expansion when venturing into new fields for investment.[20] On the other hand, the process of finding new exploited fields must be continuous to reinvest surplus capital.[21] In this situation, capitalists habitually execute the two inseparable tasks, which include encouraging the government to stipulate policies that facilitate finding new investment space[22] and increasing the pressure on the environment to produce more raw materials for production processes.[23] When they face labour shortages, one solution is to find new workers through immigration, export of capital, and transfer of labour from one city to a new city.[24] This extends the geographical range over which the capitalist is free to search for and spread out the supply of labour and raw materials.[25]

Harvey went on to argue that the formation of a new city provides a path for capitalists in navigating favourable fields for the production and absorption of surplus capital.[26] The presence of a new city, according to Harvey, provides a space for a radical transformation in a new lifestyle formation.[27] Various products are thus marketable to consumers. This new lifestyle acts as a potential market for the consumption of oil and electricity in enormous quantities.[28] As such, in Harvey's conception, the formation of a new city requires the support of the political authority, such as in the form of regulations to determine its intended location.

Harvey's concept pointed out that in the formation of a new city, the domination of capitalist political economy was found in the established cities (Paris, Mumbai, Sao Paulo), while Indonesia's IKN is a city that is still in the earliest planning stages, in which the domination of the capitalist political economy has been already detected, not only in the existing capital but also in the ongoing processes for the IKN, namely its regulations, proposed incentives, spatial plans, and other institutional designs.

The formation of a new city must involve local communities based on ethnicity, and interest groups, classified as local stakeholders. The involvement of local communities and local stakeholders is expected to foster a sense of ownership and support the implemented projects. Therefore, the formation of a new city is believed not to only have an impact on local communities based on ethnicity, but also this kind of project could affect a wider group.

Problematic IKN Development: Interview Findings

In this section, the authors discuss the technical aspects of the IKN, including reporting the key findings of their field research done in mid-2022, using

Harvey's theory as a framework. Taken together, these raise several questions about the problematic implications of the planning and work done so far and to be done on the IKN.

Domination of the Capitalist Political Economy in Planning Processes

The domination of the capitalist political economy can be detected in the planning stage, in the spatial planning for IKN, regulatory design, financial incentive and institutional design.

In terms of spatial planning, the National Strategic Area (*Kawasan Strategis Nasional*, KSN) for the IKN consists of the National Capital Region (*Kawasan Ibu Kota Negara*, KIKN), the National Capital Development Area, and the Coastal Waters of the National Capital. The State Capital Region serves as the core urban area of the KSN,[29] covering the Planning Areas (*Wilayah Perencanaan*, WP) for Central Government Core Area (*Kawasan Inti Pusat Pemerintahan*, KIPP), WP IKN West, WP IKN South, WP IKN East 1, WP IKN East 2, WP IKN North and WP IKN South. The aforementioned areas currently include Sepaku district and part of Loa Kulu district, which is part of North Penajam Paser Regency (Penajam Paser Utara, PPU). See Figure 6.1.

A series of IKN development activities have been implemented since President Widodo enacted Law Number 3 of 2022 and these are planned for at least the next two to three decades.[30] To meet water demand and flood control in the new capital, three dams were built as a water resource network system.[31] These include the Samboja Dam, Sepaku Semoi Dam, and Batu Lepek Dam. Batu Lepek Dam is located outside KSN IKN.[32]

To support logistics for the development of IKN Nusantara, the government reviewed six facilities: ITCI Hutan Manunggal Port, ITCI Kartika Utama Port, the former pier for the construction of the Balang Island Bridge, Langau Beach Pier, Buluminung Harbour, and Kariangau Harbour for their feasibility. The facility operated by PT ITCI at Manunggal was selected as the preferred choice for the main port.

In addition, four ports: one managed by the Makmur Mandiri Village Unit Business Entity (*Badan Usaha Milik Desa*, BumDes), Punggur Port by PT Tepian Benuo Paser, one managed by CV Mandiri Multi-Material, and BRM Port by PT Balikpapan Ready Mix, will join two pre-existing ones, Long Span Port of Balang Island in Tempadung, and the port managed by PT Tepian Sekapung Nusantara. Their main function is for loading and unloading logistical support for the IKN's construction and development. However, at present, only four have obtained permits from the port authority.[33]

FIGURE 6.1
Map of the State Capital of Nusantara of Indonesia

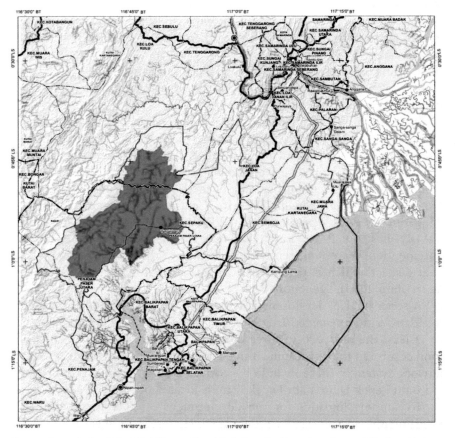

Source: Kementerian Sekretariat Negara Republik Indonesia, "Lampiran Nomor 1 Undang Undang Nomor 3 Tahun 2020 Tentang Ibu Kota Negara" [Appendix 1 of Law Number 3 of 2022 about the National Capital], *bpk.go.id*, 15 February 2022, https://peraturan.bpk.go.id/Home/Details/198400/uu-no-3-tahun-2022 (accessed 23 December 2022).

Even the land that the new IKN will sit on is controversial. WALHI in 2019 reported that IKN Nusantara is located on land riddled with pre-existing permits and concessions for mining, forestry, plantations, power plants and other business concessions, comprising 162 mining sites, forestry, oil palm plantations, and coal-fired power plants within an area of about 180 ha. This excludes concessions for the use of timber forest products and other ninety-four ex-coal mining pits. WALHI also reported that IKN

Nusantara stands on land under the control of prominent Indonesian oligarchs such as Sukanto Tanoto, Hashim Djojohadikusumo, current minister and potential 2024 presidential candidate Prabowo Subianto, Yusril Ihza Mahendra, current minister Luhut Binsar Pandjaitan, Lim Hariyanto Wijaya Sarwono and others.

Somewhat problematically, the Core Team from the regional planning agency (*Badan Perencanaan dan Pembangunan Daerah*, BAPPEDA) of East Kalimantan Province reported that the proposed capital area had undergone three changes, but in the end, its location was determined as being in PPU. From the present authors' interviews, civil society was not involved in crafting the substance of IKN Nusantara's development planning and the consultations were merely conducted as a formality to claim that there was community involvement.[34] Even worse, the East Kalimantan Provincial Ministry of Environment and Forestry was not granted official access to the Strategic Environmental Assessment Document of IKN (*Kajian Lingkungan Hidup Strategis*, KLHS) which was accessible to some others through informal channels using personal networks.

According to WALHI, the IKN Nusantara development project would benefit the owners of land concession permits, when these lands are utilized for IKN purposes. Some of the concessionaires are affiliated with companies with ties to the ruling regime. Following Harvey, the authors view the construction of dams, power plants, housing infrastructure, and other facilities as having the potential to provide space for the absorption of capital surplus from the owners of capital.

The Deputy Chairman of the Indonesian House of Representatives, Rachmat Gobel,[35] fully supports the development of IKN. He has stated that the development of IKN has the potential to have a positive impact on eastern Indonesia, which is the most underdeveloped in the country. According to Gobel, the social and environmental burdens (including crime, environmental pollution and natural damage) in Jakarta and Java are immense. Finally, Gobel has argued that the development of IKN can provide momentum to stimulate domestic investment and industry.[36]

In terms of financial design, the plans for building IKN Nusantara require a currently estimated budget of US$30.24 billion. Approximately 20 per cent of the total budget will be supported by the national budget while the rest is expected to be raised from the private sector and foreign investors. The IKN project will utilize the National Economic Recovery Programme (*Program Ekonomi Nasional*, PEN) funds which were originally allocated for post-COVID-19 pandemic recovery. Meanwhile, Jakarta has attempted to attract investors to join the IKN project by conducting promotions in international forums, including major economic summits in 2022, the year it was the G-20 chair. The appointment of international figures to help attract investment in their capacity as members of the IKN project steering committee was another arrow aimed at the investment target. Some influential names included Masayoshi Son (CEO of Softbank), Mohammad Bin Zayed (Crown Prince of Abu Dhabi) and Tony Blair (former prime minister of the United Kingdom). However, there remains huge certainty regarding investors' appetite for risk in funding the IKN. Most prominently, Softbank in March 2022 decided to withdraw its involvement from the IKN project and Masayoshi Son was replaced as a member of the steering committee.[37] Some reports suggested that Softbank's withdrawal was allegedly due to differing expectations of the proposed population of IKN: National Development Planning Agency (*Badan Perencanaan Pembangunan Nasional*, BAPPENAS) stated that IKN will be inhabited by around 1.5 million people in the first ten years[38] but Softbank expected 5 million inhabitants.

In terms of regulation design, the domination of the capitalist political economy was made obvious when the Minister of Agrarian Affairs and Spatial Planning/Head of the National Land Agency Agraria dan Tata Ruang (ATR)/*Kepala Badan Pertanahan Nasional* (BPN), Hadi Tjahjanto, extended a compromise to potential investors for the validity period of the "building rights" title (*Hak Guna Bangunan*, HGB), claiming that the validity period of the special HGB for investors in IKN could be up to 160 years. However, this directly clashes with Article 35(1) of the Basic Agrarian Law. The HGB grants the holder only the right to construct and "own" buildings on land that is not one's own for a maximum period of thirty years.[39] Contradictions like this must be resolved.

The continuing uncertainty surrounding the global economic and geopolitical fallout from the unending war in Ukraine, and Indonesia's domestic political risk factors related to leadership succession in the 2024 presidential election, also affect the IKN project's sustainability.[40]

Within the IKN development project team, a Special Working Group is chaired by Budiawan Sastrawinata, a leader of the Ciputra group, demanding incentives for investors who invest in IKN development projects in the form of cutting or eliminating taxes, increasing the duration of their concessions, and incentives for importing raw materials.[41] As this chapter will show, such requests have seemingly led the central government to compromise on other ideals, including protecting existing local community rights.

On 18 October 2022, the Nusantara Capital Authority (*Otorita Ibu Kota Nusantara*, OIKN) in collaboration with the Indonesian Chamber of Commerce and Industry (*Kamar Dagang dan Industri*, KADIN) held a Market Footprint Forum and Socialization of Nusantara Capital Investment, chaired by President Widodo. Widodo characterized the IKN as the future of Indonesia, saying that it was not just about physically moving ministry buildings and presidential palaces, but also about building a new work culture, mindset and new economic base for Indonesia.[42]

In terms of institutional design, the Indonesian government has facilitated the institutional design of IKN through the establishment of an OIKN, which is, however, considered ambiguous by some critics, due to the potential for overlapping authorities and the Agency's vague functions. This is because Indonesia's Constitution states that there are special regional government units, but higher recognition is given to units such as the Province of the Special Capital Region of Jakarta and the Special Region of Yogyakarta. In contrast, the position of the new OIKN as a regional government unit is vague or underdetermined, as the OIKN has not been regulated in detail even within the IKN Law. In the proposed IKN area, for instance, there are pre-existing subdistrict and village government units that have been operating for a long time. In addition, the relationship between these existing units and the OIKN remains undefined. The authority and provisions in the IKN Law are dominated by investment and economic considerations, not political or socio-cultural ones.[43]

To compound the matter, not many local residents in the new IKN location seem to be aware of OIKN activities. Several local government figures in PPU, Balikpapan and Samarinda are reportedly working on these activities. Various reports have also indicated the Authority's proposed function in promoting investment potential in IKN.[44] To facilitate this, the government published presidential regulation No. 62 (2022) government regulations. According to this regulation, Article 3 paragraph 2 (h and i), OIKN has the authority to "transfer, use, and/or dispose of assets over a portion of land with management rights to business actors by the agreement and holds the authority to grant and extend the terms of right to exploitation" (*Hak Guna Usaha*, HGU) and the HGB.[45]

The formation and designation of the OIKN as the institutional design for future IKN management might be compared to the development project for Batam as a commercial industrial area. Batam was constructed from the wilderness and was initially inhabited by only a few residents. Through the role of the Batam Authority, investment in the area was managed so that Batam has grown industrially and commercially to this day. The difference lies in that Batam was purpose-built for industrial and trade functions, while IKN Nusantara is planned as an environment-friendly, but much larger, government centre and smart city. The appointment of the OIKN as the IKN area manager that is directly responsible to the president would arguably create an ambiguous space for the local communities' participation. Most controversially, the IKN does not appear to have any democratic local channel like its own regional parliament (*Dewan Perwakilan Rakyat Daerah*, DPRD) in its institutional design.

Changing Landscape and Living Space

This section discusses the potential environmental and cultural heritage loss impacts of the IKN transfer on local communities in East Kalimantan. Based on the authors' field findings, there are two groups of local communities, differentiated by the area they occupy, who live in direct contact with the IKN project.

The first group comprises the local communities surrounding the main IKN area, including several indigenous groups who have inhabited this area for a long time and are highly dependent on the presence of rivers and forests. The human rights NGO AMAN's report indicates that twenty-one different indigenous peoples have inhabited the area for a long time. One of them is the Indigenous People of Balik Sepaku, considered an endangered indigenous group.[46] Other groups include migrants from Java and Sulawesi who previously participated in Suharto's New Order transmigration programme in the 1970s and 1980s. The second group comprises people who live along the coastal area of Balikpapan Bay, mostly working as traditional fishermen dependent on the condition of the bay waters as their fishing ground and who have resided for a long time there. Ethnically, this second group consists of various tribes such as Bugis, Bajo, Madurese, and Javanese.

The Balik tribe is classified as an endangered indigenous group. Based on an interview with the BAPPEDA of East Kalimantan province, the Balik tribe is included in the Paser Tribe, forming about 1.89 per cent of the latter's overall population.[47] No existing regulation acknowledges however the tribe's history or the protection of their tribal lands in the Sepaku. According to a traditional leader from the Balik Tribe, he and his family have lived in the Sepaku area since 1987 but were not at all involved nor had they received adequate information regarding the IKN transfer project. The land they own, located in the planned core area of IKN, is now planted with palm oil trees, a main source of income for their family.

Several authors have discussed the vulnerability of the Balik tribe to future development—the Multatuli Project, for instance, reported that the

Balik tribe has long been marginalized since logging companies took control of the lands that they lived on, long before the IKN transfer.[48] Massola, Rosa and Rompies argue that the arrival of logging companies since the New Order era has turned that location's forests into monoculture plantations, dominated by *sengon*, acacia, and eucalyptus plants, hindering the Balik tribe from living off forests and rivers.

Separately, mining expansion has accelerated deforestation and ecological damage on Borneo Island. Mining activities which rapidly penetrate the forest upstream has caused serious sedimentation in rivers. These activities have triggered floods and water crises. Such conditions also have the potential to turn tropical areas into desert areas.[49] With the immense expansion of oil mines, the Balik tribe was forcefully moved and fled into remote villages, despite dwelling in the Balikpapan Bay area for generations.

Mine expansion has dominated the existence and development of Balikpapan City. In fact, the commemoration of Balikpapan City on 10 February 1987 marks the first oil drilling activity in the area.[50] Then President Suharto's Decree No. 6 of 1985 allegedly disregarded the existence and history of the Balik tribe and misappropriated the Balik tribal name to claim it for the new city.

The locals have long used the Sepaku River and its various tributaries in the PPU and Balikpapan areas. Worryingly, IKN development activities are projected to have an adverse environmental impact on the Sepaku River and several tributaries. One example is the construction of a river intake project in Sukaraja Village, which threatens the water supply for ninety families in the Sepaku Lama area. Most of them are Baliknese, while the rest are immigrants from Java and Bugis. Naem and Agustiorini have argued that this project is intended to supply the IKN with clean water but instead, it has disrupted the residents' existing water supply.

For the local community, the Sepaku River also serves as one of the main transportation routes connecting the settlements to their precincts and fields. This river is an important route for marketing produce such as durian, banana, jackfruit, papaya, and various other tropical fruits to Balikpapan. Naem and Agustiorini have said that many immigrants from Java and Bugis adopted the Baliknese way of cultivating bananas in their gardens along the banks of the river. They plant fruit trees in the fields some distance behind the river. Thus, these dwellers with various ethnic backgrounds share similar spaces and create their collective experiences along the Sepaku River.

Unlike Javanese or Bugis who are considered to have "homelands" (Java Island and Sulawesi Island), it is likely that the existence and livelihoods of the Balik tribe, already experiencing several processes of marginalization, will be utterly threatened by the IKN transfer. In the face of past pressures, they have tended to relocate to avoid conflict.

In the past, the Balik tribe moved from the Balikpapan area into the hinterland of Sepaku and its surroundings. They avoided the waves of immigrants from the outside. However, one tribe member said that there are no more inland areas for any future moves.[51] For the Balik tribe, Sepaku is their last homeland—they no longer have any option to move since they were eased or forced out due to the expansion of oil fields and large plantations. Meanwhile, the current policy of relocating Indonesia's IKN threatens their last lands, eliminating their history and existence.[52]

The IKN relocation project shapes the upstream of Balikpapan Bay as a buffer zone, containing a mangrove ecosystem that stretches for 17 km. This area is a protected area for the Somber Watershed (Daerah Aliran Sungai, DAS) in Balikpapan City to Riko Watershed in the PPU Regency administrative area.[53] In total, fifty-four sub-watersheds are parented in this bay. It includes the Sein Wain watershed, which is part of the Wain River Protection Forest.[54]

Currently, there are two industrial areas in Balikpapan Bay, including Kariangau Industrial Estate (*Kawasan Industri Kariangau*, KIK) on the Balikpapan side and Buluminung Industrial Estate (*Kawasan Industri Buluminung*, KIB) on the PPU side. These two industrial areas have caused great ecological pressure on Balikpapan Bay. The existence of industrial areas has encouraged the annual shrinkage of mangrove forest cover, due to deforestation activities to build industrial ports, people's ports and palm oil processing factories. Recorded over eleven years (1995–2006), Balikpapan Bay has lost 1,000 ha of mangrove cover. This shrinkage threatens the ecological function of Balikpapan Bay as a wildlife habitat and fishing ground area for traditional fishermen.[55]

The Balikpapan Coastal Working Group stated that there have been five mangrove forest areas in Jenebora Village, PPU that have been converted. Disputes over ownership claims in the former mangrove forest have occurred since the IKN transfer project was implemented by the central government. Community groups are not given space for dialogue without adequate mitigation efforts after the forest's conversion, which further increases the ecological pressure on the area. This in turn threatens the living space of fishermen who have long lived near and depended on the waters of Balikpapan Bay.

Hardjanto pointed out that in Balikpapan Bay, about 10,000 traditional fishermen proliferate over eight fishing villages, fishing as a livelihood.[56] More than 250,000 people depend on the region's environmental services by finding cages and ponds scattered on the coast of this bay, both on the PPU and Balikpapan sides.[57] The damage to Balikpapan Bay means the destruction of the fishing grounds for traditional fishermen, as they cannot move to a more open area in the Makassar Strait. Their technology and experience are limited and thus their fishing is limited to one day of activity in the bay.

Various industrial activities including the IKN project use Balikpapan Bay as the main route for logistics delivery. The route is narrow and threatens the fishing ground area for fishermen and the coastal communities in general, due to the intense ship traffic. It is exacerbated by the high level of sedimentation from the logging of mangrove forests.[58] The IKN transfer project is inadequately supported by the study regarding the impacts on Balikpapan Bay. Thus, the IKN project poses a threat to the conservation efforts of Balikpapan Bay, performed by the local communities.[59]

Local Representatives' Responses

The authors conducted interviews with the concerned parties to record some of the responses of local representatives to the policy of the IKN's transfer to East Kalimantan. The interviews were limited in scope due to research and time constraints but still provide some useful information as to how the IKN transfer is affecting the local residents. Key interviewees consisted of representatives of the local government, civil society organizations, and residents around the IKN location. For the protection of the interviewees, the authors will identify them only using their initials (see Annex for list of interviews by date and location).

In general, the local response can be summarized as one of acceptance, critical acceptance, or even outright rejection. Some people have accepted the transfer plan of IKN to East Kalimantan and even provided support, driven by hopes for infrastructural improvements and job creation. The IKN is expected to improve the welfare of the communities. Those who reject or critically accept the move include local communities' service organizations (CSOs) such as Mining Advocacy Network (*Jaringan Advokasi Tambang*, JATAM), WALHI East Kalimantan, the Indonesian Legal Aid Institute (*Lembaga Bantuan Hukum*, LBH) Samarinda, the Coastal Working Group (*Kelompok Kerja, Pesisir, Pokja Pesisir*), and the 30 Working Group (*Kelompok Kerja 30, Pokja 30*) and local university students and academics. The latter groups see the IKN as accelerating East Kalimantan's environmental damage.

Leaders of the civil society movement focus their activities on the two cities, Samarinda and Balikpapan. Samarinda, the capital of East Kalimantan, has moderately advanced infrastructure compared to other regions. Balikpapan has excellent infrastructure due to its position as a business city. These two cities are connected by a highway, accessible by car within two hours. In addition, Samarinda and Balikpapan are centres of activity for educated people in East Kalimantan, with several universities that have fostered student movements. Samarinda and Balikpapan also serve as secretariat offices for many CSOs.

One of the nodes of the civil society movement in East Kalimantan lies in the Environmental Advocates Network (*Jaringan Advokat Lingkungan*, JAL), comprising several community alliances. They actively respond to environmental issues and act on issues in groups including the animal rescue coalition, the coastal working group, the Balikpapan Bay Care Forum, and others. JAL is highly critical of the IKN transfer policy, highlighting the threats to the protection of the Mahakam dolphin habitat, the mangrove ecosystem of Balikpapan Bay, and the biodiversity of various sub-watersheds that lead to Balikpapan Bay. JAL emphasizes the risk to the livelihoods of the coastal communities of Balikpapan Bay, as a side effect of the IKN transfer.[60]

Critical attitudes towards the IKN transfer policy emerged from community organizations with national networks such as LBH Samarinda, JATAM Kaltim, and WALHI Kaltim. Public participation and transparency have been minimal during the drafting process of the IKN Law. Echoing JAL's complaints, these groups perceive that the policy threatens the safety of people's living spaces and biodiversity. As such, the transfer of IKN is perceived as similar to the actions of mining company oligarchs, harming the people.

Activist groups formed the East Kalimantan Communities Coalition to Revoke the IKN Law in January 2022. They held several rallies and open discussions to voice their aspirations. For these actions, several figures from this group claimed to have received intimidation from an unknown source in the form of terror via threatening telephone calls. Some of the intimidation was experienced by the families of these activists.[61]

In contrast, from the authors' conversation with the management of the Balikpapan Alliance of Independent Journalists (*Aliansi Jurnalis Independen*, AJI), there was a tendency for some to accept and even support the IKN transfer policy,[62] and reasoning that there will be new points of growth in

East Kalimantan, creating jobs and improving the people's welfare. However, AJI Samarinda—a different area—had a critical attitude against the non-procedural aspects of the IKN planning process and against those which had the potential to harm the communities. Several administrators of AJI Samarinda stated that at the editor-in-chief level, the policy direction was for news to be positive and supportive of the IKN transfer policy. However, the board of AJI Samarinda continues to provide balanced coverage.[63]

An optimistic attitude was shown by the Borneo Orangutan Survival Foundation (BOSF), which has experience in processing critical land in the form of a stretch of reeds via reforestation over twenty years. BOSF claims the land covers an area of about 1,850 ha in Samboja Lestari. BOSF admitted that the head of the OIKN had visited the location incognito.[64] During the visit, BOSF presented its experience in reforestation and suggested that the IKN development adopt BOSF's strategy in performing reforestation for the Samboja Lestari area. However, in the context of the IKN transfer policy, BOSF will participate only when requested.[65]

The new IKN location in Sepaku district, PPU Regency, is accessible by land within 2 to 3 hours from the PPU capital (a similar travel time from the cities of Balikpapan and Samarinda). The newly designated IKN area is presently a village with the dominance of agricultural and plantation activities, and industrial and food crop plantations by the local communities and companies.

One of the issues that arose was the indigenous people of the Balik tribe, who have inhabited the Sepaku area for generations. Physical identification (and differentiation) for this tribe is challenging, as tribe members look like those of the immigrant population. There is no distinctive feature that distinguishes them from the non-tribal people in the Sepaku area. Hence, their claim to be indigenous people with distinctive characteristics is debatable. Several figures from the Balik tribe expressed concern regarding their fate if the IKN were relocated to Sepaku, distressed that their livelihoods would be eliminated.

In contrast, the AMAN PPU welcome the transfer of the IKN to the Sepaku area. They believe that it is a tribal myth that someday, the "centre of civilization" will move to their territory. They believe that the predictions of their ancestors as coming true when these are linked with the proposed IKN transfer.[66] However, they hope that the IKN development would involve the participation of indigenous peoples to prevent potentially damaging consequences.

Regarding the attitude of the Sepaku communities in general, there is a separate survey conducted by the Branch Executive Board of Indonesian

National Student Movement (*Dewan Pimpinan Cabang Gerakan Mahasiswa Nasional Indonesia*, DPC GMNI) Balikpapan of 104 informants distributed over five villages in Sepaku district. The author, Taufik, argues that overall, the communities accept the IKN transfer policy in their area. Nevertheless, the socialization received by the communities is inadequate. Even some local government officials did not understand the benefits of IKN transfer to Sepaku. They also have concerns about the potential for floods and droughts if the IKN development neglects environmental sustainability concerns. In addition, the local communities seem fearful of competing with the newcomers (read: immigrants) when the IKN is relocated.

Conclusion

This chapter argues that the IKN transfer policy is in line with Jakarta's interest in creating new investment space. Even though many elements of Indonesian society opposed the passage of the IKN law, the legislature still passed it on 18 January 2022 and the government ratified it on 15 February 2022. The law's hasty passage indicates the state's reluctance to listen to input from various parties who still object to this law.

Another problematic issue is how the government has unilaterally determined certain spatial designs and regional plans on the concession forest lands owned by the capitalists. The KLHS serves as a study that in theory must be applied by the local government before it grants permits for land and forest management, after determining the location of the IKN. This does not seem to have been done. However, KLHS was published after the government decided on the location of IKN. Furthermore, the public has difficulty accessing this KLHS.

In terms of funding, the state tends to provide sales and incentives that are ambiguous and may even contradict existing laws and regulations. Legal conflicts, such as the aforementioned granting of HGB for up to 160 years to IKN investors being contrary to the Basic Agrarian Law, must be resolved for fairness and consistency.

Last, the institutional design in the form of an authorized body places the prerogative mainly in the hands of the president. The absence of a legislative body in IKN potentially means that there is no counterbalancing power. The absence of space for a balance of power illustrates that the state minimizes "noise" and "resistance", long as it does not disturb the comfort and interests of investors. Even though the transfer of the new capital has not taken place yet, the domination of the capitalist political economy is evident in the design of its regulations and the preparation of spatial and regional plans, which has allegedly already caused a negative impact on the local communities.

Annex: List and Dates of Interviews

(Interviews conducted by all co-authors; individual interviewees' identities anonymised with initials)

13 June 2022: MS, Balikpapan, T, Balikpapan, HS, Balikpapan, A, Samarinda*
14 June 2022: SB, Samarinda*, AJI, Samarinda, R, Samarinda
15 June 2022: BAPPEDA Kalimantan Timur, Samarinda, R, Samarinda
16 June 2022: DLHK PPU, Penajam Paser Utara; Aman PPU, Penajam Paser Utara
17 June 2022: DLH Kalimantan Timur, Samarinda; WALHI, Samarinda; B, Samarinda
18 June 2022: D, Pemaluan, M, Pemaluan

Notes

1. Interview with M, 18 July 2022.
2. Interviews with M, 18 July 2022; D, 18 July 2022; Y, 17 July 2022; Ru, 14 July 2022; and R, 15 July 2022.
3. Mahkamah Konstitusi Republik Indonesia, "Siaran Pers Gugatan UU IKN Disidangkan" [Constitutional Court, Republic of Indonesia Press release (on) the IKN Lawsuit in Session], *mkri.id*, 25 April 2022, https://www.mkri.id/public/content/infoumum/press/pdf/press_2283_25.04.22%2053.PUU-XX.2022%20I%20UU%20IKN%20MHM.pdf (accessed 6 December 2022).
4. DPR-RI, "Siaran Pers Rapat Dengan Menteri Investasi, Nevi Zuariana Pertanyakan Investasi Untuk IKN" [Press Release: Meeting with Minister of Investment, Nevi Zuariana Questioning Investment of IKN], *dpr.go.id*, 10 June 2022, https://www.dpr.go.id/berita/detail/id/39236/t/Rapat+dengan+Menteri+Investasi%2C+Nevi+Zuariana+Pertanyakan+Investasi+untuk+IKN (accessed 27 September 2022).
5. Genta Tenri Mawangi, "Indonesian Parliamentary Center: UU IKN Minim Partisipasi Publik" [Indonesian Parliamentary Center: IKN Lawsuit has Minimal Public Participation], *Antaranews.com*, 21 January 2022, https://www.antaranews.com/berita/2658269/indonesian-parliamentary-center-uu-ikn-minim-partisipasi-publik (accessed 27 September 2022).
6. CNN Indonesia, "Formappi: RUU IKN Supercepat, Sembunyi dan Minim Partisipasi Publik" [Formappi: IKN Bill Superfast, Stealthy, and with Minimal Engagement], *CNN Indonesia.com*, 15 January 2022, https://www.cnnindonesia.com/nasional/20220114152427-32-746748/formappi-ruu-ikn-supercepat-sembunyi-dan-minim-partisipasi-publik (accessed 9 December 2022).

7. WALHI, "Ibukota Untuk Siapa?" [Whose Capital?], *walhi.or.id*, 18 December 2019, https://www.walhi.or.id/ibu-kota-negara-baru-untuk-siapa (accessed 27 September 2022).
8. S.A.F. Silalahi, "Dampak Ekonomi dan Resiko Pemindahan Ibu Kota Negara" [Economic Impact and Risks of the IKN Transfer], *Info Singkat* [Summary], vol. XI, no. 16/II/Puslit/August 2019 (DPR-RI, House of Representatives, Republic of Indonesia).
9. Reni Ria Armayani Hasibuan and Siti Aisa, "Dampak dan Resiko Perpindahan Ibukota Terhadap Ekonomi Indonesia" [The Impact and Risk of Transfer the National Capital to Indonesian Economy], *At-Tawasuth: Jurnal Ekonomi Islam* V, no. 1 (2020), pp. 183–84.
10. Wasisto Raharjo Jati, "A New Capital City for Who? Central-Local Tensions in Indonesia", *New Mandala*, 23 August 2022, https://www.newmandala.org/a-new-capital-city-for-who-central-local-tensions-in-indonesia/ (accessed 8 December 2022).
11. Bhakti Eko Nugroho, "Perlindungan Hak Masyarakat Adat dalam Pemindahan Ibukota Negara" [The Protection of the Rights of Indigenous People in the Transfer of National Capital], *Jurnal Ilmu Sosial dan Ilmu Politik Universitas Jambi* 6, no. 1 (2022), p. 64.
12. James Massola, Amilia Rosa, and Karuni Rompies, "The Tribe in the Path of Indonesia's 'Almost Impossible' New Capital", *Sydney Morning Herald*, 15 September 2019, https://www.smh.com.au/world/asia/the-tribe-in-the-path-of-indonesias-almost-impossible-new-capital-20190912-p52qu9.html (accessed 17 October 2022).
13. Maulida Rachmalia Dewi, Elin Diyah Syafitri, and Ajeng Nugraganing Dewanti, "Analisis Kesiapan Masyarakat Kecamatan Sepaku dan Samboja Terhadap Rencana Pemindahan Ibu Kota Negara Indonesia" [Analysis of the Readiness of the People of Sepaku and Samboja Districts for the Plan for the Transfer of the Indonesian National Capital], *Jurnal Pembangunan Wilayah dan Kota* 16, no. 4 (2020).
14. M. Taufik, "Policy Brief Perpindahan Ibu Kota Negara di Wilayah Kalimantan Timur" [Policy Brief on the Transfer of the National Capital in East Kalimantan], Balikpapan Branch Executive Board of Indonesian National Student Movement (Dewan Pimpinan Cabang Gerakan Mahasiswa Nasional Indonesia, DPC GMNI Balikpapan), 2022.
15. Kontras, "Catatan Kritis Pelanggaran HAM di Balik Pemindahan Ibukota Baru" [Critical Notes on the Violation of Human Rights in the Transfer of the New Capital], *kontras.org*, March 2022, https://kontras.org/wp-content/uploads/2022/03/Final_Catatan-Kritis-Pemindahan-IKN.pdf (accessed 8 December 2022).
16. David Henley and Giulia Frigo, "Lessons from Brasilia: On the Empty Modernity of Indonesia's New Capital", *New Mandala*, 14 April 2020, https://www.newmandala.org/lessons-from-brasilia-on-the-empty-modernity-of-indonesias-new-capital/ (accessed 8 December 2022).
17. David Harvey, *Rebel Cities: From the Right to the City to the Urban Revolution* (London: Verso, 2012).

18. Egi Adyatama, "Jokowi Targetkan Ada 3 Juta Lapangan Kerja Baru di Ibukota Baru" [Jokowi Targets 3 Million New Job Opportunities in the New Capital], *Tempo.co*, 26 February 2022, https://bisnis.tempo.co/read/1312546/jokowi-targetkan-ada-3-juta-lapangan-kerja-baru-di-ibu-kota-baru (accessed 25 December 2022).
19. Heather Whiteside, *Capitalist Political Economy: Thinkers and Theories* (London: Routledge, 2020).
20. Harvey, *Rebel Cities*, p. 6.
21. Ibid.
22. Bruce R. Scott, "The Political Economy of Capitalism", *Harvard Business School Working Paper* No.07-037, December 2006, https://www.hbs.edu/faculty/Pages/item.aspx?num=23129 (accessed 12 December 2022).
23. Harvey, *Rebel Cities*, p. 5.
24. Ibid.
25. Ibid., p. 6.
26. Ibid., pp. 1–12.
27. Ibid., p. 14.
28. Ibid., p. 9.
29. Kementerian Sekretariat Negara Republik Indonesia, "Peraturan Presiden Nomor 64 tahun 2022 Tentang Rencana Tata Ruang Strategis Nasional Ibu Kota Nusantara Tahun 2022–2024" [Presidential Regulation No. 64 of 2022 Concerning the National Strategic Spatial Plan for the National Capital for 2022-2024], *bpk.go.id*, 18 April 2022, https://peraturan.bpk.go.id/Home/Details/207620/perpres-no-64-tahun-2022 (accessed 06 January 2022).
30. Rayful Mudassir, "Pilah Pilih Pelabuhan Utama IKN" [Selecting the Main Port of IKN], *Bisnis Indonesia*, 7 April 2022, https://bisnisindonesia.id/article/pilah-pilih-pelabuhan-utama-ikn (accessed 8 December 2022).
31. See Article 54, Presidential Regulation of the Republic of Indonesia No. 64 of 2022 concerning Spatial Planning for the National Strategic Area of the Indonesian Capital City of 2022–2042.
32. Muhammad Ridwan, "3 Bendungan Akan Dibangun di IKN Nusantara, Inidaftarnya" [Three Dams to be Built at IKN Nusantara, Here Is the List], *Bisnis.com*, 11 May 2022, https://ekonomi.bisnis.com/read/20220511/45/1532142/3-bendungan-akan-dibangun-di-ikn-nusantara-ini-daftarnya (accessed 8 December 2022).
33. Novi Abdi, "6 Pelabuhan Siap Layani Angkutan Logistik IKN Nusantara" [Six Ports Ready to Serve IKN Nusantara Logistics Transportation], *kaltim.antaranews* 18 October 2022, https://kaltim.antaranews.com/berita/171057/enam-pelabuhan-siap-layani-angkutan-logistik-ikn-nusantara (accessed 20 October 2022).
34. Interviews with Y, 17 July 2022; D, 18 July 2022; and R, 14 July 2022.
35. Rahmat Gobel is an Indonesian businessman and politician. He is a second-generation scion of the Gobel family, which controls the former National Gobel Group founded by his father, Thayeb Mohammad Gobel. The company has changed its name to the Panasonic Gobel Group.
36. Puri Mei Setyaningirum, "3 Catatan Penting Rachmat Gobel Terkait IKN"

[3 Important Notes by Rachmat Gobel Regarding the IKN], *Warta Ekonomi*, 20 January 2022, https://wartaekonomi.co.id/read387990/3-catatan-penting-rachmat-gobel-terkait-ikn (accessed 24 October 2022).
37. Lidya Julita Sembiring, "Softbank Mundur dari Proyek IKN, Sri Mulyani Buka Suara" [Softbank Retreats from the IKN Project, Sri Mulyani Speaks], *CNBC Indonesia*, 22 March 2022, https://www.cnbcindonesia.com/news/20220322162754-4-325010/softbank-mundur-dari-proyek-ikn-sri-mulyani-buka-suara (accessed 27 September 2022).
38. Katadata, "Alasan Softbank Batalkan Investasi di Ibu Kota Negara" [Reasons for Softbank Cancelling Investments in the National Capital], 23 March 2022, https://katadata.co.id/yuliawati/berita/623a9d79a3a1e/alasan-softbank-batalkan-investasi-di-ibu-kota-negara (accessed 27 September 2022).
39. Wibi Pangestu Pratama, "Menteri ATR: Perizinan di IKN Bisa Diperpanjang Hingga 160 Tahun" [Minister of ATR: Licensing in IKNs Can Be Extended up to 160 Years], *Bisnis.com*, 7 October 2022, at https://ekonomi.bisnis.com/read/20221007/9/1585201/menteri-atr-perizinan-di-ikn-bisa-diperpanjang-hingga-160-tahun (accessed 5 December 2022).
40. Wibi Pangestu Pratama, "Ekonom Ungkap Alasan Softbank Batal Investasi IKN, Gara-gara Jokowi Presiden 3 Periode?" [Economists Reveal Reasons for Softbank Canceling IKN Investment, Because of Jokowi's 3 Term Presidency?], *Bisnis.com*, 13 March 2022, https://ekonomi.bisnis.com/read/20220313/9/1509940/ekonom-ungkap-alasan-softbank-batal-investasi-ikn-gara-gara-jokowi-presiden-3-periode (accessed 27 September 2022).
41. Rezza Adi Pratama, "Gerilya Menjaring Investor IKN" [Guerrilla Attracts IKN Investors], *katadata.co.id*, 25 August 2022, https://katadata.co.id/rezzaaji/indepth/6307305357987/gerilya-menjaring-investor-ikn (accessed 27 September 2022).
42. Kadin Indonesia, "KADIN: Investor Berperan Besar dalam Membangun Ibukota Negara Nusantara" [KADIN: Investors Play a Major Role in Building the National Capital], *Kadin.id*, 19 October 2022, https://kadin.id/kabar/kadin-investor-berperan-besar-dalam-membangun-ibu-kota-negara-nusantara/ (accessed 9 December 2022).
43. Sucipto, "Bentuk Badan Otorita IKN Nusantara Dinilai Rancu" [The Form of the Authority of IKN Nusantara Is Considered Ambiguous], *Kompas.id*, 15 February 2022, https://www.kompas.id/baca/nusantara/2022/02/15/bentuk-badan-otorita-ikn-nusantara-dinilai-rancu (accessed 27 September 2022).
44. Vendy Yhulia Susanto, "Otorita IKN—Kadin Lakukan Penjajakan Pasar Peluang Investasi di IKN" [IKN Authority—Kadin Examines the Market for Investment Opportunities in IKN], *Kontan.co.id*, 17 October 2022, https://nasional.kontan.co.id/news/otorita-ikn-kadin-lakukan-penjajakan-pasar-peluang-investasi-di-ikn (accessed 27 September 2022).
45. Syamsul Ashar, "Permudah Investasi di IKN, Pemerintah Tawarkan HGU 95 Tahun dan HGB 80 Tahun" [Facilitate Investment in IKN, Government Offers 95 Years

HGU and 80 Years HGB], *Kontan.co.id*, 17 September 2022, https://nasional.kontan.co.id/news/permudah-investasi-di-ikn-pemerintah-tawarkan-hgu-95-tahun-dan-hgb-80-tahun (accessed 27 September 2022).
46. AMAN, "Masyarakat Adat Menggugat IKN" [Indigenous Peoples Sue the IKN], 21 April 2022, https://www.aman.or.id/news/read/masyarakat-adat-menggugat-uu-ikn (accessed 29 August 2022).
47. Interview with M, 15 July 2022.
48. Abdallah Naem and Sarah Agustiorini, "Nestapa Suku Balik: Dulu Hutannya Digunduli, Kini Hidupnya Digusur IKN" [The Grief of the Balik Tribe: Formerly Their Forest Was Deforested, Now Their Lives Are Evicted by IKN], *Project Multatuli*, 1 August 2022, https://projectmultatuli.org/nestapa-suku-balik-dulu-hutannya-digunduli-kini-hidupnya-digusur-ikn/ (accessed 29 August 2022).
49. Interview with Y, 17 June 2022: The Balik tribe spreads from the Tunan watershed area to Balikpapan bordering Kartanegara. Previously, it was dominant in Balikpapan and this extended to Sepaku. The Balik tribe is considered a shy tribe as they tend to avoid crowds. However, according to tribe member Y, if they kept dodging, they would be lost, and there would no longer any history of the native tribes in the new capital.
50. A. Rahmayani, "Balikpapan Pada Awal Abad ke 20" [Balikpapan at the Beginning of the 20th Century], *Walasuji* 6, no. 1 (2015): 129–31.
51. Interview with YS, 16 June 2022.
52. Interviews with YS, 16 June 2022; M, 18 June 2022.
53. Interview with YS, 16 June 2022.
54. Y.S. Hardjanto, "Teluk Balikpapan yang Terus Tergerus Akibat Ekspansi Industri" [Balikpapan Bay Continues to Be Eroded Due to Industrial Expansion], *Mongabay.co.id*, 1 April 2015, https://www.mongabay.co.id/2015/04/01/teluk-balikpapan-yang-terus-tergerus-akibat-ekspansi-industri/ (accessed 29 September 2022).
55. Forest Watch Indonesia, *Status dan Strategi Penyelamatan Ekosistem Mangrove Indonesia: Studi Kasus: Ekosistem Mangrove di Teluk Balikpapan Kalimantan Timur* [Status and Strategy to Save Indonesia's Mangrove Ecosystem: Case Study: Mangrove Ecosystem in Balikpapan Bay, East Kalimantan] (Jakarta: FWI, 2019).
56. Ibid., p. 55.
57. Ibid.
58. Interview with MS, 14 July 2022.
59. Not only that, in the effort to protect and propose the designation of Balikpapan Bay as a conservation area, its historical aspects have not been discussed much in discourse by civil society groups, especially those carried out by the government. Meanwhile, the historical role of Balikpapan Bay, for example, in World War II battles between Japan and Australia, deserves to be considered as an important aspect of efforts to make this bay a historical, cultural, and environmental conservation area.
60. Interviews with MS, 14 July 2022; HS, 14 July 2022.
61. Interviews with Y, 17 June 2022; R, 14 June 2022; and F, 17 June 2022.

62. Interview with T, 13 June 2022.
63. Interviews with N, S, Z and I, 14 July 2022.
64. Interview with A, 13 June 2022.
65. Ibid.
66. Interview with Y, 16 July 2022.

References

Abdi, Novi. 2022. "6 Pelabuhan Siap Layani Angkutan Logistik IKN Nusantara" [Six Ports Ready to Serve IKN Nusantara Logistics Transportation]. *Kaltim.antaranews*, 18 October 2022. https://kaltim.antaranews.com/berita/171057/enam-pelabuhan-siap-layani-angkutan-logistik-ikn-nusantara (accessed 20 October 2022).

Adyatama, Egi. 2022. "Jokowi Targetkan ada 3 Juta Lapangan Kerja Baru di Ibukota Baru" [Jokowi Targets 3 Million New Jobs in the New Capital]. *Tempo.co*, 26 February 2022. https://bisnis.tempo.co/read/1312546/jokowi-targetkan-ada-3-juta-lapangan-kerja-baru-di-ibu-kota-baru (accessed 25 December 2022).

AMAN. 2022. "Masyarakat Adat Menggugat IKN" [Indigenous Peoples Sue the IKN]. 21 April 2022. https://www.aman.or.id/news/read/masyarakat-adat-menggugat-uu-ikn (accessed 29 August 2022).

Ashar, Syamsul. 2022. "Permudah Investasi di IKN, Pemerintah Tawarkan HGU 95 Tahun dan HGB 80 Tahun" [Facilitate Investment in IKN, Government Offers 95 Years HGU and 80 Years HGB]. *kontan.co.id*, 17 September 2022. https://nasional.kontan.co.id/news/permudah-investasi-di-ikn-pemerintah-tawarkan-hgu-95-tahun-dan-hgb-80-tahun (accessed 27 September 2022).

CNN Indonesia. 2022. "Formappi: RUU IKN Supercepat, Sembunyi dan Minim Partisipasi Publik" [Formappi: IKN Bill Superfast, Stealthy, and Minimal Engagement]. 15 January 2022. https://www.cnnindonesia.com/nasional/20220114152427-32-746748/formappi-ruu-ikn-supercepat-sembunyi-dan-minim-partisipasi-publik (accessed 9 December 2022).

Dewi M.R., E.D Syafitri, and A.N Dewanti. 2020. "Analisis Kesiapan Masyarakat Kecamatan Sepaku dan Samboja Terhadap Rencana Pemindahan Ibu Kota Negara Indonesia" [Analysis of the Readiness of the People of Sepaku and Samboja Districts for the Plan for the Transfer of Indonesia's National Capital]. *Jurnal Pembangunan Wilayah dan Kota* [Journal of City and Regional Development] 16, no. 4: 300–13.

DPR-RI. 2022. "Siaran Pers Rapat Dengan Menteri Investasi, Nevi Zuariana Pertanyakan Investasi Untuk IKN" [Press Release Meeting with Minister of Investment, Nevi Zuariana Questioning Investment for IKN]. *dpr.go.id*, 10 June 2022. https://www.dpr.go.id/berita/detail/id/39236/t/Rapat+dengan+Menteri+Investasi%2C+Nevi+Zuariana+Pertanyakan+Investasi+untuk+IKN (accessed 27 September 2022).

Forest Watch Indonesia. 2019. *Status dan Strategi Penyelamatan Ekosistem Mangrove Indonesia: Studi Kasus: Ekosistem Mangrove di Teluk Balikpapan Kalimantan Timur* [Status and Strategy to Save Indonesia's Mangrove Ecosystem: Case Study: Mangrove Ecosystem in Balikpapan Bay, East Kalimantan]. Jakarta: FWI.

Hardjanto, Y.S. 2022. "Teluk Balikpapan yang Terus Tergerus Akibat Ekspansi Industri" [Balikpapan Bay Continues to Be Eroded Due to Industrial Expansion]. *Mongabay. co.id*, 1 April 2015. https://www.mongabay.co.id/2015/04/01/teluk-balikpapan-yang-terus-tergerus-akibat-ekspansi-industri/ (accessed 29 September 2022).

Harvey, D. 2012. *Rebel Cities: From the Right to the City to the Urban Revolution*. London: Verso.

Hasibuan, R.R.A., and S. Aisa. 2020. "Dampak dan Resiko Perpindahan Ibukota Terhadap Ekonomi Indonesia" [The Impact and Risk of Transferring the National Capital to Indonesian Economy]. *At-Tawasuth: Jurnal Ekonomi Islam* V, no. 1: 183–203.

Henley, D., and G. Frigo. 2020. "Lessons from Brasilia: On the Empty Modernity of Indonesia's New Capital". *New Mandala*, 14 April 2020. https://www.newmandala.org/lessons-from-brasilia-on-the-empty-modernity-of-indonesias-new-capital/ (accessed 8 December 2022).

Jati, Wasisto Raharjo. 2022. "A New Capital City for Who? Central-Local Tensions in Indonesia". *New Mandala*, 23 August 2022. https://www.newmandala.org/a-new-capital-city-for-who-central-local-tensions-in-indonesia/ (accessed 8 December 2022).

Kadin Indonesia. 2022. "KADIN: Investor Berperan Besar dalam Membangun Ibukota Negara Nusantara" [KADIN: Investors Play a Major Role in Building the National Capital]. *Kadin.id*, 19 October 2022. https://kadin.id/kabar/kadin-investor-berperan-besar-dalam-membangun-ibu-kota-negara-nusantara/ (accessed 9 December 2022).

Katadata. 2022. "Alasan Softbank Batalkan Investasi di Ibu Kota Negara" [Reasons for Softbank Cancelling Investments in the National Capital]. *Katadata.co.id*, 23 March 2022. https://katadata.co.id/yuliawati/berita/623a9d79a3a1e/alasan-softbank-batalkan-investasi-di-ibu-kota-negara (accessed 27 September 2022).

Kementerian Sekretariat Negara Republik Indonesia. 2022a. "Peraturan Presiden Nomer 64 tahun 2022 Tentang Rencana Tata Ruang Strategis Nasional Ibu Kota Nusantara Tahun 2022–2024". [Presidential Regulation Number 64 of 2022 Concerning the National Strategic Spatial Plan for the National Capital for 2022-2024]. *bpk.go.id*, 18 April 2022. https://peraturan.bpk.go.id/Home/Details/207620/perpres-no-64-tahun-2022 (accessed 6 January 2022).

———. 2022b. "Lampiran Nomor 1 Undang Undang Nomor 3 Tahun 2022 Tentang Ibu Kota Negara" [Appendix Number 1, Law Number 3 of 2022 about the National Capital]. *bpk.go.id*, 15 February 2022. https://peraturan.bpk.go.id/Home/Details/198400/uu-no-3-tahun-2022 (accessed 23 December 2022).

Kontras. 2022. "Catatan Kritis Pelanggaran HAM di Balik Pemindahan Ibukota Baru" [Critical Notes on the Violation of Human Rights in the Transfer of the New Capital]. *Kontras.org*, March 2022. https://kontras.org/wp-content/uploads/2022/03/Final_Catatan-Kritis-Pemindahan-IKN.pdf (accessed 8 December 2022).

Mahkamah Konstitusi Republik Indonesia. 2022. "Siaran Pers Gugatan UU IKN Disidangkan" [Press Release the IKN Lawsuit Is Being Tried]. *mkri.id*, 25 April 2022. https://www.mkri.id/public/content/infoumum/press/pdf/

press_2283_25.04.22%2053.PUU-XX.2022%20I%20UU%20IKN%20MHM.pdf (accessed 6 December 2022).

Massola, J., A. Rosa., and K. Rompies. 2019. "The Tribe in the Path of Indonesia's 'Almost Impossible' New Capital". *Sydney Morning Herald*, 15 September 2019. https://www.smh.com.au/world/asia/the-tribe-in-the-path-of-indonesia-s-almost-impossible-new-capital-20190912-p52qu9.html (accessed 17 October 2022).

Mawangi, Genta Tenri. 2022. "Indonesian Parliamentary Center: UU IKN Minim Partisipasi Publik" [Indonesian Parliamentary Center: IKN Law has Minimal Public Participation]. *Antaranews.com*, 21 January 2022. https://www.antaranews.com/berita/2658269/indonesian-parliamentary-center-uu-ikn-minim-partisipasi-publik (accessed 27 September 2022).

Mudassir, Rayful. 2022. "Pilah Pilih Pelabuhan Utama IKN" [Selecting the Main Port of IKN]. *Bisnis Indonesia*, 7 April 2022. https://bisnisindonesia.id/article/pilah-pilih-pelabuhan-utama-ikn (accessed 8 December 2022).

Naem, Abdallah, and Sarah Agustiorini. 2022. "Nestapa Suku Balik: Dulu Hutannya Digunduli, Kini Hidupnya Digusur IKN" [The Grief of the Balik Tribe: Formerly Their Forest Was Deforested, Now Their Lives Are Evicted by IKN]. *Projectmultatuli.org*, 1 August 2022. https://projectmultatuli.org/nestapa-suku-balik-dulu-hutannya-digunduli-kini-hidupnya-digusur-ikn/ (accessed 29 August 2022).

Nugroho, B.E. 2022. "Perlindungan Hak Masyarakat Adat dalam Pemindahan Ibukota Negara" [The Protection of the Rights of Indigenous People in the Transfer of National Capital]. *Jurnal Ilmu Sosial dan Ilmu Politik Universitas Jambi* [Journal of Social Science and Political Science, Jambi University] 6, no. 1: 64–78.

Pratama, Rezza Adi. 2022. "Gerilya Menjaring Investor IKN" [Guerrilla Attracts IKN Investors]. *katadata.co.id*, 25 August 2022. https://katadata.co.id/rezzaaji/indepth/6307305357987/gerilya-menjaring-investor-ikn (accessed 27 September 2022).

Pratama, Wibi Pangestu. 2022a. "Ekonom Ungkap Alasan Softbank Batal Investasi IKN, Gara-gara Jokowi Presiden 3 Periode?" [Economists Reveal Reasons for Softbank Cancelling IKN Investment, Because of Jokowi's 3-term Presidency?]. *Bisnis.com*, 13 March 2022. https://ekonomi.bisnis.com/read/20220313/9/1509940/ekonom-ungkap-alasan-softbank-batal-investasi-ikn-gara-gara-jokowi-presiden-3-periode (accessed 27 September 2022).

———. 2022b. "Menteri ATR: Perizinan di IKN Bisa Diperpanjang Hingga 160 Tahun" [Minister of ATR: Licensing in IKNs Can Be Extended up to 160 Years]. *Bisnis.com*, 7 October 2022. https://ekonomi.bisnis.com/read/20221007/9/1585201/menteri-atr-perizinan-di-ikn-bisa-diperpanjang-hingga-160-tahun (accessed 5 December 2022).

Rahmayani, A. 2015. "Balikpapan Pada Awal Abad ke 20" [Balikpapan at the Beginning of the 20th Century]. *Walasuji* 6, no. 1: 127–38.

Ridwan, Muhammad. 2022. "3 Bendungan Akan Dibangun di IKN Nusantara, Ini Daftarnya" [Three Dams to be Built at IKN Nusantara, Here is the List]. *Bisnis.com*, 11 May 2022. https://ekonomi.bisnis.com/read/20220511/45/1532142/3-

bendungan-akan-dibangun-di-ikn-nusantara-ini-daftarnya (accessed 8 December 2022).

Scott, B.R. 2006. "The Political Economy of Capitalism". *Harvard Business School Working Paper* No. 07-037, December 2006. https://www.hbs.edu/faculty/Pages/item.aspx?num=23129 (accessed 12 December 2022).

Sembiring, Lidya Julita. 2022. "Softbank Mundur dari Proyek IKN, Sri Mulyani Buka Suara" [Softbank Retreats from the IKN Project, Sri Mulyani Speaks]. *CNBC Indonesia*, 22 March 2022. https://www.cnbcindonesia.com/news/20220322162754-4-325010/softbank-mundur-dari-proyek-ikn-sri-mulyani-buka-suara (accessed 27 September 2022).

Setyaningirum, Puri Mei. 2022. "3 Catatan Penting Rachmat Gobel Terkait IKN" [3 Important Notes by Rachmat Gobel Regarding the IKN]. *Warta Ekonomi*, 20 January 2022. https://wartaekonomi.co.id/read387990/3-catatan-penting-rachmat-gobel-terkait-ikn (accessed 24 October 2022)

Silalahi, S.A.F. 2019. "Dampak Ekonomi dan Resiko Pemindahan Ibu Kota Negara" [Economic Impact and Risks of the IKN Transfer]. *Info Singkat* [Summary], vol. XI, no. 16/II/Puslit/August 2019 (DPR-RI, the House of Representatives, Republic of Indonesia).

Sucipto. 2022. "Bentuk Badan Otorita IKN Nusantara Dinilai Rancu" [The Form of the Authority of IKN Nusantara Is Considered Ambiguous]. *Kompas*, 15 February 2022. https://www.kompas.id/baca/nusantara/2022/02/15/bentuk-badan-otorita-ikn-nusantara-dinilai-rancu (accessed 27 September 2022)

Susanto, Vendy Yhulia. 2022. "Otorita IKN—Kadin Lakukan Penjajakan Pasar Peluang Investasi di IKN" [IKN Authority—Kadin Examines the Market for Investment Opportunities in IKN]. *kontan.co.id*, 17 October 2022. https://nasional.kontan.co.id/news/otorita-ikn-kadin-lakukan-penjajakan-pasar-peluang-investasi-di-ikn (accessed 27 September 2022).

Taufik, M. 2022. "Policy Brief Perpindahan Ibu Kota Negara di Wilayah Kalimantan Timur" [Policy Brief of Transfer the National Capital in East Kalimantan]. Balikpapan Branch Executive Board of Indonesian National Student Movement (Dewan Pimpinan Cabang Gerakan Mahasiswa Nasional Indonesia, DPC GMNI Balikpapan).

WALHI, 2019. "Ibukota Untuk Siapa?" [Whose Capital?]. *walhi.or.id*, 18 December 2019. https://www.walhi.or.id/ibu-kota-negara-baru-untuk-siapa (accessed 27 September 2022).

Whiteside, H. 2020. *Capitalist Political Economy: Thinkers and Theories*. London: Routledge.

7

IDENTIFYING POTENTIAL SOCIAL CHALLENGES IN IKN
Perspectives of Civil Society and Villagers in East Kalimantan

Deasy Simandjuntak, David Meschede and Michaela Haug

INTRODUCTION

In March 2022, several activists applied for a Constitutional Court judicial review of Indonesia's Law on the State's Capital (UU IKN).[1] The law had been passed by the legislature and signed into law by President Joko Widodo in February 2022. The applicants included the Head of Legal Affairs of Muhammadiyah, Busyro Muqoddas, the Indigenous Peoples' Alliance of the Archipelago (*Aliansi Masyarakat Adat Nusantara*, AMAN),[2] the Mining Advocacy Network (*Jaringan Advokasi Tambang*, JATAM),[3] the Indonesian Forum for Living Environment (WALHI) and the people of North Penajam Paser district, whose residential area is the designated core zone of the new capital city, Nusantara.

The applicants claimed that the government had hastily passed the law without clearly stipulating the rights of the local residents; that the Parliament's deliberation of the law had been overly brief, taking only seventeen days[4] from first reading to its passage, which meant that there had been little to no public participation in the deliberations; and that this lack of public participation meant that the IKN Law conflicted with Laws No. 12/2011 and 15/2019 on the Creation of Laws.[5] The applicants, therefore, claimed that the law-making process had not sufficiently considered the constitutional rights of the affected indigenous communities in the designated IKN area at a time when the communities were struggling with the COVID-19 pandemic and economic difficulties.

Unfortunately, the Constitutional Court rejected this application[6] due to the technical reason that it was submitted on the forty-sixth day after the issuance of UU IKN, a day past the stipulated timeframe that applications for judicial review must be submitted within forty-five days after a law is first gazetted.[7]

The fact that many prominent civil society organizations (CSOs) had banded together to voice their concerns about the IKN Law has highlighted Indonesian civil society's stance against the IKN megaproject and its potential adverse impact on a range of issues and individuals. This chapter will explore civil society's concerns through the examples of AMAN's and JATAM's advocacy. Due to civil society's traditional position between "state" and "society", CSOs usually take on the task of articulating society's concerns against what they perceive as potentially unfair or detrimental state policies. It is thus crucial to understand the position of Indonesian civil society to better gauge the concerns of the local population about the planned megaproject's effect on their future lives and livelihoods.

In addition, this chapter explores the hopes and concerns of rural communities regarding the new capital, by presenting the results of a survey conducted in the upper Mahakam in 2021. The survey results provide important insights into the atmosphere of anticipation that prevails among residents of areas that are not directly affected by the construction of the IKN. Incorporating the perception of rural citizens beyond the immediate IKN region in this chapter allows for the authors' examination of the relations between the concerns of the CSOs—which primarily represent the people more directly affected by the construction of the IKN—and those of the rural communities, which, despite living further away from the IKN area, still expect the new capital to have a major impact on their lives.

Civil Society: Theoretical Considerations

A simple way to define "civil society" is by juxtaposing it against the "state" and the "market". Tocquevillian and neo-Tocquevillian scholars look at civil society as occupying the sphere between these two entities, perceiving the civil society as an "autonomous area of liberty incorporating an organizational culture that builds both political and economic democracy".[8] "Civil society" in this sense contains all the associations and networks between the family and the state in which membership and activities are "voluntary" (e.g., labour unions, political parties, churches and other religious groups, professional and business associations, community and self-help groups, social movements, and the independent media).[9]

Some scholars believe that civil society's chief virtue is its ability to act as an organized counterweight to the state.[10] As its sphere of action is independent of the state, civil society is considered capable of energizing resistance to a tyrannical regime.[11] John Keane similarly argues that "civil society is an ideal-typical category ... that both describes and envisages a complex dynamic ensemble of legally protected non-governmental institutions that tend to be non-violent, self-organizing, self-reflexive and permanently in tension with each other and with the state institutions that frame, construct and enable their activities."[12] That civil society is "permanently in tension with the state" is the main characteristic of the more politically inclined civic associations.

CIVICUS, the global alliance of CSOs and activists, which claims to have 9,000 members in 175 countries, defines civil society as the arena outside the family, the state and the market, created by individual and collective actions, organizations, and institutions to advance shared interests.[13] Building upon this, the Centre for Strategic and International Studies (CSIS) in Washington, DC proposes that civil society should be regarded as "an ecosystem of organized and organic social and cultural relations existing in the space between the state, business, and family, which builds on indigenous and external knowledge, values, traditions, and principles to foster collaboration and the achievement of specific goals by and among citizens and other stakeholders."[14]

Yet other scholars consider the above definitions rather one-sided, as "contemporary thinking gives us a picture of a global civil society that seems to be supremely uncontaminated by either the power of states or that of markets."[15] Indeed, modern-day realities show that the situation can be more complex. There are instances in which civil society is closer to, or co-opted by, the state, or even involved in politics. So-called GONGOs—government-organized non-governmental organizations—are one such example. Some civil society groups might also be working against the democratic freedoms of other groups (such as freedoms of speech, assembly or religion), leading certain scholars to dub these "uncivil" societies,[16] as they are lashing out against the very tenet that guarantees their own survival. Examples of this include conservative religious groups which threaten and mobilize negative sentiments against minority religions and communities.

Scholars have defined civil society organizations in different ways. For the purpose of this chapter, the authors use the definition proposed by the World Bank, which is "a wide array of mass organizations: community groups, non-governmental organizations (NGOs), labour unions, indigenous groups, charitable organizations, professional associations, and foundations".[17] For independent civil societies which support democracy and its related freedoms and rights, the following three principles apply: participatory engagement, constitutional authority, and moral responsibility.[18] "Participatory engagement" refers to the need for members of society to enjoy access to and the governance of resources to be used for the common good. Members of society are free to be involved in civic action and social change, and to participate in group affiliations that provide a sense of community belonging.[19] Second, "constitutional authority" protects the rights and privileges of citizens in a civil society, citizens and social groups. They are thus constitutionally legitimized and empowered to hold economic and political actors accountable for their work as community servants and trustees. Local and national decision-makers, motivated by the common good rather than self-interest, are expected to design and implement public policies that strengthen the vitality and welfare of the community.[20] Third, all community members have a moral responsibility to use their civil liberties in ways that do not violate the human rights of others, and the practice of equity, justice, and reciprocity should produce social order and stability.

As their chief strength is their ability to act as an organized counterweight to the state, CSOs mediate between the people and the state, particularly articulating and channelling the grievances of the people against the state to ensure the fulfilment of the former's rights by the latter. In the case of the IKN, two CSOs have been particularly active in observing state policies and social responses, namely the aforementioned AMAN and JATAM.

The following sections delve into AMAN and JATAM's concerns regarding the IKN megaproject. Subsequently, the chapter explores how rural communities in East Kalimantan expect the project to influence their lives and livelihoods in the future. Comparing the concerns of CSOs and the villagers' perceptions, the authors discern that the former are apprehensive about how local residents would benefit from the project, given the pre-existing unresolved problems between the local population and mining and forestry concession holders in the area, and how the IKN project will potentially add to these problems. East Kalimantan villagers, on the other hand, have a more ambivalent view: many of them express hopes that the new capital city will improve their lives, while they are at the same time anxious about potential environmental degradation and social tensions.

AMAN: Concerns about Encroachment on the Locals' Living Space

In Indonesia's draft Indigenous Peoples Bill, "indigenous peoples" refers to "the communities which have lived for generations in specific geographical areas, have a common ancestry and/or residence, cultural identity, customary law, a strong connection with the territory and environment, and value systems which determine economic, political, social, cultural and legal institutions".[21] Indigenous peoples are also recognized and regulated under Article 18B of the Indonesian Constitution. However, despite this constitutional recognition, the Indigenous Peoples' Bill has been in legislative limbo for 12 years—it has not been ratified by Indonesia's House of Representatives, the DPR. This has led to various difficulties in getting the indigenous peoples' rights, especially their customary rights to ancestral or traditional lands, fully recognized.

In 1999, AMAN was established at the First Congress of Indigenous Peoples, consolidating Indonesian indigenous peoples' groups in their understanding of and striving for their rights. During its establishment, AMAN was reported to have made a controversial statement, "If the state does not recognize us, then we will not recognize the state."[22]

This declaration has not only challenged the government to respond to indigenous demands but also stimulated a fertile and much-needed debate within indigenous communities on what kind of recognition they sought from the government.[23] In addition to domestic consolidation, AMAN forges links with international indigenous peoples' organizations. The Alliance entered the Asia Indigenous Peoples' Pact and joined the Indigenous Peoples' Caucus during the 2002 preparatory meetings of the United Nations' World Summit on Sustainable Development,[24] in addition to working closely with the International Working Group on Indigenous Affairs (IWGIA). In 2005, AMAN won the prestigious Elinor Ostrom award for working on issues concerning the world's shared resources, or "the commons".[25]

Pertaining to the IKN project, AMAN's concern is threefold:[26] first, that there has been limited public participation in the IKN policymaking; second, that the megaproject would gloss over the existing land issues between the locals and the companies holding concessions in the area; and third, that the massive influx of newcomers would lead to the encroachment on and competition for living space with the locals, resulting in the potential loss of land which is crucial for the latter to practise their way of life according to *adat* (customary law).

On 9 December 2021, Erasmus Cahyadi Terre, deputy secretary of AMAN, was invited by the Indonesian parliament's Special Committee on the State's Capital to share AMAN's views of the IKN project, with four other experts from the social, economic, investment and disaster management sectors. However, despite AMAN's warning about IKN's potential problems at this session, legislators still passed the UU IKN without making major amendments to the draft bill.

AMAN mentioned that the development of the new capital city would affect the lives of various ethnic communities, namely the Paser, Dayak Kenyah and Dayak Modang in the North Penajam Paser district; the Kutai, Dayak Modang, Benuaq, Tunjung, Kenyah, Punan, and Basap in the Kutai Kartanegara district. There are twenty-two *adat* communities in the designated IKN area which are members of AMAN, fourteen in the IKN core zone, and eight in the general IKN area, with a current population of around 16,800 people and potentially affecting 30,000 hectares of *adat* land. Due to the lack of formal or official acknowledgement of these *adat* communities' land, a large portion of the land has unclear ownership status.[27]

Concerning the lack of public participation during the IKN's planning stages, AMAN argues that the government apparently only engaged with the local elites who claimed to represent the respective *adat* communities, rather than the communities themselves. These elites at times used cultural symbols and wore traditional garb to give themselves the appearance of cultural legitimacy; they tended to be supportive of the central government's policy without advocating the local communities and their concerns. "Socialization events" by the local government, aiming to familiarize the local population with the aims, purposes and upcoming procedures of the IKN project were limited, at times including only those connected to the local administration or elites, resulting in a limited understanding of the IKN project.

AMAN has suggested that these "socializations" needed to be done more comprehensively, involving local *adat* communities whose lives and livelihoods will be directly affected by the IKN megaproject. This is so that the project can fulfil the criteria of "free, prior and informed consent" as stipulated by the United Nations on issues pertaining to the interaction with indigenous peoples.[28]

Second, AMAN highlighted existing land issues between the local population and corporate concession holders and how these issues had already accentuated the power discrepancy between the two entities.

According to AMAN's research, there are 162 concessions within what will be the proposed IKN area, for the oil palm, mining and logging industries. However, these have mostly been operating without the formal consent of the *adat* communities. This has created various structural conflicts. AMAN is concerned that the megaproject will either gloss over the existing problems or even exacerbate them, leading to the further marginalization of the already powerless local people. As AMAN's Terre mentioned, this boils down to the central government's lack of acknowledgement of *adat* communities. *Adat* communities in Indonesia are recognized in Article 18B of the Indonesian Constitution, but the long delay of the bill on their status stands in sharp contrast to the swiftness of the legislative's deliberation on and passage of the IKN Law.[29] This lack of legal acknowledgement of the *adat* communities is a factor underlying the lack of clarity on the status of their lands, despite their usage of the lands for generations past.

A third concern is about the interaction between the local population and potential newcomers to the IKN zone. AMAN mentioned that the locals were already cautious about the possibility of competition for living space with these newcomers, whom they believe will have better education, higher financial capacity and privileged access to resources. Local people are fearful that they will lose the competition and will end up being marginalized like the Betawi indigenous group which inhabited parts of Jakarta but was pushed to the fringes of society under the pressure of Jakarta's unceasing expansion in past decades.

An online interview with activists from AMAN's East Kalimantan branch revealed further concerns.[30] According to them, nine villages in the IKN's core zone will lose their land, and that more villages in the wider IKN zone will suffer from land loss, mainly due to infrastructural expansion. These include communities affected by two dam projects that will provide water to the new capital, the Sepaku-Semoi Dam and the Sepaku Dam. According to the activists, local residents at these dam construction sites had expressed fears that it would be even more difficult to prove their ownership of the land once the dams are built and their lands inundated. The activists explained that the compensation that the villagers would receive for giving up their lands, if any, would likely be very small. The villagers would get higher margins if they sold their lands to speculators on the free market, which the government prohibited.

In any case, proving ownership of customary land is difficult, as many villagers do not have formal land titles. Lacking formal land rights, many feel compelled to let go of their lands and accept relatively low compensation payments. The local AMAN representatives reported that it was also unclear where and how those who have sold their lands would be relocated. These activists further explained that those who sold their lands are deeply concerned about the consequent loss of their livelihoods and the fact that they can no longer pass down the land to their children.

An entirely different issue that increasingly concerns the local population in the IKN core zone is the oversaturation of civil society presence in their area. A plethora of civil society groups—both for and against the IKN project—have courted the villagers' support since the IKN proposed zones were declared. According to the local AMAN activists, many of the villagers are already "sick of NGOs", feeling overwhelmed by their sheer number and constant presence in the IKN area.

A specific criticism by AMAN is that while several organizations are claiming to side with the people, not all of them legitimately advocate for the people's best interests. Organizations are calling themselves "customary councils" (*dewan adat*) or something similar, but they represent local elites and businessmen hoping to land a share in IKN-related projects. According to the AMAN activists, it is these latter organizations that have conducted the aforementioned "socialization" events, which highlighted only the positive aspects of the IKN project and enticed the villagers to give up their lands.

These groups undermine the notion of "civil society", as they falsely claim to be representatives of civil society. According to AMAN activists, the central government has used these organizations to give the impression that local ethnic minorities have been consulted and are unequivocally supportive of the IKN project, when in fact those giving their support are merely local elites seeking personal profit. Some of the local elites may well be members of the ethnic minorities or *adat* communities, but they rarely speak on behalf of most of the affected villagers or advocate positions other than those from which they personally benefit. AMAN has bemoaned its growing rivalry with dubious organizations such as these, noting that many villagers are disgruntled to the point of not trusting anyone anymore, as they feel they cannot reliably judge which of the organizations that are active in their area stand for the villagers' interests.

JATAM: Existing Land Issues and the Potential Spillover of Problems Beyond the IKN Zone

JATAM was established in 1995 in Banjarmasin, South Kalimantan by forty-five institutions to address the needs for an advocacy network for organizations working on mining issues. JATAM is most concerned about the common but false assumption that the land designated for the new capital city "did not belong to anybody" or already had a clear legal status. In reality, ownership over much of this land is highly disputed between corporate concession holders and ethnic Paser, Balik, and other ethnic minorities, who own the land according to customary law (*adat*).[31]

According to JATAM's research, of the 162 concessions in the area, 158 are coal mining ones. Mining activities have left 94 uncovered former mining pits, which pose serious environmental concerns and physical danger to local inhabitants. The concessions, according to JATAM, belong to politicians and businessmen or their affiliates. JATAM believes that the IKN's establishment would benefit only these oligarchs but not the local people. An example of a concession holder is PT ITCI Hutani Manunggal (IHM), owned by lumber tycoon Sukanto Tanoto, who in 2019 released 41,000 hectares of his concessions for the proposed development of the IKN.[32] It is unclear whether the company received compensation for releasing these lands, as the lands were categorized as industrial forest plantation (*hutan tanaman industry*, HTI) which can be "returned" to the government at any time when such a need arises. JATAM mentioned that some 150 families of the Pemaluan village in the IKN core area, who previously lost land to such concessions, are afraid of losing even more land, especially when it is difficult to prove their land ownership.

JATAM thus shares some similar concerns with AMAN about the limited public participation which creates the polarization in the local society between those who support the IKN project and those who do not support it. Another shared fear is that the IKN project would "whitewash" existing "corporate crimes" (JATAM's phrase) which had earlier led to conflicts between the locals and the concessions holders. Finally, JATAM believes that it will be difficult to prove the locals' land ownership, mainly because some do not have official documents or titles and may not get proper compensation for their land if the government were to acquire it for the IKN project. Some landowners who did have titles have already sold their land to pre-empt future acquisition. Finally, JATAM highlighted that the massive influx of newcomers would lead to competition with locals over resources like living space and clean water.

The need for foreign investment has led to the current intensity of land measurement activities by those connected to the project. IKN authorities need to ensure investors that all of the prospective land for development has been lawfully purchased and its legal status is clear. JATAM highlighted how the Minister of Agrarian Affairs and Spatial Planning and Head of the National Land Agency Hadi Tjahjanto stated that he aimed to accelerate land acquisition for IKN purposes.[33] That Tjahjanto is a retired military general who was a former commander of the national armed forces, in JATAM's view, raises concerns that he might resort to coercive methods in the process of land acquisition.

JATAM members highlighted how environmental problems might occur in regions beyond the IKN zone. Dam-building activities in the IKN zone raise environmental concerns, as does the potential destruction of 160 hectares of mangrove forest in that area. This might affect Balikpapan Bay, which is 40 kilometres from the IKN core zone.[34] In addition, construction materials like sand for the IKN come from elsewhere, such as Central and Western Sulawesi. Their extraction and transportation to East Kalimantan could lead to related environmental harms like silting. Moreover, JATAM believed that as IKN is using some lands designated for concessions, the central government would have to replace these concession lands with other lands outside of Kalimantan. This means that concession activities would continue in new areas—JATAM took the example of Papua—which could potentially create new problems.

JATAM's representative in East Kalimantan voiced an even deeper concern: there has apparently been no consistent public consultation or information given as to why the new capital is being relocated at this time and to the designated IKN zone. Thus, the local population feels that they were forced to stand aside while people from the central and local governments proceeded with their land measuring and other activities in preparation for the IKN's construction. Land measurement activity has indeed intensified; landowners in the proposed IKN core zone had heard promises that they would get Rp150 million (US$9,700) to Rp1 billion (US$64,700) per hectare, depending on their proof of land ownership. Others residing in the dam project areas have received payments for their lands. There seem to be sharp discrepancies in compensation rates, as the developers held separate conversations with individual landowners: some have not received any payments. Moreover, land speculation has been rampant. It is unclear to whom the local people have been selling their land: the central government, the IKN authority, or private land speculators.

Information on the proposed relocation is similarly chaotic. Some residents have heard the news that they would be relocated, but do not know where. Others were told they would be given money to move. Some locals have stated that they would not know where to go because most of the land in the area is already concession land.

Concerning infrastructural development in the province, JATAM pointed out how the "Kayan Cascade" hydroelectric power project that is being built on the Kayan River would put two villages, Long Lejuh and Long Peleban, underwater and affect some 160 households. Simultaneously, JATAM claims that the Sepaku Semoi and Sepaku dams, which are meant to provide clean water to the IKN area, have ironically caused a scarcity of clean water during the construction process. It has forced the ethnic Balik community in the area to buy clean water for their daily use.

Like AMAN, JATAM voiced concerns about the effects of the massive future influx of newcomers, anticipating that local residents would potentially lose out on employment or other opportunities. JATAM has also heard concerns over locals not wanting to share the fate of the Betawis of Jakarta and their fears of potentially negative influences on social cohesion, and the erosion of local cultural norms and values.

Rural Communities' Hopes and Concerns

Since the Widodo administration's decision to move Indonesia's seat of government to East Kalimantan was announced in August 2019, it has been the subject of lively debates throughout the province, from urban centres to small rural communities. With the COVID-19 pandemic taking centre stage in 2020 and 2021, delaying many large-scale projects including the capital relocation, the topic temporarily faded into the background. However, with the 2022 IKN law paving the way, Nusantara has re-emerged as an important point of conversation in the rural uplands and hinterlands of East Kalimantan.

When the authors talked to people in the province about their future, the proposed new capital and its implications drew out a multitude of opinions, predictions, fears and hopes. Those who are excited about the new capital city on their doorstep are equally present as those who are worried about the challenges the megaproject will bring. However, most voices in the new capital's future hinterland have one commonality: the majority in rural East Kalimantan believe that the new capital will bring many changes that will directly impact their lives. What is striking to the authors is many people's ambivalence towards the new capital, a combination of hope and fear. The authors rarely met anyone who was either completely for or against the new capital.

IDENTIFYING POTENTIAL SOCIAL CHALLENGES IN IKN

Given the pandemic and the resulting constraints, the authors carried out a survey with the help of Emilia Gelang Timang, a local research assistant, in three neighbouring villages in the Mahakam Ulu regency in March and April of 2021. The Mahakam Ulu regency, while in the same province as the IKN, will not be directly affected by IKN-related construction activities. It is a hinterland regency bordering East Malaysia. Travelling from the coastal area that is designated for IKN to the Mahakam Ulu regency is a journey requiring several days. In the rather thinly settled regency, the majority of the roughly 35,000 inhabitants are members of various Dayak groups, such as the Dayak Bahau and the Dayak Kenyah.[35] The major aim of the survey was to gain more systematic insights into local perceptions of the new capital and explore differences in views according to age and gender. The survey included 60 respondents, comprising 20 young adults, 20 members of the first group's parents' generation, and twenty members of their grandparents' generation. There was an equal split of women and men within each age bracket. Despite the relatively small number of respondents, this survey provides valuable insight into the sentiments of anticipation in rural communities at that time vis-à-vis the proposed IKN project.

Forty-seven of the 60 respondents (or 78 per cent) knew about the capital relocation. Those who were unaware of it were mostly from the oldest or grandparents' generation (9 out of 20 were unaware), particularly the elderly women (6 out of 10 were unaware). Younger and middle-aged respondents' knowledge of the proposed capital relocation was high. Overall, 23 per cent of the respondents (14 out of 60) already felt the impact of the upcoming capital relocation on their lives. See Figure 7.1.

While the proposed IKN had very little influence on the respondents' lives at that point in time (as the survey was conducted in 2021), almost all the respondents expected major changes in the future. 47 out of 60

FIGURE 7.1
Awareness and Impact of Proposed Capital Relocation, Respondent Summary

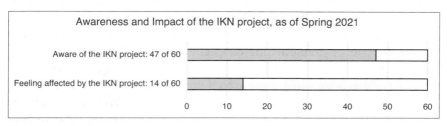

Note: Number of respondents aware of and feeling affected by the IKN project, N=60.

respondents (78 per cent) expected major disruptions in their future because of the new capital city, while 9 out of 60 (15 per cent) thought that some disruption was possible. Three did not answer the question on disruption (no clear reason why) while a sole elderly man replied that he did not expect his life to change at all.

When asked about the general theme of their future expectations, the responses revealed a mostly optimistic but notably ambivalent stance: 38 of the 60 respondents expected positive changes, while 21 expected both positive and negative changes, in their lives. Here, the 40 younger and middle-aged respondents showed an almost even split of 21 to 18 between those believing in positive changes and those expecting both positive and negative changes (one respondent's answer was missing). The older generation showed a higher tendency towards optimism here, with 17 of the 20 believing in positive changes.

The respondents were asked to enumerate more specifically their future hopes and fears. The free answers were written down by the research assistant in bullet points. An example of the full responses (summarized) of a middle-aged female respondent follows. When asked about her hopes, the respondent named three points: first, that she hoped healthcare facilities will be good and comprehensive, second, that education will be improved and third, that local infrastructure will be improved. When asked about her fears, she thought the crime rate will surely increase and that there will be conflict and litigation about land.[36]

For the authors' analysis, these bullet point responses were summarized into thematic categories. Almost all respondents expected their economic life to change. Fifty-four out of 60 respondents (90 per cent) expected some economic improvement, which was often paired with hopes for more income and job opportunities (mentioned by 39 out of 60 respondents). Another factor was easier and more affordable access to goods (mentioned by 13 out of 60 respondents). When asked what specific changes the respondents were *hoping for* (without necessarily expecting them to happen), three broad categories were regularly mentioned by all respondents: improved infrastructural access (48 out of 60), economic development (47 out of 60), and improved access to education (39 out of 60). Less regularly mentioned was the hope for a strengthening of local customs and culture (15 out of 60). No statistically significant tendencies could be distinguished between age groups or gender when it came to these hopes. See Figure 7.2.

When asked to enumerate their fears for the future in connection with the IKN construction, the respondents mostly focused on environmental degradation and forest loss as well as losing out in competition with

IDENTIFYING POTENTIAL SOCIAL CHALLENGES IN IKN

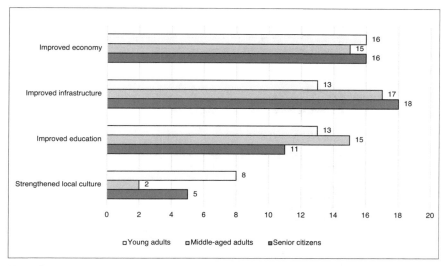

FIGURE 7.2
Respondents' Hopes for the Future, N=60

Note: Response categories as expressed by the respondents for their hopes for the IKN project.

newcomers. Two-thirds, or 41 out of the 60 respondents, spoke about these concerns. The fear of losing out to newcomers from other parts of Indonesia was notably more pronounced among the younger respondents. Some 18 out of the 20 young respondents mentioned this aspect, while only about half of the older ones (11 and 12 of the middle-aged and elder respondents respectively) did. Strongly linked to this fear are responses that can be summarized as fear of "moral degradation": 38 out of 60 mentioned the possibility of the depreciation of *adat* customary laws or a devaluation of local cultural norms, an increased crime rate, and a growing prevalence of prostitution and gambling. A smaller but still notable number of respondents were worried about future land conflicts (21 out of 60), with men mentioning this more often (14 out of 30) than women (7 out of 30). See Figure 7.3.

ANTICIPATING CHANGE: LOCAL COMMUNITIES' PERSPECTIVES ON THE NEW CAPITAL

The survey results show that local communities in the hinterland of East Kalimantan are expecting the IKN to generate changes that will directly affect their lives. The common attitude of ambivalence is particularly noteworthy.

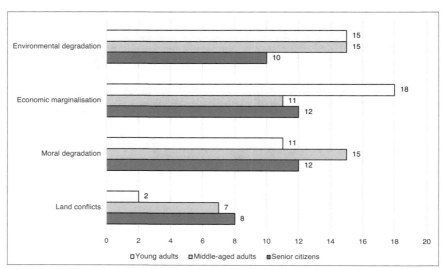

FIGURE 7.3
Fears of Respondents about Future Problems with IKN Relocation, N=60

Note: Response categories as expressed by the respondents for their fears surrounding the IKN project.

In the rural communities in the hinterland of East Kalimantan, there was hardly anyone who was completely for or against the new capital.

This ambivalent attitude towards the new capital corresponds to the ambivalence that many people in the rural hinterlands and uplands of Borneo have towards development in general.[37] Most people in rural East Kalimantan aspire towards "progress" (*kemajuan*) in the form of a well-developed road network, good quality healthcare, access to (secondary) education and reliable electricity.[38] While the provision of these infrastructural services lies within the responsibility of the state, and although local governments have invested a lot of effort and money in infrastructure since the introduction of regional autonomy in the late 1990s, it is most often the logging, mining, and palm oil companies that promise to bring this kind of progress to remote regions. Therefore, many people welcome the companies to work near their villages. At the same time, people are aware that the influx of (extractive) industries might lead to the loss of (customary) land, drive deforestation and cause serious environmental pollution, often directly affecting them. Further, extractive industries and the related influx of migrant workers, often residing in logging and mining camps, are associated with alcohol consumption, gambling and prostitution. Many villagers thus fear social conflicts and moral decline as a consequence of the intrusion of (extractive) industries into the interior regions of East Kalimantan.

From one of the co-authors' research experience, many villagers experience the resulting situation as a serious dilemma: their hopes for progress and related economic, health, and educational improvements are intertwined with fears of losing their customary land, increasing social conflicts, and environmental degradation. Many therefore desire and fear development at the same time.[39]

This ambivalence towards progress runs deep through indigenous people's lives and is currently characteristic of the general attitude towards the new capital city. Many people are proud that the new capital city is going to be built on their doorstep in East Kalimantan and hope that progress will come to the province along with new economic opportunities, health and education facilities, and improved infrastructure (e.g., roads, Internet access, and flight network). However, they also fear potential environmental pollution, social conflicts, and moral decline through more (extractive) industries and investment activities pushing into the hinterland.

Conclusion: Challenges, Anticipations and Ambivalence

By looking at the perceptions of civil society through the lenses of two selected CSOs, the chapter discerns several problematic concerns. First, there has been a woeful lack of public consultation and public participation in the policies concerning the IKN. If there were any semblance of Jakarta's "socialization" of the IKN megaproject, this was done only among limited groups. According to AMAN and JATAM representatives, these groups tended to support the government, used cultural symbols to legitimate their voices, and mainly aimed to profit from future government funding (of civil society groups).

Second, the megaproject is likely to "whitewash" existing problems connected to land concessions to large industries in the area. Local communities have had their land used by concession holders without consent and this has created a structural conflict between them. There are concerns that the megaproject would gloss over these problems and leave them unresolved, or worse, add new problems pertaining to land rights. There is potential for further unfair land acquisitions and failure to recognize customary land ownership. Looking at this trend, AMAN and JATAM consider the megaproject as benefiting the concession holders rather than the local population.

The third major concern is that the project will create problems even beyond the IKN core zone, as infrastructure projects like dam constructions are carried out in upriver areas and raw materials for the construction of the IKN will come from other Indonesian islands (e.g., sand from Sulawesi). This will result in massive extractive activities and related environmental degradation in the affected regions. It further remains unclear how (and if) the government intends to replace the concession land that will be used for the IKN with land elsewhere in Indonesia.

Fourth, local people fear the competition with newcomers for living space, jobs, and opportunities as they do not have similar levels of education, financial capacity, or access to resources as the newcomers expected to move into the IKN area from Jakarta and Java. This might ultimately lead to the marginalization of the local population.

These concerns resonate with the perception of the villagers of the Mahakam Ulu regency of East Kalimantan. From the survey, it is discernible that the villagers show a largely ambivalent stance on the new capital, expecting large changes in their personal life and their home region, tentatively hoping for improved income opportunities but simultaneously fearing environmental devastation and increased competition with immigrants.

Fifth, the lack (or absence) of local people's participation in the IKN's planning and execution has created a vacuum of information, caused by the disjuncture of understanding between the government (local and central) and the people. The former and the latter do not have the same perceptions of what this megaproject entails and how it will impact the local people's lives. This has led to several dire consequences, such as the rivalry between civil society, which is concerned about the local people's interests, and those who are a façade for the interests of investors and businesses. The activities of the latter, at times as middlemen and brokers, in general support the megaproject: these figures actively approach the local people to entice them to give up their land. The local people are familiar with this approach from their previous encounters with the large industries' concession activities.

Last, the fact that the villagers are ambivalent—partly hopeful and partly concerned—about the IKN is noteworthy. Considering their past negative experiences with projects undertaken in the name of "development" and long histories of marginalization, the willingness of rural indigenous communities in East Kalimantan to see this megaproject with some positive anticipation should not be taken for granted. It is a call for the Indonesian government to guarantee more responsible management of the capital relocation that includes, respects and empowers local communities.

The hopes of these rural communities offer a great opportunity to Indonesia's central, provincial, and local governments to engage local people in the manifold processes that are related to the IKN megaproject in a truly participatory manner. The survey findings on villagers' perceptions and the interviews with civil society representatives indicate that local communities wish to be involved in the planning of the IKN and related infrastructure projects. They do not want to be perceived only as the providers of land to be used for the project and to be left out of the policymaking. They would like to be provided with clear information, to be heard, and to become active designers of their future. Local people's hopes are a call for a more inclusive IKN project going forward, that is more responsive and sensitive to local needs and concerns, and to the actual situation on the ground.

Notes

1. Law No. 3/2022 on the State's Capital is the legal foundation for the capital city relocation. It regulates the establishment of the state's capital and its administrative authority, the organizational structure and jurisdiction of its administration, the relocation of the state's institutions from Jakarta to the new capital, and budgetary arrangements. See details of the law at https://peraturan.bpk.go.id/Home/Details/198400/uu-no-3-tahun-2022 (accessed 11 January 2023).
2. See AMAN's website, https://www.aman.or.id/
3. See JATAM's website, https://www.jatam.org/en/
4. Ermelina Singareta, the plaintiffs' attorney, claimed that it took the parliament only seventeen days to issue the IKN Law, from the day it received the official letter from the president concerning the draft of the law until the day of the issuance of the law, excluding the parliamentary recess period. See Mahkamah Konstitusi Republik Indonesia, "Kurang Partisipasi Publik, UU IKN Kembali Diuji" [Lacking Public Participation, the IKN Law Goes Through a Formal Review], 25 April 2022, https://www.mkri.id/index.php?page=web.Berita&id=18164 (accessed 19 February 2023).
5. AMAN, "Menggugat IKN" [Suing the IKN], *Gaung AMAN*, April–June 2022, https://aman.or.id/files/gaung/31616Majalah%20Gaung%20AMAN%20Edisi%20April-Juni%202022.pdf (accessed 11 October 2022).
6. In December 2022, however, Indonesia's parliament included the revision of the Law of the State's Capital in its 2023 National Legislation Programme (Prolegnas), which prioritized 39 bills and laws. See *Kompas*, "DPR Setujui Daftar 39 RUU Prolegnas Prioritas 2023, Salah Satunya Revisi UU IKN Usulan Pemerintah" [DPR Agreed to the List of 39 Bills to Be Prioritised in Its Deliberation in 2023, One of Them Is the Revision of the IKN Law as Suggested by the Government],

15 December 2022, https://nasional.kompas.com/read/2022/12/15/14161961/dpr-setujui-daftar-39-ruu-prolegnas-prioritas-2023-salah-satunya-revisi-uu (accessed 11 January 2023).
7. The application for a formal judicial review of a law must be filed within a maximum of 45 days after it is recorded in the State Gazette, according to the Decision of the Constitutional Court ("Putusan Mahkamah Konstitusi") No. 27/PUU-VII/2009.
8. Cathy McIlwaine, "From Local to Global to Transnational Civil Society: Re-Framing Development Perspectives on the Non-State Sector", *Geography Compass* 1, no. 6 (2007), p. 1256.
9. Michael Edwards, *Civil Society* (Cambridge, UK: Polity Press, 2009), p. 20. Also, Tocqueville did not include political organizations (i.e., political parties in modern times) as part of "civil society". However, he was inquisitive about the possibility that "political" organizations were more capable than "civic" organizations of being a counterweight to the state. Moreover, as civil society is supposed to be independent of the market as well, there is a question of whether professional and business associations can be categorised as civil society.
10. Michael W. Foley and Bob Edwards, "The Paradox of Civil Society", *Journal of Democracy* 7 no. 3 (1996): 38–52.
11. Ibid., p. 39.
12. John Keane, *Civil Society: Old Images, New Visions* (Stanford, CA: Stanford University Press, 1998).
13. Civicus, *State of Civil Society* (Johannesburg: Civicus: World Alliance for Citizen Participation, 2011), full report at https://www.civicus.org/downloads/2011StateOfCivilSocietyReport/State_of_civil_society_2011-web.pdf (accessed 12 January 2023).
14. CSIS, "Concept and Definition of Civil Society Sustainability", 30 June 2017, https://www.csis.org/analysis/concept-and-definition-civil-society-sustainability (accessed 18 November 2022).
15. Neera Chandhoke, "What Are the Preconditions for Civil Society?", in *Conflict, Society and Peacebuilding*, edited by Raffaele Marchetti and Nathalie Tocci (London: Routledge India, 2020), pp. 72–94.
16. Marlies Glasius, "Uncivil Society", in *International Encyclopedia of Civil Society*, edited by H.K.Anheier and S. Toepler (New York: Springer, 2010), pp. 1583–88.
17. World Bank, "Defining Civil Society", 2010, https://www.weforum.org/agenda/2018/04/what-is-civil-society/ (accessed 18 November 2022).
18. Timothy J. Peterson and John Van Til, "Defining Characteristics of Civil Society", *International Journal of Not-for-Profit-Law* 6, no. 2 (February 2004), https://www.icnl.org/resources/research/ijnl/defining-characteristics-of-civil-society.
19. Ibid.
20. Ibid.
21. *Rancangan Undang-Undang Tentang Masyarakat Adat* (the Indigenous Peoples Bill), at https://www.dpr.go.id/dokakd/dokumen/RJ2-20171106-094054-7086.pdf

22. Redaksi, "AMAN: Kalau Negara Tidak Mengakui Kami, Kami pun Tidak Mengakui Negara" [If the State Does Not Acknowledge Us, We Don't Acknowledge the State], *Sinar Keadilan*, 25 October 2019, https://sinarkeadilan.com/aman-kalau-negara-tidak-mengakui-kami-kami-pun-tidak-mengakui-negara/ (accessed 26 September 2022).
23. Sandra Moniaga, "From *Bumiputera* to *Masyarakat Adat*: A Long and Confusing Journey", in *The Revival of Tradition in Indonesian Politics: The Deployment of Adat from Colonialism to Indigenism*, edited by Jamie Davidson and David Henley (London: Routledge, 2007), p. 284.
24. Ibid., p. 283.
25. Ostrom Award, "Abdon Nababan—AMAN, winner of the Elinor Ostrom Award 2015 in the Category of Practitioners", *Youtube*, 11 August 2015, https://www.youtube.com/watch?v=DWj3ZjCgVCU and https://www.elinorostromaward.org/2015-practitioners-award (accessed 26 September 2022).
26. Based on multiple interviews with Erasmus Cahyadi Terre, Deputy Secretary of AMAN, based in Jakarta and with two local representatives of AMAN based in Samarinda, East Kalimantan in October 2022.
27. Rachmawati, "IKN Nusantara, Bagaimana Nasib Masyarakat Adat di Sekitarnya?" [IKN Nusantara, What Would Be the Fate of the Surrounding Adat Communities?], *Kompas*, 15 March 2022, https://regional.kompas.com/read/2022/03/15/122500778/ikn-nusantara-bagaimana-nasib-masyarakat-adat-di-sekitarnya-?page=all (accessed 26 September 2022).
28. United Nations, "Free Prior and Informed Consent: An Indigenous Peoples' Right and Good Practice for Local Communities—A Manual For Project Practitioners", 14 October 2016, https://www.un.org/development/desa/indigenouspeoples/publications/2016/10/free-prior-and-informed-consent-an-indigenous-peoples-right-and-a-good-practice-for-local-communities-fao/ (accessed 26 September 2022).
29. WALHI, "UU IKN Ingkari Konstitusi: Rakyat Minta Pembatalan Lewat Judicial Review" [The Law on the State's Capital Denies the Constitution: The People Asked for a Repeal Through Judicial Review], 1 April 2022, https://www.walhi.or.id/uu-ikn-ingkari-konstitusi-rakyat-minta-pembatalan-lewat-judicial-review (accessed 17 November 2022).
30. Based on interview with two representatives of AMAN's Kalimantan Timur branch, who spoke on the condition of anonymity. Interview conducted by David Meschede on 23 September 2022.
31. Based on multiple interviews with Melky Nahar, Coordinator of JATAM based in Jakarta, and Mareta Sari, representative of JATAM based in Samarinda, East Kalimantan, in October 2022.
32. See Desynta Nuraini, "Sukanto Tanoto Lepas Konsesi di Kaltim Seluas 41.000 Hektare" [Sukanto Tanoto Released 41,000 hectare Concessions in East Kalimantan], *Ekonomi*, 1 November 2019, https://ekonomi.bisnis.com/read/20191101/99/1165735/sukanto-tanoto-lepas-konsesi-di-kaltim-seluas-41.000-hektare (accessed 17 November 2022).

33. Hadi Tjahjanto mentioned that the land acquisition for the IKN project was one of his priorities, as mandated by the President. See Romys Bineskasri, "Lahan IKN Masuk Prioritas Menteri ATR Hadi Tjahjanto" [The IKN Is Among the Priorities for Minister of Agrarian Affairs and Spatial Planning and Head of the National Land Agency Hadi Tjahjanto], *CNBC*, 15 June 2022, https://www.cnbcindonesia.com/news/20220615210403-4-347469/lahan-ikn-masuk-prioritas-menteri-atr-hadi-tjahjanto (accessed 11 October 2022).
34. See Richaldo Hariandja, "Bagaimana Nasib Kawasan Mangrove Teluk Balikpapan Kala Ada IKN Nusantara?" [What Is the Fate of the Mangrove Area of Balikpapan Bay When There Is IKN Nusantara?], *Mongabay*, 7 September 2022, https://www.mongabay.co.id/2022/09/07/bagaimana-nasib-kawasan-mangrove-teluk-balikpapan-kala-ada-ikn-nusantara/ (accessed 17 November 2022).
35. Badan Pusat Statistik Kabupaten Kutai Barat, "Mahakam Ulu Dalam Angka 2021" [Mahakam Ulu in Numbers 2021], p. 66, https://mahulukab.bps.go.id/publication/2021/02/26/eb9d0cca3e988611bd3c8a70/kabupaten-mahakam-ulu-dalam-angka-2021.html (accessed 12 January 2023); Mika Okushima, "Ethnohistory of the Kayanic Peoples in Northeast Borneo (Part 1): Evidence from Their Languages, Old Ethnonyms, and Social Organization", *Borneo Research Bulletin* 37 (2006): 86–126.
36. Respondent surveyed on 27 March 2021.
37. See Liana Chua, "Gifting, Dam(n)ing and the Ambiguation of Development in Malaysian Borneo", *Ethnos* 81, no. 4 (2016): 737–57.
38. See also Morgan Harper Harrington, "Changing Exchanges: A Modern Siang Village amidst Resource Extraction in Regional Indonesia" (PhD dissertation, University of Melbourne, 2014); and Viola Schreer, "Longing for Prosperity in Indonesian Borneo" (PhD dissertation, University of Kent, 2016).
39. Schreer, "Longing for Prosperity in Indonesian Borneo", pp. 239–67.

References

AMAN. 2022. "Menggugat IKN" [Suing the IKN]. *Gaung AMAN*, April–June, https://aman.or.id/files/gaung/31616Majalah%20Gaung%20AMAN%20Edisi%20April-Juni%202022.pdf (accessed 11 October 2022).

Bineskasri R. 2022. "Lahan IKN Masuk Prioritas Menteri ATR Hadi Tjahjanto" [The IKN Is Among the Priorities for Minister of Agrarian Affairs and Spatial Planning and Head of the National Land Agency Hadi Tjahjanto]. *CNBC*, 15 June 2022.

Civicus. 2011. *State of Civil Society*. Johannesburg: Civicus: World Alliance for Citizen Participation. https://www.civicus.org/downloads/2011StateOfCivilSocietyReport/State_of_civil_society_2011-web.pdf (accessed 12 January 2023).

Chandhoke, N. 2020. "What Are the Preconditions for Civil Society?". In *Conflict, Society and Peacebuilding: Comparative Perspectives*, edited by Raffaele Marchetti and Nathalie Tocci, pp. 72–94. London: Routledge India.

Chua, Liana. 2016. "Gifting, Dam(n)ing and the Ambiguation of Development in Malaysian Borneo". *Ethnos* 81, no. 4: 737–57.

Center for Strategic and International Studies (CSIS). 2017. "Concept and Definition of Civil Society Sustainability". 30 June 2017. https://www.csis.org/analysis/concept-and-definition-civil-society-sustainability (accessed 18 November 2022).

Edwards, M. 2009. *Civil Society*. Cambridge: Polity Press.

Foley, M.W., and B. Edwards. 1996. "The Paradox of Civil Society". *Journal of Democracy* 7, no. 3: 38–52.

Glasius, M. 2010. "Uncivil Society". In *International Encyclopedia of Civil Society*, edited by H.K. Anheier and S. Toepler, pp. 1583–88. New York: Springer.

Hariandja, R. 2022. "Bagaimana Nasib Kawasan Mangrove Teluk Balikpapan Kala Ada IKN Nusantara?" [What Is the Fate of the Mangrove Area of Balikpapan Bay When There Is IKN Nusantara?]. *Mongabay*, 7 September 2022. https://www.mongabay.co.id/2022/09/07/bagaimana-nasib-kawasan-mangrove-teluk-balikpapan-kala-ada-ikn-nusantara/ (accessed 17 November 2022).

Harrington, M.H. 2014. "Changing Exchanges: A Modern Siang Village Amidst Resource Extraction in Regional Indonesia". PhD dissertation, Asia Institute, University of Melbourne.

Keane, J. 1998. *Civil Society: Old Images, New Visions*. Stanford, CA: Stanford University Press.

Kompas. 2022. "DPR Setujui Daftar 39 RUU Prolegnas Prioritas 2023, Salah Satunya Revisi UU IKN Usulan Pemerintah" [DPR Agreed to the List of 39 Bills to Be Prioritised in Its Deliberation in 2023, One of Them Is the Revision of the IKN Law as Suggested by the Government]. 15 December 2022. https://nasional.kompas.com/read/2022/12/15/14161961/dpr-setujui-daftar-39-ruu-prolegnas-prioritas-2023-salah-satunya-revisi-uu (accessed 11 January 2023).

Mahkamah Konstitusi Republik Indonesia. 2022. "Kurang Partisipasi Publik, UU IKN Kembali Diuji" [Lacking Public Participation, the IKN Law Goes Through a Formal Review]. 25 April 2022. https://www.mkri.id/index.php?page=web.Berita&id=18164 (accessed 19 February 2023).

McIlwaine, C. 2007. "From Local to Global to Transnational Civil Society: Re-Framing Development Perspectives on the Non-State Sector". *Geography Compass* 1, no. 6: 1252–81.

Moniaga, S. 2007. "From *Bumiputera* to *Masyarakat Adat*: A Long and Confusing Journey". In *The Revival of Tradition in Indonesian Politics: The Deployment of Adat from Colonialism to Indigenism*, edited by Jamie Davidson and David Henley, pp. 295–314. London: Routledge.

Nuraini, D. 2019. "Sukanto Tanoto Lepas Konsesi di Kaltim Seluas 41.000 Hektare" [Sukanto Tanoto Released 41,000 hectare Concessions in East Kalimantan]. *Ekonomi*, 1 November 2019. https://ekonomi.bisnis.com/read/20191101/99/1165735/sukanto-tanoto-lepas-konsesi-di-kaltim-seluas-41.000-hektare (accessed 17 November 2022).

Okushima, M. 2006. "Ethnohistory of the Kayanic peoples in Northeast Borneo (Part 1): Evidence from Their Languages, Old Ethnonyms, and Social Organization". *Borneo Research Bulletin* 37: 86–126.

Ostrom Award. 2015. "Abdon Nababan—AMAN, winner of the Elinor Ostrom Award 2015 in the Category of Practitioners". *YouTube*, 11 August 2015. https://www.youtube.com/watch?v=DWj3ZjCgVCU and https://www.elinorostromaward.org/2015-practitioners-award (accessed 26 September 2022).

Peterson, T.J., and J. Van Til. 2004. "Defining Characteristics of Civil Society". *International Journal of Not-for-Profit-Law* 6, no. 2 (February). https://www.icnl.org/resources/research/ijnl/defining-characteristics-of-civil-society

Rachmawati. 2022. "IKN Nusantara, Bagaimana Nasib Masyarakat Adat di Sekitarnya?". [IKN Nusantara, What Would Be the Fate of the Surrounding Adat Communities?]. *Kompas*, 15 March 2022, https://regional.kompas.com/read/2022/03/15/122500778/ikn-nusantara-bagaimana-nasib-masyarakat-adat-di-sekitarnya-?page=all (accessed 26 September 2022).

Redaksi, 2019. "AMAN: Kalau Negara Tidak Mengakui Kami, Kami pun Tidak Mengakui Negara". *Sinar Keadilan*, 25 October 2019. https://sinarkeadilan.com/aman-kalau-negara-tidak-mengakui-kami-kami-pun-tidak-mengakui-negara/ (accessed 26 September 2022).

Schreer, V. 2016. "Longing for Prosperity in Indonesian Borneo". PhD dissertation, University of Kent.

United Nations. 2016. "Free Prior and Informed Consent: An Indigenous Peoples' Right and Good Practice for Local Communities—A Manual for Project Practitioners". 14 October 2016. https://www.un.org/development/desa/indigenouspeoples/publications/2016/10/free-prior-and-informed-consent-an-indigenous-peoples-right-and-a-good-practice-for-local-communities-fao/ (accessed 26 September 2022).

WALHI. 2022. "UU IKN Ingkari Konstitusi: Rakyat Minta Pembatalan Lewat Judicial Review" [The Law on the State's Capital Denies the Constitution: The People Asked for a Repeal Through Judicial Review]. 1 April 2022. https://www.walhi.or.id/uu-ikn-ingkari-konstitusi-rakyat-minta-pembatalan-lewat-judicial-review (accessed 17 November 2022).

World Bank. 2010. "Defining Civil Society". https://www.weforum.org/agenda/2018/04/what-is-civil-society/ (accessed 18 November 2022).

8

POPULATION AND HUMAN CAPITAL REDISTRIBUTION
Understanding Opportunities and Challenges in Mass Migration to Nusantara

Meirina Ayumi Malamassam

INTRODUCTION

Law No. 3 of 2022 on Indonesia's State Capital City (*Ibu Kota Negara*, IKN) has provided a legal framework for the development of Nusantara, the new capital city of Indonesia. The IKN's development is estimated to be accompanied by the mass in-migration of construction workers, civil servants and their family members, academics and researchers, and tertiary students. Around 1.7 to 1.9 million people are estimated to inhabit the new capital by 2045.[1]

The residential mobility of around 250,000 construction workers and civil servants in 2024 would be the main feature of the initial phases of the capital relocation.[2] Public service workers from particular institutions are prioritized to move earlier to Nusantara. These include the coordinating ministries, the triumvirate of the Ministries of Home Affairs, Foreign Affairs, and Defence, government agencies supporting the offices of the president and vice president and those responsible for development planning and budgeting, and law enforcement. In addition, civil servants from ministries that directly support the development of the IKN and agencies that work on basic needs services and human capital development are also targeted to migrate earlier. However, Annex II of the law states that not all public sector workers would be posted to the IKN. Several criteria have been defined as bases to assess how qualified civil servants are for the relocation, including their highest educational attainment, retirement age and performance evaluation.

In addition to being the centre of government-related activities, the IKN is designed to provide world-class tertiary education institutions focused on science, technology, engineering and mathematics (STEM), as well as specialized skills training. Although Indonesia has become one of the largest and fastest-growing tertiary education systems in the world, with approximately 7.6 million students enrolled in over 3,100 institutions,[3] Indonesia's tertiary education system still faces problems like considerable variations in the quality of institutions. Based on the clustering of higher education institutions (HEIs) by the Ministry of Education and Culture in 2020,[4] only fifteen Indonesian universities are acknowledged to have "excellent" academic performance and are classified in the first cluster. Meanwhile, about 74 per cent of the HEIs belonged to the lowest clusters, defined as "poor". Besides that, the distribution of reputable HEIs is concentrated on Java island, resulting in low accessibility to quality tertiary education for those living outside Java. The 2020 ranking showed that only about a quarter of the top fifty universities were located outside of Java, and of these, only one HEI on Kalimantan was in the group. Therefore, the establishment of quality tertiary institutions in the IKN can be considered to be a crucial effort to provide equitable access to higher education beyond Java. The development of such institutions would require the in-migration of academic and research staff from various regions in the country, especially Java. Also, tertiary students who would pursue higher education in the IKN are expected to move to the capital city zone not only from its immediate surroundings but also from outside Kalimantan.

To achieve the estimated population size in the IKN, i.e., 1.7–1.9 million people by 2045, the population growth rate in this city should be around 9–10 per cent annually. The increase in the number of IKN inhabitants would be highly dependent on the in-migration flows. From the population planning estimates, it can be inferred that the profile of the in-migrants mainly comprises highly educated individuals. From the regional development perspective, such a considerable number of well-educated in-migrants can be seen as an opportunity to accumulate human capital and accelerate economic growth in IKN. However, highly educated migrants bring about distinctive spatial characteristics and demographic implications that require particular attention in the context of population and human capital redistribution within a country. Also, extensive development in the country's information, transportation and communication sectors has resulted in new types of mobility patterns and increased the complexity of mobility processes in Indonesia in recent years. Thus, a great challenge awaits in population dynamics and regional development in IKN.

While internal migration dynamics in Indonesia have been studied extensively,[5] exploring in-migration flows towards a newly built capital city in the Indonesian context is unknown ground. Therefore, this chapter discusses the potential implication of in-migration into the IKN by reviewing existing studies on in-migration to a newly built city in other countries. It also discusses trends and patterns of spatial mobility among migrants in Indonesia, as well as the human capital aspects of in-migration flows. This chapter uses information from previous empirical studies and research reports on this topic to establish a basis for designing social policies that can address future implications of mass in-migration to the IKN, as the latter will affect not only the IKN's economic development but also its population composition.

In the next section, several cases of migration to new cities in selected countries will be discussed, highlighting critical factors influencing migration decisions in newly established areas, as well as opportunities and challenges faced during migration processes. In the subsequent section, the chapter will explore trends and patterns of spatial mobility across regions in Indonesia. By looking at the nature of the population mobility of Indonesian workers, this chapter points out the potential mobility patterns highly associated with the IKN. Next, this chapter discusses the implication of population flows to the IKN on human capital redistribution within Indonesia.

New Capital City and In-migration: What Should We Expect?

The establishment of a new city is a natural phenomenon in urban planning development. New cities are commonly built as the country develops and its economy emerges. For example, several cities were built in Arabian Gulf countries in response to the rapid economic development in these countries.[6] Newly built cities are often considered a critical solution to overcome classic issues in urban development, such as overpopulation, traffic congestion, pollution, as well as housing and green space shortages.[7] This argument is found mainly in the narrative of moving the administrative capital to a new region, including Indonesia.[8] Several countries, such as Brazil, Kazakhstan, Australia and Malaysia, have relocated their capital cities to a new region. Moreover, Indonesia is not the only country currently planning to relocate its capital. Other countries and territories, such as South Korea, Egypt, Equatorial Guinea and Montserrat, have also announced their plans for new capital cities.[9] The relocation of government ministries and agencies to

Sejong, the new administrative capital of South Korea, started in 2012 and this process is expected to be completed by 2030.[10] In Egypt, about 30,000 state employees would be relocated to the new administrative capital by March 2023.[11] The relocation to the new capital of Equatorial Guinea was planned to take place in 2017, but the old capital, Malabo, still serves as the centre of government activities to date.[12] In Montserrat, construction work on the new capital, Little Bay, has begun in 2022.[13]

Typically, the initiative to relocate the centre of government activities to a new region is crucial to lessen the developmental gap between the region where the existing capital is located and other regions in the country. In the Malaysian context, the new administrative capital, Putrajaya, was conceived to relieve congestion and infrastructure problems faced by the old capital, Kuala Lumpur.[14] In Kazakhstan, the new capital city, Astana, is situated in the centre of the country; its location was strategically chosen to be further away from neighbouring countries.[15] Separately, the relocation of Brazil's capital city from Rio de Janeiro to Brasilia in 1960 was triggered by the unsuitability of the former capital to operate effectively as the centre of government and political activities.[16] In another example, Canberra was chosen as Australia's capital after a long dispute on the siting of the nation's capital, in a competition between Melbourne and Sydney.[17]

In the Indonesian context, Annex II of Law No. 3 of 2022 states that the establishment of the new capital city aims to achieve more inclusive economic development by accelerating regional growth in the eastern part of Indonesia. The capital city relocation from Jakarta to a newly established city outside Java is considered to be urgent due to the high population density and concentration of economic activities on Java Island, as well as the limited carrying capacity and water supply to support the high rate of urbanization in Jakarta and its surrounding areas.[18]

For newly built cities, whether they are capital cities or not, population in-migration is a critical prerequisite to further developing the region.[19] Therefore, sound planning for internal migration to new cities is important to ensure that the newly established area will be effectively populated and function as intended. Factors associated with the migrants' origin and destination areas play crucial roles in shaping migration flow between regions.[20] Although factors related to areas of origin ("push factors") generally result from an unhurried and thorough evaluation of positive or negative factors due to the long period of settlement in home regions, factors associated with areas of destination ("pull factors") are related to perceived situations in particular regions based on information obtained through the prospective migrants' social networks.

A similar set of push and pull factors can be found in in-migration flows towards newly established cities.[21] Pull factors can vary from the provision of government-subsidized housing to the creation of job opportunities and the opening of new government offices and educational institutions. Meanwhile, push factors can include the high cost of living, traffic congestion, long daily commuting time and limited housing facilities. However, some residents may reject the idea of moving to new cities due to their preference for living in areas with familiar settings or to remaining close to their family.

For capital cities, in particular, the first phase of in-migration towards these areas is highly related to the relocation and redistribution of public sector jobs. In this context, the push factor for migration is government control of civil servants' relocation. Since the capital city plays an important role as the centre of government activities, the presence of civil servants in the newly established nation's capital is necessary to carry out the central government's tasks effectively and efficiently. Relocation of public sector jobs, followed by in-migration of civil servants, could boost the economy in less developed regions and create job opportunities for local residents. In the United Kingdom, for example, while its capital city is London, there was a dispersal of 25,000 central government workers from London to peripheral regions over eight years from 2003 to 2010.[22]

The policy of public sector relocation is also expected to reduce income disparities within the country. The acceleration of the economic sector through the in-migration flows of public sector workers occurs when their presence can encourage multiplier effects in terms of creating additional local jobs. A study on the dispersal of public sector works in the UK shows that for the relocation of every ten civil servants, there would be a recruitment of eleven new workers in the private sector, particularly sectors that provide locally produced goods and services to government-driven migrants.[23] Creating such jobs may act as an important pull factor that drives additional in-migration flows towards the new centre of government activities. On the other hand, the dispersal of public sector jobs might trigger inflationary effects that result in higher local wages, costs of living and housing prices.

These inflationary effects are commonly more substantial than multiplier effects and can result in the displacement of supporting service businesses.[24] This situation occurs particularly a decade after the initiation of a new government centre.[25] The stagnation of in-migration flows of public sector workers after several years may in turn adversely affect private sector activities. This stalling population growth in a capital city highly dependent on the in-migration of civil servants occurred in Putrajaya, the administrative capital of Malaysia. Since its construction in the mid-1990s, Putrajaya has been home to federal government ministries and national-level public service workers. However, the city failed to attract additional in-migrants from other working sectors over time. Due to the city's slowdown in service sectors, its population was only 120,000 in 2021 (or about a 1.83 per cent annual growth rate) in the past ten years.[26] Moreover, this number is much lower than the intended population of 350,000 residents for Putrajaya. The challenges in managing a city dominated by governmental activities can also be seen in the case of Canberra, Australia. Its low population density, sprawling development pattern and less diversity in economic activities have made the city costly to operate and maintain.[27]

Newly established cities can be seen as a one-stop solution to overcome nations' problems of disproportionate population distribution, urban density and pollution, limited access to basic needs and economic stagnation.[28] However, not every new city succeeds in functioning according to its original plan, since the pull factors towards the unknown region may vary over time. Successful new cities have embedded economic drivers that can continually attract in-migration, while new cities that fail to follow the dynamics of labour market demand commonly struggle to excel in their economic development. Additionally, public participation in the planning of a new city is critical to have a proper estimation of in-migration flows and population growth.[29] The establishment of new cities should consider future residents' preferences, demands and choices. However, in many cases around the world, the planning and development of new cities are more likely to be carried out with a top-down approach. In such an approach, government authorities make their assumptions regarding in-migration flows without consultation. Thus, the projections for in-migration may be highly speculative given the limited public engagement in regional planning.

For in-migration flows to take place, the government must ensure there is a sufficient number of people willing to move to the planned new cities. Additionally, at the planning stage, the government should thoroughly consider the drivers of internal migration.[30] Authorities must understand that the decision to migrate is triggered not only by economic opportunities but also by complex factors including personal or emotional ones, that can affect individuals' decisions to leave or stay in their areas of origin.[31]

Migration decisions do not result from a simple calculation of positive and negative factors in the areas of origin and destination of prospective migrants. The fact that only a portion of the population eventually migrates, while factors in the place of origin and destination apply equally to all people in a given area, shows the critical role of the individual characteristics of prospective migrants.[32] Being influenced by their socio-demographic, socio-economic and socio-cultural backgrounds, some people may be resistant to changes in their living environments, while others actively look for opportunities to live in new places. For example, married individuals with school-age children are more likely to consider the provision of education facilities as an important factor when making migration decisions. For unmarried individuals, the availability of employment opportunities could be the most crucial consideration.

Heterogeneous population groups with different preferences and needs can respond differently to push and pull factors of migration to newly established cities.[33] Further, rather than directly responding to labour market opportunities in newly planned cities, decisions for internal migration have been mainly driven by indirect incentives in recent years.[34] These factors should not be ignored in the planning processes of Indonesia's new capital city. Otherwise, it may result in a costly new "ghost city" due to insufficient in-migrants.[35]

The ghost cities phenomenon is defined as the establishment of a new city accompanied by large-scale development of urban facilities and an abundance of newly built space, but a deficiency in residents. The development of new cities is usually conducted as quickly as possible, without taking into account in-migration dynamics, thus resulting in the oversupply and under-utilization of public infrastructure. In the context of newly built capital cities, some such as Brasilia, Canberra and Putrajaya, are filled with monumental and symbolic public infrastructure that is often seen as a symbol of state power.[36] This kind of development arguably makes those cities lack urban character and social dynamics. The new capital cities are also rarely regarded as the most liveable and celebrated cities in their respective countries. It is important to note that, in addition to government intervention in such in-migration, the population size in new capital cities often takes years to grow as targeted. Modelling of internal migration to new cities estimates that it takes at least three decades after their establishment to achieve the country's goals of transferring population density and mitigating any inter-regional economic development gaps.[37]

People on the Move: Internal Migration in Indonesia and Migrants' Mobility Patterns

Based on the regularity of mobility patterns and their links to the country's modernization, Indonesia is already at a late stage of its mobility transition.[38]

This stage is marked by the dominance of "circular mobility" as well as inter-urban and intra-urban movements representing major residential migration patterns.[39] Circular mobility is one of the forms of temporary spatial movement that represents multiple moves in relatively short periods of time.[40] The level of inter-regional mobility has increased considerably due to the extensive development of the information, transportation and communication sectors, as well as the implementation of decentralization and regional autonomy policies in the late 1990s. The increasing share of lifetime migrants—those whose last recorded residences are different from their birthplaces—illustrates the growing number of mobile populations in Indonesia over the years (see Figure 8.1).

Since the measurement of lifetime migration could exclude returning migrants (to their birthplaces), the lifetime migration trend could understate the actual situation of population movement within a country. However, the lifetime migration profile in Indonesia signifies the increasing importance of inter-regional mobility in the population stock across the regions. However, as highlighted in mobility transition theory, there was a decreasing trend in the share of recent migrants since 1990 (Figure 8.1). The profile of "recent" migrants—persons whose current areas of residence are different from

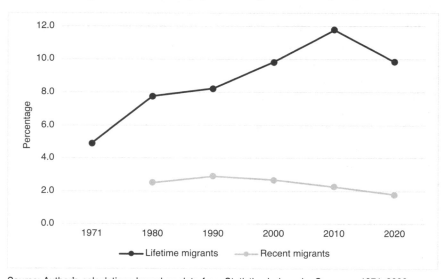

FIGURE 8.1
Migrants in Indonesia, by Percentage of Total Population

Source: Author's calculations based on data from Statistics Indonesia, Censuses 1971–2020.

where they resided five years earlier—better explains the contextual factors affecting migration flows. Despite the slight drop from about 3 per cent in 1990 to 1.8 per cent in 2020, the intensity of longer-distance movement has increased in recent years, and recent migrants were found to have a higher tendency to move further away from their areas of origin.[41] Additionally, the share of tertiary-educated migration towards rural areas in the eastern part of Indonesia has increased markedly, from 1.8 per cent in 2000 to 4 per cent in 2010.[42] Since rural east Indonesia is generally considered the least developed region, this trend may also signal the critical development of transportation modes and communication infrastructure in that part of Indonesia.

The dynamics of internal migration in Indonesia can be explained through several narratives. First, state intervention during the Suharto era through the enforcement of a population resettlement programme, widely known as "transmigration", peaked from the early 1980s until the 1990s.[43] This national policy aimed to reduce population pressure on Java Island by sending Javanese agricultural households to less densely populated regions outside Java. Transmigrants were mainly agricultural workers who did not own land and were characterized by their low level of education.[44] Internal migration in Indonesia also mainly features labour migration motivated by income differentials and employment divergence across regions.[45] Migration flows tend to focus on urban areas and this resulted in shifts to more urbanized economic environments.[46]

Cultural background or social norms related to the migratory traditions of particular communities or ethnic groups have also been influential in migration dynamics in Indonesia.[47] Some highly mobile ethnic groups in this country, such as the Minang, Batak and Bugis, view migration as a rite of passage, where young people leave their hometowns to seek knowledge and new experiences or to earn a living. However, culturally bound migration is usually seen as temporary because many of the migrants still intend to return home at later ages.

Migration in Indonesia is mainly driven by family and economic motives.[48] Family-driven migration usually takes place following a change of marital status or prior migration of one's family members, such as their spouse or parents, while economic-related migration is mainly associated with individuals pursuing work opportunities elsewhere. Education-related motives have also been important, especially among the younger population. Migration from rural to urban areas is primarily driven by youth's aspirations to earn higher wages and to have better access to education and healthcare facilities.[49] In East Kalimantan province, where the IKN would be situated, around 4 per cent of the workers are recent migrants and most of them are 15 to 34 years years old.[50] Nearly a third of these recent labour migrants have graduated from higher institutions, which is a high proportion.

It is broadly understood that once people migrate, they are more likely to be highly mobile. A 2019 study by the Research Centre for Population (LIPI) on migrants' mobility patterns in one of the major destination cities in Indonesia, Balikpapan, in East Kalimantan Province, shows that the high intensity of circular mobility is one of the prominent characteristics of migrant workers, both skilled and unskilled, in this city.[51] While a wide range of job opportunities has been the main pull factor for in-migration flows to Balikpapan, many in-migrants—particularly the highly educated ones—have shown a distinctive pattern of a "fly-in fly-out" mobility, a long-distance commuting form between employees' two residences (or more) so they do not necessarily reside full-time in Balikpapan. This pattern has emerged because the relocation of migrants' workplaces might not be accompanied by a change in their permanent residences. Although workplace relocation commonly comes with housing support, many migrants leave their family members during weekdays and fly back to their origin or home residence every weekend. In Indonesian, they call themselves *Pulang Jumat Kembali Ahad* (PJKA, "go home on Friday and back to work on Sunday").

While weekly commuting like the PJKA is a less popular form of spatial mobility compared to migration and daily commuting, its importance has recently increased significantly, particularly for workers from dual-earner households.[52] Most weekend commuters are individuals with working spouses and school-age children, and own houses in their origin areas. Weekly commuting is thus considered a close substitute for migration due to inter-regional job changes. This practice has been promoted by the rapid development of transportation networks and info-communication and technological facilities. While employers usually offer financial incentives to encourage migration following a job relocation, some employees might see migration as unfavourable and complex since it also involves their household members changing jobs or schools and also their living environment. For these individuals, weekly commuting can be a short-term practice during the first few years of their job relocation, but many workers consider this mobility pattern an established lifestyle.[53]

Migrants have voiced various considerations regarding their preferences for circular mobility. Still, the most prominent reason for their migration decision is the availability of public services and living amenities compared to their origin areas.[54] Many highly educated migrants think that their workplace relocation is only a temporary spatial movement. Their flying home every weekend is still considered financially viable and less costly than choosing to relocate their entire family. From the illustration of mobility patterns of the highly educated in-migrants in Balikpapan, a similar situation can be anticipated in relocating similar types of in-migrants to the IKN.

Human Capital Flows Towards the New Capital

The IKN is designed to reduce the population pressure in Jakarta. Moreover, in the context of regional development, migration marks an inter-regional transfer of human capital. The nature and extent of the effects of migration on human capital development are heavily subject to the socio-demographic characteristics of the migrants and their productivity in the destination areas. Therefore, migration flows—driven by educational qualification—play a critical role in the distribution of human capital in the proposed IKN. Human capital comprises two prominent components, education and health capital. Education capital manifests in an individual's educational attainment, income, and duration of employment, while health capital is represented by life expectancy in years. However, the sustainability of regional development in the IKN is largely attributed to education capital.[55] While those with a high level of human capital or highly educated migrants can choose to remain in the IKN if this new city offers them a higher income than in their origin areas, their preferences for permanent residency could be influenced by other factors. For example, they would consider their prospects for career development and upward social mobility, the presence of public amenities and leisure facilities, and the extension of social networks.[56] Tertiary-educated migrants tend to have low retention rates in their destination areas due to less social cohesion between themselves and the local communities.

The current capital city, Jakarta, and its surrounding regions have been a melting pot of human capital flows within the country due to their prominent role in accumulating and redistributing migrants with differing educational, ethnic, and cultural backgrounds. Retaining human capital stock in the migrants' destination can be a crucial challenge in developing the IKN because tertiary-educated migrants have distinctive patterns in their migration processes.[57] While the spatial structure of their migration exhibits more dispersed patterns of origin-destination pairs compared to lower-educated groups, they are also the group with the highest likelihood of conducting multiple migrations in one lifetime.

FIGURE 8.2
Predicted Probabilities of Migration by Educational Attainment

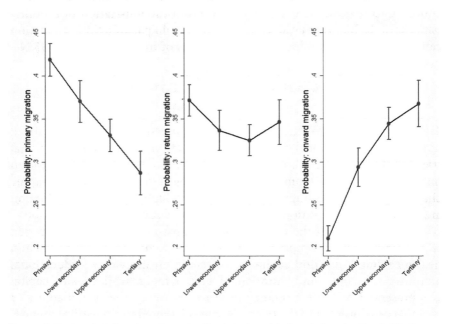

Source: Author's calculations based on migration trajectory data from Indonesian Family Life Survey (IFLS), 1993–2014.

By categorizing young adult migrants into three groups, Figure 8.2 shows that the higher the migrant's educational background, the lower the propensity of any young adult to stay permanently in their initial migration destination. The first group are primary migrants (who record one move across sub-province boundaries during the young adult period), the second is return migrants (who move more than once; residential district at age 34 is the same as any district lived in before age 15), and the third, onward migrants (who move more than once; residential district at age 34 is different from their childhood residence).

In the IKN context, the first in-migration phase of highly educated public sector workers is expected to accelerate human capital stock in the newly established IKN region. This initial move will have great potential to attract more in-migration flows into the new capital city. The agglomeration of skilled workers in an area could be a strong pull factor for the in-migration of other highly skilled individuals.[58] However, the high propensity for multiple migrations by the highly educated group—as shown in Figure 8.2—can have a negative impact on human capital accumulation in the IKN, as their migration might take the form of temporary short-term movements. Once they accumulate more soft capital, such as skills and variations in work experience, to enhance their capabilities, they might choose to migrate or return to other areas that offer better economic opportunities and living amenities.[59]

On the other hand, lowly or lower-educated migrants are shown to be more responsive to employment opportunities in destination areas.[60] For primary-educated migrants, particularly, their outflows from rural areas appear to be a response to labour demands of the informal sectors in metropolitan regions.[61] Moreover, as indicated in Figure 8.2, migrants with a primary school education or below tend to conduct permanent residential changes and their more permanent movements imply how limited human capital constrains such migrants from having additional moves.

In the context of the IKN's human capital composition, the in-flows of low-educated migrants are attributed to the migration of construction labours and informal workers. Unlike tertiary educated migrants in the IKN who would be driven by government policies, the decision to migrate to the IKN by those with primary or lower secondary education would be mainly influenced by the working opportunities in the city's construction sector and the development of supporting service sectors.

The IKN's population planning should consider the distinctive nature of spatial mobility across population groups with various educational backgrounds. The projections for population growth, in particular, must take into account the high propensity to make multiple moves of highly educated migrants and the tendency of permanent movement by lowly educated or low-skilled individuals. In the long term, this situation could negatively influence human capital composition in the IKN and have a critical effect on the slowdown of public infrastructure and living amenities development in the city.

Conclusions

In summary, migration is a crucial component of establishing a newly built city. Any new capital city, in particular, is highly dependent on the presence of in-migrants to be able to work and function as intended in its spatial planning. While the population size in the IKN during the early years of its establishment will increase largely due to the gradual transfer of civil servants and some of their families, the significant natural growth of this area will take many years and heavily depend on the developmental progress of the IKN. Therefore, the projected annual population growth rate of about 9–10 per cent until 2045 is likely overly ambitious.

The migration scheme of public sector workers from Indonesia's essential ministries and government agencies could be seen as a practical way to transfer people and human capital from densely populated and developed regions of Jakarta and its surrounding areas to the new capital. However, the main challenge in population planning in the IKN is getting other population groups, such as family members of the relocated civil servants and skilled private sector individuals to move to this city. Learning from other countries' experiences, there are multiple factors influencing successful migration to a new capital city. Beyond the provision of employment opportunities, factors such as the provision of living amenities and a vibrant livelihood will also affect the outcome of migration to the new capital.

The establishment of the IKN is designed to have a multiplier effect on population distribution and national economic development. Theoretically, the clustering of a highly educated population through the initial civil servant migration may trigger more in-migration flows through the development of supporting service sectors for public workers. This situation may accelerate human capital accumulation in the new capital. However, it remains unknown whether Nusantara will end up being a vibrant capital or a "ghost" city in the future.

Notes

1. Annex II, Law No. 3 of 2022 on Indonesia's State Capital City (Ibu Kota Negara) (accessed 20 December 2022), https://peraturan.bpk.go.id/Home/Details/198400/uu-no-3-tahun-2022
2. *CNN Indonesia*, "Penduduk IKN Akan Dibatasi Maksimal Hanya 1,91 Juta Orang", 22 November 2022, https://www.cnnindonesia.com/ekonomi/20221122 182527-92-877239/penduduk-ikn-akan-dibatasi-maksimal-hanya-191-juta-orang
3. Statistics Indonesia, "Jumlah Perguruan Tinggi, Tenaga Pendidik dan Mahasiswa (Negeri dan Swasta) di Bawah Kementerian Riset, Teknologi dan Pendidikan Tinggi/Kementerian Pendidikan dan Kebudayaan Menurut Provinsi, 2021", https://www.bps.go.id/indikator/indikator/view_data_pub/0000/api_pub/cmdTdG5vU0IwKzBFR20rQnpuZEYzdz09/da_04/1 (accessed 3 January 2023).
4. Direktorat Jendral Pendidikan Tinggi, "Klasterisasi Pendidikan Tinggi", https://klasterisasi-pt.kemdikbud.go.id/ (accessed 15 December 2022).
5. Meirina Ayumi Malamassam, "Spatial Structure of Youth Migration in Indonesia: Does Education Matter?", *Applied Spatial Analysis and Policy* 15, no. 4 (1 December 2022): 1045–74, https://doi.org/10.1007/s12061-022-09434-6; Sukamdi and Ghazy Mujahid, *Internal Migration in Indonesia*, UNFPA Indonesia Monograph Series 3 (Jakarta: UNFPA Indonesia, 2015), https://indonesia.unfpa.

org/sites/default/files/pub-pdf/FA_Isi_BUKU_Monograph_Internal_Migration_ENG.pdf; Nashrul Wajdi, Sri Moertiningsih Adioetomo, and Clara H. Mulder, "Gravity Models of Interregional Migration in Indonesia", *Bulletin of Indonesian Economic Studies* 53, no. 3 (2 September 2017): 309–20, https://doi.org/10.10 80/00074918.2017.1298719; Salut Muhidin, "An Analysis of the Relationship between Internal Migration and Education in Indonesia", Background Paper, *2019 Global Education Monitoring Report* (UNESCO, 2018), https://unesdoc.unesco.org/ark:/48223/pf0000266053

6. Nayef Alghais, David Pullar, and Elin Charles-Edwards, "Accounting for Peoples' Preferences in Establishing New Cities: A Spatial Model of Population Migration in Kuwait", *PLoS ONE* 13, no. 12 (2018): 1–31, https://doi.org/10.1371/journal.pone.0209065

7. Wade Shepard, "Should We Build Cities from Scratch?", *The Guardian*, 10 July 2019, https://www.theguardian.com/cities/2019/jul/10/should-we-build-cities-from-scratch

8. Kementerian PPN/Bappenas, *Buku Saku Pemindahan Ibu Kota Negara* (Kementerian PPN/Bappenas, 2021), https://ikn.go.id/storage/buku-saku-ikn-072121.pdf (accessed 1 October 2022),; Wilmar Salim and Siwage Dharma Negara, "Shifting the Capital from Jakarta: Reasons and Challenges", *ISEAS Perspective*, no. 2019/79, 1 October 2019.

9. Behlul Cetinkaya, "Climate Change, Growing Population Forcing 4 Countries to Move Capital Cities", *Anadolu Agency*, 4 May 2022, https://www.aa.com.tr/en/environment/climate-change-growing-population-forcing-4-countries-to-move-capital-cities/2579343

10. *dw.com*, "New South Korean President Wants to Relocate Capital City", 18 March 2022, https://www.dw.com/en/south-korea-incoming-president-yoon-wants-to-relocate-capital-from-seoul/a-61170422

11. *Ahram Online*, "New Capital Moves", 13 January 2023, https://english.ahram.org.eg/NewsContent/50/1201/484038/AlAhram-Weekly/Egypt/New-capital-moves.aspx

12. *The City Topic*, "Ciudad de La Paz: The New Capital of Equatorial Guinea Rises in the Tropical Forest", 15 October 2021, https://www.thecitytopic.com/2021/10/ciudad-de-la-paz-new-capital-of.html

13. *BBC News*, "Montserrat Profile", 17 January 2023, sec. Latin America & Caribbean, https://www.bbc.com/news/world-latin-america-20256517

14. Sarah Moser, "Putrajaya: Malaysia's New Federal Administrative Capital", *Cities* 27, no. 4 (1 August 2010): 285–97, https://doi.org/10.1016/j.cities.2009.11.002

15. Bolat Tatibekov, Kamal Fatehi, and Foad Derakhshan, "Migrants to Astana, the New Capital City of Kazakhstan", *Competition Forum* 6, no. 2 (2008): 350–56.

16. J.V. Freitas Marcondes, "Brasilia, The New Capital Of Brazil", *The Mississippi Quarterly* 12, no. 4 (1959): 157–67.

17. National Capital Authority, "The Siting and Naming of Canberra", https://www.

nca.gov.au/education/canberras-history/siting-and-naming-canberra# (accessed 1 September 2022).
18. Kementerian PPN/Bappenas, *Buku Saku Pemindahan Ibu Kota Negara*.
19. Shepard, "Should We Build Cities from Scratch?".
20. Everett S. Lee, "A Theory of Migration", *Demography* 3, no. 1 (1966): 47–57, https://doi.org/10.2307/2060063
21. Alghais, Pullar, and Charles-Edwards, "Accounting for Peoples' Preferences in Establishing New Cities".
22. Giulia Faggio, "Relocation of Public Sector Workers: Evaluating a Place-Based Policy", *Journal of Urban Economics* 111 (1 May 2019): 53–75, https://doi.org/10.1016/j.jue.2019.03.001
23. Ibid.
24. Ibid.
25. Giulia Faggio and Henry Overman, "The Effect of Public Sector Employment on Local Labour Markets", *Journal of Urban Economics*, Spatial Dimensions of Labor Markets, 79 (1 January 2014): 91–107, https://doi.org/10.1016/j.jue.2013.05.002
26. Moser, "Putrajaya: Malaysia's New Federal Administrative Capital"; Ronan O'Connell, "Putrajaya: The Capital City You've Never Heard Of", https://www.bbc.com/travel/article/20210901-putrajaya-the-capital-city-youve-never-heard-of (accessed 9 January 2023).
27. Salim and Negara, "Shifting the Capital from Jakarta: Reasons and Challenges".
28. Shepard, "Should We Build Cities from Scratch?".
29. Alghais, Pullar, and Charles-Edwards, "Accounting for Peoples' Preferences in Establishing New Cities".
30. Max D. Woodworth and Jeremy L. Wallace, "Seeing Ghosts: Parsing China's 'Ghost City' Controversy", *Urban Geography* 38, no. 8 (14 September 2017): 1270–81, https://doi.org/10.1080/02723638.2017.1288009
31. William A.V. Clark, and William Lisowski, "Extending the Human Capital Model of Migration: The Role of Risk, Place, and Social Capital in the Migration Decision", *Population, Space and Place* 25, no. 4 (2019): e2225, https://doi.org/10.1002/psp.2225; Meirina Ayumi Malamassam et al., "'Move Backward to Make a Step Forward': Understanding the Migration of the Highly Educated to Sorong City, West Papua, Indonesia", *Asian and Pacific Migration Journal* 30, no. 4 (1 December 2021): 485–99, https://doi.org/10.1177/01171968211069722
32. Lee, "A Theory of Migration".
33. Alghais, Pullar, and Charles-Edwards, "Accounting for Peoples' Preferences in Establishing New Cities".
34. Eugenia Chernina, Paul Castañeda Dower, and Andrei Markevich, "Property Rights, Land Liquidity, and Internal Migration", *Journal of Development Economics, Land and Property Rights* 110 (1 September 2014): 191–215, https://doi.org/10.1016/j.jdeveco.2013.03.010
35. Woodworth and Wallace, "Seeing Ghosts".
36. Amanda Achmadi, "After Jakarta: Imagining a New Capital", Indonesia at

Melbourne, 25 June 2019, https://indonesiaatmelbourne.unimelb.edu.au/after-jakarta-imagining-a-new-capital/
37. Alghais, Pullar, and Charles-Edwards, "Accounting for Peoples' Preferences in Establishing New Cities".
38. Aris Ananta and Evi Nurvidya Arifin, "Demographic and Population Mobility Transitions in Indonesia", PECC-ABAC Conference on "Demographic Change and International Labor Mobility in the Asia Pacific Region: Implications for Business and Cooperation", Seoul, South Korea, 2008, https://www.pecc.org/resources/labor/689-demographic-and-population-mobility-transitions-in-indonesia
39. Wilbur Zelinsky, "The Hypothesis of the Mobility Transition", *Geographical Review* 61, no. 2 (1971): 219–49, https://doi.org/10.2307/213996
40. Rosa Weber and Jan Saarela, "Circular Migration in a Context of Free Mobility: Evidence from Linked Population Register Data from Finland and Sweden", *Population, Space and Place* 25, no. 4 (2019): e2230, https://doi.org/10.1002/psp.2230
41. Sukamdi and Mujahid, *Internal Migration in Indonesia*; Statistics Indonesia, "Hasil Long Form Sensus Penduduk 2020", *Berita Resmi Statistik*, 30 January 2023, https://www.bps.go.id/pressrelease/2023/01/30/2039/hasil-long-form-sensus-penduduk-2020.html
42. Malamassam, "Spatial Structure of Youth Migration in Indonesia".
43. Riwanto Tirtosudarmo, "Mobility and Human Development in Indonesia", Human Development Research Papers (2009 to Present), Human Development Report Office (HDRO), United Nations Development Programme (UNDP), April 2009, http://ideas.repec.org/p/hdr/papers/hdrp-2009-19.html
44. Samuel Bazzi et al., "Skill Transferability, Migration, and Development: Evidence from Population Resettlement in Indonesia", *American Economic Review* 106, no. 9 (2016): 2658–98, https://doi.org/10.1257/aer.20141781
45. Gharad Bryan and Melanie Morten, "The Aggregate Productivity Effects of Internal Migration: Evidence from Indonesia", *Journal of Political Economy* 127, no. 5 (October 2019): 2229–68, https://doi.org/10.1086/701810; Sukamdi and Mujahid, *Internal Migration in Indonesia*; Wajdi, Adioetomo, and Mulder, "Gravity Models of Interregional Migration in Indonesia".
46. Gavin W. Jones and Wahyu Mulyana, *Urbanization in Indonesia*, vol. 4, UNFPA Indonesia Monograph Series (Jakarta: UNFPA Indonesia, 2015).
47. Ilmiawan Auwalin, "Ethnic Identity and Internal Migration Decision in Indonesia", *Journal of Ethnic and Migration Studies* 46, no. 13 (2 July 2020): 2841–61, https://doi.org/10.1080/1369183X.2018.1561252; Tirtosudarmo, "Mobility and Human Development in Indonesia".
48. Salut Muhidin, "An Analysis of the Relationship between Internal Migration and Education in Indonesia"; Meirina Ayumi Malamassam, "Youth Migration in Indonesia: Decision to Move and to Choose of Destination Areas", *Indonesian Journal of Geography* 48, no. 1 (2 August 2016): 62–72, https://doi.org/10.22146/ijg.12469

49. Sukamdi and Mujahid, *Internal Migration in Indonesia*.
50. Statistics Indonesia, *Statistik Mobilitas Penduduk dan Tenaga Kerja 2021* (BPS - Statistics Indonesia, 2021).
51. Meirina Ayumi Malamassam et al., *Mobilitas Penduduk Indonesia Dalam Situasi Dunia Global* (Jakarta: Pustaka Sinar Harapan, 2019).
52. Nico Stawarz, Heiko Rüger, and Thomas Skora, "Does Weekend Commuting Really Pay off? A Panel Analysis with German Data", *Population, Space and Place* 27, no. 8 (2021): e2464, https://doi.org/10.1002/psp.2464
53. A.E. Green, T. Hogarth, and R.E. Shackleton, "Longer Distance Commuting as a Substitute for Migration in Britain: A Review of Trends, Issues and Implications", *International Journal of Population Geography* 5, no. 1 (1999): 49–67, https://doi.org/10.1002/(SICI)1099-1220(199901/02)5:1<49::AID-IJPG124>3.0.CO;2-O
54. Malamassam et al., *Mobilitas Penduduk Indonesia Dalam Situasi Dunia Global*.
55. Takuya Shimamura and Takeshi Mizunoya, "Sustainability Prediction Model for Capital City Relocation in Indonesia Based on Inclusive Wealth and System Dynamics", *Sustainability* 12, no. 10 (January 2020): 4336, https://doi.org/10.3390/su12104336
56. Malamassam et al., "'Move Backward to Make a Step Forward.'"
57. Malamassam et al., "Spatial Structure of Youth Migration in Indonesia".
58. Yuming Fu and Stuart A. Gabriel, "Labor Migration, Human Capital Agglomeration and Regional Development in China", *Regional Science and Urban Economics*, Special Section on Asian Real Estate Market, 42, no. 3 (1 May 2012): 473–84, https://doi.org/10.1016/j.regsciurbeco.2011.08.006; World Bank, "World Development Report 2009: Reshaping Economic Geography" (Washington, DC: World Bank, 2009), https://doi.org/10.1596/978-0-8213-7607-2
59. Godfried Engbersen and Erik Snel, "Liquid Migration. Dynamic and Fluid Patterns of Post-Accession Migration Flows", in *Mobility in Transition*, edited by Birgit Glorius, Izabela Grabowska, and Aimee Kuvik (Amsterdam: Amsterdam University Press, 2013), 21–40, https://doi.org/10.1515/9789048515493-002
60. Malamassam et al., "Spatial Structure of Youth Migration in Indonesia".
61. Gavin W. Jones et al., "Migration, Ethnicity, and the Educational Gradient in the Jakarta Mega-Urban Region: A Spatial Analysis", *Bulletin of Indonesian Economic Studies* 52, no. 1 (2 January 2016): 55–76, https://doi.org/10.1080/00074918.2015.1129050

References

Achmadi, Amanda. 2019. "After Jakarta: Imagining a New Capital". *Indonesia at Melbourne*, 25 June 2019. https://indonesiaatmelbourne.unimelb.edu.au/after-jakarta-imagining-a-new-capital/

Ahram Online. 2023. "New Capital Moves". 13 January 2023. https://english.ahram.org.eg/NewsContent/50/1201/484038/AlAhram-Weekly/Egypt/New-capital-moves.aspx

Alghais, Nayef, David Pullar, and Elin Charles-Edwards. 2018. "Accounting for Peoples'

Preferences in Establishing New Cities: A Spatial Model of Population Migration in Kuwait". *PLoS ONE* 13, no. 12: 1–31. https://doi.org/10.1371/journal.pone.0209065

Ananta, Aris, and Evi Nurvidya Arifin. 2008. "Demographic and Population Mobility Transitions in Indonesia". PECC-ABAC Conference on "Demographic Change and International Labor Mobility in the Asia Pacific Region: Implications for Business and Cooperation. Seoul, South Korea". https://www.pecc.org/resources/labor/689-demographic-and-population-mobility-transitions-in-indonesia

Auwalin, Ilmiawan. 2020. "Ethnic Identity and Internal Migration Decision in Indonesia". *Journal of Ethnic and Migration Studies* 46, no. 13: 2841–61. https://doi.org/10.1080/1369183X.2018.1561252

Bazzi, Samuel, Arya Gaduh, Alexander D. Rothenberg, and Maisy Wong. 2016. "Skill Transferability, Migration, and Development: Evidence from Population Resettlement in Indonesia". *American Economic Review* 106, no. 9: 2658–98. https://doi.org/10.1257/aer.20141781

BBC News. 2023. "Montserrat Profile". 17 January 2023, sec. Latin America & Caribbean. https://www.bbc.com/news/world-latin-america-20256517

Bryan, Gharad, and Melanie Morten. 2019. "The Aggregate Productivity Effects of Internal Migration: Evidence from Indonesia". *Journal of Political Economy* 127, no. 5: 2229–68. https://doi.org/10.1086/701810

Cetinkaya, Behlul. 2022. "Climate Change, Growing Population Forcing 4 Countries to Move Capital Cities". *Anadolu Agency*, 4 May 2022. https://www.aa.com.tr/en/environment/climate-change-growing-population-forcing-4-countries-to-move-capital-cities/2579343

Chernina, Eugenia, Paul Castañeda Dower, and Andrei Markevich. 2014. "Property Rights, Land Liquidity, and Internal Migration". *Journal of Development Economics, Land and Property Rights* 110 (September): 191–215. https://doi.org/10.1016/j.jdeveco.2013.03.010

City Topic, The. 2021. "Ciudad de La Paz: The New Capital of Equatorial Guinea Rises in the Tropical Forest". 15 October 2021. https://www.thecitytopic.com/2021/10/ciudad-de-la-paz-new-capital-of.html

Clark, William A.V., and William Lisowski. 2019. "Extending the Human Capital Model of Migration: The Role of Risk, Place, and Social Capital in the Migration Decision". *Population, Space and Place* 25, no. 4: e2225. https://doi.org/10.1002/psp.2225

CNN Indonesia. 2022. "Penduduk IKN Akan Dibatasi Maksimal Hanya 1,91 Juta Orang". 22 November 2022. https://www.cnnindonesia.com/ekonomi/20221122182527-92-877239/penduduk-ikn-akan-dibatasi-maksimal-hanya-191-juta-orang

Direktorat Jendral Pendidikan Tinggi. 2020. "Klasterisasi Pendidikan Tinggi". https://klasterisasi-pt.kemdikbud.go.id/.

dw.com. 2022. "New South Korean President Wants to Relocate Capital City". 18 March 2022. https://www.dw.com/en/south-korea-incoming-president-yoon-wants-to-relocate-capital-from-seoul/a-61170422

Engbersen, Godfried, and Erik Snel. 2013. "Liquid Migration. Dynamic and Fluid

Patterns of Post-Accession Migration Flows". In *Mobility in Transition*, edited by Birgit Glorius, Izabela Grabowska, and Aimee Kuvik, pp. 21–40. Amsterdam: Amsterdam University Press. https://doi.org/10.1515/9789048515493-002

Faggio, Giulia. 2019. "Relocation of Public Sector Workers: Evaluating a Place-Based Policy". *Journal of Urban Economics* 111 (May): 53–75. https://doi.org/10.1016/j.jue.2019.03.001

———, and Henry Overman. 2014. "The Effect of Public Sector Employment on Local Labour Markets". *Journal of Urban Economics, Spatial Dimensions of Labor Markets* 79 (January): 91–107. https://doi.org/10.1016/j.jue.2013.05.002

Fu, Yuming, and Stuart A. Gabriel. 2012. "Labor Migration, Human Capital Agglomeration and Regional Development in China". *Regional Science and Urban Economics*, Special Section on "Asian Real Estate Market", vol. 42, no. 3: 473–84. https://doi.org/10.1016/j.regsciurbeco.2011.08.006

Green, A.E., T. Hogarth, and R.E. Shackleton. 1999. "Longer Distance Commuting as a Substitute for Migration in Britain: A Review of Trends, Issues and Implications". *International Journal of Population Geography* 5, no. 1: 49–67. https://doi.org/10.1002/(SICI)1099-1220(199901/02)5:1<49::AID-IJPG124>3.0.CO;2-O

Jones, Gavin W., and Wahyu Mulyana. 2015. *Urbanization in Indonesia*, vol. 4. UNFPA Indonesia Monograph Series. Jakarta: UNFPA Indonesia.

———, Hasnani Rangkuti, Ariane Utomo, and Peter McDonald. 2016. "Migration, Ethnicity, and the Educational Gradient in the Jakarta Mega-Urban Region: A Spatial Analysis". *Bulletin of Indonesian Economic Studies* 52, no. 1: 55–76. https://doi.org/10.1080/00074918.2015.1129050

Kementerian PPN/Bappenas. 2021. *Buku Saku Pemindahan Ibu Kota Negara*. Kementerian PPN/Bappenas. https://ikn.go.id/storage/buku-saku-ikn-072121.pdf

Lee, Everett S. 1966. "A Theory of Migration". *Demography* 3, no. 1: 47–57. https://doi.org/10.2307/2060063

Malamassam, Meirina Ayumi. 2016. "Youth Migration in Indonesia: Decision to Move and to Choose of Destination Areas". *Indonesian Journal of Geography* 48, no. 1: 62–72. https://doi.org/10.22146/ijg.12469.

———. 2022. "Spatial Structure of Youth Migration in Indonesia: Does Education Matter?". *Applied Spatial Analysis and Policy* 15, no. 4: 1045–74. https://doi.org/10.1007/s12061-022-09434-6

———, Inayah Hidayati, Bayu Setiawan, and Ade Latifa. 2021. "'Move Backward to Make a Step Forward': Understanding the Migration of the Highly Educated to Sorong City, West Papua, Indonesia". *Asian and Pacific Migration Journal* 30, no. 4: 485–99. https://doi.org/10.1177/01171968211069722

———, Haning Romdiati, Mita Noveria, and Bayu Setiawan. 2019. *Mobilitas Penduduk Indonesia Dalam Situasi Dunia Global*. Jakarta: Pustaka Sinar Harapan.

Marcondes, J.V. Freitas. 1959. "Brasilia, The New Capital of Brazil". *The Mississippi Quarterly* 12, no. 4: 157–67.

Moser, Sarah. 2010. "Putrajaya: Malaysia's New Federal Administrative Capital". *Cities* 27, no. 4: 285–97. https://doi.org/10.1016/j.cities.2009.11.002

Muhidin, Salut. 2018. "An Analysis of the Relationship between Internal Migration and Education in Indonesia". Background Paper ED/GEMR/MRT/2018/P1/5. 2019 Global Education Monitoring Report. UNESCO. https://unesdoc.unesco.org/ark:/48223/pf0000266053

National Capital Authority. n.d. "The Siting and Naming of Canberra". https://www.nca.gov.au/education/canberras-history/siting-and-naming-canberra# (accessed 1 September 2022).

O'Connell, Ronan. n.d. "Putrajaya: The Capital City You've Never Heard Of". *BBC.com*. https://www.bbc.com/travel/article/20210901-putrajaya-the-capital-city-youve-never-heard-of (accessed 9 January 2023).

Salim, Wilmar, and Siwage Dharma Negara. 2019. "Shifting the Capital from Jakarta: Reasons and Challenges". *ISEAS Perspective*, no. 2019/79, 1 October 2019.

Shepard, Wade. 2019. "Should We Build Cities from Scratch?". *The Guardian*, 10 July 2019. https://www.theguardian.com/cities/2019/jul/10/should-we-build-cities-from-scratch

Shimamura, Takuya, and Takeshi Mizunoya. 2020. "Sustainability Prediction Model for Capital City Relocation in Indonesia Based on Inclusive Wealth and System Dynamics". *Sustainability* 12, no. 10: 4336. https://doi.org/10.3390/su12104336

Statistics Indonesia. 2021. *Statistik Mobilitas Penduduk dan Tenaga Kerja 2021*. BPS - Statistics Indonesia.

———. 2023. "Hasil Long Form Sensus Penduduk 2020". Berita Resmi Statistik No. 09/01/Th.XXVI. https://www.bps.go.id/pressrelease/2023/01/30/2039/hasil-long-form-sensus-penduduk-2020.html

———. n.d. "Jumlah Perguruan Tinggi, Tenaga Pendidik dan Mahasiswa(Negeri dan Swasta) di Bawah Kementerian Riset, Teknologi dan Pendidikan Tinggi/Kementerian Pendidikan dan Kebudayaan Menurut Provinsi, 2021". https://www.bps.go.id/indikator/indikator/view_data_pub/0000/api_pub/cmdTdG5vU0IwKzBFR20rQnpuZEYzdz09/da_04/1 (accessed 3 January 2023).

Stawarz, Nico, Heiko Rüger, and Thomas Skora. 2021. "Does Weekend Commuting Really Pay Off? A Panel Analysis with German Data". *Population, Space and Place* 27, no. 8: e2464. https://doi.org/10.1002/psp.2464

Sukamdi, and Ghazy Mujahid. 2015. *Internal Migration in Indonesia*. UNFPA Indonesia Monograph Series 3. Jakarta: UNFPA Indonesia. https://indonesia.unfpa.org/sites/default/files/pub-pdf/FA_Isi_BUKU_Monograph_Internal_Migration_ENG.pdf

Tatibekov, Bolat, Kamal Fatehi, and Foad Derakhshan. 2008. "Migrants to Astana, the New Capital City of Kazakhstan". *Competition Forum* 6, no. 2: 350–56.

Tirtosudarmo, Riwanto. 2009. "Mobility and Human Development in Indonesia". HDRP-2009-19. Human Development Research Papers (2009 to Present). Human Development Report Office (HDRO), United Nations Development Programme (UNDP). http://ideas.repec.org/p/hdr/papers/hdrp-2009-19.html

Wajdi, Nashrul, Sri Moertiningsih Adioetomo, and Clara H. Mulder. 2017. "Gravity Models of Interregional Migration in Indonesia". *Bulletin of Indonesian Economic Studies* 53, no. 3: 309–32. https://doi.org/10.1080/00074918.2017.1298719

Weber, Rosa, and Jan Saarela. 2019. "Circular Migration in a Context of Free Mobility: Evidence from Linked Population Register Data from Finland and Sweden". *Population, Space and Place* 25, no. 4: e2230. https://doi.org/10.1002/psp.2230

Woodworth, Max D., and Jeremy L. Wallace. 2017. "Seeing Ghosts: Parsing China's 'Ghost City' Controversy". *Urban Geography* 38, no. 8: 1270–81. https://doi.org/10.1080/02723638.2017.1288009

World Bank. 2009. "World Development Report 2009: Reshaping Economic Geography". Washington, DC: World Bank. https://doi.org/10.1596/978-0-8213-7607-2

Zelinsky, Wilbur. 1971. "The Hypothesis of the Mobility Transition". *Geographical Review* 61, no. 2: 219–49. https://doi.org/10.2307/213996

Part III
OPPORTUNITIES FOR NUSANTARA

9

NUSANTARA THE GREEN CAPITAL
Leveraging the Moment for Improved Forest Governance

Dini Suryani, Dian Aulia and Marcellinus Mandira Budi Utomo

Introduction

On 16 August 2019, President Joko Widodo officially announced the relocation of the capital city (or *Ibu Kota Negara*, IKN) in his state address. The new IKN, named Nusantara, is in East Kalimantan's regencies of Kutai Kartanegara and North Penajam Paser. It will have an area of 256,142.72 ha, including a core city of up to 56,180.87 ha and the main government zone of 5,644 ha. It is divided into three zones, the Central Government Core Area (*Kawasan Inti Pusat Pemerintahan*, KIPP), the State Capital Area (*Kawasan* IKN, KIKN), and the National Capital Development Area (*Kawasan Pengembangan* IKN, KPIKN).[1] According to Bappenas, the goal of the IKN relocation is to realize the Golden Indonesian Vision 2045 (*Visi Indonesia Emas 2045*), one of whose aims is to create a new economic growth centre, apart from the previously Java-centric one.[2]

East Kalimantan has a large forest, covering more than half of its total provincial area.[3] However, the level of environmental damage, particularly in this forest area, is prominent. Its forest damage has reached 9.7 million ha (60 per cent).[4] Thus, many parties, especially environmental civil society groups, at local and national levels, have been resistant to the development of the IKN, which is expected to further damage the forest. However, the Indonesian government, through Bappenas, has asserted that the IKN would be built by implementing a "forest city" concept, prioritizing environmental factors, to realize the vision of a "Smart, Green, Beautiful, and Sustainable City".[5] Based on the UU IKN (IKN Law), the new capital city is managed by

Badan Otorita IKN Nusantara (Nusantara Capital City Authority, NCCA), including its environmental aspects.

This chapter discusses how the relocation of IKN, with its concepts of "Green City" and "Forest City", can be an opportunity for improved forest governance. It uses a case-study approach with a qualitative method, using in-depth interviews and focus-group discussions as primary data collection techniques complementing secondary data from published sources. Based on the data related to forest management in Kalimantan, at least three forestry issues could become the cornerstone of the management model on a broader scale. They are: (1) deforestation and forest degradation, (2) overlapping land concession, and (3) human-wildlife conflict (HWC). It is argued that the principles of a "forest city" can be achieved if IKN development can fulfil the requirements of the three pillars of forest governance, which are: policy, legal institutional, and regulatory frameworks; planning and decision-making processes; and implementation, enforcement, and compliance—as formulated by the Program on Forests (PROFOR), the World Bank.[6]

The next section discusses forest governance as the theoretical framework, while the third section presents the existing condition of the East Kalimantan forests. The following part examines the Green City and Forest City concepts as stated in the IKN Law. The fifth section explores how forest governance principles can be applied, and the sixth section concludes.

Forest City and Forest Governance: Theoretical Framework

The creation of a forest city in IKN Nusantara will be relatively easier than building the concept anew in an existing city. However, the challenge is *how* to create a forest city and address the resulting reduction in green space. It is argued that creating the IKN as a forest city is a must, given the climatic conditions of Kalimantan at the equator. Forest governance is a key principle in building a city in a tropical forest. This area is a socio-ecological system that flora and fauna, local dwellers, indigenous communities, and concession holders inhabit, so its governance reflects the Indonesian government's ability to manage its forest assets, especially natural forests. Forest governance is in the spotlight, that if successful, could become a reference and standard for other provinces.

For forests to provide sustainable benefits, they must be managed with sustainable forest management (SFM) principles as the basic forest governance based on three pillars: economic, ecological and socio-cultural.[7] However, realizing SFM in Indonesia is challenging. Two entities that suffer—

perhaps the most—from poor forest management are forest dwellers and biodiversity. Sadly, the daily struggles that the forest-dependent communities must bear are often invisible or not of global concern.[8]

Life on earth is inseparable from forests, as they are the basis of food, wood, oxygen, habitat, culture and identity.[9] They support poor people by providing subsistence goods, goods for sale, and indirect benefits.[10] Around 300–350 million people depend on forests for subsistence and income worldwide, especially those who live within or adjacent to dense forests.[11] For the benefits of this forest to be sustainable, governance is needed to ensure SFM is achieved. Having good forest governance will end up with good forest outcomes, which is indicated by the extent of forest resources, healthy forests with a capacity to provide productive, protective, and socio-economic functions, and the existence of legal, policy and institutional framework.[12]

Forest governance is a crucial building block in SFM.[13] Problems in forest governance will create forest problems,[14] such as land disputes, illegal logging, and biodiversity loss. Mayers, Bass, and Macqueen[15] note that SFM depends on the quality and extent of legal and institutional conditions and enabling policy. Stages in creating forest governance include policy and planning, implementation, monitoring, and improvement (for related legislative and institutional arrangements).[16] It is argued that socio-economic–political–historical–cultural relationships have profound roles in the creation of forest governance. Hence, the approach and results in each country and forest entity can vary.

According to the PROFOR, forest governance has three pillars and six principles.[17] The pillars are policy, legal, institutional, and regulatory frameworks; planning and decision-making processes; and implementation enforcement and compliance. The principles are accountability, effectiveness, efficiency, fairness/equity, participation, and transparency. This chapter uses the pillars and principles to elaborate on the current forest condition in East Kalimantan and as a baseline for proposing strategies to create better forest governance in IKN.

Current Condition of East Kalimantan Forests and Potential Effects of IKN

To examine how forest governance principles can be applied in the IKN, the existing condition of East Kalimantan forests and how the development of the IKN will affect them must be considered. This chapter will focus on the three aforementioned issues closely related to forest governance:

deforestation and forest degradation, overlapping land concession, and HWC.

On Deforestation and Forest Degradation

As mentioned above, the forest in East Kalimantan accounts for more than half of the province's total area. Various types of forests are present in the province (Table 9.1).

Despite the large forest area, the rates of deforestation and forest degradation[18] are high. The Ministry of Environment and Forestry (*Kementerian Lingkungan Hidup dan Kehutanan*, KLHK) notes that the province has lost more than 10 per cent of its forest over the past decade, including its habitat and other key ecosystem services.[19] Forest Watch Indonesia (FWI) reported that in 2000–13, deforestation in East Kalimantan increased,[20] resulting in a decrease in forest cover (see Figure 9.1).[21] Another study reported that the province lost 3.3 million ha of forest from 2001 to 2019, the fourth highest provincial deforestation rate after Riau, West Kalimantan, and Central Kalimantan.[22] According to FWI's report, the main driver of deforestation and forest degradation in the province was the expansion of palm oil plantations in both periods, 2009–13 and 2013–16.[23]

Besides the direct causes of deforestation,[24] such as the expansion of palm oil plantations, there are also indirect causes. According to the United Nations Development Program (UNDP), deforestation and forest degradation in Indonesia are closely related to ineffective spatial planning, tenure problems, weak law enforcement, and rampant corruption in the

TABLE 9.1
Total Forest Area of East Kalimantan in 2020

	Type of Forest Area	Area (ha)	As Percentage of Total (%)
1.	Protected forest	1,844,969	21.90
2.	Nature reserve	438,390	5.20
3.	Permanent production forest	3,027,099	35.90
4.	Limited production forest	2,908,255	34.47
5.	Water bodies	95,755	1.13
6.	Conversion production forest	120,438	1.42
Total Area		8,434,906	100.00

Source: Dinas Kehutanan Provinsi Kalimantan Timur, *Data Luas Lahan Hutan Provinsi Kaltim Tahun 2016–2020* [Data on the Forest Area in East Kalimantan Province in 2016–20], Samarinda: Pemerintah Provinsi Kalimantan Timur (East Kalimantan Provincial Government, 2021), https://data.kaltimprov.go.id/dataset/data-luas-lahan-hutan-provinsi-kaltim-tahun-2016-2020 (accessed 14 August 2022).

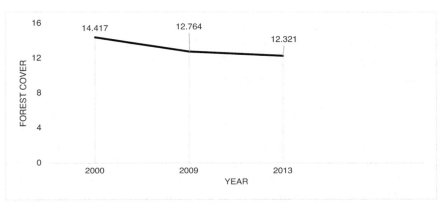

FIGURE 9.1
Forest Cover in East Kalimantan (in thousand ha)

Source: FWI, *Deforestasi: Potret Buruk Tata Kelola Hutan di Sumatera Selatan, Kalimantan Barat, dan Kalimantan Timur* [Deforestation: A Portrait of Bad Forest Governance in South Sumatra, West Kalimantan and East Kalimantan] (Bogor: Forest Watch Indonesia, 2014).

forestry and land sectors.[25] Meanwhile, FWI observed that deforestation and forest degradation continued to occur because of the assumption that natural resources, especially forests, were income sources that could be exploited for personal gain.[26] All this makes clear that deforestation and forest degradation occur because of poor forest governance.

Such poor forest governance in East Kalimantan is one reason for public resistance to the IKN relocation plan, especially from civil society groups who have concerns about forest sustainability. An academic from East Kalimantan whom the authors interviewed stated that the relocation of IKN to the province added to the current ecological crisis and was counterproductive to the government's initial intention in responding to Jakarta's environmental crisis.[27] Therefore, addressing the existing environmental and forest problems before starting the IKN megaproject in this region is vital.

There have been some studies on the potential deforestation caused by the proposed IKN development. For example, forest clearing is required to build government buildings, housing for residents, and other infrastructure.[28] The migration of large numbers of people may also lead to forest fires as a result of their burning peatlands to clear land for agricultural use.[29] Furthermore, another piece of research shows how migration can lead to deforestation in the IKN.[30] Finally, another study suggests that deforestation caused by the construction of the IKN within a radius of 200 km might result in increased carbon emissions equivalent to 126 per cent of Indonesia's greenhouse gas emissions in 2014.[31]

On Overlapping Land Concessions

Another problem is the overlapping of land permits, which includes forestry areas. In East Kalimantan, the concessions granted to the mining and plantation sectors exceed the permitted non-forest and other designated areas (*area peruntukan lain*, APL) (see Table 9.2).[32] By law,[33] the only type of forest that is allowed to be used as plantation or mining land is converted production forest (*hutan produksi konversi*, HPK). However, 2016 data show that cultivation rights (*hak guna usaha*, HGU) for plantations and mining business permits (*Izin Usaha Pertambangan*, IUP) reached more than 11 million ha, while HPK only covers an area of about 3 million ha. This means that about 8 million ha of plantation and mining permits are in permanent production and/or limited production forest areas,[34] making the overlapping of permits and misuse of forest areas for mining and plantation activities clear.

The complexity of overlapping land permits is compounded by community land tenure for economic activities. Of the 6 million hectares of land managed by local communities, 3 million are in the conservation area and two are in the production forest areas.[35] Wibowo et al.[36] show that the community-managed land is often near or precisely at the concession areas. This is very likely to lead to future tenure conflicts[37] not only between

TABLE 9.2
Natural Resources Extraction Business Permits in East Kalimantan

	Area and Concession	Area (%)
1.	Protected Forest	14.05
2.	Timber Forest Product Utilization Business Permit in Natural Forest (*Izin Usaha Pemanfaatan Hasil Hutan Kayu pada Hutan Alam*/IUPHHK-HA)	27.51
3.	Business Permit for Utilization of Industrial Timber Forest Products in Industrial Plantation Forests (*Izin Usaha Pemanfaatan Hasil Hutan Kayu pada Hutan Tanaman Industri*/IUPHHK-HTI)	14.63
4.	Area for large plantation	20.24
5.	Area for mining business permit	38.46
6.	Total area of permits (Editor's note: exceeds 100 per cent)	114.88
7.	Total area *without* permits	(−14.88)
	Total (net) area	100

Source: Agung Wibowo et al., *Potret Ketimpangan Ruang Kalimantan* [A Portrait of Kalimantan's Spatial Inequality] (Bogor: Koalisi Tanahkita.id, 2019).

companies with competing permits on the same land but also between communities and companies, both for plantations and mining.[38] Not surprisingly, tenure conflict in forest areas in East Kalimantan is among the highest in Indonesia.[39] These overlapping permits and high levels of tenure conflicts clearly indicate poor forest governance.

In the context of IKN relocation, poor governance of land permit grants is a critical point to manage. A report[40] from the civil society coalition #BersihkanIndonesia reveals that the location of IKN is actually in the area already designated for concessions. There are 162 concessions for mining, forestry, palm oil plantations, and coal-fired power plants in the IKN location. Some of these companies are connected to large conglomerates with close ties to the national political elite and even to officials within the current administration.[41]

In developing the new IKN, the areas with production forest status will be released into non-forest areas or other designated areas (APL). Hence, to maintain the total forest area coverage, the replacement land must not be a forest or production forest area so that it can be converted into a permanent forest area. This is possible according to the Government Regulation (*Peraturan Pemerintah*, PP) No. 104/2015 on Procedures for Changing the Designation and Function of Forest Areas. However, there is a high potential for natural-resource corruption[42] in this "land swap" process.[43]

In addition to company concessions in the IKN area, there will be residential areas and community-owned land. The indigenous people of Balik, the original local inhabitants, live and own land close to a location called *Titik Nol* (Point Zero), a designated spot where the government officially carried out a ritual to kick off the construction of the IKN in March 2022.[44]

One Balik resident was a casualty of a land broker who had appeared because of the rising land prices around IKN. The resident's land, located near Titik Nol, was certified by someone else and sold to another party. At the same time, like other indigenous peoples, the residents do not have a land certificate issued by the National Land Agency. The resident reported this incident to the subdistrict authorities to defend his land but, at the time of this chapter's writing, there has been no clarity. He is worried about eviction because his family and 84 others live less than 10 km from Point Zero.[45] The affected residents have made various efforts, for instance, by seeking an explanation from the village and subdistrict head, but have never received a satisfactory answer, even though the IKN development project has already started. The residents also joined the group who submitted a judicial review request for the IKN Law to the Constitutional Court.[46]

Indigenous people in Indonesia have long experienced legal uncertainty regarding the status of the land they own, including the Balik, and the construction and location of the IKN in their residential areas and land adds to the tension between the community and the government.

On Human-Wildlife Conflict

Another issue that needs attention in forest governance is human-wildlife conflict (HWC).[47] The causes of HWC include poaching, habitat degradation and fragmentation, deforestation, and forest overexploitation with the increase in the human population.[48] Due to the large proportion of forest, there are many wild animals in East Kalimantan. However, some studies show there is a tendency for conflict between humans and wild animals such as sun bears (*Helarctos malayanus*) and orangutans (*Pongo pygmaeus*).[49] The province's Conservation of Natural Resources Office (*Balai Konservasi Sumber Daya Alam*, BKSDA) indicates that 51 per cent of public reports are related to HWC issues,[50] mostly involving orangutan-human conflicts (Figure 9.2).

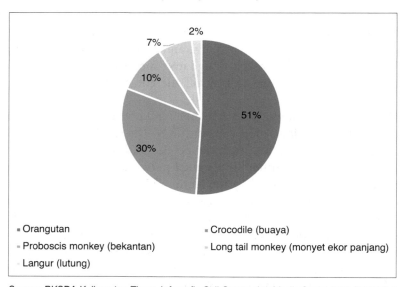

FIGURE 9.2
HWC Reports by Wildlife Species

Source: BKSDA Kalimantan Timur, *Infografis Call Center dan Media Sosial 2021* [2021 Call Centre and Social Media Infographic], (Samarinda: BKSDA Kaltim, 2021).

Rifaie et al.[51] show that HWC in East Kalimantan, especially with orangutans,[52] happens not only in forest cover areas but is even higher in the deforested zone, especially in palm as well as pulp and paper plantations. This confirms earlier[53] reports that conflicts with orangutans are due to habitat destruction and loss caused by forest conversion into concessions for mining and palm oil plantations. There are three essential ecosystem areas (*Kawasan Ekosistem Esensial*, KEE) in the province to protect wildlife: Bukit Soeharto Forest Park, Sungai Wain Protection Forest (HLSW), and the Adang Bay Nature Reserve. However, in the case of orangutans, 70 per cent of the population lives in non-protected areas.[54] This makes conservation efforts more complex.

Another study shows that infrastructure development, particularly roads and railroads across Kalimantan that will also pass through East Kalimantan, will significantly affect wildlife well-being, open up forests, and disturb forest connectivity.[55] Wildlife such as orangutans and sun bears will lose their habitat and have to travel hundreds of kilometres in search of food, mates, and new homes to survive. In addition, improving road access will make these animals more vulnerable to conflict with humans and more exposed to wildlife hunters and traders, which is a problem that has not been appropriately addressed.

This all means that East Kalimantan has already faced environmental challenges in the context of wildlife protection before IKN development. It is predicted that aside from causing deforestation which will affect wildlife homes in protected forest areas, the IKN project will reduce orangutan numbers by 38 per cent.[56] An interview with a field staff member of a government institution at the provincial level confirms that undertaking a project as big as the IKN while protecting animals is "difficult to do".[57] A well-considered and adequate policy is needed to overcome these risks, especially regarding wildlife protection.

Environmental Study of IKN: Anticipating Further Potential Environmental Degradation

Through the Ministry of Environment and Forestry, the Indonesian government has conducted a strategic environmental study (*Kajian Lingkungan Hidup Strategis*, KLHS) on the relocation of the national capital.[58] Called a "rapid KLHS" because it was conducted in just three months—for an exercise that usually takes a year—the rushed study proposes five roadmaps for environmental recovery in the new capital city area, with various timelines from between 2022 to 2030. Mining area recovery has the longest timeline (2020–30). Some critical issues related to the forest have

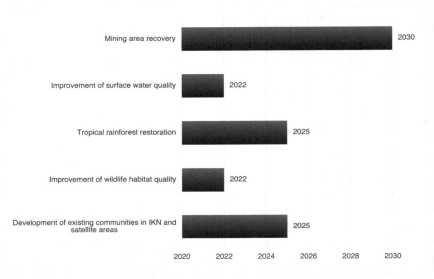

FIGURE 9.3
Roadmap Timeline for Environmental Recovery in IKN Area

Source: KLHK, *Kajian Lingkungan Hidup Strategis Pemindahan Ibu Kota Negara* [Strategic Environmental Study on the Relocation of the State Capital] (Jakarta: Kementerian Lingkungan Hidup dan Kehutanan [Ministry of Forestry and the Environment], 2019b).

been addressed, including forest restoration (2020–25) and the improvement of wildlife habitat quality (2020–22) (see Figure 9.3).

The KLHS signals that the government is aware of the environmental degradation around the proposed IKN area in particular and East Kalimantan in general. It can also be viewed as the government's first step towards manifesting the "green-forest city" of IKN. However, civil society groups in East Kalimantan have questioned the accuracy of the KLHS, given the relatively rushed drafting and evaluation process. There was also a lack of transparency, indicated by the difficulty in accessing the KLHS document experienced by relevant stakeholders at the provincial level, despite their official request to the KLHK for the report. This makes the central government's commitment towards protecting the environment questionable.

THE GREEN AND FOREST CITY CONCEPT IN IKN LAW

The development of Nusantara carries the vision of a sustainable city.[59] In Indonesia's Constitution (UUD 1945), sustainable development should focus on environmentally sound policies, as stipulated in Articles 28H(1) and 33(4).[60] However, the IKN Law does not seem to consider these articles as its legal basis (*yuridische gelding*) for environmentally sound laws and regulations,[61] although the IKN's development is said to be built with a green and forest city concept.[62]

Looking at Bappenas' 2021 Academic Paper on the IKN Bill (*Naskah Akademik Rancangan Undang-Undang tentang Ibu Kota Negara*),[63] the concept of a forest city has not been properly discussed. The term "forest city" appears just twice in the academic paper. The terms "green city" and "garden city" are mentioned more frequently in the paper but are not discussed in depth. The paper mentions other countries with the concept of a green city or garden city, like Putrajaya in Malaysia ("city in a garden") and Canberra in Australia ("garden city"). However, what the government wants as a forest city concept with IKN Nusantara in mind is not discussed at all in the paper.[64] What's more, the academic paper is apparently not used as the primary reference for the IKN Law. In Appendix II of the IKN Law, the countries referred to are not those discussed in the paper but developed countries that have applied an ideal concept that is harmonious with nature.[65]

In the legislative process in Indonesia, academic papers should ideally have a strategic role that serves as a guide in the formulation of the bill.[66] Superficial research for such papers can lead to the failure of a statutory regulation when implemented.[67] Academic papers should be based on sound research and scientifically accommodate the community's needs and expectations in order to create ownership of the legislation created.[68] In the case of the IKN Law, the relevant academic paper does not seem to have played that role well at all.

The concept of a green and forest city in the IKN Law is discussed in three parts: the law's Body and Explanation, Appendix I and Appendix II. The concept of green[69] and forest cities is however not explicitly mentioned in the body of the IKN Law. The term "forest city" appears only in the Explanation of Article 2(a), which refers to the explanation of "sustainable cities in the world".[70] Meanwhile, the concept of a forest city in IKN development as described in Appendix II[71] states that the basic principle of developing the IKN area will combine three urban concepts: a "forest city", a "sponge city" and a "smart city".

The "forest city" definitions, principles, criteria, and indicators in Appendix II were previously presented in a Bappenas working paper in 2020[72] that was eventually adopted. There are six forest city principles for IKN areas (approximately 56,180 ha): (1) conservation of natural resources and animal habitats; (2) connection with nature; (3) low carbon development;

(4) holistic, integrated and sustainable water resources management; (5) anti-sprawl development; and (6) community involvement.

Yet the achievement of the forest city concept is described differently in the Body and Appendix II of the Law, as comprising 75 per cent and 50 per cent of green areas, respectively. Furthermore, the Basic Principles for Environmental Protection and Management in Appendix II state that the target achievement for National Capital Development Area (*Kawasan Pengembangan* IKN, KPIKN) is 65 per cent of the natural areas.[73] However, in the same part of Appendix II, the IKN key performance indicators target by region puts 75 per cent as the targeted green area.[74] The differences in the listings of this target could have several negative consequences. First, legal uncertainty: a law's fundamental purpose is to guarantee legal certainty, benefit, and justice.[75] Uncertainty in the law and its appendices on what exactly the forest city green area target is will create a statutory gap that can be misused or manipulated. Second, differences in this understanding among the implementing agencies, stakeholders, and even the community regarding the green area target for the forest city concept will lead to confusion on the ground.[76] Third, these different target amounts mean that there is a lack of clarity in forest city planning and landscapes in developing the IKN, including targets for achieving green areas in the three IKN zones.

Manifesting the Green Forest City: Towards Improved Forest Governance

To manifest a forest city, policymakers must adhere to the pillars of forest governance. The implementation of forest governance is under the supervision of the Nusantara Capital City Authority (or IKN Authority), whose performance can be improved. The application of the forest city concept in the IKN must begin with improving forest governance and this could be an opportunity for the government to start doing things right.

The first pillar of forest governance relates to policy, legal, institutional, and regulatory frameworks. There are at least eight items that must be improved immediately (see Table 9.3).

The second pillar concerns the planning and decision-making process (see Table 9.4). Six issues need to be improved immediately and the principle of social justice must be initiated. One example of a potential social justice problem is how indigenous people have lost their rights in the name of IKN development, but they may not be aware of or are unable to speak out about it. The government should take the initiative to facilitate

TABLE 9.3
Pillar 1: Policy, Legal Institutional, and Regulatory Frameworks

Aspect	Status	Suggestions
Legal framework	Needs improvement	• Be based on scientific studies. • Make a forest development masterplan. • Involve local people and the public in drafting and implementing IKN regulations.
Legal framework to support the legal guarantee on land	Needs improvement	• Create technical guidance and regulations to protect land tenure, ownership, and usage rights, with recognition of the rights of indigenous peoples, local communities, and traditional forest users.
Concordance with broader development and forest policies	Needs improvement	• Establish IKN with low-carbon activities. • Reinforce and re-evaluate forest permit regulations related to environmental stewardship. • Hasten reforestation
Institutional framework	Needs improvement	• Establish form, structure, and human resources of the IKN Authority as soon as possible. • Add forest police staff.

Source: Authors' compilation.

TABLE 9.4
Pillar 2: Planning and Decision-Making Processes

Aspect	Status	Suggestions
Stakeholder participation	Needs improvement	• Map, Recognize, and Confirm original entities in IKN.
Transparency and accountability	Needs improvement	• Keep the public informed about the spatial planning of IKN. • No political pressure on forestry institutions.
Stakeholder capacity and action	Needs improvement	• Provide freedom for all stakeholders to criticize and give input (including environmental watchdogs and journalists).
Quality of decision making	Needs improvement	• Present updated long-term forest management plan.

Source: Authors' compilation from various sources.

discussion on addressing this problem rather than capitalizing on these people's weaknesses. Success in respecting the rights of indigenous people indicates that the state is willing and able to be present and side with the principles of social justice.

The third pillar considers implementation, enforcement, and compliance (see Table 9.5). The IKN project is still in the early development stage, so the implementation of these aspects cannot be seen yet but the implementation of good forest governance can be discussed. The construction of the IKN cannot be separated from political influence and how its influx accompanied by power relations[77] will threaten the objectivity of drafting and enforcing rules related to sound forest management. Without the enforcement of forestry rules strengthened by an adequate, professional, and credible legal apparatus, as well as forestry field officers such as a robust forest police force, deforestation will only recur, which leads to the destruction of the environment. The ones who will bear the most consequences of environmental damage are local communities,[78] who have limited bargaining options and positions, even though they are not involved in the process of damaging their living environment, and the wildlife and ecosystems

TABLE 9.5
Pillar 3: Implementation, Enforcement and Compliance

Aspect	Status	Policy Suggestions
Administration of forest city resources	Not available	• To have adequate staff capacity, data management, monitoring and evaluation; and the ability to adopt policies, laws, and plans.
Forest city principles enforcement	Not available	• To be fair and consistent in applying penalties for breaches of forest city principles and regulations. • To have a professional law enforcement system and apparatus.
Administration of land tenure and property rights	Not available	• Provide comprehensive and accurate documentation and access to information related to land in IKN. • Create mechanisms for resolving disputes and conflicts over tenure rights, including compensation.
Cooperation and coordination	Needs improvement	• Strengthen coordination and cooperation between national and provincial governments.

Source: Authors' compilation.

which often no longer can return to their pristine form.[79] In addition to the neglected indigenous community, indigenous people are often displaced from their land by concession holders given the lack of certainty where state and non-state land demarcations are concerned. The One Map Policy,[80] an attempt by the government to practice good forest and land governance to prevent land tenure conflicts in Indonesia, must be finalized based on participatory principles.

What matters here is the need to improve the cooperation and coordination among central institutions and between central and subnational institutions on forest issues. At this point, such improvements are needed due to the central institutions' "sectoral ego" vis-à-vis the provincial level.[81] The IKN is a central government project, but it will affect the work of institutions and the livelihoods of the local people in Nusantara. It will be unfortunate if unprofessionalism in forest governance is repeated in the IKN. It is time for the Indonesian government to devise plans and manifest these as well-directed sustainable forest management guidelines. Thus, input, opinions, and even criticisms, from the public, those who would be most affected by the IKN's development and those who are aware of the potential environmental damage that might occur, must be considered seriously in the decision-making process.

Conclusion

The development of IKN Nusantara reveals that forest land management and natural-resource governance in Indonesia require many immediate and longer-term improvements. The case of Nusantara illustrates that Kalimantan has biodiversity and ecosystem diversities that must be protected and restored because of prior, existing, and ongoing exploitative business activities. In addition, indigenous peoples who have lived in the province must be recognized as an inseparable part of the socio-ecological system of the Kalimantan forests.

The development of Nusantara, a small area compared to the total 125 million ha of forest areas in Indonesia, will prove whether the central government can realize improved forest governance for its new capital city. If so, it could strengthen the remaining 90 million ha of forested land in the country. If not, forest and environmental damage will get worse in the IKN area and East Kalimantan in general. If done properly, the development of Nusantara's "forest city" can be an example of improved forest governance and become a model for other regions and perhaps even other countries, despite entrenched challenges.

Notes

1. See Badan Perencanaan Pembangunan Nasional (Bappenas) [Ministry of National Development Planning], *Buku Saku Pemindahan Ibu Kota Negara* [The Pocket Book of Relocation of the State Capital] (Jakarta: Bappenas, 2021b), https://ikn.go.id/storage/buku-saku-ikn-072121.pdf (accessed 13 August 2022).
2. See Bappenas, "Bappenas Tekankan Tujuan Besar IKN untuk Mewujudkan Visi Indonesia 2045" [Bappenas Emphasizes the Great Goals of IKN to Realize Indonesia's 2045 Vision], 11 March 2022, https://www.bappenas.go.id/id/berita/bappenas-tekankan-tujuan-besar-ikn-untuk-mewujudkan-visi-indonesia-2045-q6ojv (accessed 12 January 2023).
3. There are differences in data calculating the area of forest areas in East Kalimantan. For example, Dinas Kehutanan Provinsi Kalimantan Timur (East Kalimantan Forestry Service) in 2021 reported that the forest area in this province was 66.2 per cent but the Earth Innovation Institute issued a report in 2020 saying that the forest area in East Kalimantan is 50.6 per cent of the total area of the province (Earth Innovation Institute, 2020).
4. Radio Republik Indonesia, "Pemerhati Lingkungan: Hutan di Kalimantan Timur Rusak Parah" [Environmental Observer: Forests in East Kalimantan Are Severely Damaged], 14 August 2022, https://rri.co.id/daerah/1581181/pemerhati-lingkungan-hutan-di-kalimantan-timur-rusak-parah (accessed 3 September 2022).
5. Bappenas, "Press Release: New State Capital to Implement Forest City Concept, Prioritizing Environmental Factors", 11 February 2020, https://ikn.go.id/storage/press-release/2020/en/eng-2-siaran-pers-terapkan-forest-city-ibu-kota-negara-pertahankan-ruang-terbuka-hijau-dan-tekan-environmental-footprint.pdf (accessed 15 September 2022).
6. Nalin Kishor and Kenneth Rosenbaum, *Assessing and Monitoring Forest Governance: A User's Guide to a Diagnostic Tool* (Washington, DC: Program on Forests, 2012).
7. Jorge Martin Garcia and Julio Javier Diez, "Sustainable Forest Management: An Introduction and Overview", January 2012, https://www.researchgate.net/publication/230710275_Sustainable_Forest_Management_An_Introduction_and_Overview (accessed 12 January 2023); and see, Sri Wahyuni, "Sustainable Forest Management In Indonesia's Forest Law (Policy And Institutional Framework)", *Jurnal Dinamika Hukum* 14, no. 3 (2014): 475–89, http://dinamikahukum.fh.unsoed.ac.id/index.php/JDH/article/view/312/328
8. Eva Wollenberg, Moira Moeliono, and Godwin Limberg, "Between State and Society: Decentralization in Indonesia", in *The Decentralization of Forest Governance Politics, Economics and the Fight for Control of Forests in Indonesian Borneo*, edited by Moira Moeliono, Eva Wollenberg and Godwin Limberg (London and Sterling, VA: Earthscan, 2009).
9. Ben Abraham, "The Roots of Forest Loss and Forest Governance", *International Institute for Sustainable Development (IISD) Earth Negotiation Bulletin*, Policy Brief #38, May 2022, https://www.iisd.org/system/files/2022-05/still-one-earth-forests.pdf (accessed 17 August 2022).

10. James Mayers and Sonja Vermeulen, "Power from the Trees: How Good Forest Governance Can Help Reduce Poverty", *International Institute for Environment and Development (IIED) Opinion*, 2022, https://www.iied.org/sites/default/files/pdfs/migrate/11027IIED.pdf (accessed 17 August 2022).
11. Abraham, "The Roots of Forest Loss and Forest Governance".
12. World Bank Group, *Roots for Good Forest Outcomes: An Analytical Framework for Governance Reforms* (Washington, DC: World Bank, 2009), https://www.profor.info/sites/profor.info/files/ForestGovernanceReforms.pdf (accessed 29 August 2022).
13. Food and Agriculture Organization (FAO), *Strengthening Effective Forest Governance Monitoring Practice*, by Arend Jan van Bodegom, Seerp Wigboldus, Arthur G. Blundell, Emily E. Harwell and Herman Savenije, Forestry Policy and Institutions Working Paper No. 29, 2012, https://www.fao.org/3/me021e/me021e00.pdf (accessed 17 August 2022).
14. James Mayers, Stephen Bass, and Duncan Macqueen, *The Pyramid: A Diagnostic and Planning Tool for Good Forest Governance* (London: IIED, 2002), https://wwfint.awsassets.panda.org/downloads/diagnosticandplanningtoolforgoodforestgovernance2002.pdf (accessed 18 August 2022).
15. Ibid.
16. FAO, *Strengthening Effective Forest Governance Monitoring Practice*.
17. Kishor and Rosenbaum, *Assessing and Monitoring Forest Governance*.
18. According to Regulation of the President of the Republic of Indonesia No. 62 of 2013 on The Management Agency for Reducing Greenhouse Gas Emissions from Deforestation, Forest Degradation and Peatland (*Peraturan Presiden No. 62/2013 tentang Badan Pengelola Penurunan Emisi Gas Rumah Kaca dari Deforestasi, Degradasi Hutan dan Lahan Gambut*), deforestation is a permanent change from a forested area to a non-forested area. Meanwhile, forest degradation is a decrease in the quantity of forest cover and carbon stock over a certain period.
19. KLHK, "Strategic Environmental and Social Assessment (SESA) Ministry of Environmental and Forestry, East Kalimantan Province", 25 August 2019, http://ditjenppi.menlhk.go.id/reddplus/images/adminppi/dokumen/mitigasi/fcpf/EKJERP_SESA_Document_Eng_v1.2_250819.pdf (accessed 20 August 2022).
20. FWI, *Deforestasi: Potret Buruk Tata Kelola Hutan di Sumatera Selatan, Kalimantan Barat, dan Kalimantan Timur* [Deforestation: A Portrait of Bad Forest Governance in South Sumatra, West Kalimantan and East Kalimantan] (Bogor: FWI, 2014). See also FWI, *Deforestasi Tanpa Henti: Potret Deforestasi di Sumatera Utara, Kalimantan Timur dan Maluku Utara* [Endless Deforestation: A Portrait of Deforestation in North Sumatra, East Kalimantan and North Maluku] (Bogor: FWI, 2018).
21. In 2016, the Kalimantan Ecoregion Development Control Centre from KLHK calculated that the rate of decline of the forest cover was 95,878.17 ha per year. It predicted that the forest cover in East Kalimantan would reach its threshold of 30 per cent per 1000 ha by 2054 (KLHK 2016).
22. See *Katadata.co.id*, "Deforestasi Paling Banyak Terjadi di Sumatera dan Kalimantan"

[Most Deforestation Occurs in Sumatra and Kalimantan], 20 January 2021, https://databoks.katadata.co.id/datapublish/2021/01/20/deforestasi-paling-banyak-terjadi-di-sumatera-dan-kalimantan (accessed 19 August 2022).
23. See FWI, *Deforestasi Tanpa Henti*.
24. KLHK has identified at least seven direct causes of deforestation and forest degradation in East Kalimantan: (1) timber plantations, (2) estate corps, (3) mining, (4) subsistence agriculture, (5) unsustainable logging practices, (6) forest and land fires, and (7) aquaculture (KLHK 2019a).
25. UNDP, *Indeks Tata Kelola Hutan, Lahan, dan REDD+ 2012 di Indonesia* [The 2012 Indonesia Forest, Land and REDD+ 2012 Governance Index] (Jakarta: UNDP Indonesia, 2013).
26. FWI, *Deforestasi: Potret Buruk Tata Kelola Hutan*.
27. According to the informant, before the IKN development, East Kalimantan had already experienced severe environmental damage, in contrast to the situation in Jakarta when it was first proclaimed as the country's capital city, which is still relatively well-maintained from an environmental point of view (retrieved from focus group discussion conducted by the authors in April 2022).
28. Luca Tacconi, "Moving Indonesia's Capital City Won't fix Jakarta's Problems and Will Increase Fire Risk in Borneo", *The Conversation*, 3 September 2019, https://theconversation.com/moving-indonesias-capital-city-wont-fix-jakartas-problems-and-will-increase-fire-risk-in-borneo-122639 (accessed 5 September 2022).
29. For example, peatland fire risk will increase and affect the population near the Mahakam River in East Kalimantan (Tacconi 2019). An earlier study shows that hunting and fishing can also cause forest fires (Tacconi 2016).
30. Aufa Hanum Salsabila and Nunung Nurwati, "Deforestasi dan Migrasi Penduduk ke Ibu Kota Baru Kalimantan Timur: Peran Sinergis Pemerintah dan Masyarakat" [Deforestation and Population Migration to the New Capital City of East Kalimantan: The Synergistic Role of Government and Society], in *Prosiding Penelitian dan Pengabdian Kepada Masyarakat* (Bandung: Universitas Padjajaran, 2020), pp. 27–39.
31. Hoong Chen Teo, Alex Mark Lechner, Saut Sagala, and Ahimsa Campos-Arceiz, "Environmental Impacts of Planned Capitals and Lessons for Indonesia's New Capital", *Land* 9, no. 11 (2020): 438, https://doi.org/10.3390/land9110438
32. Agung Wibowo, Ahmad Saini, Bimantara Adjie, Cindy Julianty, Dewi Dwi Puspitasari Sutejo, Fathur Roziqin Fen, Hilma Safitri, Imam Mas'ud, Luluk Uliyah, Muhammad Husen, and Wida Nindita, *Potret Ketimpangan Ruang Kalimantan* [A Portrait of Kalimantan's Spatial Inequality] (Bogor: Koalisi Tanahkita.id, 2019).
33. See Forestry Law No. 41/1999 (*Undang-Undang No. 41/1999 tentang Kehutanan*) and the Regulation of the Ministry of Forestry of the Republic of Indonesia No. P.50/Menhut-II/2009 on "Affirmation of the Status and Functions of Forest Areas" (*Peraturan Menteri Kehutanan No. P.50/Menhut-II/2009 tentang Penegasan Status dan Fungsi Kawasan Hutan*).
34. Wibowo et.al., *Potret Ketimpangan Ruang Kalimantan*.

35. Ibid.
36. Ibid.
37. Forest tenurial conflict could be defined as disputes or conflicting claims of control, management, use, and utilization of forest areas (see, for example, Dinas Kehutanan Provinsi Kalimantan Timur dan Yayasan Konservasi Alam Nusantara, 2020).
38. Depending on the object in dispute, tenurial conflict in forest areas can be classified into five types, namely, (1) conflict between community and the government; (2) conflict between community and companies; (3) conflict between forest management permits; (4) conflicts between communities; and (5) conflicts between government (Senoaji et al, 2020).
39. *Bisnis.com*, "Konflik Tenurial di Sektor Perkebunan Kaltim Kian Kronis" [Tenurial Conflicts in the East Kalimantan Plantation Sector are Increasingly Chronic], 30 December 2017, https://kalimantan.bisnis.com/read/20171230/409/722270/konflik-tenurial-di-sektor-perkebunan-kaltim-kian-kronis (accessed 2 September 2022).
40. See FWI, JATAM, JATAM-Kaltim, Pokja-Pesisir, Pokja-30, Trend-Asia, and WALHI-Kaltim, *Ibu Kota Baru Buat Siapa?* [New Capital City for Whom?] (Jakarta-Samarinda: Koalisi #BersihkanIndonesia, 2019), https://fwi.or.id/ibu-kota-baru-buat-siapa/ (accessed 16 September 2022).
41. For instance, PT International Timber Corporation Indonesia Kartika Utama (ITCIKU), which has a forestry concession in the KIKN area, belongs to Hasim Djojohadikusumo, brother of Prabowo Subianto, the current Minister of Defence. In addition, PT Perkebunan Kaltim Utama I, which has a concession of 17,000 ha, is connected with Luhut Binsar Panjaitan, Coordinating Minister for Maritime Affairs and Investment (ibid.).
42. Corruption in natural resources sectors occurs when there is a misappropriation of funds related to natural resources and environmental governance into private pockets through embezzlement and bribery (e.g., in environmental permitting system and inspections). Corruption can also lead to policymaking and practices that have the potential to damage the environment, as well as to the unfair allocation of environmental resources (see, for example, Winbourne 2022) In Indonesia, the Corruption Eradication Commission (*Komisi Pemberantasan Korupsi*, KPK), the state's anti-corruption agency, has a special concern to combat natural resource corruption. One method is through a campaign called the "Save Natural Resources National Movement" (*Gerakan Nasional Penyelamatan Sumber Daya Alam*, GNPSDA) which involves elements from the government, academia, and civil society. The KPK handled twenty-seven cases of natural resource corruption from 2009 to 2019. See further, *Tempo.co*, "KPK Telah Menangani 27 Kasus Korupsi di Sektor Sumber Daya Alam" [The KPK Has Handled 27 Corruption Cases in the Natural Resources Sector], 13 May 2020, https://nasional.tempo.co/read/1341909/kpk-telah-menangani-27-kasus-korupsi-di-sektor-sumber-daya-alam (accessed 18 October 2022).
43. FWI et al. (2019) highlighted this potential for corruption by using the example of

what happened in Jonggol, a subdistrict in Bogor District, West Java Province. In 2014, there was a case of forest conversion which involved PT Bukit Jonggol Asri, who bribed the Bogor District Head at that time. See further *Detik.com*, "Kasus Suap Alih Fungsi Hutan, KPK Geledah PT Bukit Jonggol Asri" [Forest Function Transfer Bribery Case, KPK Searches PT Bukit Jonggol Asri], 9 May 2014, https://news.detik.com/berita/d-2578692/kasus-suap-alih-fungsi-hutan-kpk-geledah-pt-bukit-jonggol-asri (accessed 9 August 2022).

44. See *Berita Satu*, "Erick Tohir: Titik Nol IKN Nusantara, Sejarah Kebangkitan Indonesia" [Erick Tohir: Zero Point of IKN Nusantara, The History of Indonesian Awakening], 16 March 2022, https://www.beritasatu.com/politik/903527/erick-thohir-titik-nol-ikn-nusantara-sejarah-kebangkitan-indonesia (accessed 18 December 2022). Currently, Ground Zero (or Titik Nol) is a tourist destination that attracts many visitors; see *Jawa Pos*, "Berkunjung ke Titik Nol Nusantara yang Jadi Destinasi Wisata" [Visiting Titik Nol Nusantara, which has become a Tourist Destination], 30 July 2022, https://www.jawapos.com/wisata-dan-kuliner/travelling/30/07/2022/berkunjung-ke-titik-nol-nusantara-yang-jadi-destinasi-wisata/ (accessed 18 December 2022).

45. Anonymous informant, interview by Dini Suryani and Dian Aulia, 18 June 2022.

46. See also Adrian Mulya, "Dahlia Merawat Seni Tari, Menjaga Tanah Sendiri di Megaproyek IKN" [Dahlia Caring for Traditional Dance, Protecting Her Own Land in the IKN Megaproject], 1 September 2022, *Project Multatuli*, https://projectmultatuli.org/dahlia-merawat-seni-tari-menjaga-tanah-sendiri-di-tengah-megaproyek-ikn/ (accessed on 10 October 2022).

47. This kind of conflict occurs due to interactions between humans and wild animals, which negatively impact the livelihoods of people and/or the wild animals (see, for example, Attia et al. 2018).

48. Kedar Baral, Hari P. Sharma, Bhagawat Rimal, Kum Thapa-Magar, Rameshwar Bhattarai, Ripu M. Kunwar, Achyut Aryal, and Weihong Ji, "Characterization and Management of Human-Wildlife Conflicts in Mid-Hills Outside Protected Areas of Gandaki Province, Nepal", *PLoS ONE* 16, no. 11 (2021): 1–17, https://doi.org/10.1371/journal.pone.0260307

49. Farid Rifaie, Eko Sulistyadi, and Yuli Sulistya Fitriana, "A Review of Patterns and Geographical Distribution of Human-Wildlife Conflicts in Indonesia", *Berkala Penelitian Hayati* 27, no. 1 (2021): 41–50, https://doi.org/10.23869/bphjbr.27.1.20217; Gabriella Frederiksson, "Human-Sun Bear Conflicts in East Kalimantan, Indonesian Borneo", *Ursus* 16, no. 1 (2005): 130–37; Erik Meijaard, Damayanti Buchori, Yokyok Hadiprakarsa, Sri Suci Utami-Atmoko, Anton Nurcahyo, Albertus Tjiu, Didik Prasetyo, Nardiyono, Lenny Christie, Marc Ancrenaz, Firman Abadi, I Nyoman Gede Antoni, Dedy Armayadi, Adi Dinato, Ella, Pajar Gumelar, Tito P. Indrawan, Kussaritano, Cecep Munajat, C. Wawan Puji Priyono, Yadi Purwanto, Dewi Puspitasari, M. Syukur Wahyu Putra, Abdi Rahmat, Harri Ramadani, Jim Sammy, Dedi Siswanto, Muhammad Syamsuri, Noviar Andayani, Huanhuan Wu, Jessie Anne Wells, and Kerrie Mengersen, "Quantifying Killing of Orangutans and

Human-Orangutan Conflict in Kalimantan, Indonesia", *PLoS ONE* 7, no. 3 (2012): https://doi.org/10.1371/journal.pone.0027491
50. Balai Konservasi Sumber Daya Alam Kalimantan Timur [Nature Conservation Agency of East Kalimantan] (hereafter cited as BKSDA Kaltim), *Infografis Call Center dan Media Sosial 2021* [2021 Call Center and Social Media Infographic] (Samarinda: BKSDA Kaltim, 2021).
51. Rifaie, Sulistyadi, and Fitriana, "A Review of Patterns and Geographical Distribution of Human-Wildlife Conflicts in Indonesia".
52. According to the International Union for Conservation of Nature (IUCN) Red List of Threatened Species, the Bornean orangutan is a critically endangered animal.
53. Rondang Siregar, "Practical Experience in Tackling Human-Orangutan Conflict: A Case Study in East Kalimantan, Indonesia", Workshop on "Linking Great Ape Conservation and Poverty Alleviation: Sharing Experience from Africa and Asia", CIFOR, Bogor, 2012).
54. Ibid.
55. Mohammed Alamgir, Mason J. Campbell, Sean Sloan, Ali Suhardiman, Jatna. Supriatna, and William F. Laurence, "High-Risk Infrastructure Projects Pose Imminent Threats to Forests in Indonesian Borneo", *Scientific Reports* 9, no. 140 (2021): 1–10, https://doi.org/10.1038/s41598-018-36594-8
56. Teo et al., "Environmental Impacts of Planned Capitals".
57. Anonymous informant, interview by Dini Suryani and Dian Aulia, 14 June 2022.
58. KLHK, *Kajian Lingkungan Hidup Strategis Pemindahan Ibu Kota Negara* [Strategic Environmental Study on the Relocation of the State Capital] (Jakarta: KLHK, 2019).
59. Bappenas, *Naskah Akademik Rancangan Undang-Undang Tentang Ibu Kota Negara* [The Academic Paper of the Draft Law on the National Capital City] (Jakarta: Bappenas, 2021).
60. I Gede Yusa and Bagus Hermanto, "Implementasi Green Constitution di Indonesia: Jaminan Hak Konstitusional Pembangunan Lingkungan Hidup Berkelanjutan" [Implementation of the Green Constitution in Indonesia: Guarantee of the Constitutional Right to Sustainable Environmental Development], *Jurnal Konstitusi* 15, no. 2 (2018): 306, https://doi.org/10.31078/jk1524; and see also Jimly Asshiddiqie, *Green Constitution: Nuansa Hijau Undang-Undang Dasar Negara Republik Indonesia Tahun 1945* (Jakarta: Raja Grafindo Persada, 2016).
61. Eko Nurmardiansyah, "Konsep Hijau: Penerapan Green Constitution Dan Green Legislation Dalam Rangka Eco-Democracy" [Green Concept: Implementation of Green Constitution and Green Legislation in the Context of Eco-Democracy], *Veritas et Justitia* 1, no. 1 (2015), https://doi.org/https://doi.org/10.25123/vej. v1i1.1422
62. Bappenas, "Press Release: New State Capital to Implement Forest City Concept".
63. Bappenas, *Naskah Akademik*.
64. See the section on country comparisons in the Academic Papers (Bappenas 2021a).

The paper discusses more about countries that have succeeded in moving their capital cities; however, the concept of a garden city (green area) was only briefly discussed, with Canberra, Australia; Putrajaya, Malaysia; New Kabul, Afghanistan; Abuja, Nigeria (whose garden city designs have not been realized), and South Korea, which is in the process of relocating its capital to Sejong, implementing the eco-city concept. However, Sejong remains stagnant due to an expensive development budget and an unappealing location.

65. In contrast with countries discussed in the Academic Paper, the countries cited in the IKN Law (see Appendix II) include Singapore, Japan, Paris, Germany and Austria.

66. Maria Farida Indrati, *Ilmu Perundang-Undangan Proses dan Teknik Pembentukannya* [The Science of Legislation: The Process and Techniques of Its Formulation], (Jakarta: Kanisius, 2013); Patrick Dias, Aviva Freedman, Peter Medway, and Anthony Paré, *Worlds Apart: Acting and Writing in Academic and Workplace* Contexts, (New York: Routledge, 2013); Ismet Hadi, Suslianto, and Siti Nur Setia Rahman, "The Existence of Academic Document on Development of Legal Drafting", *Journal of Asian Multicultural Research for Social Sciences Study* 1, no. 2 (2020): 107–16, https://doi.org/10.47616/jamrsss.v1i2.136

67. Yuliandri, *Asas-Asas Pembentukan Peraturan Perundang-undangan yang Baik: Gagasan Pembentukan Undang-Undang Berkelanjutan* [The Principles of Forming Good Legislation: The Idea of Establishing a Sustainable Law] (Jakarta: Raja Grafindo Persada, 2013).

68. Abdul Basyir, "The Importance of Academic Script in The Statutes Formatting to Realize Aspirational and Responsive Law", *Kajian Hukum dan Keadilan* II, no. 5 (2014): 285–306, http://dx.doi.org/10.12345/ius.v2i5.171

69. The definition of a "Green City" based on the Academic Paper for the IKN Bill is, "a concept of developing environmentally friendly cities by efficiently utilizing water and energy resources, reducing waste, implementing a more efficient integrated transportation system, ensuring environmental health, and synergizing the natural and artificial environment. Urban development aims to improve the cities and its citizens' ability to mitigate and adapt to disaster threats by balancing social activities, economic needs, and environmental sustainability. A Green City is also known as Eco City and Healthy City."

70. A sustainable city is intended as one that manages resources and provides services effectively in the efficient use of water and energy resources, sustainable waste management, integrated transportation modes, a liveable and healthy environment, and a synergistic natural and built environment. The capital of Nusantara as a forest city is envisioned as ensuring environmental sustainability with a minimum of 75 per cent green areas. The plan is woven through with the concept of a sustainable master plan to balance natural ecology, built areas, and existing social systems harmoniously. In contrast with Appendix II of the IKN Law, it is stated that the vision for IKN development is based on a "Smart, Green, Beautiful, and Sustainable" grand framework. This means that the planning for

the development of the IKN area is carried out with the concept of a forest city to ensure environmental resilience with at least 50 per cent of green areas.
71. The definition of a Forest City is one "using an integrated landscape approach is a city dominated by landscapes with a forest structure or Green Open Space (*ruang terbuka hijau*, RTH) that has the function of ecosystem services, such as forests, and aims to create a life that coexists with nature."
72. Dadang Jainal Mutaqin, Muhajah Babny Muslim, and Nur Hygiawati Rahayu, "Analisis Konsep Forest City dalam Rencana Pembangunan Ibu Kota Negara" [Analysis of the Forest City Concept in the National Capital Development Plan], *Bappenas Working Papers* 4, no. 1 (2021): 13–29, https://doi.org/10.47266/bwp.v4i1.87
73. See Appendix II of IKN Law, at p. 49.
74. See Appendix II of IKN Law, at p. 18.
75. Gustav Radbruch, "Statutory Lawlessness and Supra-Statutory Law (1946)", translated by Bonnie Litschewski Paulson and Stanley L. Paulson, *Oxford Journal of Legal Studies* 26, no. 1 (2006): 1–11, https://doi.org/10.1093/ojls/gqi041
76. Based on the authors' interviews in the field from 12 to 19 June 2022 in East Kalimantan, stakeholders have different understandings regarding the achievement of green area targets, local government agencies and private agencies. Whereas the implementation of green areas is bottom-up (see the information in the IKN key performance indicator Target Table in Appendix II of the IKN Law No. 3/2022), this means that those in the regions have a strategic role in achieving the green area target, as well as those who are most affected by the success or failure of the development of the forest city concept in Nusantara.
77. Doni Prabowo, Ahmad Maryudi, Senawi, and Muhammad A. Imron, "Conversion of Forests into Oil Palm Plantations in West Kalimantan, Indonesia: Insights from Actors' Power and Its Dynamics", *Forest Policy and Economics* 78 (2017): 32–39, https://doi.org/10.1016/j.forpol.2017.01.004
78. John F. McCarthy and Kathryn Robinson, eds., *Land and Development in Indonesia: Searching for the People's Sovereignty* (Singapore: ISEAS – Yusof Ishak Institute, 2016).
79. See, for example, Mitsuru Osaki, Bambang Setiadi, Hidenori Takashasi, and Muhammad Evri, "Peatland in Kalimantan", in *Tropical Peatland Ecosystems*, edited by Mitsuru Osaki and Nobuyuki Tjusi (Tokyo: Springer Japan, 2015), pp. 91–112.
80. Nabiha Shahab, "Indonesia: One Map Policy", *Open Government Partnership*, 2016, https://www.opengovpartnership.org/wp-content/uploads/2001/01/case-study_Indonesia_One-Map-Policy.pdf (accessed 31 July 2022).
81. Sectoral ego or institutional ego creates a situation where the intention to collaborate between or among institutions is weak.

References

Abraham, B. 2022. "The Roots of Forest Loss and Forest Governance". *International Institute for Sustainable Development (IISD) Earth Negotiation Bulletin,* Policy Brief

#38, May 2022. https://www.iisd.org/system/files/2022-05/still-one-earth-forests.pdf (accessed 17 August 2022).

Alamgir, M., M.J. Campbell, S. Sloan, A. Suhardiman, J. Supriatna., and W.F. Laurence. 2019. "High-Risk Infrastructure Projects Pose Imminent Threats to Forests in Indonesian Borneo". *Scientific Reports* 9, no. 140: 1–10.

Asshiddiqie, Jimly. 2016. *Green Constitution: Nuansa Hijau Undang-Undang Dasar Negara Republik Indonesia Tahun 1945*. Jakarta: Raja Grafindo Persada.

Attia, T.S., T. Martin, T.P. Forbuzie, T.E. Angwafo, and M.D. Cuo. 2018. "Human Wildlife Conflict: Causes, Consequences and Management Strategies in Mount Cameroon National Park South West Region, Cameroon". *Journal of Forest, Animal and Fisheries Research*, 2, no. 2: 34–49. https://dx.doi.org/10.22161/ijfaf.2.2.1

Bappenas. 2020. "Press Release: New State Capital to Implement Forest City Concept, Prioritising Environmental Factors". *Ibu Kota Negara*, 11 February 2020, https://ikn.go.id/storage/press-release/2020/en/eng-2-siaran-pers-terapkan-forest-city-ibu-kota-negara-pertahankan-ruang-terbuka-hijau-dan-tekan-environmental-footprint.pdf (accessed 15 September 2022).

———. 2021a. *Naskah Akademik Rancangan Undang-Undang Tentang Ibu Kota Negara* [The Academic Paper of the Draft Law on the National Capital City] Jakarta: Bappenas.

———. 2021b. *Buku Saku Pemindahan Ibu Kota Negara* [The Pocket Book of Relocation of the State Capital]. Jakarta: Bappenas. https://ikn.go.id/storage/buku-saku-ikn-072121.pdf (accessed 13 August 2022).

———. 2022. "Bappenas Tekankan Tujuan Besar IKN untuk Mewujudkan Visi Indonesia 2045" [Bappenas Emphasizes the Great Goals of IKN to Realize Indonesia's 2045 Vision], 11 March 2022. https://www.bappenas.go.id/id/berita/bappenas-tekankan-tujuan-besar-ikn-untuk-mewujudkan-visi-indonesia-2045-q6ojv (accessed 12 January 2023).

Baral, K., H.P. Sharma, B. Rimal, K. Thapa-Magar, R. Bhattarai, R.M. Kunwar, and W. Ji. 2021. "Characterization and Management of Human-Wildlife Conflicts in Mid-Hills Outside Protected Areas of Gandaki Province, Nepal". *PLOS One*: 1–17. https://doi.org/10.1371/journal.pone.0260307

Basyir, A. 2014. "The Importance of Academic Script in The Statutes Formatting to Realize Aspirational and Responsive Law". *Kajian Hukum dan Keadilan* II, no 5: 285–306. http://dx.doi.org/10.12345/ius.v2i5.171

Berita Satu. 2022. "Erick Tohir: Titik Nol IKN Nusantara, Sejarah Kebangkitan Indonesia" [Erick Tohir: Zero Point of IKN Nusantara, The History of Indonesian Awakening]. *Berita Satu*, 16 March 2022. https://www.beritasatu.com/politik/903527/erick-thohir-titik-nol-ikn-nusantara-sejarah-kebangkitan-indonesia (accessed 18 December 2022).

Bisnis.com. 2017. "Konflik Tenurial di Sektor Perkebunan Kaltim Kian Kronis" [Tenurial Conflicts in the East Kalimantan Plantation Sector are Increasingly Chronic]. 30 December 2017. https://kalimantan.bisnis.com/read/20171230/409/722270/konflik-tenurial-di-sektor-perkebunan-kaltim-kian-kronis (accessed 2 September 2022).

BKSDA Kalimantan Timur. 2021. *Infografis Call Center dan Media Sosial 2021* [2021 Call Center and Social Media Infographic]. Samarinda: BKSDA Kaltim.

Detik.com. 2014. "Kasus Suap Alih Fungsi Hutan, KPK Geledah PT Bukit Jonggol Asri" [Forest Function Transfer Bribery Case, KPK Searches PT Bukit Jonggol Asri]. 9 May 2014. https://news.detik.com/berita/d-2578692/kasus-suap-alih-fungsi-hutan-kpk-geledah-pt-bukit-jonggol-asri (accessed 9 August 2022).

Dias, P., A. Freedman, P. Medway, and A. Pare. 2013. *Worlds Apart: Acting and Writing in Academic and Workplace Contexts*. New York: Routledge.

Dinas Kehutanan Provinsi Kalimantan Timur and Yayasan Konservasi Alam Nusantara (YKAN). 2020. *Standar Operasional Prosedur Konflik Tenurial Kawasan Hutan* [Standard Operational Procedures for Forest Tenure Conflicts]. Samarinda: Dinas Kehutanan Provinsi Kalimantan Timur and Yayasan Konservasi Alam Nusantara.

Dinas Kehutanan Provinsi Kalimantan Timur. 2021. *Data Luas Lahan Hutan Provinsi Kaltim Tahun 2016–2020* [Data on the Forest Area in East Kalimantan Province in 2016–2020]. Samarinda: Pemerintah Provinsi Kalimantan Timur (East Kalimantan Provincial Government). https://data.kaltimprov.go.id/dataset/data-luas-lahan-hutan-provinsi-kaltim-tahun-2016-2020 (accessed 14 August 2022).

Earth Innovation Institute. 2020. "East Kalimantan Indonesia". 15 July 2020. https://forestchampions.org/jxd_reports/en_East%20Kalimantan_Indonesia.pdf (accessed 20 September 2022).

FAO. 2012. *Strengthening Effective Forest Governance Monitoring Practice*, by A.J. van Bodegom, S. Wigboldus, A.G. Blundell, E. Harwell and H. Savenije. Forestry Policy and Institutions Working Paper no. 29, https://www.fao.org/3/me021e/me021e00.pdf (accessed 17 August 2022).

Frederiksson, G. 2005. "Human-Sun Bear Conflicts in East Kalimantan, Indonesian Borneo". *Ursus* 16, no. 1: 130–37.

FWI (Forest Watch Indonesia). 2014. *Deforestasi: Potret Buruk Tata Kelola Hutan di Sumatera Selatan, Kalimantan Barat, dan Kalimantan Timur* [Deforestation: A Portrait of Bad Forest Governance in South Sumatra, West Kalimantan and East Kalimantan]. Bogor: Forest Watch Indonesia.

———. 2018. *Deforestasi Tanpa Henti: Potret Deforestasi di Sumatera Utara, Kalimantan Timur dan Maluku Utara* [Endless Deforestation: A Portrait of Deforestation in North Sumatra, East Kalimantan and North Maluku]. Bogor: Forest Watch Indonesia.

———, JATAM, JATAM-Kaltim, Pokja-Pesisir, Pokja-30, Trend-Asia, and WALHI-Kaltim. 2019. *Ibu Kota Baru Buat Siapa?* [New Capital City for Whom?]. Jakarta-Samarinda: Koalisi #BersihkanIndonesi. https://fwi.or.id/ibu-kota-baru-buat-siapa/ (accessed 16 September 2022).

Garcia, J.M., and J.J. Diez. 2012. "Sustainable Forest Management: An Introduction and Overview". January 2012. https://www.researchgate.net/publication/230710275_Sustainable_Forest_Management_An_Introduction_and_Overview (accessed 12 January 2023).

Hadi, I., S. Susilanto, and S.N.S. Rahman. 2020. "The Existence of Academic Document on Development of Legal Drafting". *Journal of Asian Multicultural Research for*

Social Sciences Study 1, no. 2: 107–16. https://doi.org/10.47616/jamrsss.v1i2.136

Indrati, M.F. 2013. *Ilmu Perundang-Undangan Proses dan Teknik Pembentukannya* [The Science of Legislation: The Process and Techniques of Its Formulation]. Jakarta: Kanisius.

Jawa Pos. 2022. "Berkunjung ke Titik Nol Nusantara yang Jadi Destinasi Wisata" [Visiting Titik Nol Nusantara, Which Has Become a Tourist Destination]. 30 July 2022. https://www.jawapos.com/wisata-dan-kuliner/travelling/30/07/2022/berkunjung-ke-titik-nol-nusantara-yang-jadi-destinasi-wisata/ (accessed 18 December 2022).

Katadata.co.id. 2021. "Deforestasi Paling Banyak Terjadi di Sumatera dan Kalimantan" [Most Deforestation Occurs in Sumatra and Kalimantan]. 20 January 2021. https://databoks.katadata.co.id/datapublish/2021/01/20/deforestasi-paling-banyak-terjadi-di-sumatera-dan-kalimantan (accessed 19 August 2022).

Kishor, N., and K. Rosenbaum. 2012. "Assessing and Monitoring Forest Governance: A User's Guide to a Diagnostic Tool". Washington, DC: Program on Forests (PROFOR).

KLHK. 2016. *25 Tahun Dinamika Tutupan Hutan Ekoregion Kalimantan* [25 Years of Forest Cover Dynamics of the Kalimantan Ecoregion]. Balikpapan: KLHK.

———. 2019a. "Strategic Environmental and Social Assessment, Ministry of Environmental and Forestry, East Kalimantan Province". 25 August 2019. http://ditjenppi.menlhk.go.id/reddplus/images/adminppi/dokumen/mitigasi/fcpf/EKJERP_SESA_Document_Eng_v1.2_250819.pdf (accessed 20 August 2022).

———. 2019b. *Kajian Lingkungan Hidup Strategis Pemindahan Ibu Kota Negara* [Strategic Environmental Study on the Relocation of the State Capital]. Jakarta: Kementerian Lingkungan Hidup dan Kehutanan.

Mayers, J., and S. Vermeulen. 2002. *Power from the Trees: How Good Forest Governance Can Help Reduce Poverty*. London: International Institute for Environment and Development. https://www.iied.org/sites/default/files/pdfs/migrate/11027IIED.pdf

———, S. Bass, and D. Macqueen. 2002. *The Pyramid: A Diagnostic and Planning Tool for Good Forest Governance International Institute for Environment and Development*. London: International Institute for Environment and Development. https://wwfint.awsassets.panda.org/downloads/diagnosticandplanningtoolforgoodforestgovernance2002.pdf

McCarthy, J.F., and K. Robinson eds. 2016. *Land and Development in Indonesia: Searching for the People's Sovereignty*. Singapore: ISEAS – Yusof Ishak Institute.

Meijaard, E., D. Buchori, Y. Hadiprakarsa, S.S. Utami-Atmoko, A. Nurcahyo, A. Tjiu, Ella, ... 2012. "Quantifying Killing of Orangutans and Human-Orangutan Conflict in Kalimantan, Indonesia". *PLOS One* 7, no. 3. https://doi.org/10.1371/journal.pone.0027491

Mulya, Adrian. 2022. "Dahlia Merawat Seni Tari, Menjaga Tanah Sendiri di Megaproyek IKN" [Dahlia Caring for Traditional Dance, Protecting Her Own Land in the IKN Megaproject]. *Project Multatuli*, 1 September 2022. https://projectmultatuli.org/dahlia-merawat-seni-tari-menjaga-tanah-sendiri-di-tengah-megaproyek-ikn/ (accessed 10 October 2022).

Mutaqin, D.J., M.B. Muslim, and N.H. Rahayu. 2021. "Analisis Konsep Forest City dalam

Rencana Pembangunan Ibu Kota Negara" [Analysis of the Forest City Concept in the National Capital Development Plan]. *Bappenas Working Papers* 4, no. 1: 13–29. https://doi.org/10.47266/bwp.v4i1.87

Nurmardiansyah, E. 2015. "Konsep Hijau: Penerapan Green Constitution Dan Green Legislation Dalam Rangka Eco-Democracy" [Green Concept: Implementation of Green Constitution and Green Legislation in the Context of Eco-Democracy]. *Veritas et Justitia* 1, no. 1: 183–219. https://doi.org/https://doi.org/10.25123/vej.v1i1.1422

Osaki, M., B. Setiadi, H. Takashasi, and M. Evri. 2015. "Peatland in Kalimantan". In *Tropical Peatland Ecosystems*, edited by M. Osaki and N. Tjusi, pp. 91–112. Tokyo: Springer Japan.

Prabowo, D., A. Maryudi, Senawi, and M.A. Imron. 2017. "Conversion of Forests into Oil Palm Plantations in West Kalimantan, Indonesia: Insights from Actors' Power and Its Dynamics". *Forest Policy and Economics* 78: 32–39. https://doi.org/10.1016/j.forpol.2017.01.004

Radbruch, Gustav. 2006. "Statutory Lawlessness and Supra-Statutory Law (1946)", translated by Bonnie Litschewski Paulson and Stanley L. Paulson. *Oxford Journal of Legal Studies* 26, no. 1: 1–11. https://doi.org/10.1093/ojls/gqi041

Radio Republik Indonesia. 2022. "Pemerhati Lingkungan: Hutan di Kalimantan Timur Rusak Parah". [Environmental Observer: Forests in East Kalimantan Are Severely Damaged]. 14 August 2022. https://rri.co.id/daerah/1581181/pemerhati-lingkungan-hutan-di-kalimantan-timur-rusak-parah (accessed 3 September 2022).

Rifaie, F., E. Sulistyadi, and Y.S. Fitriana. 2021. "A Review of Patterns and Geographical Distribution of Human-Wildlife Conflicts in Indonesia". *Berkala Penelitian Hayati* 27, no. 1: 41–50. https://doi.org/10.23869/bphjbr.27.1.20217

Salsabila, A.H., and N. Nurwati. 2020. "Deforestasi dan Migrasi Penduduk ke Ibu Kota Baru Kalimantan Timur: Peran Sinergis Pemerintah dan Masyarakat" [Deforestation and Population Migration to the New Capital City of East Kalimantan: The Synergistic Role of Government and Society]. In *Prosiding Penelitian dan Pengabdian Kepada Masyarakat*. Bandung: Universitas Padjajaran.

Senoaji, G., G. Anwar, M.F. Hidayat, and Iskandar. 2020. "Tipologi dan Resolusi Konflik Tenurial dalam Kawasan Hutan". *Jurnal Ilmu Lingkungan (Journal of Environmental Science)* 18, no. 2: 323–32. https://doi.org/10.14710/jil.18.2.323-332

Shahab, N. 2016. "Indonesia: One Map Policy". *Open Government Partnership*, 2016, https://www.opengovpartnership.org/wp-content/uploads/2001/01/case-study_Indonesia_One-Map-Policy.pdf (accessed 31 July 2022)

Siregar, R. 2012. "Practical Experience in Tackling Human-Orangutan Conflict: A Case Study in East Kalimantan, Indonesia". Workshop on "Linking Great Ape Conservation and Poverty Alleviation: Sharing Experience from Africa and Asia". Bogor: CIFOR.

Tacconi, L. 2016. "Preventing Fires and Haze in Southeast Asia". *Nature Climate Change* 6: 640–43.

———. 2019. "Moving Indonesia's Capital City Won't Fix Jakarta's Problems and Will Increase Fire Risk in Borneo". *The Conversation*, 3 September 2019. https://theconversation.com/moving-indonesias-capital-city-wont-fix-jakartas-problems-and-will-increase-fire-risk-in-borneo-122639 (accessed 5 September 2022).

Tempo.co. 2020. "KPK Telah Menangani 27 Kasus Korupsi di Sektor Sumber Daya Alam" [The KPK Has Handled 27 Corruption Cases in the Natural Resources Sector]. 13 May 2020. https://nasional.tempo.co/read/1341909/kpk-telah-menangani-27-kasus-korupsi-di-sektor-sumber-daya-alam (accessed 18 October 2022).

Teo, H.C., A.M. Lechner, S. Sagala, and A Campos-Arceiz. 2020. "Environmental Impacts of Planned Capitals and Lessons for Indonesia's New Capital". *Land* 9, no. 11: 438. https://doi.org/10.3390/land9110438

UNDP. 2013. *Indeks Tata Kelola Hutan, Lahan, dan REDD+ 2012 di Indonesia* [The 2012 Indonesia Forest, Land and REDD+ 2012 Governance Index]. Jakarta: UNDP Indonesia.

Wahyuni, Sri. 2014. "Sustainable Forest Management in Indonesia's Forest Law (Policy and Institutional Framework)". *Jurnal Dinamika Hukum* 14, no. 3: 475–89 http://dinamikahukum.fh.unsoed.ac.id/index.php/JDH/article/view/312/328

Wibowo, A., A. Saini, B. Adjie, C. Julianty, D.D. Sutejo, F.R. Fen, H. Safitri, I. Mas'ud, L. Uliyah, M. Husen, and W. Nindita. 2019. *Potret Ketimpangan Ruang Kalimantan Kalimantan* [A Portrait of Kalimantan's Spatial Inequality]. Bogor: Koalisi Tanahkita.id.

Winbourne, Svetiana. 2002. "Corruption and the Environment, November 2002". *USAID-Management Systems International.* https://pdf.usaid.gov/pdf_docs/PNACT876.pdf (accessed 1 October 2022).

Wollenberg, E., M. Moeliono, and G. Limberg. 2009. "Introduction". In *The Decentralization of Forest Governance Politics, Economics and the Fight for Control of Forests in Indonesian Borneo*, by M. Moeliono, E. Wollenberg and G. Limberg. London and Sterling, VA: Earthscan.

World Bank Group. 2009. *Roots for Good Forest Outcomes: An Analytical Framework for Governance Reforms*. Washington, D.C.: World Bank. https://www.profor.info/sites/profor.info/files/ForestGovernanceReforms.pdf

Yuliandri. 2013. *Asas-Asas Pembentukan Peraturan Perundang-undangan yang Baik: Gagasan Pembentukan Undang-Undang Berkelanjutan* [The Principles of Forming Good Legislation: The Idea of Establishing a Sustainable Law]. Jakarta: Raja Grafindo Persada.

Yusa, I.G., and B. Hermanto. 2018. "Implementasi Green Constitution di Indonesia: Jaminan Hak Konstitusional Pembangunan Lingkungan Hidup Berkelanjutan" [Implementation of the Green Constitution in Indonesia: Guarantee of the Constitutional Right to Sustainable Environmental Development]. *Jurnal Konstitusi* 15, no. 2: 306–26. https://doi.org/10.31078/jk1524

10

SUSTAINABILITY OF THE LOCAL COMMUNITY'S LIVELIHOODS AND THE IDEA OF THE MODERN CITY OF NUSANTARA

Rusli Cahyadi, Deny Hidayati, Ali Yansyah Abdurrahim, Temi Indriati Miranda and Ardanareswari Ayu Pitaloka

Introduction

When we first arrived, we felt like we were in hell. We were exiled to the jungle and isolated from the world.[1]
Do we have to repeat the same journey as our old life, even after our territory becomes the National Capital? (SN, interview, 4 July 2022)

Jakarta as Indonesia's capital has a long history of creating the idea of a modern Indonesia. Sukarno, the first president, who had architectural training, dreamed of Jakarta as a city with an ideal society. His speech in 1962 invited Indonesians to dream of an ideal city: one that was not only pleasing to the eye but that also had skyscrapers, wide streets, great monuments, and even housing with a "sense of greatness".[2] Efforts to realize said ideal modern city have been made by the governors and the central government. Unlike Sukarno, who prioritized the construction of city symbols that reflected grandness and modernity, Ali Sadikin, the governor who was considered the most successful in building Jakarta, made efforts to build better residential areas through the Muhammad Husni Thamrin (MHT) project. However, Jakarta was not built solely by engineers and regional planners with urban planning tools based on Western science (e.g., the zoning system) but also by "individuals and groups who have the authority, capital, vision and will to implement substantial new works, often breaking existing planning rules or avoiding them with the help of higher political authorities, and most importantly, built incrementally by residents".[3] In its current form, Jakarta is more like a "gigantic *Kampung*"[4] with "conflicting images"[5] and "conflicting directions".[6]

Burdened with traffic congestion issues,[7] air pollution,[8] water pollution,[9] and land subsidence[10] to the point where part of it is at risk of sinking, Jakarta can no longer be considered representative of the modern state and people of Indonesia. A new state capital (*Ibu Kota Negara*, IKN) must be built so that the vision of a developed country can be realized. This is a country that is aware of environmental problems and smart technology, and one that can improve economic development (that is, the Indonesia-centric concept of President Joko Widodo). The IKN will be a place with significant land availability, controlled by the state and private companies, and Penajam Paser Utara and Kutai Kartanegara, in East Kalimantan, are the chosen areas for the new IKN.

However, within the proposed IKN area, there are some indigenous peoples, such as the Paser[11] and Kutai.[12] However, building a new city is never straightforward. Determining the location, designing a city plan with designated zones, connecting roads, buildings and their layouts, green open spaces, and transportation systems to clean water (and other necessary facilities) are not ventures that take place in a vacuum. Designs—whether on paper or maps—are never the same as the actual conditions in which the development will be carried out. The expanse of forest, both natural and industrial plantation ones, which *de jure* should be vacant of residents, *de facto* is always occupied. Even if a forest is not physically inhabited, the forest space is connected to the livelihoods of people who may live far away from the location. Various literature on large-scale land acquisitions (LSLAs) cites this as the reason for increasing land productivity (e.g., the case of food estates), as a need for greater "development" (dam construction) and efforts to create living places (urban areas) that are better than the former ones (new city construction)[13] simultaneously disrupt the livelihoods of residents. The survival of those displaced, evicted, or compensated, and the efforts by the population to benefit from change are issues that often become the basis for the emergence of sentiment and resistance (resistance, contention, and protest) against LSLA.[14]

This chapter will seek to answer the question of how local community livelihoods can be sustainable in the context of the new IKN. The research was conducted in Kelurahan Pemaluan and Bumi Harapan Village, Sepaku Subdistrict, Penajam Paser Utara District, East Kalimantan Province. This research, carried out since 2020, was part of broader research on community roles in the collaborative management of natural resources. The chapter will discuss the continuation of the livelihoods of residents in areas that are included in the IKN's Central Government Core Area (*Kawasan Inti Pusat Pemerintahan*, KIPP). For the residents, the KIPP's construction has begun with the installation of the area markers. Part of the territory and houses in two neighbourhood associations (*Rukun Tetangga*, RT) in Kelurahan Pemaluan and two RTs in Bumi Harapan Village are included in the KIPP. The sudden arrangement has caused residents to worry about their future lives and livelihoods. This chapter will focus on the population's concerns regarding their current residence, land and work status, all of which are daily necessities.

The field data collection was carried out in July 2021 and July 2022 through focus group discussions (FGDs), unstructured interviews with residents and observations of the positions and conditions of the physical environment and their housing. This chapter is enriched by the doctoral dissertation work of a co-author who carried out field research in transmigration villages in the Sepaku Subdistrict in 1991.[15] A description of the condition of the community at the beginning of the transmigration period, and their relationships with various Paser communities and other ethnicities, has contributed to the understanding of the current condition of the community.

Area of Study and the Local Livelihoods Before IKN Development

Kelurahan Pemaluan and Bumi Harapan Village are two administrative areas that are part of the Sepaku Subdistrict (see Figure 10.1). Before becoming part of Penajam Paser Utara District (PPU District) in 2002, Kelurahan Pemaluan was part of Balikpapan City while Bumi Harapan was part of Kutai Kartanegara District. Pemaluan and Bumi Harapan consist of six and 10 RTs, respectively.[16]

The *Sepaku dalam Angka* document[17] describes Kelurahan Pemaluan and Bumi Harapan Village as being on the edge of, or around, the forest, functioning as a production forest area. The relevant population and regional data in the two regions can be seen in Table 10.1.

The discussion on the livelihoods of the residents will be limited to the conditions in the four RTs that are part of the KIPP area as mentioned in Presidential Decree 64 of 2022 on the Spatial Plan of the National Strategic Area of the IKN (2022–2024). The areas referred to are RT 05 and RT 06

FIGURE 10.1
Map of the Existing Administrative Boundary of the IKN

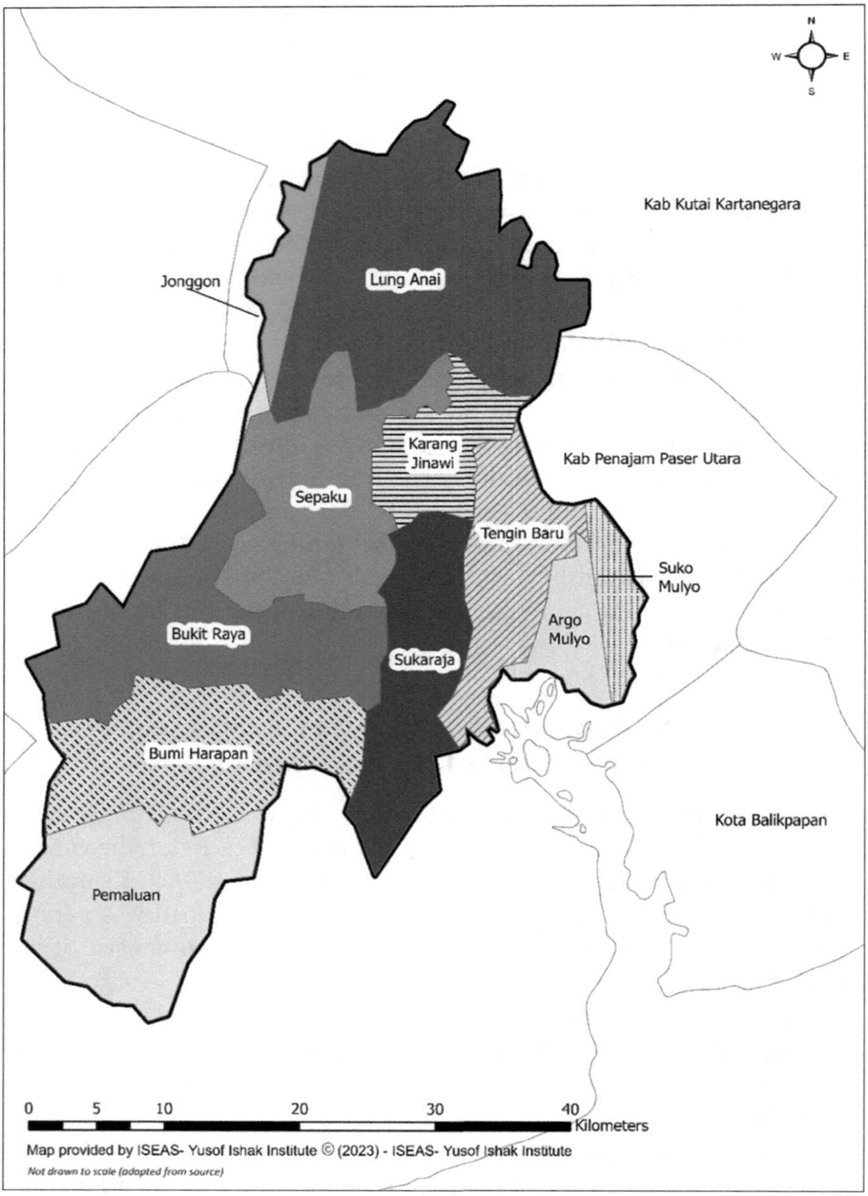

Source: Appendix II, Law No. 3 of 2022 (IKN Law).

TABLE 10.1
Basic Population and Area in Kelurahan Pemaluan and Bumi Harapan Village

	Kelurahan Pemaluan	Bumi Harapan Villlage
Number of RT	6	10
Number of residents	1,643*	2,071*
Number of family cards	440**	671**
Area of region (in km2)	367.18*	15*
Population density (per km2)	3.98***	130.87***

Source: Data from *BPS PPU District (2021), **Ministry of Home Affairs (2022), and ***BPS PPU District (2020).

in Kelurahan Pemaluan, and RT 02 and RT 10 in Bumi Harapan Village. The approximate locations of the four RTs are indicated in Figure 10.1.

It was not easy to identify residents in the four RTs who own houses and/or land in the KIPP area. As the IKN development project is a National Strategic Project (*Proyek Strategis Nasional*, PSN) it is tightly guarded. The (psychological) tension is very strong with the apparent presence of police intelligence even in FGD activities with residents.

Bumi Harapan Village, known before 1999 as Sepaku IV Village, was a second-tier village in the history of transmigration to the Sepaku area, which began in 1975. This village is a further development of the transmigrant area in Sepaku starting from Bukit Raya Village (Sepaku I), Sukaraja Village (Sepaku II), and Tengin Baru Village (Sepaku III). According to several residents, the residents of Bumi Harapan are the children of transmigrants in Sepaku I, II, and III, along with the Paser people. At the time, the government allowed local people (including Paser) to transmigrate to this location. Meanwhile, the residents of the Pemaluan are more heterogeneous because this area has been developed by the residents spontaneously or independently. In both areas, the residents are mainly farmers, casual daily labourers, private employees, and entrepreneurs.

The occupations listed in Table 10.2 reflect the population's crucial dependence on two sectors: agriculture and plantations. Many are self-employed, which includes those who are small traders (e.g., owners of grocery stalls). The table reveals that the types of work in Kelurahan Pamaluan (formerly part of Balikpapan City) are more diverse than in Bumi Harapan Village. The residents in the four RTs that are part of the KIPP area generally do various types of work as listed in Table 10.2 but are more concentrated in the agriculture and plantation sectors, with oil palm

TABLE 10.2
Occupations in Kelurahan Pemaluan and Bumi Harapan Village, by Gender

Occupation	Kelurahan Pemaluan			Bumi Harapan Village		
	Male	Female	Total	Male	Female	Total
Farmer	159	17	176	296	129	425
Day labourer	162	10	172	300	0	300
Private sector	57	13	70	33	7	40
Self-employed	26	12	38	17	10	27
Small, medium and large business owners	18	11	29	0	0	0
Mechanic	12	0	12	10	0	10
Civil servant/Military/Police	2	4	6	7	12	19
Animal husbandry	6	0	6	6	0	6
Private school teacher	1	4	5	1	1	2
Carpenter	4	0	4	26	0	26
Tailor	0	3	3	0	0	0
Fisherman	2	0	2	0	0	0
Security personnel	2	0	2	0	0	0
Midwife	0	1	1	0	1	1
Barber	1	0	1	2	0	2
Travelling merchant	0	1	1	0	15	15
Artist	0	1	1	0	0	0
Retiree	1	0	1	0	0	0
Total	453	77	530	698	175	873

Source: Ministry of Home Affairs (2022).

plantation workers being predominant. While population profiles based on ethnicity cannot be found in the official village or subdistrict statistics, residents occasionally group themselves into four categories: transmigrants (predominantly Javanese), indigenous people (Paser), migrants from Sulawesi (Bugis), and migrants from other parts of Indonesia. Among these community groups, long-standing socio-cultural and economic relationships have been developed. Before the formation of Bumi Harapan Village (Sepaku IV) and Sepaku I, II, and III Villages in the late 1970s, there were indigenous people (Paser people), Banjarese, and Bugis groups in the area. The Banjar and Bugis people are the earliest migrants to the Sepaku area. Meanwhile, Kelurahan Pemaluan, which is part of the municipality of Balikpapan and previously known as part of Balikpapan Seberang, has a relatively heterogeneous population and its administrative status as a subdistrict also supports this diversity.

The relationships among the various categories of residents span up to fifty years (using the arrival of transmigrants as a reference point) and together they have formed a functional livelihood system. An account of the history of the relationships between the groups can be found in Hidayati's doctoral dissertation.[18] According to her, the relationships between transmigrants and indigenous people are based on "knowledge acquisition and information flows"[19] and the "adoption and adaptation of indigenous cultivation practices",[20] where the knowledge and practice of agricultural land management and plant varieties are the results of the combination of knowledge and practices learned and exchanged among community groups.

Hidayati explains that although it was initiated by the "Paser people's resentment of the transmigrants, [because of their] language and cultural differences, and the settlement pattern", the transmigrants from Java acknowledged that "the indigenous people were the most useful source of information about local conditions". Through their observations of the Paser's farming system, Javanese transmigrants learned how and when to cultivate mountain rice through shifting cultivation.[21] The transmigrants also learned from Bugis migrants who previously inhabited the area between Balikpapan and Samarinda, especially about pepper cultivation.[22] This knowledge was then further adapted by the transmigrants.

Companies which have Forest Concession Rights (HPH), also referred to as Industrial Plantation Forest (HTI) companies, in addition to the existing mining companies operating in the area around Balikpapan and Samarinda, were also agents that brought together transmigrants and the Bugis and Paser people. Those who worked together in the companies exchanged information, including on pepper cultivation techniques or procedures.[23]

The interaction and exchange of knowledge that occurred between the different groups in the population led residents in the Sepaku transmigration area to share the same characteristics in relation to land management. Namely, they implemented shifting cultivation systems for planting mountain rice and converted "rice field" land located in residential areas (the villages) into cash crop plantations. The adoption of shifting cultivation caused agricultural areas to be used not only as forest land for spontaneous transmigrants but also as land owned by the HPH companies.[24] The practice of agriculture and plantations developed along with the entry of new commodities of high economic value. From the late

1990s to the early 2000s (especially 1997–98), pepper and rubber became the mainstay cash crop commodities. Then oil palm became the mainstay crop of the people.[25]

The Paser people have adopted an economic system for transmigrants that has been integrated with the market, especially in the city of Balikpapan. The pattern of sedentary life, especially that which followed after roads were built by the government and the HPH and HTI companies and the pattern of the transmigrants' residence was followed by the Paser people. This can be seen, for example, by the number of local transmigrants in Bumi Harapan (Sepaku IV) who hail from the Paser tribe.

Currently, most of the people in Pemaluan and Bumi Harapan depend on plantation activities, including oil palm, rubber and other crops, for their livelihoods. The relationships between various categories of the local population and with other entities such as companies (which own plantations and mines) and the government, although conflict-ridden, have been regarded as functional. In this local context, the conflicts that often arise concern land ownership, especially when determining which are forest areas and which are not (*Area Penggunaan Lain*, APL). Conflicts between residents are usually about the formal legal status of land ownership, while conflicts that occur between the transmigrants and Paser people are generally in the forest areas that were cleared spontaneously. Typically, the forest areas cleared by transmigrants might be claimed by the Paser people as their own. Facing such claims, transmigrants have stated that they handed the land to the claimant. Nevertheless, there has never been an open conflict over land ownership. Cahyadi et al. (2021) describe the pattern of land ownership and uses in the IKN area as interdependent, albeit with unequal relationships.[26]

There are several important characteristics of land management in Pemaluan and Bumi Harapan as well as other areas in Sepaku. First, overlapping land use is functional and does not reach the point of disturbing the functions (of land) desired by competing stakeholders. The entry of transmigrants and the Paser people into the forest areas or HPH concession areas, and later the HTI, is to some extent tolerated. This compromise came about for many reasons: limitations of the area, its use for subsistence needs, and the relevant company's dependence on local workers.

In addition, the land controlled by the population is, in many cases, assessed as a place to grow crops and other forest products. Hidayati has reported that the early transmigrants who came to Sepaku adopted a shifting cultivation pattern without providing markers for the landowners after the land was no longer productive.[27] Furthermore, the use of forest land by the state and companies could reach up to 3 to 5 kilometres from village boundaries.[28] Second, lands are usually sold in times of need such as for school fees, medical treatment (at hospitals), or major life-cycle ceremonies. Horne et al. state that livestock also functions as a source of income "in times of urgent needs or for school costs and social events".[29] Third, the difference in the legal status of the land is less relevant to buyers and sellers. The value of land is determined by its maturity level (e.g., whether it has rice fields, yards or gardens) or its position relative to the highway. Before the Sepaku area was designated as an IKN location, the land was seen more in terms of use values, especially by local residents.

The residents in the four RTs that are the focus of this chapter generally work in three main sectors: work related to land, work related to the road network, and other formal jobs. The first category includes residents who cultivate oil palm plantations, rubber plantations, rice fields and fruit orchards, and labourers (freelance) in industrial forest plantation companies or agricultural labourers (in plantations or residents' rice fields). Land for residents in this category is a necessity for their livelihood and a daily source of income. The second category is dominated by small businesses like grocery stalls, vehicle repair shops and restaurants, which require exposure to foot traffic and need to be easily accessible. Therefore, jobs of this type will mostly be found along main roads. The third category includes those in government or private sector jobs. The first two categories of workers will be greatly affected by the change in the status of the area to an IKN zone.

IKN and Local Livelihoods

In a sense, the discourse on moving the national capital began in 2017, when Bappenas conducted a study to assess possible locations for the new national capital. (Editor's note: This discussion focuses on the most recent history of discourse under President Joko Widodo; cf. Chapter 1.) This discourse and various policies had a direct impact on local livelihoods, as illustrated in the two cases below.

> *Case 1:* BD, a healthcare worker who lives in Kelurahan Pemaluan, signed a land sale deed for her 1-hectare piece of land located in the Kelurahan Pemaluan area on 26 August 2022 morning. She received cash worth approximately Rp60 million. In the evening, she received news on the President's establishment of Penajam Paser Utara District and Kutai Kartanegara District, East Kalimantan as the location of the new State Capital. She then confided to her relatives that the transaction made that

morning was a regrettable one because the value of the land immediately increased after the announcement. In her words, "If only I didn't think about my pride, I would immediately return the money I received." (BD, interview on 4 July 2022)

Case 2: On 26 August 2019, the President announced the location of the IKN. A month earlier, HR, a civil servant who lives in Bumi Harapan, bought a 1-hectare piece of land for approximately Rp60 million. When the authors met him in 2021, he expressed, "I would not even consider selling the land if the price reached Rp1 billion." (HR, interview on 7 June 2021).

The above cases show the significant increase in land prices that occurred long before the central government officially announced the precise location of the KIPP IKN. The establishment of the Penajam Paser Utara District and Kutai Kartanegara District has sharply escalated the economic value of land in Sepaku Subdistrict. Land prices skyrocketed. Until the early 2010s, land per hectare was around Rp15–30 million, depending on the location and the level of maturity of the land. The highest price was around Rp50 million per hectare. After the KIPP IKN was announced and established, land prices have increased to hundreds of millions of rupiah per hectare. In some cases, residents had even sold their land for up to Rp300 million/ha. At the time of the field data collection in 2021, members of the present research team were often offered land at prices in the range of Rp300–400 million/ha. There is a risk of a land speculation bubble. According to information provided by the Temporary Head of the Sepaku Subdistrict, around January 2022 the price of land per hectare was Rp130 million but by July 2022, it had reached the price of Rp1.1 billion per ha. The shocking increases in the price of land as described above reflect the deep uncertainty of the impact of the KIPP's establishment on the local community.

Land transactions after the establishment of the IKN increased rapidly and stories about land sales among residents are common. This phenomenon led to the community's effort to legalize their land parcels, either by registering for Freehold Title Certificate (*Sertifikat Hak Milik*, SHM) or by registering locally, which refers to the Statement of Land Ownership (*Surat Pernyataan Kepemilikan*), locally known as *surat segel* (statement of ownership ratified by the village government and subdistrict government) and/or *surat adat* (statement of ownership ratified by a local customary leader). These letters determine the economic value of the land. SHM, *surat segel*, and *surat adat* are important as proof of control and ownership. Ownership of these documents can increase the value of land exchanged and is part of residents' strategies to strengthen their land claims.[30]

The letters of proof of ownership have the strongest legal power. The land's status corresponds with its position on the regional map. Land with certificates is generally located in non-state forest areas (APL) and associated with land belonging to transmigrants. Of lower status are the *surat segel* and *surat adat*, which are often correlated with forest areas (and associated with the local Paser). The increase in the selling and buying of land and the ratification of various types of land "legality" certificates has been marked by higher sales of stamp duty documentation in local grocery stores. One shop owner explained that before 2019 he did not even sell stamp duty documents but since the establishment of the IKN, stamp duty has become one of the commodities with a fast turnover.

The increase in land sales is obvious: notice boards for land sales can be found along the main road from Samboja to Pemaluan. Newcomers in the Sepaku area would likely be asked to buy land if they interact with residents for long enough. One of the most striking changes is the increasing number of land sales in the form of *kavling*, which refers to a land area of between 150 to 300 square metres, sold for housing purposes. *Kavling* is usually on the side of the main road, but since the IKN's announcement, they can also be in an area far from such roads. In the village of Bukit Raya, developers who advertise and sell their land as part of the state's civil apparatus (ASN) *kavling* can be found. In the Kelurahan Pemaluan, there are also relatively large *kavling* that are located on the side of the main road for sale.

On 2 September 2019, the Regent of Penajam Paser Utara signed the Regent's Regulation No. 22 of 2019 regarding the supervision and control of land sales, purchase transactions and the transfer of land rights. This was then supported by the Governor of East Kalimantan who issued Governor Regulation No. 6 of 2020 on the control of transfers, land use, and licensing in IKN candidate areas and its buffer zones. The two regulations were later strengthened by the Ministry of Agrarian Affairs and Spatial Planning/National Land Agency through a circular from the Regional Office of the National Land Agency of East Kalimantan Province number HP.01.03/205-64/II/2022. The first two regulations emphasized the control of buying and selling transactions and permits related to land, while the last more explicitly prohibits the Land Offices of PPU and Kutai Kartanegara from providing services or recording sales and purchases (transfer of rights) and sale and purchase agreements (see Figure 10.2). Land certificate makers (PPAT) and notaries are also prohibited from performing similar services. These government regulations are known by the residents as "land freezing" or the prohibition of sales. The issuance of these three regulations cannot be separated from the craze for land

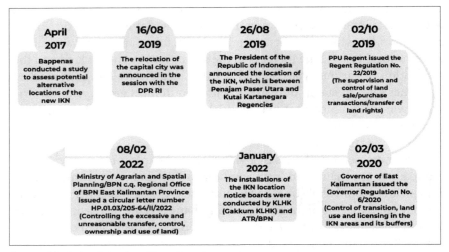

FIGURE 10.2
Policies Related to IKN

Source: Adapted and developed by authors from various sources.

buying and selling and the emergence of the seeds of conflict over land ownership.[31]

Discussion: Local Impact of the IKN

"A month before Jokowi's arrival (at Sepaku on 16 February 2022]" (KR, interview, 5 July 2022)—that is how the residents in RT 5 and 6 Kelurahan Pemaluan refer to the time of the installations of the large billboards (called *patok* by the citizens) for the KIPP. There are two types: those installed by the Ministry of Environment and Forestry (*Kementerian Lingkungan Hidup dan Kehutanan*, KLHK) or as Sepaku residents say, "the KLHK Gakkum" (see Figure 10.3-Left below) and those installed by the Ministry of Agrarian Affairs and Spatial Planning/National Land Agency (*Kementerian Agraria dan Tata Ruang/Badan Pertanahan Nasional*, ATR/BPN) (see Figure 10.3b).

There was tension between the local government and the residents whose yards were attached to the posted KIPP area markers, especially those posted by KLHK. This is because the boards read, "It is forbidden to enter, carry out activities, use and/or occupy the forest area illegally" (see Figure 10.3a). The residents thought that this warning meant that they could no longer live on or cultivate their land behind the billboards. Despite the misunderstanding, the installation activities were carried out and all the

SUSTAINABILITY OF THE LOCAL COMMUNITY'S LIVELIHOODS

FIGURE 10.3
Two Notice Boards in KIPP IKN installed by KLHK (left) and ATR/BPN (right)

(a)　　　　　　　　　　　　　　(b)

Source: Photos taken by authors on 2 July 2022 in Bumi Harapan (left) and in Pemaluan (right).

residential areas in the four RTs within the KIPP zone had these boards installed. This was after the head of their RT and village officers clarified that the installations of the KIPP notice boards served only as markers. Nothing would be different for them, and the boards would not affect the status of their land and houses.

However, the residents' bafflement cannot be separated from the short socialization period for the installation of the notice boards. The *lurah* and village heads, as well as RT heads in Pemaluan and Bumi Harapan, received a call to arrive at the subdistrict office the same morning to be given instructions about the installations of the notice boards. By the afternoon, the boards were installed, before the heads of the RTs had time to inform the residents whose land or yard would be affected.

The residents perceived these installations of the notice boards, as a prohibition to perform tasks on the lands attached. This was especially for the prohibition to build houses, which came as a shocking revelation. A middle-aged female resident (S) who owns a small house that also functions as a stall questioned how her life would continue. She asked, "What will my house be like [will I be evicted]?" She continued, "Please leave a little bit of my house, so I can stay there." (SU, interview on 5 July 2022). She was worried as this was her only residence as well as her only source of income; she could not imagine moving to another place.

Another question asked by S was related to the sustainability of her livelihood. Together with her husband, S runs a small shop in front of their house which is on the side of the main road. She hopes that she can still do the only job she knows how to do even if she must move elsewhere.

The increase in land prices, from many of the authors' conversations with residents, is often associated (only) with the benefits that may be obtained by residents. The cases of residents selling or buying land before the establishment of the IKN show that there are economic benefits from the changing status of the Pemaluan and Bumi Harapan areas. Land prices that increase up to five to ten times (or more) are likely to benefit the landowners. Moreover, according to the residents' recollection, President Jokowi had stated that the price of land in the IKN locations could reach up to Rp2 million per square metre. However, behind these fantastic figures, there are deep concerns related to the sustainability of their livelihoods.

The perceptions of the sustainability of livelihoods in the four RTs are, to some extent, strongly influenced by the resident's type of house and land ownership, and whether it is within or outside of the KIPP area. Table 10.3 categorizes the population into five groups.

Those in category C are the largest in number. In RT 05 and RT 06 of Kelurahan Pemaluan, of the 44 heads of household, 31 fall into this category. Those in the other categories number less than 10. Those who fall into category A, as represented by the female stall owner S above, are the ones most affected by the change in the continuity of their livelihood, as the houses which fall under the KIPP area are their only property. *Ganti untung* (a term used by residents, which means "compensation") for their houses is not an option for them. It is difficult for them to imagine continuing

TABLE 10.3
Population Category by House and Land Location

Category	Explanation
A	Residents who own a house in the KIPP area.
B	Residents who own a house and land in the KIPP area.
C	Residents who own a house and land in the KIPP area and own land outside the KIPP area.
D	Residents who own land in the KIPP area but own a house outside the KIPP area.
E	Residents who own a house in the KIPP area but own land outside the KIPP area.

Source: FGD, 2 July 2022.

their way of life with any replacement money they will get if they must move. Being at home while minding their small store and socializing with neighbours they have known for their whole life, are things they could not imagine giving up. Residents in category B have similar concerns, although they can accept compensation. For those who fall into categories D and E, even though living in the IKN is still within the realm of possibility, as they can build a new house from the compensation money, many wonder about the amount of money they will receive. Notably, they are excited about the amount of replacement money.

In general, the concern that arises among the residents is whether they, as residents who have lived in the area for a long time, will still be able to enjoy the advantages of Sepaku as part of the community of the IKN. they consider that they have put their blood, sweat, and tears into the Sepaku area for it to be a decent place in which to live and to do business. They recall the time when they had to carry people who were sick with malaria using cloth poles and walk to the mouth of the river, to bring patients to Balikpapan by the river for medical help.[32] The population at that time was mostly struggling to clear forest land because the transmigration land promised to them was still forest, instead of open land that was already cleared. Forest, wild animals, and malaria-carrying mosquitoes were difficulties that some of the early transmigrants had to overcome. Several areas in the Sepaku Subdistrict were only able to use electricity in 2019.

Residents in the four RTs questioned whether in future they will be part of the citizenry that enjoys the facilities and infrastructure of the IKN.

They also asked whether the compensation they receive will be enough to buy similar land in the KIKN area or the IKN buffer areas. Most residents who work as farmers wanted to still be able to keep their occupation while the IKN was established. With such aspirations, they generally rejected the relocation plan. To them, it did not guarantee that they would get new land which satisfies their needs. The experience of transmigration showed them that the plots for land distribution could be very different; the new plots could require extra effort to make them suitable for farming. Even if relocated, they demanded to inspect the potential location first, saying that they should be the ones who decide whether the location was acceptable or not.

The idea of differences in land characteristics has caused some residents in the four RTs to propose that the compensation method is prioritized as an option. In this regard, the government's prudence in determining the level of compensation needs to take into account the following conditions. According to FGDs and interviews, there are three important expectations from the affected residents. First, the residents want to stay in the IKN area. They do not want to be relocated because they have made great sacrifices in building the Sepaku area into what it is today. To that end, they want to be able to enjoy IKN-class facilities and infrastructure. Second, they want to maintain the way of life they have known so far. Farming, gardening and trading are jobs they are used to. Compensation for lands and houses in the KIPP area, therefore, must be done in such a way as to enable them to be able to buy the land they desire (according to their occupation) in a larger area. Third, they wish for the government to maintain the social and neighbourly lifestyles that they have enjoyed so far.

Conclusion

The construction of the IKN affects the continuity of the KIPP's current residents' livelihoods. Local residents who will be affected by land use change have a high risk of losing their assets (especially houses and land) and access to land and natural resources and economic resources (like business premises). They cannot refuse land acquisition when regulations dictate that the location of their residence, business, and agricultural activity are now part of the KIPP area. Land-based jobs for the majority will experience turbulence due to the conversion of these lands into central government areas with infrastructure and facilities. This poses serious risks to the continuity of the local residents' livelihoods, especially if they do not have alternative sources of income. At the time of research (July 2022), information on relocation and compensation was scarce. The actual risks are likely higher now.

Various socio-cultural relations that were formed from land-based livelihood activities have also changed, which has the potential to cause conflicts of interest between residents and stakeholders. This is due to lands which tended to be seen in terms of their use value until the establishment of the IKN. Land use value in this area has never been determined by its legality but rather, by location and maturity. Despite comprising many ethnic backgrounds and living amid longstanding competition for land use, the people of Kelurahan Pemaluan and Bumi Harapan have been able to live together and learn from one another. Although land ownership disputes have occurred, these clashes were tolerable due to their mutual dependence. The establishment of the IKN has changed the use value of the land and the dynamics of these two population groups. This sudden and drastic increase caused the previously latent conflicts to rise to the surface, even though it still has not manifested into open conflicts.

This study recommends that the government re-evaluate the importance of policies and regulations that specifically support the sustainability of local people's livelihoods. The effort to increase the capacity of local residents is urgently needed for them to participate in the development of the IKN. Local residents' participation must be accompanied by an ability to adapt to newcomers with diverse socio-economic and cultural backgrounds and lifestyles. It is necessary to carry out further studies on livelihood resilience, policy and regulation, and land tenure conflict and its resolution.

Notes
1. Deny Hidayati, "Striving to Reach 'Heaven's Gate': Javanese Adaptations to Swamp and Upland Environments in Kalimantan" (PhD dissertation, The Australian National University, 1994), https://openresearch-repository.anu.edu.au/bitstream/1885/116778/4/b18877400_Hidayati_Deny.pdf (accessed 20 September 2022).
2. S. Abeyasekere, *Jakarta: A History* (Singapore: Oxford University Press, 1987); Abidin Kusno, *Behind the Poscolonial: Architecture, Urban Space and Political Cultures in Indonesia* (London: Routledge, 2000).
3. Pratiwo and Peter J.M. Nas, "Jakarta, Conflicting Directions", in *Directors of Urban Change in Asia*, edited by Peter J.M. Nas, pp. 78–95 (London: Routledge, 2005), p. 68.
4. Gumilar Rusliwa Somantri, *Looking at the Gigantic Kampung: Urban Hierarchy and General Trends of Intra-City Migration in Jakarta* (University of Bielefeld, Faculty of Sociology, Sociology of Development Research Centre, 1995).
5. Anthony Sihombing, *Conflicting Images of Kampung and Kota in Jakarta: The*

Differences and Conflicts, and the Symbiotic Links between Kampungs and Kota (LAP LAMBERT Academic Publishing, 2010).
6. Pratiwo and Nas, "Jakarta, Conflicting Directions".
7. Tomoo Kikuchi and Shunta Hayashi, "Traffic Congestion in Jakarta and the Japanese Experience of Transit-Oriented Development" (S. Rajaratnam School of International Studies, 2020), http://hdl.handle.net/11540/12462 (accessed 26 September 2022).
8. Kusumaningtyas, Sheila Dewi Ayu, Edvin Aldrian, Trinah Wati, Dwi Atmoko, and Sunaryo Sunaryo, "The Recent State of Ambient Air Quality in Jakarta", *Aerosol and Air Quality Research* 18, no. 9 (2018): 2343–54.
9. Pingping Luo, Kang Shuxin, Zhou Meimei, Lyu Jiqiang, Siti Aisyah, Mishra Binaya, Ram Krishna Regmi, and Daniel Nover, "Water Quality Trend Assessment in Jakarta: A Rapidly Growing Asian Megacity", *PloS One* 14, no. 7 (2019): 1–17.
10. Lisa-Michéle Bott, Tilo Schöne, Julia Illigner, Mahmud Haghshenas Haghighi, Konstantin Gisevius, and Boris Braun, "Land Subsidence in Jakarta and Semarang Bay: The Relationship between Physical Processes, Risk Perception, and Household Adaptation", *Ocean and Coastal Management* 211 (2021): 105–75.
11. L.G.H Bakker, "Land and Authority: The State and the Village in Pasir, East Kalimantan", *IIAS Newsletter* 40 (Spring 2006): 15.
12. Vice Admira Firnaherera and Lazuardi Adi, "Pembangunan Ibu Kota Nusantara: Antisipasi Persoalan Pertanahan Masyarakat Hukum Adat", *JSKP: Jurnal Studi Kebijakan Publik* 1, no. 1 (2022): 71–84.
13. Marcel Mazoyer and Laurence Roudart, "A History of World Agriculture: From the Neolithic Age to the Current Crisis" (New York: NYU Press, 2006); Jan Sändig, "Contesting Large-Scale Land Acquisitions in the Global South", *World Development* 146, October (2021): 1–13.
14. Sändig, "Contesting Large-Scale Land Acquisitions in the Global South", p. 2.
15. Hidayati, "Striving to Reach 'Heaven's Gate'".
16. BPS, Statistics of Penajam Paser Utara, "Sepaku Subdistrict in Figures 2021".
17. Ibid.
18. Hidayati, "Striving to Reach 'Heaven's Gate'".
19. Ibid., p. 143.
20. Ibid., p. 184.
21. Ibid., p. 164.
22. Ibid., p. 175.
23. Ibid., p. 176.
24. Ibid.
25. Bayu Eka Yulian, Arya Hadi Dharmawan, Endriatmo Soetarto, and Pablo Pacheco, "Dilema Nafkah Rumah Tangga Pedesaan Sekitar Perkebunan Kelapa Sawit di Kalimantan Timur", *Sodality: Jurnal Sosiologi Pedesaan* 5, no. 3 (2017): 242–49.
26. Rusli Cahyadi, Herry Yogaswara, Syarifah Aini Dalimunthe, Deny Hidayati, Robert Siburian, Dedi Supriadi Adhuri, Herman Hidayat, Terry Indrabudi, Masyhuri Imron, Ary Wahyono, Laely Nurhidayah, Sudiyono, Ratna Indrawasih, Luis Feneteruma,

Dwiyanti Kusumaningrum, Annisa Meutia Ratri, Dicky Rachmawan, Tria Anggita Hafsari, Ali Yansyah Abdurrahim, Letsu Vella Sundary, Andini Desita Ekaputri, Temi Indriati Miranda, and Sanusi, "Policy Brief: Broker Tanah dan Potensi Eskalasi Konflik Berbasis Lahan di Lokasi Ibu Kota Negara Baru", OR IPSH BRIN, unpublished report.
27. See Hidayati, "Striving to Reach 'Heaven's Gate'".
28. Ibid., p. 203.
29. P.M. Horne, W. Stür, P. Phengsavanh, F. Gabunada, and R. Roothaert, "New Forages for Smallholder Livestock Systems in Southeast Asia: Recent Developments, Impacts and Opportunities", in *Grasslands: Developments Opportunities Perspectives*, edited by Stephen Reynolds, pp. 357–82 (Boca Raton: CRC Press, 2019).
30. Louis Albrechts and Seymour Mandelbaum, "Organization of Space and Time: Challenges for Planning and Planners", in *The Network Society*, edited by Louis Albrechts and Seymour Mandelbaum, pp. 141–42 (London: Routledge, 2007); Nancy Lee Peluso, "Seeing Property in Land Use: Local Territorializations in West Kalimantan, Indonesia", *Geografisk Tidsskrift-Danish Journal of Geography* 105, no. 1 (2005): 1–15; Nancy Peluso and Jesse Ribot, "Postscript: A Theory of Access Revisited", *Society & Natural Resources* 33, no. 2 (2020): 300–6, https://doi.org. 10.1080/08941920.2019.1709929
31. Cahyadi et al, "Policy Brief: Broker Tanah dan Potensi Eskalasi Konflik Berbasis Lahan di Lokasi Ibu Kota Negara Baru"; Yanuar Nugroho and Dimas Wisnu Adrianto, "The Nusantara Project: Prospects and Challenges", *ISEAS Perspective*, no. 2022/69, 7 July 2022.
32. See Hidayati, "Striving to Reach 'Heaven's Gate'", pp. 125–51 for a description of malaria in the Sepaku area from 1987 to 1991.

References

Abeyasekere, S. 1987. *Jakarta: A History*. Singapore: Oxford University Press.
Albrechts, L., and S. Mandelbaum. 2007. "Organization of Space and Time: Challenges for Planning and Planners". In *The Network Society*, edited by Louis Albrechts and Seymour Mandelbaum, pp. 141–42. London: Routledge.
Bakker, L.G.H. 2006. "Land and Authority: The State and the Village in Pasir, East Kalimantan". *IIAS Newsletter* 40 (Spring): 15.
Bott, Lisa-Michéle, Tilo Schöne, Julia Illigner, Mahmud Haghshenas Haghighi, Konstantin Gisevius, and Boris Braun. 2021. "Land Subsidence in Jakarta and Semarang Bay: The Relationship between Physical Processes, Risk Perception, and Household Adaptation". *Ocean and Coastal Management* 211: 105–775.
BPS-Statistics of Penajam Paser Utara. 2020. "Sepaku Sub-District in Figures 2020".
———. 2021. "Sepaku Sub-District in Figures 2021".
Cahyadi, Rusli, et al. 2021. "Policy Brief: Broker Tanah dan Potensi Eskalasi Konflik Berbasis Lahan di Lokasi Ibu Kota Negara Baru". OR IPSH BRIN. Unpublished report.
Firnaherera, Vice Admira, and Adi, Lazuardi. 2022. "Pembangunan Ibu Kota Nusantara:

Antisipasi Persoalan Pertanahan Masyarakat Hukum Adat". *JSKP: Jurnal Studi Kebijakan Publik* 1, no. 1: 71–84.

Hidayati, Deny. 1994. "Striving to Reach 'Heaven's Gate': Javanese Adaptations to Swamp and Upland Environments in Kalimantan". PhD dissertation, The Australian National University. https://openresearch-repository.anu.edu.au/bitstream/1885/116778/4/b18877400_Hidayati_Deny.pdf (accessed 20 September 2022).

Horne, P.M., W. Stür, P. Phengsavanh, F. Gabunada, and R. Roothaert. 2019. "New Forages for Smallholder Livestock Systems in Southeast Asia: Recent Developments, Impacts and Opportunities". In *Grasslands: Developments Opportunities Perspectives*, edited by Stephen Reynolds, pp. 357–82. Boca Raton, FL: CRC Press.

Kikuchi, Tomoo, and Shunta Hayashi. 2020. *Traffic Congestion in Jakarta and the Japanese Experience of Transit-Oriented Development*. Singapore: S. Rajaratnam School of International Studies. http://hdl.handle.net/11540/12462 (accessed 26 September 2022).

Kusno, Abidin. 2000. *Behind the Postcolonial: Architecture, Urban Space and Political Cultures in Indonesia*. London: Routledge.

Kusumaningtyas, Sheila Dewi Ayu, Aldrian, Edvin, Wati, Trinah, Atmoko, Dwi, and Sunaryo. 2018. "The Recent State of Ambient Air Quality in Jakarta". *Aerosol and Air Quality Research* 18, no. 9: 2343–54.

Luo, Pingping, Shuxin Kang, Meimei Zhou, Jiqiang Lyu, Siti Aisyah, Mishra Binaya, Ram Krishna Regmi, and Daniel Nover. 2019. "Water Quality Trend Assessment in Jakarta: A Rapidly Growing Asian Megacity". *PloS One* 14, no. 7: 1–17.

Ministry of Home Affairs. 2022. "Sistem Informasi Desa dan Kelurahan". http://www.prodeskel.binapemdes.kemendagri.go.id/mdesa/ (accessed 2 July and 2 September 2022).

Mazoyer, M., and L. Roudart. 2006. *A History of World Agriculture: From the Neolithic Age to the Current Crisis*. New York: NYU Press.

Nugroho, Yanuar, and Dimas Wisnu Adrianto. 2022. "The Nusantara Project: Prospects and Challenges". *ISEAS Perspective*, no. 2022/69, 7 July 2022.

Peluso, N.L. 2005. "Seeing Property in Land Use: Local Territorializations in West Kalimantan, Indonesia". *Geografisk Tidsskrift-Danish Journal of Geography* 105, no. 1: 1–15.

———. 2007. "Violence, Decentralization, and Resource Access in Indonesia". *Peace Review: A Journal of Social Justice* 19, no. 1, 23–32.

Peluso, Nancy, and Jesse Ribot. 2020. "Postscript: A Theory of Access Revisited". *Society & Natural Resources* 33, no. 2: 300–6. https://doi.org.10.1080/08941920.2019.1709929

Pratiwo, and Peter J.M. Nas. 2005. "Jakarta, Conflicting Directions". In *Directors of Urban Change in Asia*, edited by Peter J.M. Nas, pp. 78–95. London: Routledge.

Sändig, J. 2021. "Contesting Large-Scale Land Acquisitions in the Global South". *World Development* 146, October 2021: 1–13.

Sihombing, Anthony. 2010. *Conflicting Images of Kampung and Kota in Jakarta: The Differences and Conflicts, and the Symbiotic Links between Kampungs and Kota*. LAP LAMBERT Academic Publishing.

Somantri, Gumilar Rusliwa. 1995. *Looking at the Gigantic Kampung: Urban Hierarchy and General Trends of Intra-City Migration in Jakarta*. Vol. 236, University of Bielefeld, Faculty of Sociology, Sociology of Development Research Centre.

Yulian, Bayu Eka, Arya Hadi Dharmawan, Endriatmo Soetarto, and Pablo Pacheco. 2017. "Dilema Nafkah Rumah Tangga Pedesaan Sekitar Perkebunan Kelapa Sawit di Kalimantan Timur". *Sodality: Jurnal Sosiologi Pedesaan* 5, no. 3: 242–49. http://journal.ipb.ac.id/index.php/sodality/article/download/19398/13499 (accessed 20 September 2022).

11

PROJECTING A GLOBAL IDENTITY AS A MARITIME NATION IN THE NEW CAPITAL CITY

Lidya Christin Sinaga and Khanisa

INTRODUCTION

Indonesia has decided to relocate its capital city (*Ibu Kota Negara*, IKN) to East Kalimantan, in the Penajam Paser Utara and Kutai Kartanegara regencies, with Law No. 3 (2022) confirming the decision. The government has named the IKN "Nusantara", which according to the Minister of National Development Planning, Suharso Monoarfa, reflects the reality of Indonesia: a maritime country in which the islands are united by the sea.[1] Additionally, the minister stated that the name was chosen because it reflects Indonesia's geography and is internationally iconic.[2]

In building a new capital, the government has highlighted several characteristics representing Indonesia's identity. The IKN Law states that it will be built as a forest city, a sponge city, and a smart city. Beyond the three characteristics, maritime identity—an identity that Indonesia has claimed through its archipelagic status, has yet to be adopted as the main characteristic of the new IKN.

It will be unfortunate if Indonesia fails to make the new IKN reflects the country's maritime identity. The location for the IKN is strategically situated near the coastal area of East Kalimantan. It has proximity to the Makassar Strait, a central feature of the second of Indonesia's archipelagic sea lanes (*Alur Laut Kepulauan Indonesia II*, ALKI II) which is also connected to the Lombok Strait. As one of the world's choke points, these straits directly connect the Indian and Pacific oceans. The nearest designated port, Semayang Port in Balikpapan Bay, has been built to facilitate international shipping and long-distance sea routes. It is estimated that 420 large ships mostly sail through the Lombok and Makassar straits each year, carrying around 36 million tons of cargo.[3]

On maritime identity, Indonesia has politically recommitted to its maritime development aspect by launching the Global Maritime Fulcrum (GMF) vision in 2014, at the beginning of President Joko Widodo's administration. This vision aims to build up Indonesia's maritime capacity at the national and international levels. From building infrastructure that connects ports to building international shipping hubs and driving a regional and international maritime-centred foreign policy agenda, Indonesia has been proving its seriousness in embracing its maritime identity.

Within the new IKN framework, however, such excitement towards the sea seems to be limited. In the supporting document for the IKN Law, the words "maritime" or "sea" can only be found in the sections on connectivity and defence. This can be understood because connectivity and defence are crucial matters in the early phases of the development of the IKN. While connectivity ensures the flow of logistics, defence is important to guard the process of building the city and beyond.

This chapter argues that Indonesia's maritime identity, although only represented in limited aspects for now, can effectively merge with the ideas and vision for the IKN so that the new capital can continue to embody the spirit of Indonesia as a GMF. It will address three main research questions: what constitutes Indonesia's maritime identity, how the new IKN can fit with this identity, and what are the challenges in ensuring that this maritime identity will be represented in the new IKN framework?

In answering those questions, this chapter offers three main analyses and is structured as follows. After the introduction, it will unpack Indonesia's maritime identity framework. Next, it explains how this identity can be incorporated into the new IKN, focusing on maritime infrastructure and security and defence aspects. It will then discuss the challenges in operationalizing such incorporation before summing up some future prospects in embedding this maritime identity within the larger ideas and vision for the new IKN.

On Indonesia's Maritime Identity

Indonesia has long been known for its identity as an archipelagic state. Then Prime Minister Djuanda in 1957 in his "Djuanda Declaration" defined Indonesia's national interests as those of an archipelagic state in law, politics, economy, culture, and the protection of territorial integrity and national unity.[4] It was a "declaration of territorial unity that comprised the unity between the land, the sea, its seabed and subsoil area, the airspace and all the resources contained therein".[5] With the Djuanda Declaration, the concept of Nusantara was born and this was used as a symbol for the unity and integrity of the Indonesian nation.[6]

The developmentplan of this Nusantara concept reached its final stage with the enactment of "Wawasan Nusantara" as a concept of national unity that views the state and nation of Indonesia as a unit.[7] The New Order administration formulated this Archipelagic Outlook (the Wawasan Nusantara) in 1966 and started campaigning for the acceptance and recognition of Indonesia's archipelagic status in international deliberations on the United Nations Convention on the Law of the Sea (UNCLOS 1982).[8] Together, the Djuanda Declaration and Wawasan Nusantara contained core maritime policy principles guiding Indonesia's strategic thinking.[9]

Nonetheless, during the New Order (1966–98) maritime issues were long neglected. National economic development and defence strategy were terrestrially based, with less political attention paid to their maritime aspects.[10] Marine resources were under-utilized, affecting the way the government (and military) supervised and secured the seas and developed infrastructure. Consequently, Indonesia's limited control of its archipelagic territory led to several serious challenges to its maritime security, not only from illegal fishing but also smuggling and illegal trade in its archipelagic waters.[11] As an example of how long it took for such matters to reach national attention, maritime development was formally incorporated into the Sixth Five-Year Plan only in 1994.[12]

After the New Order, maritime development was institutionally sustained. In 1999, during Abdurrahman Wahid's brief presidency, the Department of Sea Exploration (*Departemen Eksplorasi Laut*) was established.[13] A month later, its name was changed to the Department of Sea Exploration and Fisheries (*Departemen Eksplorasi Laut dan Perikanan*) and in 2000, it was renamed the Department of Marine Affairs and Fisheries (*Departemen Kelautan dan Perikanan*), partly in response to the rapid growth in illegal fishing.

During the Yudhoyono presidency (2004–14), two major events occurred in Indonesia's maritime development. First, the government upgraded the Department of Marine Affairs and Fisheries to a Ministry of Marine Affairs and Fisheries, based on Presidential Regulation (*Peraturan Presiden*, Perpres) No. 47 (2009). Second, the government launched its Master Plan for Accelerating and Expansion of Indonesia's Economic Development 2011–25 (Masterplan *Percepatan dan Perluasan Pembangunan Ekonomi Indonesia*, MP3EI 2011–25), based on Perpres No. 32 (2011). This was part of an ambitious plan to accelerate Indonesia's economic development by cultivating the whole potential of all provinces,[14] one of which was the marine and fisheries sector. As stated in Annex I of Presidential Decree No. 48 (2014), an amendment of Perpres No. 32 (2011) concerning MP3EI:

> As the largest maritime and archipelagic country in the world, Indonesia has enormous marine and fishery potential ...With the vast seas and maritime wealth in Indonesia, the potential income of the maritime sector per year can reach seven times the state's current income. It is estimated that with its maritime potential and with good management of marine resources from the fisheries, mining, marine tourism, maritime industry and sea transportation sectors, each year it will produce Rp7,400 trillion. (Authors' translation, excerpts from pp. 9–10)

Besides addressing the marine and fisheries sector's potential, the MP3EI highlighted Indonesia's strategic geographical location astride global container shipping lanes. As part of accelerating the masterplan, Indonesia Port Corporations (*PT Pelabuhan Indonesia, Pelindo*) in 2012 formulated the concept of "Pendulum Nusantara", which was intended to connect six main ports as part of a National Logistics System, to reduce the disparity between the western and eastern parts of Indonesia, where the latter lags economically and developmentally.[15]

The presidency of Joko Widodo in 2014 marked a developmental change for Indonesia's maritime identity through the aforementioned GMF vision. For the first time in the *reformasi* era, a presidential candidate had articulated a maritime vision in his Election Manifesto. In their vision and mission statement, team Joko Widodo–Jusuf Kalla wanted to see Indonesia become a maritime country which is independent, advanced, powerful, and based on national interests.[16] Widodo utilized his presidential campaign to build up nationalism as his source of legitimacy by reviving the old value of Indonesia as an archipelagic nation.[17] As argued by Saha, "The central idea of (the) GMF is to reassert the age-old archipelagic identity that recognizes the link between the country's geography, identity, and livelihood."[18] Accordingly, the GMF concept seeks to reinvigorate Indonesia's age-old identity as an archipelagic state.

At the domestic level, there are several new maritime policies. Institutionally, the Widodo government formed the Coordinating Ministry of Maritime Affairs in 2015. In 2019, its nomenclature was changed to the Coordinating Ministry of Maritime Affairs and Investment. In addition to these institutional arrangements, in 2017 the government issued Presidential Decree No. 16 (2017) concerning Indonesian Ocean Policy (*Kebijakan*

Kelautan Indonesia, KKI). As the country's general guidelines on ocean policy, the KKI consists of a National Document and Plan of Action. In 2018, the Coordinating Ministry of Maritime Affairs issued Ministerial Decree No. 128 on a Maritime Diplomacy White Paper.[19]

The KKI can be seen as the cornerstone of a maritime nation. As mentioned, the GMF is Indonesia's vision to become a maritime country that is sovereign, advanced, independent, strong, and able to make a positive contribution to regional and world security and peace in accordance with national interests.[20] There are seven pillars of the KKI: marine and human resources development; marine security, law enforcement and safety at sea; ocean governance and institutions; maritime economy development; sea space management and marine protection; maritime culture; and maritime diplomacy.[21]

In addition, Indonesia has established the 115 Task Force (*Satuan Tugas 115*, Satgas 115) as a special task force with an important role in the defence of the marine and fisheries sector. The Task Force has succeeded in sinking or seizing hundreds of illegal foreign fishing vessels (*Kapal Ikan Asing*, KIA) operating in the Republic of Indonesia Fisheries Management Area (*Wilayah Pengelolaan Perikanan–Negara Republik Indonesia*, WPP–NRI). The Task Force has also played an active role in rescuing the enslaved crew members in Benjina, Aru Islands, Maluku.[22] Besides, the government also prioritizes maritime infrastructure to ensure a more equitable distribution of logistics networks, especially between western and eastern parts of Indonesia, through a programme of "maritime highways" (*tol laut*).

Although some have argued that the idea of building maritime highways resembles the pre-existing concept of a "Pendulum Nusantara" and that the maritime infrastructure agenda of President Widodo is only a revised version of the MP3EI,[23] the Widodo presidency has made a difference in articulating Indonesia's maritime identity. President Widodo adopts a more proactive approach to implement the vision.[24] In his first state address entitled "Di Bawah Kehendak Rakyat dan Konstitusi", President Widodo explicitly reaffirmed his desire to make the maritime area one of his development foci. He said,

> We have to work as hard as we can to restore Indonesia as a maritime power. The oceans, the seas, the straits and the bays are the future of our civilization. For far too long, we have turned our backs on the seas, the oceans, the straits and the bays. Now is the time to restore *Jalesveva Jayamahe* [At sea we are victorious], the motto of our forefathers. We should return back to sailing the seas. (Translation by *Jakarta Post*).[25]

At the regional level, Indonesia has paved the way to mainstream its maritime vision in ASEAN. President Widodo consciously used the East Asia Summit in Naypyidaw, Myanmar in November 2014 to announce his vision of GMF. The use of this forum was a strategic step, not only to assert that the rise of the GMF vision was in the context of Indonesia's foreign policy but also to indicate the magnitude of the expected impact of its implementation, especially in Asia.[26] In 2017, when Indonesia became the chair of the Seventh ASEAN Maritime Forum (AMF) and the Fifth Expanded ASEAN Maritime Forum (EAMF), Indonesia brought to the table the issues of safety and security at sea; illegal, unreported and unregulated (IUU) fishing activities; human trafficking; and environmental protection. When the ASEAN Outlook on the Indo-Pacific (AOIP) was launched in 2019, the issue of maritime connectivity was one of four priority sectors for cooperation.

However, the continuity of this vision became uncertain in President Widodo's second term. Some argue that President Widodo lost his interest in the maritime vision, as indicated by the fact that he did not mention this vision as often as in his first term. Maritime issues were no longer visible in his campaign materials, victory speeches, and his first speech as President of the Republic of Indonesia in his second term.[27] The present authors would argue that President Widodo's vision of the GMF in his second term has actually entered the "harvest" period, as the programmes carried out in his first term were expected to start showing positive results.[28] During President Widodo's state visit to Beijing in July 2022, Indonesia and China signed a renewed memorandum of understanding on jointly advancing cooperation related to China's Belt and Road Initiative and the GMF. President Widodo called for strengthened alignment between the two nation's strategies to make more effective use of Indonesia's vast seas for the national economy, through port infrastructure, sea transport, and the sustainable production of maritime-related resources.

Overall, the development of Indonesia's maritime identity from one administration to the next shows that the continuity of the idea is critical. Despite its flaws, the rise of the GMF must be recognized as a significant development of Indonesia's maritime identity which will not go away with the end of the political regime. One way for the maritime vision to go beyond Widodo's presidency is to ensure that it is manifested in the IKN's development plan. First, Indonesia is an archipelagic and maritime country not only geographically, but also historically, in that it is an identity that was fought for so that the nation could benefit economically, politically, and socio-culturally. Hence, Indonesia can project its national identity as a maritime country globally. Second, as argued by Khanisa and Sinaga, Indonesia has been aiming to strengthen its maritime identity regionally and globally through the GMF, which is an important basis for formulating the AOIP, launched in President Widodo's second term.[29] Therefore, this maritime vision is significant and continuously revived and adopted, given the dynamics that continue to indicate the importance of the maritime domain in great power politics, especially in the Indo-Pacific. The geographical location of Nusantara as the new capital of Indonesia reflects a long-term projection of making it the region's maritime hub.

ON MARITIME IDENTITY AND THE NEW CAPITAL CITY

The continuity of Indonesia's vision to strengthen its maritime identity will lay upon the decision of the government to keep this agenda alive. In the context of building the new capital, there are several ways in which Nusantara can represent this identity. First, by observing the choice of location, and second, by looking at maritime aspects in the IKN Law. Regarding the location, as the new IKN is located in Penajam Paser Utara, with Balikpapan at its north and Samarinda in its east, it lies in a strategic spot where the mountains meet the sea, and where rivers connect those who live in the area. As the historical record shows, both cities are no strangers to water transportation. In Samarinda, boats have been cruising the Mahakam River to transport goods and people since ancient times. In Balikpapan, its bay has received domestic and international ships as it is located near the busy Makassar Strait. With this background, Nusantara already has the modalities to support the national maritime identity.

Nusantara is divided into two areas, the area of the new capital city (*Kawasan IKN*, KIKN) and the development area of the new capital city (*Kawasan Pengembangan IKN*, KPIKN). Both areas have different accesses to the sea. The KIKN, where the central government zone will be located, is close to the downstream of the rivers flowing into Balikpapan Bay. This area, although it still needs to be developed, has many river ports which are actively used by companies to transport logs and other goods. Meanwhile, the KPIKN directly faces the Makassar Strait, with 68,189 ha of maritime area.

In terms of maritime connectivity, Nusantara has the potential to be developed further. Currently, as stated in Annex II of the IKN Law, Semayang Port and Kariangau Terminal in Balikpapan will become two significant maritime connectivity spots for the new IKN as they meet certain requirements. Port Semayang's pier is 489.5 metres long and 21 metres wide. It has been categorized as a first-class port by Indonesia's Ministry of Transportation.[30] Meanwhile, Karingau Terminal, a container-focused port, has a 270-metre-long pier and can serve ships of up to 35,000 deadweight tonnages (DWT).[31] Aside from these two ports, Balikpapan has Kampung Baru Port, a small port that serves fast boats to several districts in East Kalimantan.[32]

Aside from the ports, the government must give special attention to building maritime defence and security around the IKN. Referring to Annex II of the IKN Law, the maritime aspect is a significant part of Indonesia's national defence posture. It states, "The development of national defence is carried out to implement military defence and non-military defence towards (building) a regional maritime power that is respected in the East Asia region with the principles of active and layered defence in order to guarantee national interests."[33]

Specifically, this document mentions a concept of a "virtual maritime gate" whose function will be to scan the movement of people, goods, and other items such as ships on the surface or underwater. It will be placed in the Makassar Strait and its objective is to identify objects that cross the strait towards the new IKN.

With the current arrangement, the new IKN area is under the protection of Naval Base (*Pangkalan Angkatan Laut*) Balikpapan which comes under the First-Class Naval Base (*Pangkalan Utama Angkatan Laut*) XIII located in Tarakan. Alongside the new IKN's development, the Indonesian Navy plans to upgrade Balikpapan Naval Base to a First-Class Naval Base.[34] The Navy is also proposing to upgrade the First-Class Naval Base into future Maritime Area Commands (*Komando Daerah Maritim*, Kodamar) headed by a *Laksamana Muda* (Rear Admiral).[35] These Kodamar will be located in Samboja, East Kalimantan and Tarakan, North Kalimantan.[36]

As discussed, it is feasible for the new IKN to accentuate its maritime identity. In the effort to embody the spirit of GMF, it does not mean that the capital needs to be completely maritime in its outlook. However, the government must be ready to optimally pursue substantive projects that convey Indonesia's identity as a maritime nation. A well-designed maritime infrastructure and improving the IKN's maritime defence and security capacities are two areas that need attention.

Challenges in Strengthening Maritime Identity in the New IKN

Challenges lie ahead in reinforcing the logistical and defence and security infrastructure of the new IKN. Arguably, the government needs to evaluate the existing status of and acknowledge problems in each aspect so that future projects can be designed effectively. On maritime infrastructure, Indonesia has been facing a serious infrastructure gap between the western and eastern parts of the country. Major maritime infrastructure developments have been dominant in the western part. While almost 80 per cent of national economic growth is attributed to this region, the lack of maritime infrastructure development in the east has contributed to the country's high logistics costs.[37]

When President Widodo came up with the vision of GMF, maritime infrastructure was one of its five pillars. In the context of developing maritime connectivity, the KKI has emphasized that connectivity must be the backbone of development that is Indonesia-centric, not just Java-centric. It has been explicitly stipulated that building infrastructure and inter-regional connectivity should be carried out by optimizing sea transportation. Good connectivity between regions in Indonesia is expected to facilitate the increased movement of people, goods, services, and capital. Therefore, the development of maritime infrastructure such as ports as hubs for trading activities and the provision of international standard means of transportation, especially in peripheral eastern Indonesia areas, must be a key concern.

Maritime infrastructure will gain importance as IKN Nusantara is located in the epicentre of maritime connectivity. East Kalimantan province is located along ALKI II, which cuts across the Sulawesi Sea, Makassar Strait, Flores Sea, and the Lombok Strait which connect the Indian and Pacific Oceans. International commercial ships sail through ALKI II to East Asia and the Pacific from the Lombok Strait through the Makassar Strait, between the islands of Kalimantan and Sulawesi, and then towards the Sulu-Sulawesi Sea before continuing to the Pacific Ocean or the South China Sea.[38] In this regard, Makassar is known as "a gateway to Eastern Indonesia", for goods and people to Indonesia's eastern regions.[39]

With one of the aims being the development of IKN Nusantara to be a superhub for the regional economy, strengthening connectivity domestically and in synergy with outward-looking connectivity architectures must be carried out.[40] One of them is by improving maritime infrastructure in accordance with the GMF vision. With a city of such magnitude in the making, the two proposed ports, Semayang and Kariangau, will not be enough for the IKN's purposes. Therefore, the government is preparing several other ports to support logistics delivery. According to the Head of Balikpapan Port, six ports will be prepared.[41] Unfortunately, many of them are not in good condition and have narrow road access that needs to be upgraded.[42] Therefore, improving this maritime infrastructure and connectivity should be the main narrative in planning the development of the IKN.

Another challenge comes from security and defence aspects. Sonny Harmadi, Head of the Demographic Institute, Faculty of Economics, at the University of Indonesia, cited in a 2010 interview, explained that one of the criteria for determining a new IKN was that it would be safe from the perspective of defence and national resilience.[43] Determining a region to be the nation's capital requires geographical considerations because these aspects affect the vulnerability of the capital.

Historically, the most attacked capitals have been those located close to land and sea borders and which have high topographical complexity.[44] IKN Nusantara has a 2,062-kilometre land border with eastern Malaysia.[45] In terms of maritime borders, the eastern part of IKN borders the Makassar Strait, the heart of ALKI II.[46] These key geographical features arguably expose IKN Nusantara to several interrelated challenges, especially with regard to maritime security. In line with the importance of the sea as one of Indonesia's economic lifelines, the government is faced with the challenge of maintaining the security of the seas and waterways.

Recent studies show how Indonesia's seas are increasingly prone to maritime and other potential crimes.[47] A security issue that needs to be taken seriously is the transnational crime on the northern and eastern coasts of Kalimantan Island. On the northern coast, there are border areas between Indonesia and Malaysia where many illicit activities such as the smuggling of people, drugs, and other unregulated items are common. Based on a 2017 unpublished research study by BRIN's ASEAN Research Team, although both governments have set up bilateral cooperation and regional collaboration, such crimes cannot be eradicated easily as they already have complex networks. Many times, the perpetrators will cooperate with people from the area. On the eastern coast where the new IKN is located, although it is not the centre for transnational crime, the effect of existing networks surrounding it might influence the future security of the new capital. Its open maritime area close to ALKI II can also face problems if security measures are not well designed.[48]

Kapiarsa has conducted a study on the potential threats of terrorism in the new IKN: East Kalimantan is potentially vulnerable to terrorism.[49] The province is not far from Central Sulawesi where the main East Indonesian Mujahidin (*Mujahidin Indonesia Timur*, MIT) groups operate. In addition, it is quite close to the Philippines' border, especially in the Sulu Archipelago, Palawan, and Mindanao where the Moro Islamic Liberation Front (MILF) is located. The new IKN is located along ALKI II, which is an international shipping lane but also where terrorists traverse through the Makassar Strait. The Kapiarsa study shows that the route used by these terrorists is by sea. This is also in line with BRIN's unpublished ASEAN Research Team study in 2018 which found that the geographical proximity between the islands in the border areas of Indonesia, Malaysia, and the Philippines has facilitated the flow of people, goods, and weapons from the Southern Philippines region to Indonesia. The position of the North Kalimantan region, which is close to Malaysia and the Philippines, including the Sulu Sea area, makes it vulnerable to becoming a crossroads for terrorists and other criminals.[50]

As stated by Widjajanto, IKN Nusantara has a high external vulnerability in the dimensions of land, sea and air.[51] Given these conditions, the government must have a solid grand design for the defence of the new IKN while improving its defence infrastructure. In his writing, Suryanto emphasizes the need for the IKN to have an integrated and interoperable system under Network Centric Warfare. Such a system requires the development of defence forces in their capacity, defence force exercises, and an overall grand zoning design and development plan.[52]

Therefore, the relocation of IKN needs to be accompanied by broadening Indonesia's defence paradigm. According to Widjajanto, Indonesian defence, which has tended to focus on land-based defence relying on an in-depth defence strategy, is not in line with its geographical conditions and vulnerabilities.[53] Since the location of IKN Nusantara has maritime features which also expose its vulnerabilities, the maritime defence should be considered. It is time for Indonesia to strengthen its maritime defence capabilities. The Navy has historically played a role in securing the voyages of trading ships. The Navy is also responsible for ensuring the security of Indonesia's maritime borders.

As the complexity of problems in maritime security increases with various cases of transnational crime, the Navy needs to work closely with other bureaus of security to ensure a holistic approach to securing the sea. According to Widjajanto, strengthening the forward presence to safeguard the sovereignty of IKN Nusantara, especially from maritime threats, is absolutely necessary.[54] Another defence consideration that will have a significant effect on the whole framework is cyberspace: the decision-makers need to pay attention to the cyber dimension in ensuring a holistic defence framework.[55]

In this context, the new IKN seems to be on the right track to incorporate Indonesia's maritime vision. However, more discussions are needed to ensure that the development of the new IKN will genuinely uphold Indonesia's commitment to its maritime vision. Noir Purba has asserted his concern on the lack of maritime focus in Annex II of the IKN Law.[56] The document emphasizes land-oriented development and has a limited acknowledgement of the IKN's maritime-oriented aspects. The Chairman of the Indonesian Association of Planners Hendricus Andi Simarmata, in a January 2022 interview with Mikrefin, considered that during the preparation for the IKN's relocation, the government discussed more about building a new city instead of the narrative of a maritime nation in its development plans.[57] These criticisms show that the government might need to consider strengthening its maritime outlook in developing IKN Nusantara.

In the future, the development of IKN needs to pay more attention to highlighting its maritime aspects, not just connectivity and defence. In this regard, Presidential Decree No. 64 of 2022 on Spatial Plan for the National Strategic Area of the Nusantara Capital City 2022–2024 (*Rencana Tata Ruang Kawasan Strategis Nasional Ibu Kota Nusantara Tahun* 2022–2024) is a complementary document as it has a wider maritime perspective. Later, renewed commitment is expected so that IKN Nusantara can represent Indonesia's global identity as a maritime nation.

Conclusion

It can be seen that Indonesia's maritime identity has the potential to be manifested in the government's ideas and vision for the IKN. The country's strong maritime character can be used for state branding in the new IKN, which is not only symbolic but has a political, economic, and sociocultural power that can be projected as Indonesia's global identity in the future.

The prospect of further incorporation of a maritime identity into the new IKN's ideas and vision can be done in two important ways. First, by observing the choice of location, it can be argued that the geographical location of Nusantara as the new state capital reflects a long-term projection of making it Indonesia's maritime hub. Second, this can be done by looking at what maritime aspects are planned to be built. This chapter has argued that at least there are two aspects representing Indonesia's maritime identity in the new IKN: infrastructure, and security and defence.

However, these aspects provide opportunities and challenges. For a long time, Indonesia's planning and development paradigm has been land-based, as reflected in Annex II of the IKN Law, which emphasizes land-oriented development and has a limited acknowledgement of the maritime aspects. Therefore, the Indonesian government needs to consider the maritime outlook in developing the new IKN, first by renewing its commitment so that IKN Nusantara can represent Indonesia's global identity as a maritime country. The continuity of Indonesia's vision to strengthen its maritime identity, recently enforced by the rise of the GMF vision, lays upon the decision of the government to keep the agenda alive. One way is to ensure that the vision is manifested in the IKN's development plan.

Notes

1. Petir Garda Bhwana, "Nusantara Name Emblematic of Indonesian Nation, Says Minister", *Tempo.co*, 18 Januari 2022, https://en.tempo.co/read/1551074/nusantara-name-emblematic-of-indonesian-nation-says-minister (accessed 20 October 2022).
2. BBC, "Indonesia Names New Capital That Will Replace Jakarta", 18 January 2022, https://www.bbc.com/news/world-asia-60037163 (accessed 20 October 2022).
3. Evan Laksamana, "The Military and Strategic Implications of Indonesia's New Capital", *ASPI The Strategist*, 22 January 2022, https://www.aspistrategist.org.au/the-military-and-strategic-implications-of-indonesias-new-capital-2/ (accessed 20 October 2022).
4. Nugroho Wisnumurti, "Legal Regimes of Archipelagic States", *Jakarta Post*, 4 March 2014, http://www.thejakartapost.com/news/2014/03/27/legal-regimes-archipelagic-states.html (accessed 20 October 2022).
5. Djalal, Hasyim. 2011. "Regime of Archipelagic State". *ASEAN Regional Forum*, March 2011, https://aseanregionalforum.asean.org/wp-content/uploads/2019/10/Annex-K-Prof-Hasjim-Djalal-Regime-of-Arch-States.pdf (accessed 20 October 2022), p. 3.
6. Chairul Anwar, *ZEE di Dalam Hukum Internasional* [EEZ in International Law] (Jakarta: Sinar Grafika, 1995), p. 154.
7. Ibid., p. 158.
8. Evan Laksmana, "The Enduring Strategic Trinity: Explaining Indonesia's Geopolitical Architecture", *Journal of the Indian Ocean Region* 7, no. 1 (2011): 100–1.
9. Ristian Atriandi Supriyanto, "Developing Indonesia's Maritime Strategy Under President Jokowi", *The Asan Forum*, 22 February 2016, http://www.theasanforum.org/developing-indonesias-maritime-strategy-under-president-jokowi-1/ (accessed 20 October 2022).

10. Ministry of National Development Planning, *Konsep Mainstreaming Ocean Policy ke Dalam Rencana Pembangunan Nasional* [The Concept of Mainstreaming Ocean Policy into the National Development Plan], p. 5.
11. Hasyim Djalal, "Maritime Dimensions of a New World Order: Security Experiences in South East Asia", in *Negara Kepulauan Menuju Negara Maritim: 75 Tahun Prof. Dr. Hasjim Djalal*, edited by Chandra Motik Yusuf (Jakarta: Lembaga Laut Indonesia, 2010), 100–3.
12. Ministry of National Development Planning, *Konsep Mainstreaming Ocean Policy*, p. 3.
13. Ministry of Maritime Affairs and Fisheries, "Sejarah KKP" [History of KKP], https://kkp.go.id/page/6-sejarah
14. Tan Khee Giap et al., *Competitiveness Analysis and Development Strategies for 33 Indonesian Province* (Singapore: World Scientific Publishing, 2013), p. 28.
15. Tabita Diela, "Lino: Tol Laut Jokowi Mirip Pendulum Nusantara Pelindo", *Kompas.com*, 4 September 2014, https://money.kompas.com/read/2014/09/04/115316326/Lino.Tol.Laut.Jokowi.Mirip.Pendulum.Nusantara.Pelindo (accessed 20 October 2022).
16. Joko Widodo and Jusuf Kalla, "Jalan Perubahan Untuk Indonesia yang Berdaulat, Mndiri, dan Berkepribadian, Visi Misi dan Program Aksi Jokowi-Jusuf Kalla 2014" [Path to Change for a Sovereign, Independent, and Distinctive Indonesia, Vision and Mission and Program of Action Jokowi-Jusuf Kalla 2014], KPU, May 2014, https://www.kpu.go.id/koleksigambar/Visi_Misi_JOKOWI-JK.pdf
17. Lidya Christin Sinaga, "Indonesia's China Foreign Policy under President Joko Widodo: Projecting the 'Global Maritime Fulcrum'", (Master's thesis, Flinders University, 2016), p. 18.
18. Premesha Saha, "Indonesia's New Maritime Doctrine: Continuity and Change", in *Maritime Perspectives 2015*, edited by Vijay Sakhuja and Gupreet S. Khurana (New Delhi: National Maritime Foundation, 2016), p. 79.
19. See decree and the White Paper at https://jdih.maritim.go.id/cfind/source/files/keputusan-menteri-marves/kepmenko-no.-128-tahun-2019-tentang-buku-putih-diplomasi.pdf (accessed 6 March 2023).
20. Sekretariat Kabinet Republik Indonesia, "Presiden Jokowi Teken Perpres Kebijakan Kelautan Indonesia" [President Jokowi Signs Presidential Regulation on Indonesian Ocean Policy], *Sekretariat Kabinet Republik Indonesia*, 1 March 2017, https://setkab.go.id/presiden-jokowi-teken-perpres-kebijakan-kelautan-indonesia/ (accessed 20 October 2022).
21. Coordinating Ministry For Maritime Affairs Republic of Indonesia, *Indonesian Ocean Policy* (Jakarta: Coordinating Ministry for Maritime Affairs, Republic of Indonesia, 2017), p. 3, https://maritim.go.id/konten/unggahan/2017/07/offset_lengkap_KKI_eng-vers.pdf (accessed 20 October 2022).
22. Fika Nurul Ulya, "Satgas 115: Dibentuk Era Susi, Sempat Mati Suri, Kini Hidup Lagi [Task Force 115: Formed in the Susi Era, Once in Near-Death Experience, Now Alive Again], *Kompas.com*, 22 May 2020, https://money.kompas.com/

read/2020/05/22/074600926/satgas-115--dibentuk-era-susi-sempat-mati-suri-kini-hidup-lagi?page=all (accessed 20 October 2022).
23. Ristian Atriandi Supriyanto, "Developing Indonesia's Maritime Strategy Under President Jokowi".
24. Premesha Saha, "Indonesia's New Maritime Doctrine: Continuity and Change", p. 83.
25. *Jakarta Post*, "Work, Work, Work to Restore Maritime Power", 21 October 2014, https://www.thejakartapost.com/news/2014/10/21/work-work-work-restore-maritime-power.html (accessed 20 October 2022).
26. Khanisa Krisman and Lidya Christin Sinaga, "Menakar Keberlanjutan Visi Poros Maritim Dunia di Tengah Agenda Pembangunan Maritim Regional" [Measuring the Sustainability of the Global Maritime Fulcrum Vision Amidst the Regional Maritime Development Agenda], *Jurnal Penelitian Politik* 17, no. 1 (2020), p. 105.
27. Ibid., p. 111.
28. M. Riza Damanik, "Menakar Kelanjutan Visi Maritim Jokowi" [Measuring the Continuity of Jokowi's Maritime Vision], *KataData*, 2 February 2019, https://katadata.co.id/opini/2019/02/02/menakar-kelanjutan-visi-maritim-jokowi (accessed 20 October 2022).
29. Krisman and Sinaga, "Menakar Keberlanjutan Visi Poros Maritim Dunia", p. 113.
30. Kementerian Perhubungan Republik Indonesia, Direktorat Jenderal Perhubungan Laut, *Kantor Kesyahbandaran dan Otoritas Pelabuhan Kelas I Balikpapan*, [Port Office and Class I Port Authority of Balikpapan], Kementerian Perhubungan Republik Indonesia, https://hubla.dephub.go.id/ksopbalikpapan/page/services-facilities/facilities
31. Kaltim Kariangau Terminal, Fasilitas & Peralatan [Facilities and Equipment], https://info.kariangauterminal.co.id/fasilitas-peralatan/.
32. Pelindo (n.d.). *Pelabuhan Balikpapan* [Balikpapan Port], https://www.pelindo.co.id/port/pelabuhan-balikpapan
33. Authors' translation of Annex II, Law No. 3/2022 on the State Capital (Lampiran II UU Ibu Kota Negara), p. 87.
34. Flori Sidebang, "TNI AL Akan Perkuat Lanal Balikpapan Jadi Lantamal" [TNI AL Will Strengthen Lanal Balikpapan to Lantamal], *Republika*, 30 June 2022, https://www.republika.co.id/berita/rea534430/tni-al-akan-perkuat-lanal-balikpapan-jadi-lantamal (accessed 20 October 2022).
35. Maulana Riezky, "Usul Lantamal Diubah Jadi Kodamar, KSAL: Dipimpin Bintang 2" [Suggestion of Lantamal Changed to Kodamar, KSAL: Led by 2 Stars], *Sindo News*, 2 March 2022, https://nasional.sindonews.com/read/701455/14/usul-lantamal-diubah-jadi-kodamar-ksal-dipimpin-bintang-2-1646226225 (accessed 20 October 2022).
36. Iwan Sutiawan, "TNI AL Akan Dirikan Dua Kodamar untuk Cegah Serangan dari Laut ke IKN" [TNI AL Will Establish Two Kodamar to Prevent Attacks from the

Sea on the IKN], *Gatra*, 1 July 2022, https://www.gatra.com/news-547103-nasional-tni-al-akan-dirikan-dua-kodamar-untuk-cegah-serangan-dari-laut-ke-ikn.html (accessed 20 October 2022).

37. *Global Business Guide Indonesia*, "Indonesia's Maritime Infrastructure: Key Challenges Remain", 2018, http://www.gbgindonesia.com/en/services/article/2018/indonesia_s_maritime_infrastructure_key_challenges_remain_11873.php (accessed 20 October 2022).

38. Rizki Roza, "Keamanan Laut Sulu-Sulawesi: Kaji Ulang Kerja Sama Trilateral?" [The Security of Sulu-Sulawesi Sea: Review of Trilateral Cooperation?], *Info Singkat* X, no. 20 (2018): 9.

39. Andrew M. Carruthers, "Developing Indonesia's Maritime Infrastructure: The View from Makassar", *ISEAS Perspective*, no. 2016/49, 30 August 2016, p. 4.

40. Andi Widjajanto, "IKN dalam Dinamika Keamanan Regional" [IKN in Regional Security Dynamics], slides presented at webinar "IKN dalam Dinamika Keamanan Regional dan Refleksi Identitas", Global Indonesia, Research Centre for Politics-BRIN", Jakarta, 12 May 2022.

41. *CNN Indonesia*, "6 Pelabuhan Akan Layani Bongkar Muat untuk Pembangunan IKN Nusantara" [6 Ports Will Serve Loading and Discharging for the Development of the IKN Nusantara], 18 October 2022, https://www.cnnindonesia.com/ekonomi/20221018113541-92-862027/6-pelabuhan-akan-layani-bongkar-muat-untuk-pembangunan-ikn-nusantara (accessed 20 October 2022).

42. *Kaltim Post*, "Proyek IKN Butuh Banyak Dermaga" [The IKN Project Needs Many Piers], 27 June 2022, https://kaltimpost.jawapos.com/utama/27/06/2022/proyek-ikn-butuh-banyak-dermaga (accessed 20 October 2022).

43. Ade Mayasanto, "Enam Syarat Ibukota Negara Baru" [Six Requirements for a New State Capital], *Tribunnews*, 4 Agustus 2010, https://www.tribunnews.com/nasional/2010/08/04/enam-syarat-ibukota-negara-baru (accessed 20 October 2022).

44. Andi Widjajanto, "Pertahanan Laut di Era Geopolitik V" [Maritime Defence in the Geopolitical Era V], slides presented at "Seminar Nasional Seskoal 2022", Jakarta, 27 July 2022.

45. Mikhael Lefri, "Pemindahan Ibu Kota Negara dalam Tinjauan Geografi Pertahanan" [State Capital Relocation in Geography of Defense Review], *Pusat Riset Politik*, 10 March 2022, https://politik.brin.go.id/kolom/pemilu-partai-politik-otonomi-daerah/pemindahan-ibu-kota-negara-dalam-tinjauan-geografi-pertahanan/ (accessed 20 October 2022).

46. *Detik*, "Letak Ibu Kota Baru Indonesia Bernama Nusantara, Ini Detil Lokasinya" [The Location of Indonesia's New Capital City Named Nusantara, Here are the Location Details], 21 January 2022, https://news.detik.com/berita/d-5908269/letak-ibu-kota-baru-indonesia-bernama-nusantara-ini-detil-lokasinya (accessed 20 October 2022).

47. Destructive Fishing Watch Indonesia, "Laut Indonesia Rawan Kejahatan Maritim" [Indonesian Seas are Prone to Maritime Crime], *Destructive Fishing Watch*

Indonesia, 27 January 2021. https://dfw.or.id/laut-indonesia-rawan-kejahatan-maritim/ (accessed 20 October 2022).
48. Khanisa Krisman and Faudzan Farhana, *ASEAN dan Penanganan Kejahatan Transnasional di Laut: Studi Kasus Indonesia-Malaysia* [ASEAN and Handling Transnational Crime at Sea: Case Studies of Indonesia-Malaysia] (Jakarta: BRIN Press, forthcoming).
49. Asa Bintang Kapiarsa, "Penanganan Potensi Ancaman Terorisme di Ibu Kota Baru Indonesia Studi Kasus: Kabupaten Kutai Kartanegara dan Penajam Paser Utara" [Handling Potential Threats of Terrorism in Indonesia's New Capital City Case Study: Kutai Kartanegara and North Penajam Paser Regencies], *Jurnal Manajemen Pertahanan* 6, no. 2 (2020), p. 25.
50. Khanisa and Farhana, *ASEAN dan Penanganan Kejahatan Transnasional di Laut*.
51. Andi Widjajanto, "IKN dalam Dinamika Keamanan Regional".
52. Sugeng Suryanto, "Pemindahan Ibu Kota Negara ke Kalimantan Timur dari Tinjauan Aspek Pertanan dan Keamanan" [State Capital Relocation to East Kalimantan from a Defense and Security Review], *WIRA* 1 (2022), p. 28.
53. Andi Widjajanto, 2022. "IKN dalam Dinamika Keamanan Regional".
54. Ibid.
55. Ibid.
56. Noir Primadona Purba, "Bias Daratan Megaproyek IKN: Bagaimana Ruang Laut Terlupakan Dalam Perencanaan Ibu Kota Baru" [Land Bias of the IKN Megaproject: How Sea Space Is Forgotten in Planning for a New Capital City], *The Conversation*, 18 October 2022, https://theconversation.com/bias-daratan-megaproyek-ikn-bagaimana-ruang-laut-terlupakan-dalam-perencanaan-ibu-kota-baru-192527 (accessed 20 October 2022).
57. Nuhansa Mikrefin, "Ahli Tata Kota Kritik Minimnya Narasi Negara Maritim di Ibu Kota Baru" [City Planning Expert Criticizes the Lack of Narrative of the Maritime State in the New Capital City], *Katadata*, 27 January 2022, https://katadata.co.id/yuliawati/berita/61f20656dabe0/ahli-tata-kota-kritik-minimnya-narasi-negara-maritim-di-ibu-kota-baru (accessed 20 October 2022).

References

Anwar, Chairul. 1995. *ZEE di dalam Hukum Internasional* [EEZ in International Law]. Jakarta: Sinar Grafika.
BBC. 2022. "Indonesia Names New Capital That Will Replace Jakarta". 18 January 2022. https://www.bbc.com/news/world-asia-60037163 (accessed 20 October 2022).
Bhwana, Petir Garda. 2022. "Nusantara Name Emblematic of Indonesian Nation, Says Minister". *Tempo.co*, 18 January 2022. https://en.tempo.co/read/1551074/nusantara-name-emblematic-of-indonesian-nation-says-minister (accessed 20 October 2022).
Carruthers, Andrew M. 2016. "Developing Indonesia's Maritime Infrastructure: The View from Makassar". *ISEAS Perspective*, no. 2016/49, 30 August 2016.
CNN Indonesia. 2022. "6 Pelabuhan Akan Layani Bongkar Muat untuk Pembangunan IKN Nusantara" [6 Ports Will Serve Loading and Discharging for the Development

of the IKN Nusantara]. 18 October 2022. https://www.cnnindonesia.com/ekonomi/20221018113541-92-862027/6-pelabuhan-akan-layani-bongkar-muat-untuk-pembangunan-ikn-nusantara (accessed 20 October 2022).

Coordinating Ministry for Maritime Affairs, Republic of Indonesia. 2017. *Indonesian Ocean Policy*. Jakarta: Coordinating Ministry for Maritime Affairs, Republic of Indonesia. https://maritim.go.id/konten/unggahan/2017/07/offset_lengkap_KKI_eng-vers.pdf (accessed 20 October 2022).

Damanik, M. Riza. 2019. "Menakar Kelanjutan Visi Maritim Jokowi" [Measuring the Continuity of Jokowi's Maritime Vision]. *KataData*, 2 February 2019. https://katadata.co.id/opini/2019/02/02/menakar-kelanjutan-visi-maritim-jokowi (accessed 20 October 2022).

Destructive Fishing Watch Indonesia. 2021. "Laut Indonesia Rawan Kejahatan Maritim" [Indonesian Sea is Prone to Maritime Crime]. *Destructive Fishing Watch Indonesia*, 27 January 2021. https://dfw.or.id/laut-indonesia-rawan-kejahatan-maritim/ (accessed 20 October 2022).

Detik. 2022. "Letak Ibu Kota Baru Indonesia Bernama Nusantara, Ini Detil Lokasinya" [The Location of Indonesia's New Capital City Named Nusantara, Here Are the Location Details]. 21 January 2022. https://news.detik.com/berita/d-5908269/letak-ibu-kota-baru-indonesia-bernama-nusantara-ini-detail-lokasinya (accessed 20 October 2022).

Diela, Tabita. 2014. "Lino: Tol Laut Jokowi Mirip Pendulum Nusantara Pelindo" [Lino: Jokowi's Sea Toll Road Is Similar to Pelindo's Nusantara Pendulum]. *Kompas.com*, 4 September 2014. https://money.kompas.com/read/2014/09/04/115316326/Lino.Tol.Laut.Jokowi.Mirip.Pendulum.Nusantara.Pelindo (accessed 20 October 2022).

Djalal, Hasyim. 2010. "Maritime Dimensions of a New World Order: Security Experiences in South East Asia". In *Negara Kepulauan Menuju Negara Maritim: 75 Tahun Prof. Dr. Hasjim Djalal*, edited by Chandra Motik Yusuf, pp. 100–3. Jakarta: Lembaga Laut Indonesia.

———. 2011. "Regime of Archipelagic State". *ASEAN Regional Forum*, March 2011. https://aseanregionalforum.asean.org/wp-content/uploads/2019/10/Annex-K-Prof-Hasjim-Djalal-Regime-of-Arch-States.pdf (accessed 20 October 2022).

Global Business Guide Indonesia. 2018. "Indonesia's Maritime Infrastructure: Key Challenges Remain". 2018. http://www.gbgindonesia.com/en/services/article/2018/indonesia_s_maritime_infrastructure_key_challenges_remain_11873.php (accessed 20 October 2022).

Jakarta Post. 2014. "Work, Work, Work to Restore Maritime Power". 21 October 2014. https://www.thejakartapost.com/news/2014/10/21/work-work-work-restore-maritime-power.html (accessed 20 October 2022).

Kaltim Post. 2022. "Proyek IKN Butuh Banyak Dermaga". 27 June 2022. https://kaltimpost.jawapos.com/utama/27/06/2022/proyek-ikn-butuh-banyak-dermaga (accessed 20 October 2022).

Kapiarsa, Asa Bintang. 2020. "Penanganan Potensi Ancaman Terorisme di Ibu Kota Baru Indonesia Studi Kasus: Kabupaten Kutai Kartanegara dan Penajam Paser Utara"

[Handling Potential Threats of Terrorism in Indonesia's New Capital City Case Study: Kutai Kartanegara and North Penajam Paser Regencies]. *Jurnal Manajemen Pertahanan* 6, no. 2: 16–37.

Krisman, Khanisa, and Lidya Christin Sinaga. 2020. "Menakar Keberlanjutan Visi Poros Maritim Dunia di Tengah Agenda Pembangunan Maritim Regional" [Measuring the Sustainability of the Global Maritime Fulcrum Vision Amidst the Regional Maritime Development Agenda]. *Jurnal Penelitian Politik* 17, no. 1: 103–16.

———, and Faudzan Farhana. Forthcoming. *ASEAN dan Penanganan Kejahatan Transnasional di Laut: Studi Kasus Indonesia-Malaysia* [ASEAN and Handling Transnational Crime at Sea: Case Studies of Indonesia-Malaysia]. (Jakarta: BRIN Press).

Laksmana, Evan. 2011. "The Enduring Strategic Trinity: Explaining Indonesia's Geopolitical Architecture". *Journal of the Indian Ocean Region* 7, no. 1: 95–116.

———. 2022. "The Military and Strategic Implications of Indonesia's New Capital". *ASPI The Strategist*, 22 January 2022. https://www.aspistrategist.org.au/the-military-and-strategic-implications-of-indonesias-new-capital-2/ (accessed 20 October 2022).

Maulana, Riezky. 2022. "Usul Lantamal Diubah Jadi Kodamar, KSAL: Dipimpin Bintang 2" [Suggestion of Lantamal Changed to Kodamar, KSAL: Led by 2 Stars]. *Sindo News*, 2 March 2022. https://nasional.sindonews.com/read/701455/14/usul-lantamal-diubah-jadi-kodamar-ksal-dipimpin-bintang-2-1646226225 (accessed 20 October 2022).

Mayasanto, Ade. 2010. "Enam Syarat Ibukota Negara Baru" [Six Requirements for a New State Capital]. *Tribunnews*, 4 August 2010. https://www.tribunnews.com/nasional/2010/08/04/enam-syarat-ibukota-negara-baru (accessed 20 October 2022).

Mikhael, Lefri. 2022. "Pemindahan Ibu Kota Negara dalam Tinjauan Geografi Pertahanan" [State Capital Relocation in Geography of Defense Review]. *Pusat Riset Politik*, 10 March 2022. https://politik.brin.go.id/kolom/pemilu-partai-politik-otonomi-daerah/pemindahan-ibu-kota-negara-dalam-tinjauan-geografi-pertahanan/ (accessed 20 October 2022).

Mikrefin, Nuhansa. 2022. "Ahli Tata Kota Kritik Minimnya Narasi Negara Maritim di Ibu Kota Baru" [City Planning Expert Criticizes the Lack of Narrative of the Maritime State in the New Capital City]. *Katadata*. 27 January 2022. https://katadata.co.id/yuliawati/berita/61f20656dabe0/ahli-tata-kota-kritik-minimnya-narasi-negara-maritim-di-ibu-kota-baru (accessed 20 October 2022).

Ministry of National Development Planning. (December 2014). *Konsep Mainstreaming Ocean Policy ke Dalam Rencana Pembangunan Nasional* [The Concept of Mainstreaming Ocean Policy in the National Development Plan]. Jakarta: Ministry of National Development Planning.

Pelindo. N.d. *Pelabuhan Balikpapan* [Balikpapan Port]. https://www.pelindo.co.id/port/pelabuhan-balikpapan

Purba, Noir Primadona. 2022. "Bias Daratan Megaproyek IKN: Bagaimana Ruang Laut

Terlupakan Dalam Perencanaan Ibu Kota Baru" [Land Bias of the IKN Megaproject: How Sea Space Is Forgotten in Planning for a New Capital City]. *The Conversation*, 18 October 2022. https://theconversation.com/bias-daratan-megaproyek-ikn-bagaimana-ruang-laut-terlupakan-dalam-perencanaan-ibu-kota-baru-192527 (accessed 20 October 2022).

Roza, Rizki. 2018. "Keamanan Laut Sulu-Sulawesi: Kaji Ulang Kerja Sama Trilateral?" ["The Security of Sulu-Sulawesi Sea: Review of Trilateral Cooperation?"]. *Info Singkat* X (20): 7-11.

Saha, Premesha. 2016. "Indonesia's New Maritime Doctrine: Continuity and Change". In *Maritime Perspectives 2015*, edited by Vijay Sakhuja and Gupreet S. Khurana, pp. 79–85. New Delhi: National Maritime Foundation.

Sekretariat Kabinet Republik Indonesia. 2017. "Presiden Jokowi Teken Perpres Kebijakan Kelautan Indonesia" [President Jokowi Signs Presidential Regulation on Indonesian Ocean Policy]. *Sekretariat Kabinet Republik Indonesia*, 1 March 2017. https://setkab.go.id/presiden-jokowi-teken-perpres-kebijakan-kelautan-indonesia/ (accessed 20 October 2022).

Sidebang, Flori. 2022. "TNI AL Akan Perkuat Lanal Balikpapan Jadi Lantamal" [TNI AL Will Strengthen Lanal Balikpapan to Lantamal]. *Republika*, 30 June 2022. https://www.republika.co.id/berita/rea534430/tni-al-akan-perkuat-lanal-balikpapan-jadi-lantamal (accessed 20 October 2022).

Sinaga, Lidya Christin. 2016. "Indonesia's China Foreign Policy under President Joko Widodo: Projecting the 'Global Maritime Fulcrum'". Master's thesis, Flinders University.

Supriyanto, Ristian Atriandi. 2016. "Developing Indonesia's Maritime Strategy Under President Jokowi". *The Asan Forum*, 22 February 2016. http://www.theasanforum.org/developing-indonesias-maritime-strategy-under-president-jokowi-1/ (accessed 20 October 2022).

Suryanto, Sugeng. 2022. "Pemindahan Ibu Kota Negara ke Kalimantan Timur dari Tinjauan Aspek Pertahanan dan Keamanan" [State Capital Relocation to East Kalimantan from a Defense and Security Review]. *WIRA* 1: 22–29.

Sutiawan, Iwan. 2022. "TNI AL Akan Dirikan Dua Kodamar untuk Cegah Serangan dari Laut ke IKN" [TNI AL Will Establish Two Kodamar to Prevent Attacks from the Sea on the IKN]. *Gatra*, 1 July 2022. https://www.gatra.com/news-547103-nasional-tni-al-akan-dirikan-dua-kodamar-untuk-cegah-serangan-dari-laut-ke-ikn.html (accessed 20 October 2022).

Tan, Khee Giap, Mulya Amri, Linda Low, and Tan Kong Yam. 2013. *Competitiveness Analysis and Development Strategies for 33 Indonesian Provinces*. Singapore: World Scientific Publishing.

Ulya, Fika Nurul. 2020. "Satgas 115: Dibentuk Era Susi, Sempat Mati Suri, Kini Hidup Lagi" [Task Force 115: Formed in the Susi Era, Once in Near-Death Experience, Now Alive Again]. *Kompas.com*, 22 May 2020. https://money.kompas.com/read/2020/05/22/074600926/satgas-115--dibentuk-era-susi-sempat-mati-suri-kini-hidup-lagi?page=all (accessed 20 October 2022).

Widjajanto, Andi. 2022a. "IKN dalam Dinamika Keamanan Regional" [IKN in Regional Security Dynamics]. Slides presented in webinar "IKN dalam Dinamika Keamanan Regional dan Refleksi Identitas", Global Indonesia, Research Centre for Politics-BRIN, Jakarta, 12 May 2022.

———. 2022b. "Pertahanan Laut di Era Geopolitik V" [Maritime Defence in the Geopolitical Era V]. Slides presented at "Seminar Nasional Seskoal 2022", Jakarta, 27 July 2022.

Widodo, Joko, and Jusuf Kalla. 2014. "Jalan Perubahan Untuk Indonesia yang Berdaulat, Mandiri, dan Berkepribadian, Visi Misi dan Program Aksi Jokowi-Jusuf Kalla 2014" [Path to Change for a Sovereign, Independent, and Distinctive Indonesia, Vision and Mission and Program of Action Jokowi-Jusuf Kalla 2014]. *KPU*. May 2014. https://www.kpu.go.id/koleksigambar/Visi_Misi_JOKOWI-JK.pdf (accessed 20 October 2022).

Wisnumurti, Nugroho. 2014. "Legal Regimes of Archipelagic States". *Jakarta Post*, 4 March 2014. http://www.thejakartapost.com/news/2014/03/27/legal-regimes-archipelagic-states.html (accessed 20 October 2022).

Regulations

Decree of the Coordinating Minister for Maritime Affairs No. 128 of 2019 on the Maritime Diplomacy White Paper [Keputusan Menteri Koordinator Bidang Kemaritiman No. 128 Tahun 2019 tentang Buku Putih Diplomasi Maritim].

Law No. 3 of 2022 on the State Capital [Undang-Undang No. 3 Tahun 2022 tentang Ibu Kota Negara].

Law No. 3 of 2022 on the State Capital, Annex II [Undang-Undang No. 3 Tahun 2022 tentang Ibu Kota Negara, Lampiran II].

Presidential Decree No. 48 of 2014, Annex I [Keputusan Presiden No. 48 Tahun 2014 tentang Perubahan atas Peraturan Presiden Nomor 32 Tahun 2011 tentang Masterplan Percepatan dan Perluasan Pembangunan Ekonomi Indonesia 2011–2025, Lampiran I].

Presidential Decree No. 64 of 2022 on Spatial Plan for the National Strategic Area of the Nusantara Capital City 2022–2024 [Keputusan Presiden No. 64 Tahun 2022 tentang Rencana Tata Ruang Kawasan Strategis Nasional Ibu Kota Nusantara Tahun 2022–2024].

Presidential Decree No. 16 of 2017 concerning Indonesian Ocean Policy [Keputusan Presiden No. 16 Tahun 2017 tentang Kebijakan Kelautan Indonesia].

Presidential Regulation No. 32 of 2011 [Peraturan Presiden No. 32 Tahun 2011 tentang Masterplan Percepatan dan Perluasan Pembangunan Ekonomi Indonesia 2011–2025].

Presidential Regulation No. 47 of 2009 [Peraturan Presiden No. 47 Tahun 2009 tentang Pembentukan dan Organisasi Kementerian Negara].

CONCLUSION
Shaping Nusantara

Yanuar Nugroho and Julia M. Lau

"The future is neither predicted, nor forecasted. The future is shaped."
The Many Faces of Foresight, Miles et al. (2008)

This book has provided a collection of academic writings examining the various aspects of the historic and momentous relocation of Indonesia's capital city from Jakarta to Nusantara. In this sense, this edited volume serves as the first academic summation of the myriad challenges and opportunities involved in the IKN's transfer, and simultaneously, as a call to Indonesia's policymakers and leaders to build or develop their new capital in a more balanced, more inclusive, and more sustainable fashion.

From the key takeaways and policy recommendations provided by the authors, there are a few central themes. First, as the overall level of practitioner and research knowledge on the IKN's relocation and development is still limited, this volume will hopefully inspire other researchers and organizations to conduct more detailed and focused studies on all aspects of the IKN's future development. This is particularly for areas related to the IKN's human and social capital, including the livelihoods and well-being of East Kalimantan's local and indigenous communities, the proposed physical and infrastructural development, existing and future environmental and ecological concerns and threats, and evolving social dynamics. Any future studies will need to be sensitive to the potential for unintended or unexpected consequences of IKN development, including widening socio-economic inequality and environmental degradation.

The editors hope that the present volume provides some direction for how the above themes and research questions might pan out, especially if certain recommendations are ignored or dismissed prior to the actual transfer of the national capital from Jakarta to Nusantara.

Generally, development initiatives need three frameworks for execution: a regulatory and policy framework, an institutional framework, and a system to trace and enforce accountability. While Indonesia's IKN Law is a start, the regulatory and policy framework and the actual implementation of the transfer still need regulations to operationalize the move at the ground level. Likewise, while the establishment of the IKN Authority marked the development of the IKN's institutional framework, this Authority is not fully operational yet and its accountability mechanism is not developed. This book calls for the Indonesian government to address these challenges; the three frameworks need to be put in place given the complexity of the transfer and the IKN's overall development. To succeed, the IKN will require multiple levels and stages of intricate construction and development projects, and above all, financing. The necessary bureaucracy or state apparatus also needs to be set up, to ensure the smooth running of related processes.

As the authors of several chapters have warned, the central government's consultation and engagement with East Kalimantan or the proposed Nusantara's local communities and groups including CSOs, and local or subnational government and society, have been and are minimal if not non-existent. For Nusantara to fairly and adequately manage the real concerns of locals, especially the indigenous communities who might be most affected by the expected influx of newcomers from Jakarta and other parts of Indonesia when the IKN is up and running, much more needs to be done on this front.

It is an open question whether subsequent administrations after Joko Widodo's will show the same political commitment to continue with the IKN's development. From the view of the private sector, certainty in politics and the external environment must improve before investment can be pledged. At the same time, civil servants in Jakarta are rightfully concerned about how the physical transfer of their service might affect their future career trajectory and even their children's education and personal well-being, given the lack of existing infrastructure and facilities in East Kalimantan and the proposed IKN zone. Given this, some incentives must be carefully designed for the private sector as well as civil servants to support the IKN's development.

In an ideal scenario, the IKN transfer will eventually create a new Indonesian civilization and not a mere city. How will Nusantara's identity and social fabric evolve and strengthen? How will local and central governance be conducted when the new capital city emerges from the forest lands? These are longer-term questions that will await answers and analyses from future researchers and scholars.

Last, as the IKN's highly complex development will likely span the next three to four or even five decades, Indonesia's leaders and policymakers might consider proactively mapping megatrends, anticipating changes and identifying drivers, and developing scenarios and potential roadmaps to shape the IKN's future. This is important as the megaproject embodies and affects various perspectives, including socio-economic, cultural, and environmental trajectories and discourses. Lively and open engagement, including that of scholars and experts knowledgeable about local developments as IKN's construction proceeds apace, will help to secure future political and financial commitment to ensure the continuation of IKN development. It will also address challenges during the transition to a new capital city and perhaps even help to pre-empt and resolve serious risks like potential environmental degradation and human rights violations before they are unmanageable. All this can be an opportunity for growth, rather than be seen as limitations.

We hope this book will be a resource for all who are interested in and care about the future of Nusantara and Indonesia. The findings and recommendations of the authors who have contributed to this volume are among the first published scholarly reflections on this broad subject. May the path that they have forged lead more to follow.

Reference

Miles, I., J. Cassingena, L. Georghiou, M. Keenan, and R. Popper. 2009. "The Many Faces of Foresight". In *The Handbook of Technology Foresight: Concepts and Practice*, edited by L. Georghiou. Cheltenham: Edward Elgar Publishing Ltd.

Index

A
A.A. Baramuli, 18
Abdurrahman Wahid, 11, 248
Academic Paper on the IKN Bill
 (*Naskah Akademik Rancangan
 Undang-Undang tentang Ibu Kota
 Negara*), 207
Adang Bay Nature Reserve, 205
adat (customary) community, 5, 42, 44,
 155–57, 234
 see also customary law
Advisory Council (*Dewan Penasihat*),
 42
agricultural land, loss of, 25, 108–9, 115
Ahmad Doli Kurnia Tandjung, 42
AJI (*Aliansi Jurnalis Independen*),
 138–39
Ali Sadikin, 58, 225
ALKI II (*Alur Laut Kepulauan
 Indonesia II*), 246, 254–56
All-Indonesian Provincial Government
 Association (APPSI), 21
AMAN (Alliance of Indigenous Peoples
 of the Archipelago), 49, 114, 126,
 134, 139, 150–51, 153–57, 160, 165
 see also indigenous people
Anderson, Benedict, 58
Andrinof Chaniago, 12, 23
animal rescue, 138
APBN (*Anggaran Pendapatan dan
 Belanja Negara*), 76–77, 82, 88, 93
 limitations of, 78
APL (*area peruntukan lain*), 202–3, 232,
 235

Arab Spring, 55
Archipelagic Outlook, 248
ASEAN, 14, 251
ASEAN Maritime Forum (AMF), 251
ASEAN Outlook on the Indo-Pacific
 (AOIP), 251
ASEAN Research Team, 255–56
Asia Indigenous Peoples' Pact, 154
Asian Games, 13, 18
Astana, 21, 176
asymmetrical elections, 62
Aung San Suu Kyi, 63
authoritarianism, 65
autocratic legalism, 61
automobile industry, 57, 110

B
B2B (business to business) funding, 88
Bajo, ethnic group, 134
Balang Island Bridge, 129
Balik, ethnic community, 114, 125,
 134–36, 139, 145, 157, 160, 203–4
Balikpapan Alliance of Independent
 Journalists, *see* AJI
Balikpapan Bay, 127, 134–38, 145, 159,
 246, 252
Balikpapan Bay Care Forum, 138
Balikpapan City, development of, 125,
 135
Balikpapan Coastal Working Group,
 136–37
Balikpapan Naval Base, 253
Balikpapan Port, 255
Bambang P.S. Brodjonegoro, 23

Bambang Soesatyo, 62
Bambang Susantono, 47, 76
Bambang Triatmodjo, 13, 18, 20
Banjarese, ethnic group, 230
BAPPEDA (*Badan Perencanaan dan Pembangunan Daerah*), 131, 134
Bappenas (National Development Planning Agency), 12, 18, 23, 48, 78, 132, 197, 207, 233
Basab, ethnic group, 44, 155
Basic Agrarian Law, 132, 140
Basuki Tjahaja Purnama (Ahok), 60
Batak, ethnic group, 181
Batam, as commercial industrial area, 133
Batam Authority, 133
Batu Lepek Dam, 129
Belt and Road Initiative, 251
Benuaq, ethnic group, 44, 155
#BersihkanIndonesia, 203
Betawi indigenous group, 156
Bhima Yudhistira, 78
biodiversity, 119, 138, 199, 211
Bisnis.com, 78
B.J. Habibie, 11, 21
BKSDA (*Balai Konservasi Sumber Daya Alam*), 204
Blair, Tony, 132
Borneo Orangutan Survival Foundation (BOSF), 139
bottom-up policy, 12, 219
Brasilia, 16, 39–40, 48, 56, 176, 179
BRM Port, 129
Budiawan Sastrawinata, 132
Bugis, ethnic group, 134, 136, 181, 230–31
building rights title, *see* HGB
Bukit Jonggol Asri, consortium, 18
Bukit Soeharto Forest Park, 205
Buluminung Harbour, 129
Buluminung Industrial Estate, *see* KIB
BumDes (*Badan Usaha Milik Desa*), 129

Bumi Harapan Village, area study of, 227–30, 232–34, 238–41
Bumi Serpong Damai, 21
Busyro Muqoddas, 150

C
Canberra, 70, 176, 179, 207, 218
population, 178
capital city
countries, and relocation of, 175–76
political space, and, 54–56
roles of, 55
see also IKN (*Ibu Kota Negara*); Nusantara
capitalist political economy, 132
concept of, 127–28
domination of, 129–34
Center for Economic and Legal Studies (CELIOS), 78
Central Government Core Area, *see* KIPP
centralization, 25, 32–37, 39, 47
see also decentralization; recentralization
Centre for Strategic and International Studies (CSIS), 152
Ciputra Group, 21, 132
circular mobility, 180, 182
citizen participation, 75, 89–90
city manager, 62
civic capital, 61
civic crowdfunding, 80–81, 89, 91–93
civic participation, 75
CIVICUS, 152
civil society, 5, 35, 53, 60, 64, 69, 131, 157, 167, 201, 206
definition, 151–52, 168
principles of, 153
civil society organizations (CSOs), 5, 41–42, 137–38, 151–53, 165, 268
"clean and clear" development, 117
clientelism, 65
coal mining, 130, 158

Coastal Waters of the National Capital, 129
colonialism, 15–16, 24, 109
Conservation of Natural Resources Office, *see* BKSDA
Constitution, of 1945, 32, 40, 48, 126, 206
constitutional authority, 153
Constitutional Court, 34, 40, 126, 150–51, 204
converted production forest, *see* HPK
Coordinating Ministry of Maritime Affairs and Investment, 249–50
corporate crimes, 158
corruption, 11, 35, 47, 61, 64, 68, 92, 200, 203, 215
Corruption Eradication Commission (KPK), 47, 60–61, 68, 215
Council of Community Representatives (*Konsil Perwakilan Masyarakat*), 42
COVID-19 pandemic, 78, 131, 150, 160
creative financing, 76, 78
crime rate, 162–63
criminal code (KUHP), 61
crowdfunding, 4, 75–77
　civic, 80–81, 89, 91–93
　expert opinion on, 87–88
　IKN (*Ibu Kota Negara*), and, 78–95
　laws, 82–83
　literacy on, 89–90
　risks, 79–80, 91–92
　survey, 83–86
crowdsourcing, 78, 93
customary councils (*dewan adat*), 157
customary land, 114, 117, 119, 156, 165
customary law, 126, 154, 158, 163
　see also adat (customary) community
CV Mandiri Multi-Material, 129

D

DAS (*Daerah Aliran Sungai*), 136
Dayak Bahau, ethnic group, 161
Dayak community, 13–14
Dayak Kenyah, ethnic group, 44, 155, 161
Dayak Modang, ethnic group, 44, 155
debt crowdfunding, 79
debt trap, 78
decentralization, 4, 21, 32, 34, 36, 180
　democracy, and, 35, 56
　see also centralization; recentralization
decolonization, 11, 15, 25
deconcentration, meaning, 48
deforestation, 5, 114, 135–36, 164, 198, 200–1, 204–5, 213
　causes of, 214
　rules enforcement, 210
delegation, defined, 48
democracy index rating, 62
Democratic Party, 40–41, 68
democratic regression, 61
de Oliveira, Juscelino Kubitschek, 39
Department of Marine Affairs and Fisheries, 248
Development Commission for the New Capital, *see* NOVACAP
Dhony Rahajoe, 47
diaspora community, 75
direct election, 11, 21, 33, 37, 62, 69
direct government budget, *see* APBN
Djamaluddin Surjohadikusumo, 20
Djuanda, 17, 247
Djuanda Declaration, 247–48
dolphin habitat, 138
DPC GMNI (*Dewan Pimpinan Cabang Gerakan Mahasiswa Nasional Indonesia*), 139–40
DPD (regional representatives), 62
DPRD (Regional House of Representatives), 33, 41, 43, 62, 134
DPR (House of Representatives), 34, 37–38, 40–42, 48, 62, 126, 154

E

Earth Innovation Institute, 212
East Asia Summit, 251
East Indonesian Mujahidin (MIT), 256
East Kalimantan
　forest area, 197, 200, 205, 211–12
　forests condition of, 199–206
　population, 1
East Kalimantan Communities Coalition to Revoke the IKN Law, 138
East Kalimantan Forestry Service, 212
Eco City, 218
economic crisis, 59
ecosystem, 108, 112, 117–18, 200, 205, 210–11, 219
　mangrove, 136–38
　see also KEE
Elinor Ostrom award, 154
Environmental Advocates Network, see JAL
environmental degradation, 118, 153, 164–66, 206, 267
environmental study, of IKN (*Ibu Kota Negara*), 205–6
Erasmus Cahyadi Terre, 49, 155–56
essential ecosystem areas, see KEE
Expanded ASEAN Maritime Forum (EAMF), 251

F

family-driven migration, 181
feudalism, 16
Financial Service Authority (OJK), 82, 92
First Congress of Indigenous Peoples, 154
flood, 2, 12, 21, 25, 57, 110, 129, 135, 140
fly-in fly-out mobility, 182
focus group discussions (FGDs), 227, 229, 240
foreign direct investment (FDI), 109
foreign loans, 88
Forest City, 107, 113, 117, 197–98, 246
　concept of, 207
　definition of, 219
Forest Concession Rights (HPH), 231–32
forest degradation, 198, 200–201, 213
　causes of, 214
forest fire, 201, 214
forest governance, 198–99, 201, 204, 211
　pillars of, 208–10
forest tenurial conflict, 215
Forest Watch Indonesia (FWI), 200–201
Freehold Title Certificate, see SHM

G

G-20, 132
G2G (government to government) funding, 88
garden city, 207
General Spatial Plan for the IKN, 107
Germany, and capital city, 12–13
ghost city, 179, 186
Global Maritime Fulcrum (GMF), 6, 247, 249–54, 258
Golden Indonesian Vision 2045, 197
Golkar, 41
GONGOs (government-organized non-governmental organizations), 152
Government and Business Entity Cooperation, see PPP
Government Regulation, 22, 47, 203, 235
Governor Regulation, 235
green capital city, 77
Green City, 198, 207
　definition of, 218
green-forest city, 206
Green Open Space (RTH), 219
Guntur Soekarno Putra, 13

H

Hadi Tjahjanto, 132, 159, 170

Hashim Djojohadikusumo, 131, 215
Healthy City, 218
Hendricus Andi Simarmata, 257
HGB (*Hak Guna Bangunan*), 132–33, 140
HGU (*Hak Guna Usaha*), 133, 202
higher education institutions (HEIs), 174
Hong Kong, pro-democracy protests, 55
HPK (*hutan produksi konversi*), 202
HTI (*hutan tanaman industry*), 158, 231–32
human capital, 173–75, 267
  migration flows, and, 183–86
human trafficking, 251
human-wildlife conflict (HWC), 5, 198, 200, 204–5, 216

I
IKN Authority (*Badan Otorita Ibu Kota Nusantara*), 34, 37–39, 42–43, 94, 197, 268
  Chief of, 47, 62
  structure of, 40–41
  see also OIKN (*Otorita Ibu Kota Nusantara*)
IKN government, structure of, 38–41
IKN (*Ibu Kota Negara*), 1, 3, 12, 33–34, 197, 226, 246
  crowdfunding, 78–95
  environmental study of, 205–6
  financing scheme, 77–78
  governance system, 43–45, 62–63
  survey on proposed, 161–64
  see also capital city; Nusantara
IKN Law of 2022 (UU IKN), 2, 12, 23, 36–41, 94, 133, 155–56, 160, 268
  forest city, and concept of, 197–98, 207, 218–19
  judicial review of, 150–51, 168, 204
  maritime aspects, 246–47, 252–53
  public participation, 42–43, 126, 138, 150

ratified, 126, 167
  see also Law No. 3 of 2022 on the State Capital City
IKN Nusantara, *see* Nusantara
IKN Special Region, 37–38
illegal, unreported and unregulated (IUU) fishing activities, 251
illiberalism, 53, 61
imagined communities, 58
imperialism, 16
Imron Bulkin, 48
Independence Day, 3
indigenous people, 203–4, 226, 230–31
  exclusion of, 44, 63, 126–27
  groups of, 134
  identification, 139
  recognition of, 154–55
  rights of, 208–9, 210–11
  see also AMAN (Alliance of Indigenous Peoples of the Archipelago)
Indigenous People of Balik Sepaku, 134
Indigenous Peoples Bill, 154
Indigenous Peoples' Caucus, 154
Indonesia
  GRDP (gross regional domestic product), 1, 70
  internal migration in, 179–83
  islands in, 108
  maritime identity, 247–52, 254–57
  population, 108–9
Indonesia Port Corporations (Pelindo), 249
Indonesian Association of Planners (IAP), 110, 257
Indonesian Chamber of Commerce and Industry, *see* KADIN
Indonesian Communist Party (PKI), 17
Indonesian Forum for Living Environment, *see* WALHI
Indonesian Legal Aid Institute (LBH), 137–38
Indonesian National Party (PNI), 17

Indonesian National Student Movement, *see* DPC GMNI
Indonesian Ocean Policy, *see* KKI
Industrial Plantation Forest, *see* HTI
information asymmetry, 90–91
in-migration flow, 5, 174, 182, 186
  new capital city, 107, 113, 119, 175–79, 184
  see also migration; transmigration programme
institutional ego, 219
International Union for Conservation of Nature (IUCN), 217
International Working Group on Indigenous Affairs (IWGIA), 154
Islamists, 61
ITCI Hutan Manunggal Port, 129
ITCI Kartika Utama Port, 129
IUP (*Izin Usaha Pertambangan*), 202

J
Jakarta
  capital, declared as, 18
  environmental challenges, and, 2, 11
  gigantic Kampung, as, 226
  liveability index, 110
  parliament, 41
  population, 21, 58, 126
  protests in, 53, 55, 57, 60, 63
  riots, 59
  showpiece, as a, 57, 67
  special region status, 32, 37
  urban areas, 109
Jakarta's burden, 13, 19
JAL (*Jaringan Advokat Lingkungan*), 138
JATAM (*Jaringan Advokasi Tambang*), 137, 150–51, 153, 159–60, 165
  establishment of, 157–58
Java-centrism, 63
Java, population, 1
Javanese dominance, 17
Javanese, ethnic group, 134, 136, 230–31

job creation, 33, 61, 137
Joko Widodo, 3, 6, 42, 47, 67, 127, 129, 133, 150, 226, 233
  capital relocation, 4, 14–15, 22–26, 77, 107, 111, 197, 268
  infrastructure development, 61
  maritime development, 247, 249–54
  recentralization, 33, 45
  rise of, 62
Jonggol, and relocation plan, 13–15, 18–21, 26, 216
Jusuf Kalla, 249

K
KADIN (*Kamar Dagang dan Industri*), 131–32
Kalimantan Ecoregion Development Control Centre, 213
Kampung Baru Port, 253
Kariangau Harbour, 129
Kariangau Industrial Estate, *see* KIK
Kariangau Terminal, 252–53, 255
kavling, land sales, 235
"Kayan Cascade" hydroelectric power project, 160
Kazakhstan, and capital city, 21, 53, 63, 176
Keane, John, 152
KEE (*Kawasan Ekosistem Esensial*), 205
  see also ecosystem
Kelurahan Pemaluan, area study of, 227–35, 238–41
KIB (*Kawasan Industri Buluminung*), 136
Kickstarter.com, 80–81, 90
KIK (*Kawasan Industri Kariangau*), 136
KIKN (*Kawasan IKN*), 129, 197, 240, 252
KIPP (*Kawasan Inti Pusat Pemerintahan*) 111–12, 114, 129, 197, 227, 229, 234
  area markers, 236–38
kitabisa.com, 80–81

INDEX

KKI (*Kebijakan Kelautan Indonesia*), 249–50, 254
KLHS (*Kajian Lingkungan Hidup Strategis*), 131, 140, 205
Kodamar (Maritime Area Commands), 253
Kompas, 13
Kontras, 127
KPBU (cooperation with business entities), 76
KPIKN (*Kawasan Pengembangan KPIKN*), 129, 197, 208, 252
KSN (*Kawasan Strategis Nasional*), 129
Kuala Lumpur (KL), 2, 12, 176
Kutai, ethnic group, 44, 155, 226

L
labour union, 151–52
land acquisition, 114, 159, 165, 170, 226, 240
land certificate makers (PPAT), 235
land concession, 5, 131, 165, 198, 200, 202
land conversion, 118
"land freezing", 235
land ownership, 117, 158–59, 165, 232, 234, 238, 241
land permits, overlapping, 202–3
land speculation, 159, 234
land swap, 203
Langau Beach Pier, 129
large-scale land acquisitions (LSLAs), 226
Law No. 3 of 2022 on the State Capital City, 33, 129, 167, 173, 176
  see also IKN Law of 2022 (UU IKN)
Law No. 10 of 1964, 18
Law No. 11 of 2020 on Job Creation, 33
Law No. 22 of 1999, 47
Law No. 23 of 2014 on Regional Government, 37, 47
Law No. 27 of 1959, 13
Law No. 28 of 2009, 33
Law No. 29 of 2007, 33
Law No. 32 of 2004, 33
Law No. 33 of 2004, 33
Law No. 34 of 1999 on the Provincial Government of the Special Capital Region of Indonesia, 32–33
life expectancy, 183
lifetime migration, measurement of, 180
lighthouse agenda, 14, 22–24
Lim Hariyanto Wijaya Sarwono, 131
local government structure, 34
local spatial planning, *see* RTRWK
Long Span Port of Balang Island, 129
Luhut Binsar Pandjaitan, 62, 76, 131, 215

M
Madurese, ethnic group, 134
Mahathir bin Mohamad, 39
Majapahit empire, 16
Makassar Strait, 246, 252–56
Makmur Mandiri Village Unit Business Entity, *see* BumDes
Malaysia, and capital city, 2, 12, 176
mangrove ecosystem, 136–38
Maphilindo, 13
Maritime Area Commands (Kodamar), 253
Maritime Diplomacy White Paper, 250
maritime highways, 250
maritime identity, 247–52
  challenges, 254–57
Market Footprint Forum, 133
massa, 57, 60
Master Plan for Accelerating and Expansion of Indonesia's Economic Development, 248
Mayor of London, 76
megaphonic function, 53
Megawati Sukarnoputri, 11, 21
micro, small and medium enterprises (MSMEs), 78
middle class, 61, 67

migration
  family-driven, 181
  forest fire, 201
  human capital, 183–86
  internal, 44, 179–83
  lifetime, 180
  new capital city, 107, 113, 119, 175–79, 184
  population, 20
  see also in-migration flow; transmigration programme
Minang, ethnic group, 181
Mining Advocacy Network, see JATAM
mining concession, 114–15, 130
Ministerial Regulation, 116
Ministry of Agrarian Affairs and Spatial Planning, 116, 132, 235–36
Ministry of Defence, 173
Ministry of Education and Culture, 174
Ministry of Environment and Forestry (KLHK), 131, 200, 213–14, 236
Ministry of Foreign Affairs, 173
Ministry of Home Affairs, 34, 173
Ministry of Marine Affairs and Fisheries, 248
Ministry of Transportation, 253
Mohammad Bin Zayed, 132
monoculture, 135
moral degradation, 163–65
moral responsibility, 153
Moro Islamic Liberation Front (MILF), 256
Muhammad Husni Thamrin (MHT) project, 225
Muhammadiyah, 150
Mulawarman University, 42
Multatuli Project, 134
multiscalar integration, 116
multisectoral integration, 116
Myanmar, 53, 63

N
Nahdlatul Ulama, 64
nation in microcosm, 54
National Awakening Party (PKB), 41
National Capital Development Area, see KPIKN
National Capital Region, see KIKN
National Conference (*Muswayarah Nasional*), 17
National Council, 17–18
national debt, 78
National Development Planning Agency (Bappenas), 12, 18, 23, 48, 78, 132, 197, 207, 233
National Economic Recovery Programme, see PEN
national general spatial plan, see RTRWN
National Gobel Group, 143
national identity, 12
National Land Agency, 132, 203, 235–36
National Logistics System, 249
National Mid-term Development Plan (RPJMN), 107
National Monument (Monas), 57, 60
National Strategic Area, see KSN
National Strategic Project, see PSN
national symbolism, 53
nationalism, 88, 249
nationalist urbanism, 58
Naypyidaw, 53, 63, 251
NCICD Master Plan, 109
Negara Rimba Nusa, 112
neighbourhood associations, see RT
Network Centric Warfare, 256
New Order, 18, 21, 57–60, 62, 68–69, 109, 134–35
  maritime issues, 248
NGOs (non-governmental organizations), 60, 134, 152, 157
NOVACAP (*Companhia Urbanizadora da Nova Capital do Brasil*), 39–40
Nursultan, 53
Nusantara, 12, 76, 107
  concept, 248

core government area, *see* KIPP
cost, 2, 131
customary lands, 114, 117, 119
defence strategy, 256–57
funding schemes for, 76
geographical features, 255
incentive, to move to, 70
indigenous community in, 114
map of, 130
meaning of, 1, 22, 246
population projection, 113, 173–74, 186
public participation in, 41–43, 53, 154–55, 165, 178
relocation, benefits of, 1–2
spatial planning, 115
urban design, 111–13
see also capital city; IKN (*Ibu Kota Negara*)
Nusantara Capital Authority, *see* OIKN
Nusantara Capital City Authority (NCCA), *see* IKN Authority

O

Occupy movement, 54–55
OIKN (*Otorita Ibu Kota Nusantara*), 132–34, 139
see also IKN Authority
oligarchs, 131
Omnibus Law on Job Creation, 61, 68
One Map Policy, 211
115 Task Force, 250
other designated areas, *see* APL
overlapping land permits, 202–3
overpopulation, 1, 175

P

Pakistan, and capital city, 16
Palangkaraya, as capital city, 13–18, 26
palm oil plantation, 114, 130, 156, 200, 203, 205, 232–33
Panasonic Gobel Group, 143

Panitia Agung (Supreme Committee), 16
"participatory engagement", 153
Paser, ethnic group, 44, 49, 134, 155, 157, 226, 229–32, 235
peatland fire, 201, 214
Peckham Coal Line, 76
Pemuda Pancasila, 64
"Pendulum Nusantara", 249–50
PEN (*Program Ekonomi Nasional*), 131
Philippines, and Muslim elites, 35
PKB (National Awakening Party), 41
Planning Areas, *see* WP
plantations and mining business permits, *see* IUP
PNKN (*Poros Nasional Kedaulatan Negara*), 126
political autonomy, 32–33
political contracts, 67
pollution, 2, 65, 110, 131, 164, 175, 178
population migration, 20
poverty, 56, 63–64
power plants, 130–31, 203
PPAT (land certificate makers), 235
PPP (public-private partnership), 76–77
Prabowo Subianto, 68, 131, 215
presidential campaign, 79
Presidential Decree, 114, 227, 249, 257
presidential election, 11, 132
Presidential Palace, 111
Presidential Regulation (*peraturan presiden*), 37, 42–43, 48, 77, 133, 248
Program on Forests (PROFOR), 198–99
Prosperous Justice Party (PKS), 40–41
provincial spatial plan, *see* RTRWP
PSN (*Proyek Strategis Nasional*), 229
PT Balikpapan Ready Mix, 129
PT Bukit Jonggol Asri, 20, 216
PT International Timber Corporation Indonesia Kartika Utama (ITCIKU), 215
PT ITCI Hutani Manunggal (IHM), 158

PT Pelabuhan Indonesia (Pelindo), 249
PT Perkebunan Kaltim Utama I, 215
PT Tepian Benuo Paser, 129
PT Tepian Sekapung Nusantara, 129
public consultation, 5, 42, 44, 61, 63, 75, 159, 165
public participation, 33–34, 45, 117, 158
  IKN Law, and, 42–43, 126, 138, 150
  Nusantara, 41–43, 53, 154–55, 165, 178
public transport, 57, 59, 107, 110, 112, 117
pulp and paper plantation, 205
Punan, ethnic group, 44, 155
Punggur Port, 129
purpose-built capital cities, 52, 54, 56, 64
Putrajaya, 2, 12, 39, 48, 176, 179, 207
  population, 178
Putrajaya Authority (*Perbadanan Putrajaya*), 40

R
Rachmat Gobel, 131, 143
RDPU (*Rapat Dengar Pendapat Umum*), 126
RDTR (*Rencana Detail Tata Ruang*), 116
recentralization, 33, 35–36, 45
  see also centralization; decentralization
reforestation, 139, 209
reformasi, 21, 45, 109, 249
regional autonomy, 45, 47, 164, 180
regional planning agency, *see* BAPPEDA
Republic of Indonesia Fisheries Management Area, *see* WPP–NRI
Research Centre for Population (LIPI), 182
Revolutionary War, 17
right to exploitation, *see* HGU

Riko Watershed, 136
"Road to Nusantara: Process, Challenges and Opportunities, The", conference papers, 3
Robocop statue, 80
Roeslan Abdul Gani, 18
Rossman, Vadim, 12, 25
RPJMN (National Mid-term Development Plan), 107
RT (*Rukun Tetangga*), 227, 229
RTRWK (*Rencana Tata Ruang Wilayah Kabupaten/Kota*), 116
RTRWN (*Rencana Tata Ruang Wilayah Nasional*), 115–16
RTRWP (*Rencana Tata Ruang Wilayah Provinsi*), 116
rubber plantation, 232–33

S
Samboja Dam, 129
satellite city, 20
satgas (task force) units, 60
Save Madeira Terrace, 80
Save Natural Resources National Movement (GNPSDA), 215
SBSN (*Surat Berharga Syariah Negara*), 77
sectoral ego, 211, 219
Sein Wain watershed, 136
Semayang Port, 252–53, 255
Sepaku dalam Angka document, 227
Sepaku Semoi Dam, 129, 156, 160
SHM (*Sertifikat Hak Milik*), 234
Sidik Pramono, 78
Sinar Mas Land, 47
Singapore, 67
Sixth Five-Year Plan, 248
smart city, 6, 207, 246
Smart, Green, Beautiful, and Sustainable City, 197, 218–19
socialization events, 155, 157, 165
Socialization of Nusantara Capital Investment, 133

INDEX 281

SoftBank Corporation, 76, 93, 132
Sofyan Djalil, 23
Somber Watershed, 136
Son, Masayoshi, 132
Sonny Harmadi, 255
Soviet Union, 13
Spacehive.com, 80
Spatial Planning Act, 115
Special Committee (*Panitia Khusus Dewan*), 126
special status regions, 62
sponge city, 207, 246
stamp duty, 235
State Capital Area, *see* KIKN
State Capital Region, 129
state debt securities, *see* SUN
Statement of Land Ownership, 234
state sharia securities, *see* SBSN
Strategic Environmental Assessment Document, *see* KLHS
Suharso Monoarfa, 246
Suharto, 134–35, 181
    capital relocation, 11–14, 18–22, 24–26
    toppled, 59, 109
Sukanto Tanoto, 131, 158
Sukarno
    capital relocation, 4, 11–18, 22, 24–26
    Jakarta, and, 57, 65, 225
Sultanate of Kutai Kartanegara, 42
SUN (*Surat Utang Negara*), 77
Sungai Wain Protection Forest (HLSW), 205
Supreme Committee (*Panitia Agung*), 16
surat adat, 234–35
surat segel, 234–35
Susilo Bambang Yudhoyono (SBY), 69, 248
    capital relocation, 11–12, 21–22, 24–26
    recentralization, 33

sustainable city, 218
sustainable development goals, 117
sustainable forest management (SFM), 198–99
Sutiyoso, 60
Synergistics approach, 108, 117–18

T
Team of 11, 23
terrorism, 256
tertiary education, 174
Thayeb Mohammad Gobel, 143
Third World country, 11
30 Working Group, 137
timber forest, 130, 202
Tim Visi Indonesia 2033, *see* Vision Indonesia 2033
Tito Karnavian, 62, 69
Tjilik Riwut, 13, 15, 17–18
top-down policy, 11–12, 39, 178
totalizing projects, 52
transfer-oriented development (TOD) design, 117
transmigration programme, 109, 134, 181
    see also in-migration flow; migration
transnational crime, 255–56
Tunjung, ethnic group, 44, 155
Turkey, and recentralization, 36
Twitter, 85–86
212 Movement, 60, 63

U
Ukraine, war in, 132
"uncivil" societies, 152
United Kingdom, and dispersal of government workers, 177
United Nations, 154–55
United Nations Convention on the Law of the Sea (UNCLOS), 248
United Nations Development Program (UNDP), 200

University of Indonesia, 255
Urban+, design firm, 112
urban area, 63, 129, 181, 226
  expansion of, 108–9, 117–19
urban design, of Nusantara, 111–13
urban rationality, 58
urban symbolism, 14

V
van Klinken, Gerry, 13
Velix Wanggai, 21
virtual maritime gate, 253
Vision Indonesia 2033, 12, 24

W
Wain River Protection Forest, 136
WALHI (*Wahana Lingkungan Hidup Indonesia*), 126–27, 130–31, 137–38, 150
water resource network, 129
Wawasan Nusantara, 248
whitewash, 126, 158, 165
wildlife-human conflict (HWC), 5, 198, 200, 204–5, 216
World Bank, 152, 198
World Summit on Sustainable Development, 154
World War II, 145
WP (*Wilayah Perencanaan*), 129
WPP–NRI (*Wilayah Pengelolaan Perikanan–Negara Republik Indonesia*), 250

Y
Yusril Ihza Mahendra, 131